KEATON

KEATON

THE SILENT FEATURES CLOSE UP

DANIEL MOEWS

UNIVERSITY OF CALIFORNIA PRESS

BERKELEY • LOS ANGELES • LONDON

43532

University of California Press
Berkeley and Los Angeles, California
University of California Press, Ltd.
London, England
Copyright © 1977 by
The Regents of the University of California

Library of Congress Catalog Card Number 75-27930
Printed in the United States of America

Contents

43532

Preface

AFTER what must have been one of history's most agreeable childhoods, spent traveling with his family's knockabout act and learning the tricks of the comic trade on turn-of-the-century vaudeville stages, Buster Keaton as a young man entered the movies. First serving several apprentice years, he performed from 1917 through 1919 as a supporting actor with Fatty Arbuckle's Comique Film Corporation, and in 1920 as the leading actor in one Metro feature, *The Saphead*. Then, in the decade that followed, the last great golden-tinted years of the silent screen, he became both the star and principal creator of nineteen two-reelers and twelve feature-length films.

Except for the last two features, produced under growing difficulties after Keaton had been contracted to Metro-Goldwyn-Mayer, these movies of the twenties are all independent Keaton creations. He and his crew in the Keaton Studio controlled every aspect of the films' making and were under no constraints to please anyone but themselves. They ended up pleasing not only themselves but a large contemporary audience, and, since the rediscovery of Keaton in the nineteen-sixties, a new and growing audience, which still laughs in all the funny places.

One center of the current rediscovery is the National Film Theatre in London, and at a retrospective staged there in the summer of 1966, I first saw most of Keaton's films. Since then I have seen all that are available for viewing, many times, either whenever I was where they were being shown; or, when they were not being shown by someone else, whenever as a teacher I could book them myself for a course or a campus film series.

For nearly a decade I have continued to watch them because I like them, all of them. I like the two-reelers, released from 1920 through 1923, even though they vary considerably in quality, and I am impatiently awaiting the day when I finally manage to see the rarest Keaton short, *The Love Nest,* and the still lost *Hard Luck.* I also like the first of the features, *The Three Ages* (1923), which consists of three two-reeler love stories cut in pieces and then pasted together, this done in parodic imitation of the parallel editing that simultaneously presented the four stories of D. W. Griffith's *Intolerance.* My liking continues right up through the final silent features, *The Cameraman* (1928) and *Spite Marriage* (1929), though these show signs of Keaton's MGM difficulties. Both suffer from a slight but diminishing change in the nature of the hero and from a blurring of narrative form, which no longer progresses as economically and efficiently as before.

If the last MGM features are noticeably imperfect, however, the nine independent features that precede them, from *Our Hospitality* in 1923 through *Steamboat Bill Jr.* in 1928, are nearly flawless. They are the culminating works of Keaton's silent art. Or, in other and already often used words, I like them: of all the Keaton films I like them the best. They are therefore the subject of this study, to be considered as a group in an introductory essay and then individually in the chapters that follow. Though they have been happily and enthusiastically rediscovered and acclaimed, they have not yet been adequately understood, at least to the satisfaction of one demanding Keaton fan. They have not yet been viewed in a sufficiently objective and detailed way to reveal them—to demonstrate exactly what they are about and why they are funny; clearly to explain, to the extent that such things are explicable, why after half a century so many viewers still find them so enjoyable that they must now be placed among the few certain classics of the American screen.

Given an intricate and amusing mechanical toy, a certain type of mind immediately wants to take it apart to see how it is put together. That is essentially what is done here. The nine features are analyzed for their structural and functional principles; their cogs and gears and springs are exhibited and explained as parts of a complicated and entertaining mechanism. After finishing the book, an attentive and enterprising reader should have gained sufficient practical knowledge of the films so that if he wants, he can immediately go forth and make a Keaton silent comedy. One major flaw in my explanation is that I do not provide directions for finding another Buster Keaton to star in such a production, but then criticism cannot do everything.

While I am responsible for what is said, I am indebted to a number of people—friends, former students, and former colleagues—without whose encouragement and assistance I almost certainly would not have begun this book. Whether they read and criticized parts of the manuscript at various early stages in its composition, provided me with access to the films or other Keaton materials, worked with me in the promotion and staging of two Keaton film series, subsidized the deficits of those series, or were just Keaton fans who were always happy to watch and talk about his movies, I thank them for their support. In the hopes that some of them might be motivated to buy a copy of the book, I will even list their names: Cindra Anderson, Tom Birmingham, John Black, Steve Blakesley, Tom Buegge, Frances Clements, Eleanor Crandall, Madie Deutsch, Jim Green, Elmer Havens, Paul Kores, Greg LeDuc, Mike Murphy, Illyana Portella, Pete Poplaski, Irene Schneider, Karl Terens, Mike Weber, Jarrell Yarbrough.

From a later period, when the completed manuscript was slowly working its way through the due deliberations of the University of California Press, I am also particularly appreciative of my editor, Ernest Callenbach, and of several prudently anonymous consultants for the Press, whose careful examinations and sensible advice for improvement are largely responsible for making the finished book, whatever its limitations, the best that I am capable of producing. For me, and I hope also for the present reader, that is a source of great satisfaction. Wherever the writing approaches an exact, elegant, economical Fowlerian perfection that I am not capable of producing, the grateful reader should thank copy editor Muriel Bell.

1.

A Preview of
Coming Attractions

W ITHIN five years, Buster Keaton released nine features. In
November 1923, there was *Our Hospitality*; in 1924, *Sherlock
Junior* and *The Navigator*; in 1925, *Seven Chances* and *Go West*; in
1926, *Battling Butler* and *The General*; in 1927, *College*; and in May
1928, *Steamboat Bill Jr*. Nine films rapidly made and also nine successes. Though one of them, *College*, falls slightly below the others in
quality, the series as a whole represents an astonishing record of
sustained excellence.

Apart from genius, which cannot be explained, the most obvious
reason for this serenely unmarred record of speed and accomplishment
is that Keaton did always only what he could do well. To state the point
less amiably, he made one good movie and released it under nine different titles. If he avoided the sentimental conventions of his age, which
have reduced some of Chaplin's otherwise timeless masterpieces to
period pieces, he was like Chaplin working in the Hollywood of popular
and mass-produced art. These feature films, which regularly rolled out
from his assembly line, are all constructed to the same basic design.
Fortunately, there is enough variety and zest in Keaton's application of
the design that the last feature is as fresh and entertaining as the first;
nevertheless, the formulas for character and conflict in *Our Hospitality*
are still being reworked in *Steamboat Bill Jr*.

Most basically, Keaton's customary formulas are dramatic adapta-
tions of adolescent experience, though the aspects of adolescence
stressed in the films are always farcically exploited for what is funny in

1

them rather than being realistically or uncritically presented. The Keaton hero and his adventures are intended to be taken seriously, but never too seriously and never entirely seriously. The need for laughter is primary, and that need controls all. To describe the films, therefore, it is necessary first to note the adolescent character of the Keaton hero and the varieties of adolescent experience that constitute the standard Keaton plot, and then to demonstrate how both character and plot are comically shaped, extravagantly exaggerated into the laugh-producing forms of Keaton's favorite silent-screen gags. Such a description will not completely explain the films, but it will provide a necessary beginning for any accurate and adequate understanding of them.

The Youthful Hero

The Keaton hero is almost always a young hero, initially presented as untried, unformed, and decidedly callow. In *Sherlock Junior* and in *Steamboat Bill Jr.*, the juvenile status proclaimed in the titles is emphasized in the eponymous leading characters. In *Sherlock Junior* and *College,* the hero is even labeled "the boy," though in the first film there are some parodic complications in the use of the word. In *The Navigator* and *Battling Butler,* if the hero seems a little older, he is initially shown as childishly spoiled and inexperienced; and in the second film his parents deliberately send him off on a camping trip in the hope "it will make a man" of him. Even in *Seven Chances,* where the hero is a mature and sophisticated twenty-seven, when a title describes him as a partner in a law firm, he is predictably a junior partner. Only in *The General* is the hero initially given completely adult status, though even there his name, Johnnie Gray, follows a diminutive pattern set in *Our Hospitality* and *Seven Chances* by Willie McKay and Jimmie Shannon, all apt appellations for characters played by the diminutive Keaton, whose small size often makes him resemble some strange adult child. And though he is an adult, Johnnie's character includes a major adolescent quality, one common to all Keaton's heroes, that of change.

Basic to the Keaton heroes is a psychological dynamic of essentially adolescent transformation. They always make some traditional move from youth to maturity, from being a novice in life to being an expert. They invariably begin as despised raw rookies and wind up as seasoned and respected pros. And as they so change and succeed, there is concentrated in them much agreeable adolescent feeling, which is the primary source of the films' emotional appeal. The heroes are all charged with youthful expectancy, that state in which the young are continually conscious that they are growing up into something and continually hopeful that the something will turn out to be wonderful, heroic rather than commonplace. The transformations that dynamize the heroes, in fact, owe as much to the hopes of adolescent dreams as to the realities of adolescent achievements. The transformations are adroit and inviting mixtures: in substance they are often acceptably realistic, involving the sorts of improving changes actually realizable by the young and most common to them; but the accomplishment of the changes is always wonderfully fictitious, managed with a rapidity possible only in the realm of fantasy. By the end of the films, the improved heroes always shine with the realistic light of plausible youthful development. They also always glow with the pleasing but implausible aura of a very young man's desire for instantly and extravagantly achieved growth and glory.

The fantasy element is most evident in a formula central to the structure of the features: the Keaton hero must fall asleep halfway through his adventures. Following a prologue, which quickly establishes characters and situation, the main action of the films is neatly balanced about this sleep, an action that, with classical deference to the unity of time, usually occupies one day or, if the sleep is at night, two consecutive days. The sleep is generally elliptical, abbreviated into a few shots and a single title, and it is always pivotal to the action, marking a brief but decisive turning point for the hero. Waking, he will have undergone one of two possible kinds of change. In the six films where he is closest to being a conventional comic underdog, he will in the first half do no more than bumble and fail at something, and then in the second half, after he wakes, he will be astonishingly improved and will therefore astonishingly succeed. In three more complicated films (*Seven Chances, Battling Butler,* and *The General*), he awakens first into a major role reversal, an unpleasant new identity, which absurdly causes him to be or do the opposite of what he was or did before, but in these films, too, he eventually improves and then succeeds where he earlier had failed.

In all nine films, though most noticeably in those moving simply and directly from failure to success, the sleep of the hero not only provides a natural and dramatic pause before the coming transformations, but also in a curious causal way seems responsible for them. Though other explanations are always offered, the sleep alone seems a sufficient and satisfactory reason for the changes the hero and his fortunes undergo. He has only to fall asleep to wake up to another and better or at least far different day, most often to a kind of waking dream of wish-fulfillment and success, occasionally first to a comic nightmare of exchanged identities and goals, though that, too, always turns into a dream of success and a triumphant assertion of his own heroic self. After the sleep, his subsequent adventures take place in a world of happily egoistic imagining, in what becomes a projected youthful reverie in which the winning of glory and the establishing of an admirable adult identity should be and always are quickly achieved—in less than a day. If the films look real, they seem dreamt. The recurring sleep does curiously bring about the changes in the second half in the sense that the films all develop as objective realizations of daydreams or occasionally incipient nightmares, developments that the hero, if he were an actual person, might easily have fantasized for himself as he rested. Even though the hero wakes up, the films invariably proceed as though he had not. They are or soon become dreams of glory, and to participate in them as a viewer is, as is the case with our own dreams of glory, a very cheerful, very inspiriting, slightly escapist, and slightly transcendent experience.

The basic fantasy pattern of failing, sleeping, waking, and winning is best exemplified in *Steamboat Bill Jr.* After graduating from an effete Boston college, the hero returns to River Junction, a small southern town, where his father is owner and captain of an old paddlewheel boat. On the first of the film's two days, he quickly proves a major disappointment to Steamboat Bill Sr., presenting himself as a foppish and callow collegiate, an incompetent at all work on the boat, and the inappropriate wooer of a rival riverboat-owner's daughter. Then night and sleep charitably end a day of multiplying failures, and in the morning a better day, at least for the hero, dawns. When a climactic cyclone strikes, he expertly man-euvers his father's boat, in contrast to the previous day's bungling, and one by one, in a comic apotheosis of the heroic, he rescues from the flooding river his girl, his father, her father, and even, in preparation for the happy ending, a priest.

Other films introduce variations in the pattern, though recognizably holding to it. In *Sherlock Junior,* the usually disguised fantasy and wish-fulfillment elements are made explicit. In the course of a morning the young hero, who is mistakenly accused by his girl's father of stealing a watch, tries and fails to solve the crime. In the afternoon, he falls asleep, and in this film he does not wake up. The dream of glory that follows is actually the hero's dream of glory, starring himself as the world's most famous and successful detective. In *The Navigator,* many nights' sleep are compressed into one. On the first day the hero and heroine find themselves alone on an otherwise empty ocean liner and drifting across the Pacific. Both of them are rich and foolish and unused to waiting on themselves, and the day's events are a comedy of bumbled efforts to secure food and shelter and of infantile frights over imagined terrors. In the last shot of the day, they uncomfortably sleep, sitting up side by side at a table, and then there is a fadeout to a title that begins "Weeks later . . . ." This is immediately followed by the film's second and final day, in which they rise from comfortable staterooms and, since the title's few seconds' duration has provided them with ample time to learn, credibly proceed to perform with incredible competence all the tasks they had so badly bungled the seeming though not actual day before. In a concluding chase and battle, they even adultly meet and conquer real and savage dangers, to replace the first day's Halloween frights, and the film is then happily over.

Seven Chances is one of the films in which the dream of glory begins as a nightmare. About noon on his twenty-seventh birthday, the hero learns that he must be married by seven P.M. that day in order to inherit a seven million dollar fortune, so all afternoon he actively seeks a wife, asking every woman he meets and being rejected by each of them. At five he goes to a church, where a friend has promised to secure him a bride if he still needs one by then, and there, exhausted by seventeen strenuous and unsuccessful proposals, he falls asleep. What the friend has done is to place a story in a newspaper describing the situation and suggesting that any girl who would like to marry a millionaire should come to the church in bridal attire and ready to wed. An uncomely throng of would-be brides respond, and when the hero wakes, he finds the church filled with them and himself surrounded. Where he had proposed before, they all usurp the male's courtship role and propose now; and where he had single-mindedly sought a wifè, he must now flee some seven hundred of them, as they chase him from the church, through the city, and into the hills. He does not stop running, in fact, for the entire second half of the film, though by the end, which is about one minute before seven, the nightmarish chase has turned into a triumphant trial of endurance, and having passed this test, the hero is rewarded with a wedding to the girl he loves.

Though *Battling Butler* doubles the format, being divided into two parts that each feature a transforming night's sleep, only one of the films, *College,* noticeably departs from the customary pattern of a unified period of one or two days centering on a restful pause that changes or refreshes. Nevertheless, even *College* contains a curious analogue. After spending much of his freshman year unsuccessfully trying out for various athletic teams, the hero has one last sporting chance. On the orders of a friendly dean, he is appointed coxswain of his college's rowing crew just before the big annual meet with another college. When the angry coach slips some sleeping powder into his cup of coffee, so that the former and better coxswain can replace him, it is the regular coxswain who accidentally drinks the drugged brew and passes out. At the hero's turning point, therefore, there is as always a sleep, though here it is that of a surrogate. With no other substitute available, the coach reluctantly sends the hero off with the crew, and while the coxswain snoozes, his formerly inept rival is transformed into an athletic wonder and a glory. Ably if somewhat eccentrically, he coaxes the rowers to victory, and afterward, in a running, leaping, throwing, tackling rescue sequence, he further succeeds at all the athletic events in which he previously had failed.

Even in *College,* though the hero stays awake, force of habit seems to have led the film makers to put someone else to sleep. The dream of glory that concludes the film requires a sleeping presence to inaugurate and sustain it. In *College* as in the other films, the incredible changes undergone by the hero after he or his substitute falls asleep seem right and reasonable because they are shaped to the demands of an emotional logic, that of dream or reverie or wish-fulfillment fantasy. Like much popular art, including many later Hollywood movies, the films mirror and manipulate their audience's emotional needs and fantasy life. They are every man's, at least every young man's, dream of instant success, in which reality always acquiesces to the heart's desires and what should be immediately is. A severely unimaginative realist might resist their appeal; most daydreamers would be quickly and cheerfully drawn into them.

While the pattern of wish-fulfillment fantasy is central to the films and has been accurately abstracted, it is not the only form of youthful experience stressed in them. Like many objects subjected to meta-morphosing gags by Keaton—for example, the shovel that instantly becomes an oar when the hero of *Our Hospitality* is dropped into a river—wish-fulfillment fantasy can easily be turned into something else if seen from a different point of view.

If we focus on the acts of failure and success instead of the glory-producing sleep between them, other youthful experiential patterns reveal themselves. The two most important of these are closely related, even though the subjects that distinguish them, work and etiquette, seem to have little in common. Both patterns—the first a pattern of learning and the second of self-transcendent identity development—involve expansive and cheerful movements from ineptitude to mastery, from restraint to freedom, and from external control to self-assertion. In part, failure in the early scenes of the films either is failure to execute the steps required in a learned activity, often a work routine, or is associated with the gestures of etiquette, which are also learned and systematized motions. In either case, the hero's initial actions are imposed upon him from without. His very movements are dictated either by the skilled labor he is amateurishly trying to master or by the rules of social decorum. In the first case because he does not really know how to perform the steps required by the work routine, and in the second case because he does not really want to make the polite gestures society requires, his movements, whether inept or polished, are similar in producing a wildly ironic comedy of enforced automation. There is an always felt and always funny discrepancy between the prescribed moves called for by routine or manners and the ambivalent feelings of the puppet who ignorantly or unwillingly performs them. Only later, when ignorance and rote have been replaced by understanding, or when the codes of decorum have been repealed, are his now capable and unfettered actions fully willed from within and self-asserting. They then become expressions of his own improved being, as he makes a liberating and individuating advance to autonomous action.

The pattern of work and learning, from the initial essaying to the final mastery of a new discipline, recurs in seven films. In these the hero is quickly involved in some programmed physical activity, an occupation or a sport or something that at least resembles them, where proficiency in handling professional tools or gear is required and professional routines or movements must be expertly executed. In *Go West* a young eastern tenderfoot starts work as a cowboy herding cattle. Saddles, horses, lariats, guns, branding irons, holsters, spurs, and chaps constitute the inventory of a cowboy's equipment and working dress, and the routines involving these items, from saddling a horse to roping a steer to pulling a gun from a holster, are learned rather than natural activities. They are also activities that the farcically bumbling beginner of a hero must perform for what is obviously the first time in his life, without benefit of study or practice. As he goes through the required steps, his execution of them is either so miserably ineffectual that it leads quickly to failure or else so eccentrically and precariously performed that the resulting success is more a parody of achievement than an actual accomplishment.

In six other films, other professions with other routines employing other tools of the trade are featured. When the landlubber hero of *Steamboat Bill Jr.* is introduced to the engine room of his father's riverboat, he twice accidentally pushes the forward control lever, causing two collisions; on deck he is continually tripped up by guy wires and ropes and often nearly falls overboard. In *The Navigator*, having never labored in his idle life, the hero must suddenly perform all the work on an empty ocean liner, from making breakfast in the galley to sending up signal flags to repairing a propeller, in the last activity fully rigged out in an air-tight rubber suit, plentifully supplied with tools, and even advised by a small booklet entitled *Instructions for Deep Sea Divers*. In *Battling Butler* and *College*, in the latter once again armed with instruction books, the hero tries his inept hand at sports and athletics—hunting, fishing, professional boxing, baseball, and track (including most of the events of the decathlon)—and also in *College* manages to stumble through the dexterous routines of a soda jerk and a waiter. In *Sherlock Junior,* having been introduced with a magnifying glass, fake mustache, and yet another book of instructions, which he frequently consults, he labors at the tasks of a private detective, primarily at the art of secretly and surely following a suspect. Finally, in *The General*, he works for most of the film as a railroad engineer, though this time, in what is a unique variation on the formula, he is from the beginning an accomplished professional at his job. In two railroad chases and a concluding battle sequence, however, he conventionally first bungles and then masters the work routines of a soldier, which is what from the start he has desired to become.

Though work, expanding the term to include the labors of an athlete, is a topic not much explored in most of the arts, it is obviously basic to the art of Keaton. Work is for him a way of creating in silence a distinctive and highly individual hero, for while the Keaton character does not indiscriminately support the work ethic, usually limiting himself to jobs with a strong heroic potential and much youth appeal, he is likely to be identified by his career and its activities. He is a man employed, frequently a man in the easily identifiable uniform of his profession, even if there is a ludicrously visible gap between the knowledge the uniform proclaims and the ignorance of the young novice who wears it.

Work also provides Keaton's imagination a necessary and desirable foundation of reality; upon its solid base credible fantasies of comic ineptitude can airily soar. He is in particular taken with work's real and predictable routines, whether they are the orderly steps and precise movements of skilled labor or the fixed moves required by the rules of a game. Because the patterns of such work and worklike play exist for the viewer in expectation, and because they are highly visible, the movements they require being the acts that hold our attention on the screen, they furnish golden ground for the economical mining of laughter in silent-screen comedy. Without necessarily requiring establishment by prior presentation in the film, their known patterns can be instantly varied to produce a surprising departure from the expected. Skilled moves will be bungled or unpredictably performed in what is always a farcical variation on the norm.

The work routines are also, to come back to the point of departure in considering them, initially exploited for a comedy of frustrated automation, which finally becomes a comedy of triumphant learning. In his first performances of them, the human hero is always forced to execute what is for him an arbitrary and mechanical program. The moves are not of his choosing, nor are they the expression of any mental or physical understanding, of any skill, he may possess. Rather, for some comically sufficient reason, he must ignorantly execute them and always ignobly fail. Their actions are not yet his actions, and when he gives himself up to them, like a hopeful puppet whose strings are about to be pulled by a nonexistent puppeteer, he soon flails his way into the tangles of disaster. If the actions are imposed and mechanical, however, the comedy of their bungled performance is funny precisely because the performer remains and is perceived as all too human. The face may be cast in stoic stone, but its chiseled fortitude is always pained. The eyes simultaneously express awareness that something is going wrong, a perplexed inability to remedy the situation, and a grim and foolish determination to carry through anyway to a ludicrous end. What is automated, they reveal, is a conscious being, whose mind and feelings remain his own while his body enacts a fated routine in which he is doomed to failure—though also, since the films' learning patterns are all cheerfully affirmative, in which he is eventually destined for success. Usually after the sleep, which can now be seen as an abbreviated and fictional substitute for lengthy and laborious practice in real life, an experiential pattern of learning so dubiously begun concludes with achievement and mastery. There is at some point an instantaneous leap and wild comic contrast from the first bumbling attempt to the final accomplished performance, a change that marks not only the acquiring of a skill but also a progression to a more competent and autonomous state of being, where actions are now willed from within and self-expressing rather than childish mimicking controlled from without.

The best example of such a change is the hero of *Battling Butler*. In this film the hero, in order to impress his girl, first pretends to be a boxer. Then, following some unlikely plot twists, he wakes up one morning to discover that he has actually become one. Soon afterward he is shoved into a boxing ring for the first time in his life and must fight with a sparring partner. When he displays a total ignorance of what to do, his coach, at a distance, demonstrates for him the proper defensive moves to make with his gloved hands. His eyes fixed on his teacher, he dutifully and tardily repeats them, a puppet whose strings are never quite pulled in time, for as he attempts to ward off a blow the next one is already falling. After the initial disaster of this training match, there is at the film's conclusion a second, real bout. The hero is provoked into a genuine grudge fight with a champion boxer, who wants to flatten him. In the crisis, ignorant timidity instantaneously gives way to knowledgeable action, first expert defense and then slaughterous offense, as the hero physically asserts and in the process discovers and creates himself.

He also wins the fight, and in the other films early disasters are similarly superseded by final victories. The many bungled routines of work or athletics are almost all repeated and mastered, though often, in contrast to *Battling Butler,* in laughably eccentric ways. The eccentricity, however, never detracts from the hero's new proficiency. Instead, it makes his accomplishments more completely and individually his, the expression of a self that remains oddly and engagingly comic while suddenly and heroically improving. To take the most extreme example of autodidactic professional competence, at the end of *Go West* the formerly tenderfoot hero expertly performs a cowboy's labor as he single-handedly leads an entire herd of cattle to the Los Angeles stockyards. What makes the accomplishment uniquely and eccentrically his is that he herds the cattle not along a trail but along the city streets, through which they all bullishly chase after him, for he is dressed in a red devil's costume. But if his methods are comical, his competence is sound. He delivers every last head of cattle to the stockyard pens.

In the two remaining films a similar pattern of development and self-assertion is present in a different way. In *Our Hospitality* and *Seven Chances* the hero is never sentenced to forced labor, but in the first half of each film he is constrained to do things he does not want to do, and, further, his actual movements as in work routines are in part prescribed and imposed upon him, though now the constraints are dictated by etiquette. Each film begins as an ironic comedy of manners, in which the rules of formal behavior are rigidly adhered to even though the situation and feelings of the characters involved in it are at comic odds with decorous formality.

In *Our Hospitality,* a Romeo and Juliet story about two young lovers in the antebellum South, the hero soon learns that his girl's relations, the Canfields, want to kill him to settle an old family feud; but both he and they, when the code of southern manners and hospitality calls for it, are constrained to be polite. When they meet, there is much bowing and tipping of hats, and such patterns of politeness override inner feelings of hate and fear. Etiquette controls all the moves of all the performers, especially when the girl innocently invites the hero to dinner and he becomes an uneasy guest in the Canfield house, saved there only by his hosts' rigorous sense of southern hospitality. In *Seven Chances,* the hero must acquire an instant wife, and in a country club sequence during the first half of the film, he is forced, against his will and without success, to propose marriage to eleven different women. His approaches to them are all marked by decorous restraint, are all conventionally gestured meetings of the sexes, most of them involving the polite removal of his hat, but these formalized motions are increasingly inauthentic. The unvarying social routine conceals an unsociable reluctance to perform it and a growing desperation over its repeated failure; in addition it belies its own conclusion, the proposal of marriage, which is an unexpected and farcical termination of what begins as a ritual of polite restraint.

In these two films, as in the seven others, the hero is initially presented in scenes like these as a comically unwilling puppet, making moves that are not genuinely his and inwardly suffering as he performs them. In both films, too, a change to authenticity and self-assertion occurs when the restraining walls of manners collapse. In *Our Hospitality,* hospitality ends when the hero is driven from the Canfield home. Chased by three gun-waving Canfields, he is suddenly running for his life, temporarily escaping his pursuers only to fall into a river, where he must then struggle to survive against rapids and a waterfall. When his girl turns up to be swept across the falls, he must also rescue her. And as he now moves, it would be hard to imagine actions that are more authentic, more the outward expression of inner will, or more assertive of physical courage and competence. No longer protected and limited by manners, he expansively acts and learns his heroic worth, though always of course in ways that are funny as well as heroic. Similarly, in *Seven Chances,* when the hero awakes to find himself surrounded by an army of angry women determined to marry or demolish him, he must once again run for his life. In this film, too, human threat is eventually replaced by natural threat. Racing down a long, long hill, he is soon pursued by an avalanche of monumental boulders, and must heroically and existentially assert and prove himself against the elemental hostility of a rocky universe.

In both films the hero's final and urgently willed if often defensive actions replace with their magnificent motion the earlier restrained gestures of etiquette. They visually represent a development in character and ability as the hero becomes a new, more assertive, more competent self, in a change that parallels the mastery of work or athletic routines in the seven other films. The parallel is in fact even closer than the description of work in those films may have indicated. They also conclude in a battle or chase, building up to a climax of high-speed action as well as to the mastery of earlier bungled labors. In *Steamboat Bill Jr.,* where as in *Seven Chances* the most comic and characterizing of the hero's early gestures involve his hat, near the end a cyclone strikes, blowing away both hats and the limitations of character they represent. In what resembles an adolescent Indian's initiatory ordeal into manhood, a test of physical prowess that proves his maturity, the hero is battered about by the winds and in a solitary trial of endurance survives the destructive test of the storm. Having survived, having come of age in River Junction, he can then with a convincing and competent adultness for the first time expertly manage his father's riverboat, and with it perform the multiple rescues that end the film. To take a less spectacular and elemental example, when the hero in *College* at last succeeds in the athletic events he had earlier gone out for, he succeeds in them almost inadvertently as he races along, hurdling over hedges, broad-jumping over a pool, and finally pole-vaulting into a second-story window, in order to rescue his girl and then fight a villainous rival, who is holding her captive in her room. In so doing, he not only succeeds at learned athletic activities where he earlier had failed, but he also triumphantly breaks loose into intense and sustained action, in a sequence of sufficient length and weight to credibly allow for the creation and discovery of a new and higher self.

At this point, before one last formulaic pattern is discussed, a brief recapitulation is desirable. The nine Keaton feature films are all variations on a single ideal Keaton comedy, which contains in its structure several major experiential and emotional patterns most common to adolescence. The films all follow the emotional curve of wish-fulfillment fantasy—of failing, sleeping, and miraculously waking to a day of glory. In a highly compressed way, if we consider only the beginning and the end, they also utilize the pattern that most learning follows, from bumbled beginning at a new job or task to final proficient accomplishment. Similarly, there is in the films a pattern of identity development, of a transcendent move from a lesser to a higher level of being, in which potentialities of character are for the first time realized and expressed. This pattern is most evident in the progression from constrained and imposed gestures to unrestrained, self-willed, and self-proving actions.

The final form of youthful experience in the films, a last cheerful variation on the hero's instantaneous leap from failure to success, is that of frustratedly wooing and then happily winning a girl. Though such a romance is always featured, however, its presentation is usually such as to make it subordinate to the patterns just summarized, an important but secondary emphasis in most films.

Though the Keaton hero invariably loves a heroine, she generally remains a somewhat distant and dramatically underdeveloped figure. She is used in a stylized and simplified way to provide a primary motivation for him, an initial impetus for his subsequent actions. Either she or her family or both will disapprove of him, and he therefore has to win her or their approval, which he accomplishes in a manner appropriate to an adolescent ego, by becoming a heroic hero in an adventurous fantasy, someone they will all have to admire, as in the end they always do. In seven of the nine films, when the heroine is kidnapped or threatened by death or by a chaste and comically underplayed sexual assault, he is even called upon to perform dangerous feats in her rescue, an ultimate means of securing her admiration and love without ever transferring the center of action and interest from himself. If the films are all love stories, the major focus still remains exclusively on the hero. The girl is apt to be reduced to a sketchy background figure, designed not to compete for attention with the hero but rather to serve simultaneously as a football-like prop to be carried by him across some athletic battlefield, as an admiring cheerleader to look on and applaud while he victoriously shines, and as a coveted silver prize finally to be won. In these respects, she seems to be only limitedly there, present merely to fulfill the requirements of a love object as needed by an immature and self-centered male. In the dream world of the films, though the hero's feelings are often fiercely projected toward her, somehow they still remain egoistically within and actually fixed upon himself. To describe the same state of things from a point outside rather than inside the films, in movies that are vehicles for Keaton, the camera and consequently the audience are required to concentrate on only one person, the star.

The General provides both a good exemplification of this pattern and, in one sequence, one of Keaton's two modest departures from it. A southern railroad engineer at the outbreak of the Civil War, the hero wants to enlist but is turned down because there is more need for him to drive a train than to fight. His girl and her father and brother, both of whom have immediately joined the army, angrily condemn him as a slacker. To win her approval and to prove to himself his own worth, he must therefore become a soldier. And over a two-day period, he does. While he and the other passengers disembark at a lunch stop, his train and his girl, who is a passenger on it, are abducted by a group of northern spies. He chases after them in a second locomotive, all the way into northern-held territory, and on the first day rescues his girl. On the next day, after an uncomfortable night's sleep, the two of them also recover the train. Hero and heroine then speed south, now pursued by the northerners, and manage to warn a southern division of an approaching attack. In the attack, a major battle, the hero so shines that he is rewarded with a lieutenant's commission in the army and with his girl's final admiring approval.

That is the pattern: the heroine scornful, the heroine in danger, the heroine rescued as the hero adventurously triumphs, the heroine grateful and in love. The modest departure from it occurs in the chase south. As happens also on the steamship in *The Navigator,* the heroine in this sequence is continually on screen with the hero; and assisting him in the locomotive, she like him acquires a reality through action, developing as a character with a presence of her own. Except for *The Navigator* and the sequence here, however, the Keaton heroines rarely act. In *Battling Butler* the hero's love is unusually intensified, made an urgently felt rather than a simply conventional source of motivation, but even there the heroine, like most Keaton heroines, never becomes any more than an onlooker, a cheerleader to stand by and admire the hero's boxing feats. Though the cause of, she is also always secondary to, his own dramatic development.

The high priority placed on the hero, and the hero alone, partially explains Keaton's often perfunctory depiction of romance. A respect for comic decorum is a second reason, for in film any realistic and extended presentation of love is apt to be too emotionally involving for an audience to find it funny. A historical perspective on the transitional period in which Keaton worked also reveals a third cause. While some silent films, like *Flaming Youth* or *Our Dancing Daughters* or Clara Bow's *It, The Primrose Path,* and mildly blasphemous *My Lady of Whims,* reflected a jazz age emancipation that points to the present—a reflection, however, much more faint than the audience-luring titles would suggest—others, like the films of Griffith, Pickford, Chaplin, and Keaton, are backward-looking, mirror what was still Victorian in American culture, and seem in many ways more of the nineteenth century than our own. Youthful romance in a Keaton film is therefore circumscribed by a Victorian attitude, the attitude of a culture somewhat more restrained than ours, which stressed love and sex as an adult privilege to be earned rather than an instant proof of adulthood to be enjoyed as soon as biology permits. Ideally, a young man of the respectable middle class was expected to prove his adulthood in nonsexual areas before being allowed the joys of love or its presumed equivalent, marriage. As a potential suitor of a middle-class young lady, he was calvinistically required to prove his worth as a provider, as someone with a job or a career who could properly maintain a wife, before he would be accepted by her and her parents. Only after such proof were an engagement, marriage, and the pleasures of marriage allowed. Generally depicted as a still untried youth who has not yet fought the battle of life and in some way proved himself, the Keaton hero as a late-Victorian survival must first do that before he is allowed the joy of having his girl. And it is upon his first victory, upon a proper Victorian young man's first demonstration of his adult worth in various nonsexual arenas (themselves equally Victorian in their

Alger-like concern with work and self-improvement), that the films most intensively dwell, to the moderate exclusion and partial deferment of a love interest. Only at the end, at the puritanical threshold of adult love, is the virginal hero rewarded with an actual or promised wedding.

Although lingering Victorian attitudes about what activities of adolescence should or should not be encouraged on the screen have a sadly retardant effect on the Keaton hero's love life, they do not adversely affect the Keaton movies. The latter simply concentrate on what was allowed, and what they can do they do well. The conclusion to be drawn from this description of the narrative and character formulas in the films is that the major patterns of self-transcendent adolescent experience, which are stressed in plot and hero, are not only what the films most intensively dwell upon, but also what they most significantly and successfully are about. The triumphant exploitation of these formulas, the convincing if comic dramatization of them, is a basic source of the films' greatness (a point especially in need of making because other commentators on Keaton, preoccupied with tracking bigger thematic game, have missed or ignored it).

The major patterns do not quite function in a conventional thematic manner. It is impossible to abstract from the films any set of ideas and attitudes that compose a didactic statement on adolescence, any sort of moral or sociological lesson on growing up, because Keaton has no such message to deliver. These patterns do, however, endow the films with a kind of meaning, make them communicate, to borrow a phrase from the aesthetics of Susanne Langer, as presentational symbols, as nonverbal ways of allowing us to conceive of something which is important to us and which we wish to speak about but which cannot adequately or easily be signified in words. The ineffable and important something that the films symbolize, that they nondiscursively present to us for our comprehension, is a strongly felt sense of the adolescent experiences contained in the major patterns. Existing simultaneously and unseparated in the films, highly compressed within the visual statements, the patterns wordlessly define for us certain limited but universal adolescent truths. They convey the felt idea of what it is like to dream of glory or genuinely to achieve it, of what it is like to learn and to grow, of what it is like suddenly to transcend an old self and expansively to enter into a new one. Within the films and the films' patterns, the feelings of these youthful experiences are caught and preserved in accomplished art, are fully realized and made accessible to us. Though the films have no conscious didactic concern, they do in this way speak to us about life, about some of the major experiences of all people's lives, which they present to us for contemplation. To watch them is not only to enjoy the experiences but to be better informed about them, even though the informing takes place in a symbolic code that is visual and felt rather than in a verbal code that can be conceptually apprehended.

At the very least, the major patterns endow the Keaton hero with a compelling emotional reality. The patterns are so dense in feelings which young people especially can respond to that they infuse the hero with a sympathetic inner emotional life, despite his and the films' frequently affectless surface. That surface, with its farcical exaggerations and stylized, even mechanized, comic actions, may often appear resolutely unfeeling, the construction of an assembly-line mind whose business is the regular production of laughter and nothing more, but at the heart of the efficiently running comic machine there is something deeply felt and cheerfully human.

Why We Laugh

If the sleep in a Keaton feature functions as the turning point for the patterns of plot and character development, it also exists for the sake of a morning or waking joke. In *The Navigator,* there is the comic surprise of seeing the hero and heroine emerge from far more comfortable quarters than those in which they fell asleep. In *The General,* when the hero and heroine spend a night cowering in the woods, there is the equivalent but opposite surprise of seeing them wake up in the same uncomfortable crouching position into which they had collapsed the evening before. And the other films also mark the passage of a night or a rest with an unexpected comic revelation. When the hero then goes on to succeed, moreover, he does not do so straightforwardly but in a farcical series of gags and chases, achieving his glory in eccentric, extreme, and fantastic ways that are in themselves always funny, though no more so than the equally eccentric, extreme, and fantastic ways in which he earlier had failed. Throughout, laughter always dominates.

If audiences still go to Keaton movies, it is because the movies still make them laugh. Keaton is a master of most traditional ways of being funny: from fundamental low humor, pratfalls and double-takes, through clownish burlesque, to more subtle parody; from outrageously active farce, through restrained social comedy, on up to the luminous heights of comic irony, comic paradox, and the comically absurd, where the humor is not only funny but becomes almost a metaphysics, a way of interpreting the world and explaining man's place in it. He is simply a master laugh-maker, and his films are so packed with comic turns and touches that many viewings are required to see and respond to them all.

While the full confirmation of this eulogistic assertion will be left to the chapters on individual films, where the laughs occur, it must be added in this introduction that the Keaton hero and his fate, like nearly all other elements in the films, are the practical laugh-producing creations of a professional and pragmatic comedian. It is therefore necessary to shift perspective once again and to describe Keaton's customary patterns of plot and character from one last new point of view: the Keaton hero is a gag, one more gag among many, and his adventures are all gags, too. If both are based on universal adolescent experience, they also have a second origin in the comic possibilities available to the silent screen, possibilities Keaton develops in several of his best and most characteristic gag routines.

A gag is a basic unit of laughter, a technical term for some formulaic construction, verbal or visual, that produces a laugh. The labor of a craftsman, a well-made gag has a clear and functional form and operates with maximum efficiency, rapidly obtaining its laugh and, if possible, simultaneously building on a previous laugh and setting up a subsequent one. Many viewers have noted what cannot be missed, that Keaton, who was trained in the laugh-a-minute school of vaudeville routines, tells a story with gags, that he conscientiously constructs his narrative out of closely spaced laughs. What has not been observed is how much that story and the hero of it themselves resemble the gag building blocks. To describe the forms of the latter, which is to explain why they are funny, is to describe the forms of character and plot, which are also always structured as gags, as causes of laughter.

The possibilities for evoking laughter on the silent screen, to make the simplest of categorizations, are two: Keaton can move in funny ways, or else he can see and show things in funny ways. Less monosyllabically, in some of his best gags he is a master of comic choreography, adept at arranging motions on the screen into uniform and mechanized patterns, whose striking and unexpected regularities are always risible. He is also a master of gags based on visual surprise, of making what we see funny by suddenly altering or doubling our perception of it. In the blink of an eye, while the audience stares and laughs in momentary disbelief, people and things and the states in which they exist will metamorphose into the opposite of what they at first appear to be.

The many action gags based on mechanized movement, as characteristically used by Keaton, are comic because paradoxical, because they result in an unexpected stasis. In them, however frenzied the moves on the screen, there is no consequent progression. Like running on a treadmill, the motions they subject the hero to carry him nowhere, and in any Keaton movie the hero is likely to exert himself in a strenuous excess of such treadmill activity. In a similar and complementary way, the many sight gags based on a double identity are paradoxical and funny because they produce an unexpected alteration. Looking at something generally results in our seeing it for what it clearly is, fixing its identity. In Keaton comedy, however, many things have progressive identities, and simply to be shown them is to be constantly stunned and surprised into laughter by the transformations they undergo.

When combined in Keaton's concentrated and distinctive manner, such trademark action gags and sight gags as these help create a dense and vital surface in the films, one where the causes of laughter are always in conflict and tension with one another, in a comically precarious alliance of simultaneous and equally unlikely fix and flux. Such gags, also, both in combination and individually, reiterate in their structure the larger forms, the larger gags, of the hero and his fate, his initial and often unbelievably prolonged state of farcically active but unchanging failure and then his sudden transformation into surprising success.

Keaton's comedy of fixation, of unmoving motion, is character-istically created through the arranging of movements into either repetitive or symmetrical forms. A symmetrical uniformity is the cause of the laughs in many short gags and also contributes to the continuing comic ambience of many long sequences and even entire films. When controlled by symmetry, comic movements in the films, whether brief or lengthy, all follow a self-canceling pattern. They are conceived as dysteleological structures of action, which, whatever the original intention of the performer, ultimately serve no function or purpose except that of their own completion, for their symmetry is the result of a reversal, which causes them to turn back upon themselves and to end where they have begun.

About the briefest action gag of this sort is an inept attempt by the hero of *Battling Butler* to leap into a boxing ring. Running toward the ring, he grabs the top rope with both hands and propels himself up and over it in a neat arc that almost becomes a circle. Coming down, still revolving about the rope axis, he has gained enough momentum so that he does not halt when he hits the floor but instead slides under the ropes, stopping only where he had started, still outside the ring and still wanting to get in. In *The General,* the major chase sequences have an equally symmetrical form imposed upon them. First the hero speeds north in one locomotive, chasing the Union spies who have stolen his train and kidnapped his girl. The chase pattern having reached its northern extremity, there is then an exchange of elements and a mirrorlike reversal. Now the hero, in his recovered train and with his discovered and rescued girl, speeds south, this time pursued by the Union spies, who follow in the other locomotive. An entire film that is structured in this way is *Seven Chances.* The whole first half is a series of approaches and marriage proposals to unreceptive and beautiful women, the second a series of hairbreadth escapes from matrimonially inclined old maids, both movements in the film being visually simplified into walking toward and running from. And because the proposals all fail and the escapes all succeed, the hero, at the completion of each set and also of the symmetrical pair, is left exactly as he started, single and financially in desperate need of a wife.

Such symmetrical arrangements as these, a mechanical pendulum-like swing first in one direction and then in the opposite, whether they result in prolonged smiling delight or in the momentary response of loud laughter, are funny at least in part because they are absurd. They are simultaneously meaningful and meaningless, rational and mad. In the short action gags, such symmetrical movements are meaningful in that they possess a shape that can be intellectually perceived and understood. There is a foreordained and self-contained causality built into their structure, expressible at times as an elementary law of mechanics, Newton's "Every action must have its equal and opposite reaction." But in Keaton's application of the law, the reaction often cancels the action. The combination is self-destructive, and therefore, since the action is generally intended to produce a change, like the leap into the boxing ring, it is finally meaningless. If the total movement possesses an internal logic, the mechanical law that informs it, it is a logic that necessarily results in an external illogicality, a defeat of the purpose for which the action was begun.

To provide another example, there is the shot in *The Navigator* where the heroine attempts to rescue the hero, who is swimming in the water beside the ocean liner. She drops him a line, which passes over a pulley, and begins ineffectually to pull on it. Then she slips and herself falls overboard, and in a classical demonstration of Newton's law, there is an instantaneous reversal. Logically enough, she falls down and he flies up, but illogically, even though the rescue is a success, it ends with someone still floundering in the water. And that, like the circular leap that carries a person nowhere, is absurd. Like the ultimate dadaist machine, carefully designed and put together so that when started it will take itself apart, the many action gags of symmetrical motion in the films are all purposefully and absurdly planned to autodestruct, and they never fail to get a laugh when they do.

The longer symmetrical sequences are absurd and funny through a slightly different combination of meaning and madness. Rather than being demonstrations of Newton's actual law, they are seemingly based on irrational applications or arbitrary extensions of it. They belong to an alternative universe conceived by a more imaginative Newton, one where motions are controlled by such metamechanical laws as "Every move to the north must have its equal and opposite move to the south," or "Every stationary and matrimonially negative woman must have her highly kinetic and positive counterpart." However unreal, such laws are rigorously applied. A mad world of necessarily symmetrical movement, movement that takes the hero nowhere, is somehow logically and absurdly built upon them. It is a world, not surprisingly, that has occasional striking resemblances to Lewis Carroll's *Through the Looking Glass,* a fantasyland where moves are also governed in a logically illogical way. Like the Red Queen and Alice, Keaton characters frequently have to run as fast as they can just to stay where they are. In *Seven Chances,* anyway, when the hero's friend wants to talk, the only manner in which he can establish and maintain a stable and proximate position in relation to the hero is to begin running as fast as he can, for that is what the hero, pursued by the spinsterly mob, is himself vigorously doing.

Keaton's second way of creating laughter through the transforming of action into stasis is by means of repetition, the recurrence in a temporal series of some single basic activity. As with symmetry, repetition is intensively employed as a structural technique, and many brief gags, many scenes, and again even very long sequences obtain their laughs from it. It is with the last, in fact, that Keaton's use of what is a common laugh-producing device becomes impressively unique. Once a theme action has been established by him, it is apt to be repeated in an incredibly long line of variations, and each added repetition will become a gag, an economical laugh-producing unit, because in defiance of all probability it continues a patterned entertainment the audience has learned to enjoy and also because it provides something new and ingenious in its execution. To provide a single example, in *College,* when the hero suits up for track practice, the theme act is the misperformance of an athletic act. One after another, he doggedly attempts the events of a track meet—running, the shot put, discus throw, javelin throw, high jump, broad jump, hurdle race, hammer throw, and finally the pole vault—and at one after another he fails. Several events are even attempted more than once, as with three demonstrations of how to meet disaster while pole-vaulting, and the result is an astonishingly sustained demonstration of abject athleticism, some two dozen comic variations on how to finish last. Eventually, it seems, the hero must succeed; comically, he never does.

If such extended series—the seventeen unsuccessful marriage proposals in *Seven Chances,* the thirteen hats tried on and rejected in *Steamboat Bill Jr.*—are the high points in Keaton's use of comic repetition, they are by no means his only use of the device. Small gags of more briefly repeated actions are employed almost everywhere, so extensively that they nearly become an automatic means of developing narrative. The Keaton hero could be described as a man who is required to do everything at least three times, for in such gags three presentations of an action is generally the minimum number required to obtain a laugh—the first to introduce the action, the second to establish it as a pattern, and the third to provide the comic variation or climax. In *Go West,* when the hero attempts to rope a calf, he first swings his lasso and becomes entangled in it, he swings it a second time and knocks his hat off, and for the climactic third time he whirls it so heftily that he becomes unbalanced, falling from his saddle to the ground.

The only modest diminution of repetition in such short action gags comes when Keaton's comic narrative is proceeding most elegantly and efficiently, at which times the number of presentations between consecutive comic climaxes is adroitly reduced by making the capping or third presentation of one action serve simultaneously as the introductory presentation of the following action, which also will be performed three times as it builds to its comic climax. In this way, several different gags resulting from triply repeated actions will be interwoven to provide maximum density and continuity of laughter. Again to provide a single example, one of the most appropriate length, there is a brief sequence in *The Navigator* where three such triadically structured gags are merged into one another.

The hero and heroine, alone on the abandond ship, bunk down in adjacent cabins. In hers, staring evilly at her, is a large framed photograph of a scowling seaman. Bothered by its presence, she carries it out and throws it overboard. The wire on which it is hung, however, catches on the ship's side, and the picture starts swinging back and forth in front of an open porthole. It is naturally the porthole of the hero's cabin, directly beside his bunk, and the first of the three triply presented actions begins. In the initial presentation, the picture swings by the porthole, the ugly life-size face looking in at the hero, who lies facing the camera, his eyes blinking in an intuitive perception that something is wrong. In the establishing presentation, the face swings by again, and this time the hero is restless and stirs. In the capping presentation, it swings by once more and this time he looks up and sees it and is satisfactorily frightened. This laugh-producing climax introduces the second triadically structured action. The hero sees the picture and is frightened but lies trembling in his bunk. Another swing into view and he is more frightened, hiding himself under the sheet. A third swing, and this time, in the most comic of the three frightened responses, he leaps out of bed, covered by the sheet, and runs through the cabin door. This ending presentation is again also a beginning presentation, the first of three frights and runs. He is terrified into flight first. Second, when he bursts into the hall, tangled ghostlike in his sheet, he terrifies the girl, who now takes off in a similar dash for safety. Untangled, he peers back into his cabin just in time to see the face pass by the porthole once more, and he too scurries away—the third run from danger.

Whether present as an aggregation of consecutive action gags of triplicated motion or as a single, impressively sustained gag series of variations on a basic theme action, the gags of repetition, like the gags of symmetry, are also a comedy of paradoxical and therefore laughable stasis. Logically, an action, having been completed, should lead to a new action, not to its own repetition. It is absurd, too, that despite all the frenetic movement on the screen in the course of a repeated action, the hero often does not appreciably alter his position, at least not until the very end of such a series, and not always even there. If the repetitions in any series are consecutive, this rarely means that they are therefore also sequential. There is in fact usually no development to them, for it is the failure of any particular action to accomplish something that necessitates its being performed and failed again, as with all the bungled athletic feats at the track meet or the futilely repeated frights and runs on the boat.

When so forced to repeat himself without progression, the Keaton hero becomes a recognizable relation of the tragically frustrated Sisyphus, like him absurdly doomed forever to be pushing a stone to the top of a hill, since each time, just before the summit is reached, the stone rolls all the way back down. The gag chains the Keaton hero is bound to are even often based on a Sisyphus-like torment of blocks and frustrations, the most exemplary of them being perhaps the chase north in *The General*. There the blocks are exactly that and little more, actual obstructions from logs to burning freight cars that the fleeing northerners place on the railroad track in front of the advancing hero. Each must be removed—shunted aside or heaved away—but each is also immediately succeeded by a new block, some new stone of frustration.

The Keaton hero, however, is a comic Sisyphus. At times he seems destined forever to repeat himself, but the gag chains of necessity are limited, not infinite, and sooner or later the repetitions end. The comic pattern of repetition is also a pattern of restraint and release, happily resembling the movements of a theatrical chorus line, where the restrictive stasis of one, two, three, abruptly and wonderfully gives way to a liberating, explosive kick. In the brief gags of triply enacted repetition, the explosive impact is particularly strong, the final enactment decisively and comically both filling and breaking the mold, as was the case in the examples from *The Navigator*. And in the longer gag chains, though there is no linearly developing progression within the series, movement forward is apt to be introduced at the end, in a final variation extreme enough to become a kind of evolutionary leap ahead, sending the hero on, even if only to some new trial of painfully repeated labors.

Such a chorus-line rhythm, comic repetition ending in comic release, is not only the rhythm of some of Keaton's most characteristic action gags and gag chains, but also the basic rhythm of the Keaton plot, of the hero's fate. In fact, it is indistinguishable from his fate. Like the gags in the films, the larger structure of action that is the plot always requires the hero to do the same things over and over like a bobbing yo-yo; both gags and plot skillfully reduce the progressions of action into a treadmill to nowhere but laughter. If the films are based on the real life experiences of adolescent learning, growth, and self-transcendence, these experiences are always given a comic shape. When the hero develops in some way, his development is not realistically progressive. He is instead someone who tries and tries and tries and tries and tries again, who is forever being sent all the way back to Go in his farcically frustrated effort to improve himself or his situation. Or else his development is first comically blocked by the symmetrically reversing moves he is forced to make. Moreover, when it occurs, the development itself is likely to proceed as a perfect symmetrical reversal, one that requires the hero to absurdly retrace his steps and do the same things all over again.

In *Seven Chances,* the hero does nothing for the entire film but first propose marriage and then symmetrically avoid it; in *The Navigator* and in *Steamboat Bill Jr.,* he bungles the work of a ship and then repeats and masters it; in *The General,* he laboriously goes first north and then south. Or in two films, *Battling Butler* and *College,* where repetition dominates over symmetry, he simply and unceasingly fails at something, the failures being monumentally multiplied and prolonged right up to the final minutes. As a result, all the many action gags, even the shortest of them, recapitulate and reinforce in their comic repetitions and reversals the plot of most or all of a Keaton film, for the plot too has the clear, economical form, the repetitive and reversing structure, of a mammoth action gag of seemingly unending Sisyphean labors.

The only difference is that in the larger gag form which is the hero's fate, when the inevitable release from repetition comes or when the film's major symmetrical reversal is reached, it often brings with it a striking and comic transformation in the character of the hero. And it is in the hero's customary change, the surprising, quick, and occasionally total reversal which he undergoes, that he is clearly related to another set of trademark Keaton gags, so closely related that he can easily be subsumed into the set and seen as one of them. These are the many gags of visual surprise in the films, where the audience is startled into laughter by an unlikely but convincing alteration in what it is seeing. The greater the alteration in such gags, the greater the laugh, and Keaton is adept at producing complete transformations, turning people, things, relationships, states of being, whatever, into their opposites. If his action gags and sequences, though they may end explosively, generally create the impression of a simplified, cyclical, and unchanging world of comically frustrated fixation, it is one opposed by the equally numerous visual gags, which counter it with an anti-world of total flux, one subject to a law of comic metamorphosis that denies a substantial and single fixed identity to everything. Fortunately for the Keaton hero, and greatly adding to his laugh-producing value, he belongs to both worlds.

While an exhaustive list is impossible here, some characteristic gags of visual surprise can be reviewed, each a miniature version of the similar if larger gag, the paradoxically combined doublenesses revealed by his transformation, which are the hero.

First and most distinctive, there is a much described Keaton favorite, the visually conceived pun. Just as similarities in sound allow words to be heard in a double, punning way, so too similarities in shape allow Keaton visually to create transforming puns with objects. By altering through camera placement or movement the point of view from which we see something, or else by placing it in a new context where it functions in a new manner, he can surprise us into seeing one thing as two. In *College,* when carried in a new way, a coconut for a comic moment becomes a football, and in *The General* even an action is similarly transformed. As the two flee south in the recovered locomotive, the hero, irritated by the heroine's spectacular ignorance and incompetence as a fireman, grabs her by the neck and starts to give her a violent shake, which he then instantly converts into an embrace and a kiss. In so shifting emotional gears, he comically demonstrates that the same gesture serves equally well for anger or affection, and can momentarily be the punlike expression of both.

Other characteristic Keaton gags based on surprising changes in our perception of things involve a rapid transformation of the states in which they exist. The narrative line of the films is marked by a constant comic fluctuation and reversal in which a situation of safety can in a moment become one of danger, the dry become the wet, success become failure, high become low, or as often happens, a man pursuing become a man pursued. In *The General,* the last transformation takes place the instant the northerners discover the hero is the only person on the train chasing them. As the hero's perception of the situation also dawns in a doubletake, the audience suddenly sees him in a new and completely opposite way, and the total change causes laugher.

To cause laughter by surprising an audience with a metamorphosing view of things does not always even require a change. Keaton is also adept at something like a metaphysical pun, where instead of multiplying the identity of a single object, he can make us see several things as one thing, unity within dissimilarity. This happens most often in single, casually inserted, almost accidental shots, where two objects are shown, juxtaposed on the sides of the screen, an arrangement which surprisingly discloses a synthesis of things radically unlike.

In *Go West,* as the camera pans across a boxcar full of steers, it ends on the faces of the hero and a cow. With a wide-eyed, heavy-lidded stare, the two gaze from the side of the car, both equally expressive of an unreflective, inner-directed placidity. For a moment, there is no difference between animal and human; if the man remains a man and the cow remains a cow, at some level they are deeply and mysteriously the same. At some level they are also comically the same, for the twinlike pairing of the two always gets a laugh.

To provide a more extreme example, one where the elements paired have seemingly nothing in common, there is a throwaway shot in *The Navigator* of the heroine operating an air pump, while the hero is under water, repairing the propeller. Looking down the camera reveals the heroine on one side of the screen and the open works of the pump on the other. Both her hands grasp a handle attached to the rim of a large flywheel. As she turns the wheel, her body turns with it, and the oscillations of her elbows and hips as she bends and unbends parallel the angular moves of the camshaft and pistons inside the pump. Here the woman remains a woman and the pump remains a pump, but also, for a moment, they are the same, comically transformed and merged through a unity of motion.

Other gags related to metamorphosis stress not so much a doubleness within an object as a doubleness in the viewer's perception of it. Often this involves a momentary and paradoxical crisis of judgment, in which something is confoundingly seen as both right and wrong, altering instantly from one state to the other and probably back again. Most simply, what seems an appropriate gesture can have its suitability simultaneously undercut by being performed in an inappropriate place. In *Our Hospitality,* having fallen off a cliff, the hero stands and begins to reconnoiter, looking about for a promising direction to set out in. He looks left, he looks right, and then he also looks up. Since he happens to be standing on the bottom of a lake, up is the choice he reasonably makes, though under the circumstances making a choice is itself simultaneously an unreasonable activity. To take another watery example, water being Keaton's favorite inappropriate context, there is a scene in *Battling Butler* in which the hero, following the rules of social decorum, tips his hat to a passing lady. She, however, passes in a boat, and he is standing, as Keaton heroes often do, immersed neck-deep in a river.

Similar in confusing and compounding an audience's perception of an action by creating a gap between it and its context, is the tendency of Keaton characters to inappropriately transfer the rules of one activity or routine to another. In *Go West,* when he has to call two bellicose steers back into a pen, the hero whistles and slaps his knee, as if he were trying to attract a friendly puppy. In *The General,* when the heroine is throwing boards into the engine's firebox, she picks up one with a large knothole in the center. Judging by a builder's rules, she condemns it as defective, tossing it out onto the track rather than into the fire. Her action is perceived by the viewers simultaneously in two different contexts, that of a carpenter and that of a locomotive fireman, and therefore it simultaneously seems both right and wrong, somehow vacillating between the two in a metamorphosing gag of absurdly shifting identity.

If the gags of surprising change or of double vision, of ironically perceived discrepancy, as described so far, are common to most comedians, another means of separating an action from its setting, of making it seem both right and wrong there, is much more distinctively Keaton's. He is adept at creating such a discrepancy with a highly elliptical cut. A sustained action, like running, will be begun in one setting, with the hero perhaps racing off screen to the right, and then continued in the next shot but in a far different place as he instantly races on screen from the left. Since the action is so carefully matched, one at first assumes that the cut is instantaneous in film time and that the running is an uninterrupted sequence, but so viewed, the second shot has incredibly accelerated the hero's motion. Whipping around a tree in a wood, as in *Our Hospitality,* he will suddenly have propelled himself onto the edge of a distant rocky cliff. In a quickly reached correction, the cut must then be adjusted to and accurately interpreted as an elliptical one, which conventionally enough has abbreviated an action into its initial and final moments, omitting everything in between. The confusion and its resolution force the viewer actively to see the action in a double way, and the change in perception of the setting after the cut from wrong to right produces one of the most impressive and distinctive of Keaton laughs.

If in such ways Keaton startles an audience into laughter by making it alter the ways in which it sees things, in what is another of his trademark gags, he can even alter seeing itself into a different sense impression. He does this through synesthesia, evoking sound out of silence as he transforms a visual image into a simultaneously aural experience. He generally manages the feat by showing a sound being produced in some strikingly visual way and also by showing a hyperactive response to it, the response of someone who can only hear the sound and who does not himself see it being made. The result is that the audience both sees the sound and, in sympathetic response with him, hears it, too. When a tray full of silver is dropped behind the nervous hero in *Our Hospitality,* he leaps up, and as he leaps, the sound is actually produced.

The technique also works with dialogue. In this case, a conversation is so arranged that at some point only one word can be spoken, a word the audience can anticipate, usually with eagerness. Futher, it is a word that will produce a marked response from the screen listener, a strong visual proof of its having actually been sounded. In *Seven Chances,* rehearsing a proposal to his girl, the hero sits on a bench in her yard and pantomimes the gestures of courtship. He also speaks, the words appearing in titles, some customary preliminary pleas and the final and decisive "Will you marry me?" He sits facing left, and therefore he does not notice as his girl enters from the right and sits beside him, listening eagerly to his words. The proposal stated in the title, the next shot shows them still sitting together, he looking left and she staring straight into the camera. Silently, she mouths her reply, "Yes," and he is startled into a responsive spin as he hears and turns to confront her. Subjectively at least, the audience hears her, too, so strongly has her reply been visualized; and hearing, it laughs.

The proliferation of such gags, from visual puns through synesthesia, all based on metamorphosis, on sudden, surprising, and extreme alterations in things or in the perception of things, may have had only a pragmatic origin. Keaton obviously knew a good, that is a funny, thing, and never hesitated to get a laugh with it whenever opportunity and ingenuity allowed. Nevertheless, after a certain point, which Keaton decidedly passes, the quantitative becomes the compulsive, and his comedy is obsessed with or at least strongly informed by the duplicities and transformations of identity. In a medium stressing comic motion, it seems as if everything must somehow be made animate, endowed with a protean urge to reshape itself. Movements on the screen become sounds. People, objects, actions, relationships, settings, all constantly transform or reverse their meanings and appearances. Not only is a change in them possible, not only is it probable, it is actually a necessity. They belong to a comic world that denies stability and complacency, one where nothing can be taken for granted, and one where the eye of the viewer is always being fooled. What the changes demonstrate is that what we see is how we see, that the identity of people and things is never fixed or at least never single. What they are at any moment depends as much on the point of view of the observer, on the amount of information provided him about them, or on the context in which they are placed, as it does upon the people or things themselves. They are inherently dynamic and manifold, and the only certainty they allow of is the certainty that some sudden, surprising, and unexpected change will instantly occur, some transformation or reversal that will alter them and shock the audience into laughter.

There are sequences in the films where such moments occur in unusually dense profusion, where gags based on rapid change or double perception follow upon one another so frantically that both the hero and also the audience become disoriented. What seems real becomes surreal and dreamlike, ordinary objects become extra-ordinary, and everything both is and is not. Of all such sequences, the best is the storm near the end of *Steamboat Bill Jr.* When the cyclone strikes River Junction, the hero is blown about in a series of mind-boggling reversals. He is inside a hospital one moment, and the next he is outside, the building having instantly disappeared, pulled into the air above him and as quickly and easily discarded as if it were no more than a porkpie hat. Again, in reversal of this, when he is outside, a building falls on him and he is suddenly inside again, though when he exits through the door and then looks back, the building disintegrates as quickly as it earlier had appeared and suddenly is no longer there. At one point, seeking refuge in the ruins of a theater, he wanders on stage and confusedly tries to leap into a lake, which turns out to be a painted backdrop. Soon it is not even a painted lake, for the backdrop falls and on screen becomes nothing at all. Standing on a magician's platform, the hero pulls a cord, and he himself instantly disappears, though he manages a return as he climbs up through a trapdoor. At the climax of the episode, he seeks safety and stasis by clinging to a large tree, whereupon what should be rooted takes flight, and he is soaring through the air across the ruins of the town.

Following his ordeal the hero of *Steamboat Bill Jr.* himself changes in line with the adolescent experiential patterns of wish-fulfillment, learning, and self-transcendence. Displaying a heroic competence that earlier he had conspicuously lacked, he ably pilots his father's riverboat through the course of a triple rescue. Not only does he change in this respect, he changes completely and instantly, for he is simply one more transformation in a comic world where the urge to total reversal is fundamental and widespread. Viewed reductively, the Keaton hero is just one more gag—one among many—of surprising alteration. The changes he undergoes, which in real life would be gradual and incomplete, must in the film be most immediate and most extreme. That is what makes them funny.

Most of Keaton's other heroes also suddenly and comically meta-morphose into their opposites. Like the hero of *Steamboat Bill Jr.*, they quickly move from an incredibly exaggerated state of incompe-tence and inactivity, relieved only by clumsy, feeble, or childish gestures, to one of incredibly competent activity, in which all moves are intense, athletic, and supremely sure. Though some viewers, including this one in the chapter on *College,* are occasionally moved to complain about the improbability of a Keaton hero's surprising change for the better, the complaint is, in a way, irrelevant. The films are obviously not concerned with realistically depicting the experiential patterns of youthful character development, and there-fore cannot be faulted for an unconvincing reproduction of them. Rather, they are concerned with exaggerating these patterns into gags, into sources of laughter. And this they skillfully and surely do.

Such total transformations, to further stress their origin in the crowd-pleasing jokes of popular entertainment, are similar in their effects to what used to be a basic comic moment in a much used circus routine. In it, a performer would first appear in a clown's baggy dress and in keeping with his costume proceed to stumble and bumble as the audience condescendingly laughed. Eventually, however, he would trip his way to the edge of a trampoline or a high wire, and then, discarding his oafish costume, reveal himself in an acrobat's tights and proceed to perform with insouciant ease astonishing feats of athletic dexterity. And the moment of sudden change, at least if enough children were present, would always be greeted with laughter, a naive joy in the surprising metamorphosis, followed by a cheerful switch from condescending amusement to admiring awe. For an audience, such a performer combined two opposite appeals. They could both laugh at him and feel superior to him and then they could also admire him as a heroic figure, though never perhaps entirely losing their own initial sense of superiority. And on such terms as these, the metamorphosing Keaton hero is also founded. He, too, is shrewdly calculated to have a maximum audience appeal, being first fragile and incompetent and clownlike, the most untried and unformed of youths, and then, following a crucial joke of surprising change, metamorphosing into a hero's hero.

The comic gag of the transforming Keaton character, it might as well be added, is one whose humor is intensified, perhaps even made possible, by a unique quality of Keaton's face. Along with its other and often described wonders—its sublime blankness and its frequent, absurd suggestion of frozen seriousness or melancholy in the middle of frenetic comic action—it is also perfectly designed to promote the characteristic Keaton metamorphosis. Though handsome, it is not quite handsome. It presents the unusual combination of a jaw that tends to be square (inherited from his mother) and a chin that tends to retreat (inherited from his father). Depending on camera angle or on physiognomic posturing, it can look either resolute and strong or timid and weak. Often and easily, it can shift from one to the other, in a rapid alteration from uncertainty to competence, from cowardice to courage, from clown to acrobat. Keaton's frail-forceful face is itself a striking visual gag of unlikely opposites combined, the ultimate expression and perhaps source of the metamorphosing gag that is the Keaton character.

Why Keaton's Comedies Endure

In summary, what these nine Keaton features most basically are are farcical comedies about essentially adolescent and ultimately pleasant experience. The experience is not only affirmative; it is even affirmed. The films are all white rather than black comedies, and their invariably happy endings are all undeniably there. At the same time, the youthful hero and his triumphs are never naively indulged in. The power of positive comedy, Keaton demonstrates, lies in always subordinating the positive to the comic. His features do not provide any sentimentally approving or tediously realistic simulation of youth and its character-forming activities. Instead, subjected to the shaping of an intelligent and detached comic mind, both plot and hero are stylized into a continuous source of laughter, exaggerated into the same kinds of circularities, repetitions, and surprising contrasts that underlie the films' many action and sight gags. The farcical exaggerations do not keep the Keaton hero from genuinely learning and growing and winning his wished-for glory (and his girl); the dramatization of his experiences is seriously intended, but the seriousness is always happily and subserviently merged with the comic. The serious base of the films exists more to provide an experientially and emotionally credible ground for the luxuriant growth of laughter than for its own sake.

When handled too positively, as many mediocre films have shown, positive subjects can easily be incorporated into at best mildly depressing movies. At worst, as with *The Sound of Music,* the relentlessly proclaimed affirmative can be made so irritatingly negative as to provoke, in one viewer anyway, a murderously misanthropic desire to go forth and stomp on children and nuns and Rodgers and Hammerstein. Keaton's features are about positive experience, but they never cross the dangerous line separating the sensibly cheerful, which invites emotional acquiescence, from the fatuously optimistic, which repels it. The affirmative youthful experiences that are the subjects of his films are only one aspect of the more complex affirmative impact of the films themselves. If the adolescent triumphs and transformations have a universal experiential credibility, are sufficiently real and basic to provide a solid emotional foundation for the witty comic extravaganzas developed from them, endowing Keaton's comedy with a dramatic power lacking in mere mechanical farce or parody or burlesque, at the same time it is precisely the thoroughgoing comic interpretation of these universal experiences that makes them successfully affective. It is because they are first made entertaining and funny in a hard-headed, hard-hearted, farcical way that they encourage and earn an affirmative response to the cheerful feelings contained in them.

The approach to youthful experience in the films is primarily that of a thinking mind. The films are comedies of wit, of a particularly fine, almost metaphysical wit, which delights in such conceits as the creation of visual puns and startling juxtapositions, in the discovery of an unexpected *concordia discors,* or in the synesthetic mutation of motion into sound—all ways in which the intellect can startle itself into laughter. Not only the visual gags but also the paradoxically funny action gags of nonprogression have a basically witty appeal. Further, in the great gag chains, like the multiple track events in *College,* even though the hero's actions are frequently dumb ones, the prolific variety of his dumbness is so brilliantly conceived, so obviously the result of an intelligent delight in the active play of mind with movement, of the ceaseless analyzing of actions for their possible comic constituents, that the laughter provoked by the repetitions is never dumb laughter. It is rather a shared joy in witty, intelligent, and unwearied comic creativity. And it is because a similar exuberant wit is primarily concerned with intensifying the commonplace patterns of adolescent growth and development into absurd extravaganzas that the banal and potentially boring patterns are made entertaining and convincing, more wonderful and real than life. The dull conservative center of things, universal and normal experience, becomes as odd and attention-attracting as the most extreme fringe behavior. Wittily handled and exaggerated, it holds our interest, and because it does that, what is affirmative in it is finally entertainingly affirmed. Keaton is able to assert and to make us happily feel and accept the pleasures of his common experiential patterns because he is able to make us laugh at them, too.

If the films are just farces of adolescence, they are also major comic accomplishments, complexly satisfying demonstrations of some of the joys of living, and in themselves an infinitely watchable joy.

This summarizing proclamation of Keaton's achievement having been issued, by way of modest and necessary disclaimer it must also be admitted that his accomplishment is not quite unique. So far I have been following Matthew Arnold's somewhat premature advice to a would-be film critic, premature because delivered before movies were invented. "The function of criticism," he said in 1851, "is to see the object as in itself it really is," and I have therefore with a single-minded concentration stared only at Keaton, attempting to see him steadily and to see him whole. And, as I will soon observe, I think I have seen and described his features more clearly and accurately than has previously been managed. At the same time, it must be admitted that a larger angle of vision, placing him in the context of his movie-making contemporaries—Chaplin, Lloyd, Linder, Langdon, Fairbanks, Pickford, Normand, Lillie, and others—would reveal that both in subject matter and in comic techniques he is only one in a crowd, all doing something rather similar.

Keaton's comedy, his gags, are a professional, hard-working comedian's adaptive blend of contemporary pantomine, vaudeville turns, and theatrical farce, and not really much more. All the source routines, admittedly, are liberated and enlarged by the transforming possibilities of the new medium, so that there is in the films, even with the oldest gags, always a sense of comic discovery, as if new ways of making us laugh were being invented for the first time, as in places, of course, they were. Nevertheless, though vitalized on the screen, the basic comic moves and presentations are mostly those of the performing arts of Keaton's day, or more accurately, as Rudi Blesh has biographically demonstrated, of Keaton's vaudeville childhood. And further, the same gags, the same routines, are used by all the other silent-screen comics. Keaton employed them because they were best suited for causing laughter on the silent screen, and so reasonably enough did everyone else, all of them borrowing from one another in such a confusion of comic creativity that it is impossible to say who originated what or even if anybody actually originated anything.

Similarly, the experiential patterns of adolescence must have been adopted by Keaton as equally stock frameworks upon which the stock comedy could be developed. They belong to an innocent age in popular art, when many of the Hollywood stars, even the elderly ones, were playing children's or adolescents' roles, an age in which, judging by the *American Film Institute Catalog,* most of the some 6,000 feature films released in the nineteen-twenties had an inexperienced and adolescent hero or heroine busily meeting and overcoming melodramatic dangers and winning glory at the end. Even Keaton's characteristic stress on the dramatic and comic transformation of his youthful hero was a much used period convention, a customary gimmick for creating an interesting and engaging character. In his features, like *The Freshman, Grandma's Boy,* and *The Kid Brother,* Harold Lloyd was also a callow adolescent, either a brash and foolish rookie who changed under the stress of desperate action into a glory-achieving pro, or a timorous twerp who became a Goliath-slaying David. Douglas Fairbanks, too, at first used the same formula (his *The Mollycoddle* could easily have starred Keaton), though he is better known for his later handling of a different but closely related adolescent fantasy. It is one much exploited in the next decade by the superheroes of pulp fiction and comic books, the dream of a secret identity, of the beggar or milquetoast by day who becomes the Thief of Bagdad or Zorro by night. Though Lloyd, Fairbanks, and Keaton are all distinctively different, all are making Hollywood factory features, best-selling, mass-production products, whose unpatented formulas were the property of everyone in the industry. All portrayed a favorite period type; to rephrase the Biblical analogy, a little David who himself grew up to become Goliath.

These disclaimers allowed, it remains true that the stock twenties' formulas of adolescent fantasy and experience in Keaton are so well conceived, the handling of them so capably comic, that it is not surprising to find his films among the few that have survived to tell us what the popular arts were like in their day. Like many other great works of art that have been labeled classic, Keaton's classics of silent-screen comedy are enduring masterpieces not for any highly individual means of expression, nor for any intense personal vision (biography, except for showing how Keaton learned his comic craft, adds little to an understanding of his work); rather they are classic because they so brilliantly sum up the themes and means of expression characteristic of their age. The subject matter of popular American farce and melodrama, the comic techniques characteristic of vaudeville and the early movies—these receive in Keaton's films their highest realization.

At their best, the popular performing arts of his day obviously were very good. Their stock themes and plots and characters, their common dramatic and comic techniques, when viewed in the perspective of the age's greatest movie masterpieces, like Keaton's, can be taken as seriously as the stock themes and plots and characters and dramatic conventions of Elizabethan drama, when viewed in the eminently typical but supreme work of Shakespeare rather than in that of the many minor (a polite synonym for hack) Elizabethan playwrights. The American accomplishment, like the culture, was much more limited than the Elizabethan, and it also was largely restricted to comedy, but in that mode it is as high as any age or art has achieved.

Even more completely than the films of Chaplin, Lloyd, and Fairbanks, Keaton's films both transcend and preserve their golden age, silently speaking, with no decline in interest or in comic volume. Since silent-screen comedy is now a lost art in a dead medium from a vanished time, nothing like them, it is certain, will ever be made again.

2.

Keaton Commentary and This Commentary

I N SEVERAL places in the opening ·chapter, I observed that no one, till now, has adequately and accurately seen the Keaton features. By way of introducing the chapters that follow, I want to develop that assertion, and also in the process to do what film critics like to do even more than criticize films, that is, to knock the competition.

There are two major faults to which most writing on Keaton, in fact most writing on film, is liable. The first is simply inaccuracy. Not just an occasional wrong detail, but major errors of omission or transposition or total invention are likely to mar any description of any film. I have rarely seen anyone acknowledge the difficulty of accurately recalling a film, but I have certainly read many inaccurate and misleading film summaries. In what is an excellent biography and one of my favorite books, Rudi Blesh's *Keaton* (New York, 1966), the descriptions of individual films are disastrously weakened in this way. There are transpositions of scenes from one film to another, nonexistent titles are invented along with nonexistent action, including the killing of a character who is never even hurt in *Go West* (p. 263), and now and then Blesh's memory is so inaccurate, as with a never-occurring elopement thrown into the description of *Our Hospitality* (p. 228), that he seems to be talking about the wrong film altogether. The result, to say the least, considerably undermines one's confidence in his interpretive comments, based as they are on such a faulty recollection of what he once saw, evidently much too long ago.

In the best critical introduction to Keaton, David Robinson's *Buster Keaton* (Bloomington, Ind., 1969), there is evident a much more conscientious effort to be accurate, but even Robinson slips on details. He adds a nonexistent frock coat to the concluding joke on the oddly dressed hero of *Battling Butler* (p. 137). The hero of *Go West* travels west on many freight trains rather than one (p. 132), and the steamship in *The Navigator* does not as in the film run into a sandbank but instead is described as having an anchor caught in its propeller (p. 110). An Englishman, Robinson is also frequently guilty of a rather endearing but still dismaying insular ignorance of things American. In *Seven Chances* two football teams are described as playing rugby (p. 124), and at the beginning of *Go West* Horatio Alger rather than Horace Greeley is named as the speaker of the title (p. 129). My favorite mistake of this sort, however, is in the chapter on *The General*. The film is based, though from a southern point of view, on the actual adventures in the Civil War of a northern spy named Pittenger, which leads Robinson to explain that Keaton "insisted that the film be shot in the original Oregon locations so that the breathtaking pine forests and mountains are the same ones that Pittenger and his companions traversed sixty-five years earlier" (p. 149). As one reads that, the scenery in the Confederate state of Oregon is not the only thing that takes one's breath away.

The almost inevitably inaccurate recollection and description of a film is related to the second major fault of film criticism, much evident in serious writing on popular American movies such as Keaton's—a strong tendency to make them more meaningful, more thoughtful, than they actually are. Generally, this occurs when a culturally insecure critic, probably an American, feels uneasy about promoting silent farcical comedies and therefore attempts to associate Keaton with whatever currently fashionable tradition in the higher arts the critic feels is most significant, most relevant, or most intellectually respectable. Blesh, for example, in his biography invariably searches in the films for a philosophical profundity, an absurdist's tragic sensibility, that places Keaton in the company of many conspicuously dropped names like Sartre and Kafka. One likes seeing Keaton joined with those two, they are worthy of him, but still the comparisons are not really the most appropriate. They are not entirely arbitrary, the films provide some modest support for them, but only a distorted and peripheral view, one that ignores most of what is in his movies, makes Keaton look like a sad existential sage. (Someone, though, who has for similar elevating reasons already allied Keaton with Shakespeare, and who will very soon do so again, cannot afford to be too disdainful about Blesh's name-dropping.)

An even better example of the critical temptation to inflation, most prevalent in academics, who are professionally obliged to believe and to tell one another that they are seriously dealing with serious stuff, is that of Gerald Mast. Though he has written a good textbook, he is, in his weaker moments, the type of genteel academic critic, a pedant as preacher, who believes that art must inculcate lofty moral truths, edifying lessons about life for drowsy student congregations. A sensibly toadying academic moralist, however, he also usually preaches lessons the young will want to hear, and so in his *A Short History of the Movies* (New York, 1971), he reads out of *The General* a morality sermon from the sixties, calling it a resolutely anti-war movie, an early day *M*A*S*H* denigrating military heroics. He details a "moral thrust" (p. 157), an intended statement that all armies are infernal machines engaged in pointless battles, whose outcome the hero's victories prove is the result of accident and luck rather than courage or skill.

Unfortunately, though Mast is expressing a good morality for the sixties, it is not Keaton's. *The General*, as the later chapter on it will demonstrate, is no more anti-war than *Go West* is anti-cowboy or *Battling Butler* anti-boxing. In all three, the professional activities in which the hero bumbles his way to success are similarly treated, exploited for laughs but also seen as proving grounds for his final genuinely heroic achievements.

In a more recent and less successful book, *The Comic Mind* (New York, 1973), Mast similarly and incorrigibly strains to find a "moral edge" (p. 136) in *Our Hospitality*, describing it as a Hemingway-like exercise in the modernist literary tradition of the artist as an angry moral revolutionary, the upholder of a humanistic individualism in the face of immoral establishment values. In the film, the criticized establishment value is a southern one, that of family honor. Honor, we are solemnly told, is a dangerous abstraction opposed to true individual worth. Though it may have the appearance of virtue, Keaton strips and reveals it as an ugly reality. Its codes of hospitality and revenge, when inconsistently applied to the same person, obviously ignore his true goodness or worth and are therefore revealed as arbitrary, inadequate, and immoral guides for conduct.

The film, to be sure, does have some moral content; in a twice repeated line of Biblical advice, it piously says you should love your neighbor. It does not, however, set out to examine the moral structure of the South and to show it as wanting. What it does is take a standard dramatic situation, one whose tradition extends from turn-of-the-century melodrama back through Shakespeare to the Greeks, and develop this in a conventional, though comically farcical, way. When the hero is unintentionally invited to his enemies' house, their traditional dramatic conflict between hatred and the moral imperative of protecting a guest under their roof is similar to Macbeth's. Unlike Macbeth, however, they admirably and rightly do the hospitable thing. Though they comically hate themselves for doing it, they are punctiliously pleasant to the vulnerable hero and thus prove themselves likable, moral, and worthy to be his future in-laws. Similarly, though the feud is a bad thing, involving many deaths, the code of revenge behind it is not dissected and condemned. Rather, the feud is simply presented in a traditional manner as a dangerous but inescapable legacy of past generations, which can only be brought to an end, like the demands for revenge that entrapped Orestes, in some extraordinary way. This happily occurs when the hero saves the life of his enemy's daughter and then marries her.

To seriously question the southern concept of family honor and its derivative codes of hospitality and revenge is to undermine the hero. As with the war in *The General*, the adventurous activities resulting from the concept and the codes are so essential to the hero's glorification that the film cannot question them without questioning and debunking him as well. And this it emphatically does not do. Only the most humorless professional moralizer would do that; one, moreover, whose bookish fund of morality is limited to a few simplistic commonplaces of literary studies.

Again, too, as with his modish interpretation of *The General*, Mast seems to be engaged in a temporally provincial effort to turn

Keaton into a tract for the times. His denunciation of honor is evidently a repetition of recent editorial cries, the angry responses of a decade whose leading politicians too often dishonorably used and cheapened the word. In movies made fifty years ago, however, Keaton's comic but unquestioning approach to honor looks backward rather than forward. *Our Hospitality* does not foresee or share Mast's narrowly modern anger over the term.

If one looks hard enough for something in any movie, one will probably find it, but the Keaton films do not belong among the works of art possessing significant social themes. They do not fit into the schools of modernism, existentialism, or contemporary protest, and the attempt to make them fit, to force a social or philosophical commentary out of them, is to do violence to their real nature, to the fact that even though they are very intelligent comedies, there is in them no serious interest in ideas, no desire to make a didactic statement about war or morality or any other aspect of the human condition.

Among the many functions of criticism, surely that of telling lies about art is one not to be encouraged. Yet in talking about films, it is very difficult not to tell lies. Since they are not apt to be generally available for ready reference, they are, in fact, almost nondiscussable. Too often, one is instead talking about one's fallible memory of them, a memory easily distorted by one's own current preoccupations, moral or aesthetic predilections, or fantasizing proclivities. The result is that what is talked or written about is rarely the same thing as the actual film, though without the film at hand for immediate inspection, few readers, even among those who have seen it, are in a position to judge the accuracy of what they are told. They are not apt even to suspect how misleading are the comments of someone like Mast on *The General* or *Our Hospitality*.

Considering the two related and mutually reinforcing faults that serious film criticism on Keaton has so far shown itself liable to—imprecise and often highly selective recollection and description, combined with the imposition of borrowed and inappropriate meanings upon the films—what I have tried to present in the following chapters is a genuinely accurate description and explanation of the nine Keaton features. Each is summarized, the key scenes in great detail, and each is simultaneously analyzed in an effort to reveal its main structural principles, its inherent meanings, and the functions and interrelationships of significant individual elements. All other comments are developed within the context of these complete and analytic descriptions, carefully tied, I hope, to what is actually there. If nothing else, such a format should at least ensure that everything said is said of the films, that they are seen and explained for what they are and not for what someone would like them to be or imagines them to be. Though it is sure to be a long way from the end of Keaton criticism, what follows is intended to be an equally sure foundation for a responsible beginning.

In the film chapters, I have also attempted, along with accurate analytic description, nine different ways of looking at a Keaton movie. In continuation of the emphases in the opening chapter, the approaches stress either comedy, some traditional theory of comedy or standard comic type or technique, or else subject matter, primarily though not exclusively Keaton's basic theme of youthful character transformation. Since the Keaton features are all very similar, whatever the particular approach taken reveals about one of them is usually in some degree a revelation about the others as well.

In the chapter on *Our Hospitality,* the approach is structural, analyzing further the architecture of Keaton's films, the way in which they are built up of seemingly independent, self-contained sequences, which, however, are skillfully integrated to shape and then to alter the audience's perception of the hero. In *Sherlock Junior,* the main topic is the film's peculiar and intentional mixture of fantasy and reality, a characteristic confusion of comedy and of Keaton, and one best demonstrated here. In *The Navigator,* there is more on the use of symmetry as a distinctive governing principle in the Keaton films and as a classic narrative form in much comedy, a form that serves as comedy's cheerful equivalent of tragedy's fate. Though I have criticized Mast for attempting to make the socially unconcerned Keaton into a critic of society, in *Seven Chances* I could not myself resist trying to approach him in this way, and therefore analyze the film, not too successfully, for the social commentary, or at least social implications, it contains. In *Go West,* Keaton's relation to contemporary sentimentality, his half-parodic, half-serious, use of it, is explored. In *Battling Butler,* which is something of an anomaly for Keaton, I consider how in this film his stylized and simplified comedy moves away from the conventions of farce toward the realism and fullness of drama, particularly in the development of character and character relationships. In *The General,* I take up the inescapable Keaton topic, the importance to his comedy of machines. In *College,* for the sake of variety after much unremitting praise, there is a cautious and palinodic admission of Keaton's limitations, including comments on his unfortunate racial jokes and on the oppressed Keaton heroine. In *Steamboat Bill Jr.,* there is a shift back to fulsome praise. In an exercise in mythic criticism, the customary transcendence achieved by the Keaton hero is analyzed for its relationship to genuinely transcendent and mystic experience. Following the film chapters, there is also a brief summing up and some inevitable speculation on why, within a few years after these films were released, the laughter stopped and with it Keaton's career.

Before the film descriptions and commentary, an apology. Though what are summarized and analyzed are among the classic film comedies, the greatest humorous works produced by any American artist since Mark Twain, the summaries and analyses themselves contain few laughs. The comedy is explained, not reproduced. Keaton's films should certainly be taken seriously, but for the sin of making them serious, may he forgive me.

3.

Our Hospitality

THE STRUCTURING OF CHANGE

O NE OF THE original glass slides advertising Keaton's films
describes *Our Hospitality* as a film in seven parts. At the time
parts must have meant reels, but the film does break down into seven
major divisions. Like all his subsequent features, it is composed of
independent but interconnected sequences, seven separate cogs
grinding away together in a carefully contrived mechanism for the
regular production of laughter. Like the subsequent features, it is
also essentially a one-man movie. A title in an earlier two-reeler, *The
Playhouse,* proclaims "This guy Keaton is the whole show," and
what is true there is true here, and everywhere else for that matter.
All of which is simply to say that an analysis of *Our Hospitality* is a
good place to begin making further observations on the architectonics of a Keaton film and the nature of a Keaton hero. The
principal observation will be that in the film a strong structural sense
is at work, that all the parts are subordinated to the whole and
function within it, primarily to shape and then to alter the audience's
perception of the changing hero.

Though the lightest of comedies, *Our Hospitality* begins heavily.
Its first sequence is a six-minute prologue of serious melodrama, so
starkly tragic that it seems an unlikely prelude to laughter. Only the
first four words of the first title imply the pastoral romance that will
later follow: "Once upon a time in certain sections of the United
States there were feuds that ran from generation to generation." The
second and third introductory titles continue solemnly: "Men of one

47

family grew up killing men of another family for no other reason
except that their fathers had done so. Our story concerns the old-
time feud between the Canfield and McKay families as it existed
about the year 1810.'' A fourth title then sets the scene: ''The
humble home of John McKay—the last of his line—except his infant
son.''

In their one-room cabin, John McKay's apprehensive wife and his
baby are introduced, and then McKay himself enters, from a stormy
night outside. He announces that Jim Canfield is in town, which
means trouble. Trouble named, there is a cut to the ''fiery'' Jim in
the mansion of his brother, Joe Canfield, who attempts to calm him,
to make him ''forget this feud.'' But vowing that he ''came a long
way to kill,'' Jim runs off. Prompted by his wife's urging and by a
sampler he notices on the wall that reads ''Love thy neighbor as
thyself,'' Joe sets out to prevent the murder. But he is too late. John
MaKay is ready for the confrontation, he and Jim meet outside the
cabin, and in the dark, illuminated only by lightning flashes, they
shoot and kill each other. Mrs. McKay is left crouching fearfully by
the fireplace, pressing her infant son to her, while Joe carries home
the body of his brother, sadly telling his wife, ''Now the feud must
go on and on. My two sons must be taught to avenge this deed.''
After this, in a brief scene Mrs. McKay departs, taking her son to a
''sister's home in New York, where he may grow up in ignorance of
the feud.'' And the prologue to the comedy is over.

Totally unfunny, the prologue's melodramatic contents, though
stereotyped, have been vividly, seriously, and successfully developed. ''Successfully'' is a word worth stressing. Watching the
film with many audiences, I have never heard anyone laugh during
the prologue, even though most of the viewers must have been expecting immediate amusement. In Chaplin's *The Circus*, by contrast,
where the opening shots are also seriously melodramatic (a villainous ringmaster bullies his daughter and finally hits her, knocking her
into a paper hoop), someone in the audience always laughs. The
blow, intended to arouse pity, always strikes a few viewers as funny.
The mustachioed villain, the circus setting, the clown extras, and
that paper hoop all confusingly and unintentionally signal an immediate comic tone. Keaton's self-contained miniature melodrama, how-

ever, never misfires. Its terrors are real, its deaths are real, its grief is real. Watching it, no one could ever mistake it for a comedy, and no one ever laughs.

The successfully melodramatic prologue is intentionally out of place in the film, a strong contrast to the parody melodrama that follows, whose dangers will be comic and threaten no one. Its opening reminder of what melodramatic conventions are like when seriously handled is there to point up the cheerful mockery of their later parodic treatment. Its presence also makes that parody more than just a parody, provides it with some of the depth to be found in Shakespearean pastoral romance. As in *The Tempest* or *The Winter's Tale,* the heavy sense of past grief and wrong that dominates the opening intentionally establishes a discord that will then rapidly modulate into a pastoral strain of edenic joy, a vision of life as a charmed adventure advancing irresistibly toward a happy ending. And in both Shakespeare's plays and Keaton's film, the initial tragic counterpoint keeps the following pastoral and parodic comedy from being mere escapist entertainment, gives to it a solid enough base so that we can take it seriously, even though we continually laugh. The film that follows is a deliberate creation of an innocent and harmless world, an hour-long ideal abstracted from a less happy reality, whose imperfections are there at the beginning so that they may be transcended by the end.

Present in these ways as counterpointing melodrama, the prologue also functions to establish the basic conflict of the following story and further points ahead to its final resolution and a reconciliation. Parallels between the alternating shots in the McKay cabin and the Canfield mansion imply a potential unity behind the violent divisions of the feud. In both cabin and mansion, despite the horrifying killings, a similar picture of family and familial love is stressed: McKay parents and their baby, Canfield parents and their two small sons. In nearly identical shots, too, Joe Canfield attempts to restrain his angry brother, and Mrs. McKay her husband. At the end, a unity is also suggested through grief, with two climactic shots of the prologue again parallel—McKay's wife holding dead husband, Joe Canfield his dead brother. There is finally that sampler, "Love thy neighbor as thyself," hanging on the Canfield wall. It will turn up once more in the film's seventh and last sequence to be seen again by Joe Canfield, and its reappearance will remind us that the world of the prologue has been overcome.

In all these ways, the prologue is integrated into the film, though only after its end does the comedy begin, in "New York City— twenty years later." A title informs us that "young McKay was raised by an aunt after his mother had passed away," which makes him an authentic if elderly orphan hero, one appropriate to melo-drama, real or comic. Then a deceptive note at the bottom of the title adds, "Broadway and Forty-Second Street as it was in 1830. From an old print." Instead of the verbally promised view of Times Square, however, a long shot discloses two country dirt roads, Broadway and Seventh Avenue, empty except for a man leading a cow. The roads are crossed by a foot path, which is Forty-Second Street, and just beyond it is the pleasant rural home where Willie McKay lives with his Aunt Mary. Following this opening joke, with its combination of gentle irony and nostalgia, subsequent shots confirm a new and potentially comic mood: the smiling old aunt, who gathers flowers in her yard, the friendly neighbor, who greets the aunt as he passes by, and the neighbor's contented cow. All are details of a pastoral and now daylight world, even if at first the rural charm incongruously belongs to New York City.

The next title is the hero's name, "Willie McKay," and he is introduced in a medium shot, looking down at a sealed letter he holds. He places the letter inside the crown of his very tall, foppishly elegant hat, puts the hat on his head, and steps forward. A long shot reveals that he is on the porch of a post office, and when he steps down from it, he mounts a pedalless bicycle of the kind known as a gentleman's hobbyhorse, and rides off, propelling himself by push-ing his feet against the ground. The bicycle is a slim, elegant machine, as is the dandified young man riding it. It is also comic in its fragility and inefficiency, a child's toy rather than a man's means of getting around, and Willie's motions as he propels it emphasize these qualities. He begins with long-legged strides, which have some purpose to them, but then switches to moving both legs simultane-ously as they curve forward in a lackadaisical arc and then curve back again inefficiently to skim the ground. His head also moves from side to side in precise but negligent rhythm with his legs. The total effect is comic but impressive. It is eccentric, ineffectual, and childish, but so simply and surely created that it is beautiful and admirable as well.

So introduced, Willie is a characteristic Keaton hero in two major respects. First, as the diminutive ending of his name suggests, he is a juvenile, a very young man, at twenty-one as much child as adult. In a film that seems an adolescent dream of glory, the small-sized Willie is initially presented as immature and ineffectual, and then, a comic underdog triumphant, he proves his adultness and superiority in ways appropriate to an adolescent's daydreams. He overcomes older and larger enemies, he performs courageous acts of bodily strength and athletic skill, and as a result of such activities, he impresses and wins a girl. As in most adolescent fantasy, however, even though the girl is won, the main center of interest is on the dreamer himself. The girl is there primarily for his ego enhancement, as object and audience, a combination of prize to be won and admirer of the hero's success. The success itself comes first, and it is for Willie, as for most other Keaton heroes, a very young man's dream of success. To succeed is to be accepted as an adult by conquering an adult world, and further by conquering it with the only weapon an adolescent has, himself—his wits, his strength, his courage, his physical endurance. And that is what Willie will do.

Second, Willie is also a characteristic Keaton hero in that he is immediately associated with a machine of transportation and starts traveling on it, beginning a journey that will keep him moving till the final scene. In a film where plot development is equated with spatial movement, Willie is always going from here to there and frequently back again. Like all Keaton heroes, he is a kinetic hero. He rarely stays where he is or stands still, and it is his continual journeying, as either quest or flight, that sweeps us along in the film. In fact, he moves about so fast and so continuously, either on a machine, on foot, or driven by a natural force, that twice he finds he does not know just where he is, a puzzlement that results in a trademark Keaton gesture, for Willie then stands, his right hand shading his eyes, and looks about him. The hero of a silent film that employs minimal titles, he gains his identity primarily through his movements. He is, in a modest way, a comic existential hero, one who genuinely creates himself by his actions. As happens with the bicycle, he also is generally in so close an association with his means of locomotion that it is difficult to separate him from it. In short, Willie is how he moves and what he moves upon, for these are the elements used to define and develop his character.

At this point, he continues to move on his comic bicycle. Willie is stopped briefly at an intersection by an elderly traffic cop, who is separating a horse-drawn bus and a carriage that have collided, but then proceeds to his aunt's house, where, with some difficulty, his legs braced and his feet digging into the ground, he stops again. Inside, followed by his dog, which will continue to follow him for most of the movie, he walks over to a window and reads his letter. It announces that he is the legal heir to the estate of John McKay and that he should come to Rockville to claim his inheritance. Hurrying to his aunt, who is arranging the flowers she was earlier shown picking, he hands her the letter, and while she reads he has a vision of an antebellum southern mansion with a pillared two-story porch. His aunt then says, "Before you go—there is something I must tell you." A following title adds, "And she told him the story of the feud." With this, the short New York sequence is over.

The film's third sequence, the journey to Rockville, like the second begins with a deceptive title, "The outbound-limited." When it is shown, however, the cross-country express is more a toy than a streamliner, an authentic recreation of an eighteen-thirties' vintage train. The passenger cars, both of them, are like old horse-drawn carriages, with large spoked wheels, a curved underbody, and seats on top for spare riders. The small engine is a rickety contraption of spindly poles and pistons and outsize smokestack. Like the bicycle, the entire train seems ineffectual, delicate, more fantastic than real, a toy that under any stress is likely to fall apart.

It therefore seems an appropriate vehicle for the dandified and childish hero's continuing travels, and he soon arrives, carrying an umbrella and a carpet bag, two props to be employed in many small gags. He is also accompanied by his aunt, who is seeing him off, and his dog, which unnoticed will follow and easily keep up with the train. Then, just as an antiquated conductor climbs to the roof-top seat of the last carriage and blows his horn to signal the train's departure, a late passenger hurries up, ''a fair visitor to New York on her way back home.'' Willie, now in the last carriage, steps out, helps her in, and then sits next to her on the two-passenger-wide rear seat. In the first of a series of interior closeups that delineate the modest progression of an incipient romance, they look briefly at each other but then diffidently turn their eyes away. The conductor blows his horn again, and the train jerks to a start.

After this beginning, the trip to Rockville develops in crosscut shots featuring three centers of interest. There are the closeups of Willie and the girl, there are a few shots of Willie's dog running beneath or behind the train, and third, most numerous, there are shots of the train itself. It becomes in fact the real hero of the journey sequence, which, like the prologue, develops as a self-contained miniature film within the larger work.

In the train shots, we see first a crossroad, where a small crowd runs up and gawks as the train and a frightened cow go past, the bystanders all struck with wonder by this new mechanical marvel. Besides being one more example of the film's frequent use of ironic nostalgia, the shot also displays the train's peculiar and Keatonesque charm. As it passes, the humans on the train are assimilated to the machine and seem to be parts attached to it. The engineer, played by Buster's father, Joe Keaton, is the most fully mechanized. Here and in many of the later shots, he has a single stance. Legs are spread apart, forming a long narrow triangle, the right hand grips the throttle, and the left arm forms a rigid and rarely altered second triangle as the hand rests on the hip. It is a stance of long lines and angularities, which seem extensions of the rigidly, fragilely constructed train. Like the train's structure, it is not a stance apparently designed for going around curves and over frequent bumps. This unpromising design makes incongruous and comic the unyielding ease with which it does surmount the bumps, with as few flexes and twists as are necessary to maintain its stability—as is true also of the train. Similarly assimilated to the train are the passengers and the conductor seated on the coach roofs. As they bob and sway, they look like loose parts that threaten to fall off, though that happens only once during the journey, when the conductor and the rear wheels go

together, and then again at the end, when a collision sends all parts—
human, metal, and wood—flying.

The result of this merging of men into machine is to make the train
humanly heroic. A cheerful half-mechanical, half-human contraption, it presents itself as an ineffectual and accident-prone underdog.
It also becomes a fantastic hero that will, however unlikely it first
seems, surmount all obstacles, until finally, in a climactic race, it
reaches its destination in triumph. So viewed as the hero of the
journey sequence, the train has much in common with Willie as the
hero of the entire film; and our developing perception of its comic
heroism parallels and in fact helps shape our developing awareness
of Willie's heroic potential. He is an immature and childish dandy
and it is a fragile toy, but the train proves capable of far more than
first seems possible, and Willie, who is how he travels and what he
travels upon, similarly changes, acquiring at least a potential for
heroic development.

The obstacles the train encounters on its comically adventurous
journey are first obstreperous human beings—an angry tramp, who is
stealing a ride, and then a foxy grandpa, who throws rocks at the
engineer to provoke him into retaliating with firewood for an
evening's supply of kindling. Next there are difficulties with the
track, seeming obstacles like a tree that it suddenly bends around,
incredibly loose sections, incredibly bumpy sections, a donkey obstinately blocking the way till the loosened track is bent around it, and
finally, most surprisingly and comically, a complete absence of
track, when the engineer, preoccupied with cooking his dinner over
the firebox, allows the train to move somehow from the track to an
adjacent road. Third and last, the train itself causes problems. The
rear wheels of the second carriage fall off, going through a tunnel the
engine's smoke coats all the passengers and crew with a sooty
blackface, and in the journey's climactic crisis, caused by a man who
fiddles with a switch as the train passes, the sidetracked carriages are
detached from the engine and return to the main track ahead of it.
Out of control and backward, the outbound limited rushes toward
Rockville. The carriages crash into the barrier at the end of the line
there, and then, for good measure, the pursuing engine crashes into
them. But still, the last obstacle has been overcome, and the train,

which at first seemed too fragile to succeed, has triumphantly, if also always comically and eccentrically, reached its goal. And the diminutive Willie has been sufficiently identified with the diminutive train to make its real though amusing glorification an element promoting our changing recognition of him. Like the train, which he has been a part of while traveling on it, he will not be stopped.

During the journey, two cutaway shots to Rockville are particularly important for maintaining a sense of the train's triumphant and unstoppable progression. Leaving the track for the road and losing a pair of wheels are both accidents that would lengthily delay movement, so repair activity is omitted and the passage of time in which it might be undertaken is covered by cuts to the Canfield mansion. Here we learn that the girl on the train is Joe Canfield's daughter, one of the film's many uses of dramatic irony, which allows us to enjoy a comic Romeo and Juliet situation long before any of the characters are aware of it. And just as important for the train sequence is the fact that the cuts allow the train's progression to be presented as an unflagging one. Even major catastrophes do not keep it from credibly and almost continually rolling for all the time we see it on the screen.

The catastrophe of leaving the track, which editing allows the train instantly to triumph over, is also the occasion for one of the first demonstrations of Willie's potential as an athletic adventurer, the first sign of his individual unstoppability. He is the one who notices, and in order to point out the problem to the conductor, who is riding on his roof-top seat, Willie must climb through the window and stand on the sill outside the carriage. The feat is performed so quickly, so effortlessly, that it does not seem a feat, but performing it obviously takes considerable strength and coordination and a foolish disregard of danger, all factors that help make its casual accomplishment by the foppish Willie seem incongruous and funny. Moreover, it is performed as a pure and instant action, carried through without the adulteration or hesitation of thought, which further adds to its combined air of comic nonchalance and athletic heroism. A similar leap to the window sill is repeated at the switch when the carriages roll in front of the engine, and then an even better example of such underplayed and comic athleticism occurs. The conductor and the other passengers at this point turn in their roof-top seats or lean out the windows to wave at the laggard engineer. Willie, however, does more. Again instantly, he leaps outside the carriage, and while the others wave only an arm, he transforms his entire body into an angular, mechanical signaling device, a living extension of the train that seems almost a regular part of it. Hanging on by one hand and foot, his other arm and leg stretched out, he forms a giant waving X. His whole being is thus engaged in the action, becomes the act of signaling, and this total commitment to an action, this ability to embody an action, reveals in him unexpected depths of kinetic intensity, of physical determination and intelligence.

When the journey ends, there is a final such throwaway motion, like the others so quickly and casually accomplished that it almost passes unseen. As the engine collides into the carriages, passengers, baggage, and train parts go flying, and Willie at the door of his carriage flies farthest. In a seated position he executes a giant arc in the air, landing still seated with enough momentum to propel him scooting along the ground behind a wood pile. It is his character and his fate to move more, higher, farther, faster, than anyone else. And when he so moves, his motions are no longer the superficial and ineffectual gestures of the childish dandy on the bicycle. Like the train he is in, which in these acts he has employed as a kind of traveling gymnasium, he is capable of much more significant movement than at first appears likely. When he acts, he acts instinctively and intensively, if also casually and thoughtlessly, and that is heroic as well as comic. In the shots described, all of which are briefer than the description of them, the comedy outweighs the heroism, but the full development of the latter has been prepared for and pointed to. When he next rides on the train near the film's end, on the day of his glory, he will perform even more spectacular acrobatic feats upon it, and what is only intimated now will be explicitly developed then.

In the journey there is still to be considered the first group of shots mentioned, the interior closeups of Willie and the girl. Early in this series, they both look demurely ahead, reticent, decorous, each reserved in the presence of a stranger. Willie then puts on his tall hat, politely removed before when he helped her into the carriage. It just manages to fit in the cramped space, though the top touches the ceiling and he must scrunch down in order to bring his head up into it. Next, his eyes move from side to side just beneath its brim, first attracted to the girl and then reluctantly turning away. Their motion emphasized, attention drawn to them, his eyes are suddenly eclipsed as a heavy jolt drives the hat down over Willie's ears. The girl for the first time now looks curiously at him, which in a comedy of reticent coutship is a major romantic response and her initial demonstration of interest. As she watches, he struggles out of the hat and, reaching into his carpetbag, replaces it with the trademark flat-crowned Keaton porkpie.

When the tall hat is removed, it leaves behind two heavy black marks on Willie's forehead, resembling a second pair of eyebrows, where his thick white facial makeup has been scraped off. With Keaton, such makeup is more than just the customary period response to an orthochromatic film stock insensitive to flesh tones. Working like Chaplin in the tradition of the clown developed in circus, pantomine, and vaudeville, he carries on the tradition of a clown's white face, with accented eyes and lips, as he does with the porkpie hat and occasionally worn slap shoes also borrowed from a clown's costume. Generally, the more stylized and unreal the film, as with *Go West,* the heavier the clown's makeup, though there is a casualness about Keaton's use of the convention that keeps it from being easily explained. Frequently, the makeup will come and go, doing the latter in the more watery scenes that regularly appear in Keaton features, only later to be applied once again. Further, the makeup can even change from shot to shot, turning up where a comic effect can be obtained from heavily rimmed eyes, which probably pop or stare, and then instantly disappearing.

In this film, where the makeup throughout is moderately heavy, and in this series of closeups, where it is much thicker than anywhere else, three additional reasons for it are also apparent. First, it is part of an idyllic and pastoral world, in which everything is idealized, where scenery, sets, and people are all beautiful. Even Joe Roberts as Joe Canfield and Joe Keaton as the engineer, both generally comic-looking actors in the two-reelers, are prettied up, the first in white flowing locks, the other in what may be a bright black wig.

Second, in this series of closeups, the first prolonged view of Willie, the extra-heavy makeup turns his face into a flawless white porcelain oval, establishing an initial impression of weakness and fragility to be comically overcome later. In fact, so beautifully white is the perfect oval of his face that it visually equates him with the girl at his side, whose face is also a perfect white oval. And that is the third reason for the makeup. Their facial similarity is so striking that it becomes the major means of implying an affinity between them. They look so much alike they must be destined for each other, and the comedy of reticent courtship is made funnier because the identical appearances already predict its end. The reticence, their twinlike faces announce, is unnecessary, is bound to be overcome, and therefore is slightly absurd.

The closeups continue, and in them the comic obstacles in the train's journey are transformed into the impetus for romance. In the Keaton universe of double identities, where what seems to be one thing is frequently another, the difficulties the train encounters outside become inside encouragements to love. Looking out the window, the girl sees a tree, apparently in the center of the curving track but actually just beside it; frightened, she momentarily holds to Willie. Following a jolt over rough track, she holds even tighter to him, and then, when she lets go, the reserves of strangeness have been sufficiently broken down so that he can speak to her. When another bump causes him to bounce and strike the carriage roof, he chivalrously protects her head from a similar fate by stretching his hand above her, in a gesture very close to an embrace.

In further shots, they continue to talk, and finally, as the journey nears its end, she sleeps, her head resting on his shoulder. And he, after looking down at her, leans his head against hers and sleeps, too—the pair forming a tableau of sentimental and innocent but still marginally physical and marginally erotic love. In fact, the shot has such a sentimental charm to it, that, as is customary in Keaton, it must be undercut to preserve the primacy of laughter over feeling. At this point, then, the train goes through the tunnel, and in their next closeup Willie and the girl wake to find themselves covered with soot, their porcelain figurine faces comically smudged, with noses and cheeks blotched a deep black. In their final closeup, as the carriages race out of control into Rockville, they are united in fright, and he for the first time holds her as the restraints of decorum give way in the crisis. Once in Rockville, following the collisions, he helps her from the carriage as before he had helped her in. She runs off to her father and brothers, who have come to meet her, and the preliminary and tentative but still firmly established courtship is over—a comedy of manners and of minimal lovemaking, where the greatest laughs arise from the most politely restrained and hesitant gestures of passion.

The journey sequence then ends with the culmination of its third and last group of shots, those of the dog, which has been running behind the train all the way to Rockville. Willie wipes the dust off his face, picks up his bag, turns, and sees the dog. He blinks, he squints, he stares, an eyebrow raised in disbelief, and then he walks up and examines its paws, which prove to have nicely survived the cross-country run. This discovery scene has been long prepared for, and the doubletake by Willie is one of the major comic moments of the film, the culmination of one major strand in its structure of multiple, overlapping, and lengthily sustained dramatic ironies.

The last of the journey jokes concluded, the film's fourth sequence begins. It consists of Willie's wanderings around Rockville, and it is inaugurated with the creation of a new source for comic dramatic irony, which, like the dog joke in the train sequence, will run all the way through. As he starts to walk into town, Willie meets one of the Canfield brothers, and when asked for directions to the McKay estate, the brother learns who Willie is. For the remainder of the Rockville sequence, he and the other Canfield men will be out to kill their new-found enemy, though ironically Willie will never learn who they are or even notice their attempts on his life.

The first attempt begins immediately. As the two men stroll past a store, the brother with a few deceptively polite gestures indicates he must enter. Once inside, he asks the proprietor, "Have you a pistol handy?" When the answer is no, he comes out again, and after more polite gestures, of apology for delay on the brother's part and agreeable acquiescence on Willie's, the two men resume their walk. As in the train closeups, the forms of etiquette conceal strong emotions, creating an incongruous and comic effect. Another pause, a second store entered, still no gun procured, the walk continues. Then, as the brother goes into a third store, a variation occurs. Waiting outside, Willie sees a man knock down his wife and hurries to her rescue. As it turns out, she resents being saved and quickly flattens Willie, who rises and runs for safety. Though the encounter at first seems a disaster, it is suddenly revealed as his salvation. Back at the store, the brother now comes out, this third time successfully armed with a gun. But Willie is gone, so the brother hands the gun back to the store owner and angrily departs.

Hurrying home, he there proclaims his discovery, and the three Canfield men step to a gun rack to arm themselves. With the threat on his life just tripled, Willie immediately and comically appears outside the Canfield yard, ignorantly and ironically moving to the point of maximum danger, which of course is also the point of maximum attraction. The girl is there gathering flowers, and when in good southern style she asks, ''Would you all come over to supper tonight,'' he happily accepts the invitation. Inside, the Canfield men are now armed and ready for the hunt, though they are momentarily delayed when the girl enters with the news but not the name of her guest. Joe responds by embracing her, at the same time winking at one of his sons, humorously implying that the girl, if still regarded as a child, is beginning to grow up. He also approves of her invitation in a wonderfully prophetic title, ''Splendid! He'll never forget our hospitality.'' When the girl leaves, however, all smiles and good-natured approval disappear. The men set out to kill the family enemy, and their grim looks recall the serious melodrama of the prologue, momentarily replacing the film's comic and parodic tone with a sense of genuine danger.

At this point, another long-prepared-for laugh occurs. Still wandering, Willie reaches the McKay estate, a decrepit shed. In closeup, he stares at the ruin, and there is a fadeout and a fadein to the porticoed mansion he had imagined back in New York. The mansion blows up, an illusion shattered, and Willie in closeup again stares at his actual inheritance. It immediately starts disintegrating, and after twice being nearly hit by falling beams, he takes off, running to safety. Where he unintentionally runs to is once more the point of maximum danger; for the second time he pulls up in front of the

Canfield house. Slowing to a walk, he looks in at the gate as he passes, and this causes him to bump into Joe Canfield and the brother who has not yet met him, as the two of them approach from the opposite direction. With polite bows, the three excuse one another, but when the two Canfields reach the house door, the other brother comes out and identifies the now distant Willie. Comic manners instantly give way to comic madness. Both brothers fire from the porch, but Willie is too far away to be hit, even if he is puzzled by whatever it is that whizzes by his head. The brothers then take out after him, followed by Joe.

In a beautifully composed shot, half light and half dark, one of the brothers is next shown waiting behind the dark wall of a building, ready to ambush Willie, who walks forward in the light half of the frame, stopping just as he reaches the building corner. The brother pulls the trigger, but in the first round of what will be a much repeated gag, his gun jams. He tries again and again, shaking the gun violently, whereupon Willie, now fully past the corner, suddenly sees his predicament. Helpfully, he grabs the gun and instantly succeeds in firing it into the ground. Returning the now empty weapon, he casually continues on his way, having unknowingly disarmed an enemy, an act that on the next day will be consciously and courageously repeated.

While the Canfield brother is preoccupied with reloading, Willie's wandering takes him into the countryside, where, after buying a pole from two passing boys, he soon sits to pass the time till supper in fishing. The episode that follows is the last in the Rockville sequence, and like the prologue and the adventurous journey of the train, it is developed as a self-contained miniature film within the larger one, and in fact seems at first an arbitrary insertion, a comic indulgence included for its own entertaining sake. Like the others, however, it actually works within the larger structure in several important ways. The unity of the film to some extent derives from its similarity to its parts, which like the train sequence seem miniature models of the whole, and the fishing episode is another microcosm of the film's entire world. What happens to Willie in its few minutes is an abbreviated version of what happens to him throughout, and helps to establish and reinforce the metamorphosing nature of his comic fate. There operates throughout both the episode and the film a law of reversal, a kind of comic necessity demanding change, which keeps Willie active, making him a kinetic hero, even when he is seeking rest. Like much of the film, the episode develops through a series of rapid reversals, from triumph to failure to triumph and back again, becoming a sort of near-perpetual motion comedy machine, which never comes to a full stop in any position until the end.

With the basic situation established, Willie fishing as he sits on a ledge at the base of a cliff, the episode begins with the planting of a customary charge of dramatic irony, something to keep the audience in a state of comic expectation till it finally goes off. Here it is established in a cutaway shot of two men with a dynamite keg at the base of a dam. One of them implausibly observes, "It's a shame to blow up this dam, but we must irrigate." They light the fuse and run, and then in a long shot of a miniature set, the dam explodes and water rushes through it. The rest of the episode is Willie's, and he immediately starts his comic reversals and transformations, which proceed densely, almost one to a shot. First he sits, patiently fishing. Then, disgusted at the lack of a nibble, he throws his pole into the water. Reversal, he threw it away too soon; something large is hooked on it, for the bob wiggles violently. Reversal, it is not too late. Setting aside his hat, he leaps into the water and at the cost of a dunking retrieves the pole. Reversal, it was not a big fish after all, merely an outsize minnow at the end of the line, and he was a fool to leap in to retrieve it. Reversal, he instantly converts the fish from undersize catch to oversize bait, impaling it on the hook and beginning to fish all over again with this improved equipment. Reversal, as he resumes fishing, bent over the pole, his hat, kept dry till now, falls off toward the water. Reversal, he adroitly manages to catch it just before it hits the surface. Reversal, water from the cliff behind begins to drip on him, wetting the carefully preserved dry hat. Reversal, he grabs his umbrella and puts it up, expecting to stay dry. Reversal, the drops are not rain but water released from the dynamited dam, which now comes down in a flood, soaking hat and all despite the umbrella. Reversal, the flood may drench him but it also hides him from the Canfield brothers, who now pass by in front of the newly created falls. Reversal, the Canfield brothers pass by but Willie is being nearly drowned in the deluge (emphasized in a medium shot). Reversal, he leaps into the water, holding onto his hat, umbrella, and pole, and swims to the foreground bank, where soon he stands safely on dry land. Ironic triumph and reversal, he at last catches something as a large fish chooses this moment to be caught on his line, but its unexpected tug tumbles him back into the water for another drenching, and it gets away. Final reversal, Willie quickly climbs back on the bank. Happy end, though he is wet and his pole is gone, at least his hat, an object of concern throughout, has damply survived through everything. He sits and puts it on, a climaxing act, as the episode fades out.

In its few minutes there have been fourteen comic reversals, each one good for a laugh, and each one helping to establish the larger film world of sudden and surprising change, in which the hero continually oscillates between triumph and disaster, safety and danger, dry and wet. Moreover, the fishing routine is further integrated into the film in that the episode itself, as a whole, is the before half of a demonstration of major change. It is a comic preview of the last episode in the coming day's climactic action sequence, a chase that, like Willie's walk, begins in town and moves to the country, ending again in a setting of rocks and water. Here these natural elements are parts of a low-keyed and minor comedy, in which Willie is featured as bumbling fisherman and ignorant victim, further examples of his first day's ineptitude. But his comic movements on the ledge and in the pool, like his casually performed comic feats on the train, have a strong potential for heroic development, a potential that will be realized in the parallel situation of the film's second day. The hero who comically leaps and tumbles among rocks and water now will much more spectacularly leap and tumble later. A comic fall guy for a waterfall now, he will reverse this situation and at the film's end achieve his glory, heroically triumphing over a much larger falls and its literal brink of doom.

Willie's wanderings around Rockville finished, the film's fifth sequence, the story of a man who came to supper, begins. In Willie's wanderings, he was twice led to the Canfield gate, and now, for the third and climactic time, he reaches and passes through it. Met by the girl at the door, he is unnecessarily introduced to the Canfield men, who stare aghast at their guest, even though he remains blissfully ignorant of their identity (the film's silence making temporarily credible introductions where no last names are mentioned). While the unsuspecting Willie strolls off with the girl, therefore, the two knowledgeable brothers head for the gunrack. Fortunately, Joe, a true southern gentleman, follows them and prevents an instant massacre, saying, "Wait boys! Our code of honor prevents us from shooting him while he's a guest—in our house."

Also helping maintain peace is Rockville's "kindly old parson," who now enters for his weekly visit. A white-haired old man with a shawl over his shoulders, he is also a little man, one whose diminutive size makes him an automatic ally of Willie and the girl and visually predicts that he will later come to the aid of their romance. As the parson is greeted, however, all thoughts of romance are temporarily curtailed. Briefly left on his own, Willie steps back by a drape and overhears one of the brothers complaining beyond it, "Father won't let us kill him in the house—but wait 'till he gets outside." Hurrying over to a butler, Willie for the first time asks whose house he is in. The answer is a one-word title, an unnecessary one, for both the butler's response and Willie's surprised repetition of the name can easily be lipread and almost heard—excellent examples of Keaton's ability to create audible silent speech.

For the remainder of what will be his first day at the Canfields, Willie is pesented as a timid and nervous victim, anxious to leave but afraid to do so. His first escape attempt is immediate. He runs out a side door, but the brothers notice and follow, chasing him around the house and firing after him. When he reaches the front door, all he can do to save himself is to go back in. Completing a circular, symmetrical move, which has taken him nowhere, he returns to the uneasy safety of the hall and Canfield hospitality.

When supper is served, it features three jokes on Willie's uneasy predicament. First, the girl asks the parson to pray, and as he does, the men all sit with heads bowed but only one eye closed. Willie's open eye glances nervously about, encountering as it does the steady, baleful, one-eyed glare of all his Canfield enemies. The butler next enters and clumsily drops a tray full of silver behind Willie, who responds by leaping nearly across the table. After that, there is a carving routine. A large turkey is set before Joe, who begins to sharpen a long knife, swinging it as he does so in a wide arc that ends just before Willie's neck. The gesture is repeated three times, with Willie's flinch a shade stronger each time. And then supper is over. A closeup of the turkey dissolves into a closeup of the turkey skeleton, and conspicuously full, all rise from the table and move to the hall.

An obvious place for some obvious gags, the hall becomes the setting for a series of comic variations on the theme of how to avoid leaving. They begin with a prolonged farewell handshake, as Willie shakes Joe's hand, then the girl's, then everyone's, then the girl's again—only with painful reluctance letting go of each of them. Next, he deliberately mislays his hat, throwing it under a bench, but his dog, who waits for him there, retrieves it. So he has the dog perform tricks for the unappreciative Canfield audience. Then, just as all delays seem exhausted, the parson is escorted to the door and discovers that it is raining. Joe observes ironically and hospitably, "It would be the death of any one to go outside tonight," and the girl leads the parson up the hall stairs so he can settle down till morning. Willie, by the door, watches all of this and takes the hint. He reaches outside on the porch for his carpetbag and umbrella, left there earlier, and soon in imitative motion is following the girl and the parson up the stairs, tipping his hat to the Canfield men below, one more polite gesture in a comedy of barely maintained manners.

A night instantaneously passes in a fadeout and a fadein to a title, but it is a crucial night and the film's central turning point, one that cuts across its seven divisions and establishes a major interrelationship between those that come before and those that come after it. In the remainder of the visiting sequence and in the following chase sequence, what happens will parallel or echo much of what has happened before. Where Willie before was inept, ignorant, or timid, however, at best a potential hero as in his feats on the train, he will now appear sublimely heroic and triumphant. A night's sleep is sufficient to transform Willie into the hero of a waking dream of adolescent glory, for in the world of Keaton comedy, tomorrow is always not only another day but a better day. Because of the incredibly tidy structure of the film, tomorrow is, in fact, almost the same day, only redeemed. The first day's hesitant courtship on the train will be initially repeated as a masterful wooing, and this will be followed once again by a pursuit, only now all out and deadly dangerous, a fact that makes a hero of Willie, just as the craftily concealed and hospitably curtailed earlier pursuit had reduced him to an ironically ignorant and absurd victim. As before, too, the chase will move from town to country and will again end with Willie by himself tumbling through rocks and water and even encountering a second waterfall, after which he will for the second time pay an evening's visit, a much more satisfying visit, to the Canfield home.

A title announces, "By the next day young McKay had decided to become a permanent guest," and the second day's continuation of the man-who-came-to-supper sequence is then presented in a single extended scene. In it, Willie is now self-assured and in control of the situation, no longer the frightened and reluctant visitor. From timid admirer of the girl, he has also turned into a bold and confident suitor. Further, helping to make his change both credible and more apparent, two comic acts performed unwillingly or in ignorance the day before will be performed again by him in more impressive ways. What Willie did before can easily be accepted as something he can do again, though now he will commit the acts consciously and courageously, elevating them and himself to a more heroic level.

The scene starts with the girl playing the piano. Willie stands beside her, romantically attentive; seated at a distance, watching both of them, are the three Canfield men. Discomposed but determined, Willie solves the problem of an unwanted audience by suddenly racing outside through a pair of French doors. The men all follow, in repetition of the previous day's chase around the house, but this second time Willie has already re-entered by an adjacent door as they are beginning their run outside. Very quickly back at the piano and alone with her at last, he once more leans intimately over the girl, though their romantic seclusion is somewhat undercut when he discovers the piece she plays is "We'll Miss You When You're Gone."

Soon, too, the Canfield men have circled the house, and one of the brothers positions himself by the now open doors, prepared for a second escape attempt. When a breeze blows the girl's music outside the parlor sanctuary, she asks Willie to fetch it for her, and he does. Walking up to the inattentive sentry, Willie calmly grabs his gun, fires it into the ground, returns it with mock courtesy, and then proceeds to retrieve the music and casually stroll back inside. The earlier ignorant disarming of the same brother in the same way in Rockville has thus been heroically repeated, and it is appropriately followed by a display of similar heroic determination in love. For the first time in the film, Willie kisses the girl.

The kiss, however, ends this phase of his courtship, for it is viewed by Joe, who angrily approaches. Willie retires to another room, and in several serious and emotional closeups, shots belonging to the world of real melodrama, Joe tells his daughter who her suitor is. She is stunned, and Willie, believing himself rejected, sadly leaves, so disconsolate that he even forgets the danger outside. Reminded by a gunshot, accidentally fired by the brother on sentry duty, he tumbles into a pratfall and then reverses direction, going not only inside but into an open closet. In a short scene building comic anticipation of what he will be like when he comes out of the closet, the girl, now recovered from her initial shock, runs up to her father and the brother with him. As they stand, towering and intransigent, their hands resolutely folded behind their backs, she, a small white form between them, pleads for Willie. It is another of the several emotional shots belonging to real melodrama, and when she finally asks, "You surely don't intend to kill him," Joe's tight-lipped failure to respond melodramatically answers her question.

As also happened in the prologue, after a shot in which Jim Canfield vowed to kill, this point of maximum threat is followed by a dramatic cut to the intended victim, who unlike his father is comically rather than melodramatically prepared. Willie leaves the closet, clothed in a poke bonnet and a long, bustled dress. His head down, his hands demurely folded before him, he reaches the front gate, but then the brother outside notices that the back of Willie's dress is hitched up and fails to cover his trousers. The brother fires, Willie runs, the two men inside race out, and the girl follows. Pursued by everyone, the man who came to supper is finally gone, and the film's sixth sequence, its major chase, has begun. The relatively contained indoor scenes now give way to frenetic action

outdoors, and the earlier comedy of manners, of politeness restraining violent feelings, is now replaced by magnificently hostile
motion, all of it totally unrestrained.

The chase sequence begins in town, at the end of the railroad line,
where the train is pulling out for its return to New York. From this
point, in the center of town, exactly the same place where his
wanderings began the day before, Willie will repeat and improve
upon his previous moves. His flight will gain in heroic intensity as he
progresses again to the country and to locations that grow more and
more wild and elemental.

The chase starts as Willie runs up and leaps into the second
carriage, the same one he had traveled in the day before. But then he
immediately leaps out, for the Canfields have also run up and are
searching the train. His leap accidentally landing him on the back of
a handy horse that stands by the window, Willie next gallops off into
the countryside, still followed by the gun-shooting Canfields. He
gallops anyway till his billowing hoop skirt and self-opening
umbrella topple him. When the Canfields run up, therefore, they see
him, now standing on the ground, his back to them and the umbrella
over his shoulder. Just before Joe fires, however, the figure turns
around and also turns from human to animal. It is not Willie but the
horse, dress and umbrella arranged over its rear and the bonnet on its
head.

At this point the elements take over. After whipping through a
wood, Willie races to a cliff. When he begins to crawl down it, he
inaugurates an episode among rocks and water, one recalling the
previous day's fishing trip, though in deliberate contrast to that, the
elements and his actions among them are now glorified and become
spectacular and heroic, if still satisfactorily comic.

Struggling along the massive cliff, Willie is soon trapped halfway
down, when a rocky ledge partially collapses beneath him. Hearing
his cries for aid, the Canfield brother who has been most actively
trying to shoot him secures one end of a rope (borrowed from a
handy prospector) to his own waist and drops the other end to Willie.
Willie also ties the rope around his waist and swings to a solider and
safer ledge—safer at least till he looks up and discovers his rescuer
preparing to shoot him. Instinctively, Willie attempts to flatten him-

self against the cliff but then stumbles, which causes him inadvertently to jerk on the rope. It plummets past him as he curiously watches, and when the brother passes too, he suddenly realizes what is about to happen. He braces himself in the most unmovable of stances and so posed is instantly yanked off his ledge. Falling past the brother, who has landed in a tree, he in turn topples the latter. Both, or two dummy substitutes, plunge into the water below.

Swimming to shore first, Willie climbs a bank, crosses a railroad track, and starts straining at the rope, an easy target for the brother, now also by the bank, who raises his gun. The New York train at this moment naturally comes by, effecting an accidental rescue. Its wheels sever the taut rope, and the brother splashes back into the water. Willie, however, is caught by the train and dragged along till a carriage wheel is derailed by the entangled rope. After being kicked at by the angry engineer (an incredibly high back kick, a specialty of the limber Joe Keaton), who walks back to examine the situation, Willie scurries for safety to the water side of the train. There he discovers, as he often has, that safety is a very relative thing, for he is once more a target threatened by the brother's gun.

Responding quickly, Willie leaps on the engine and rides off with it and its tender. Standing between the two, a leg resting on each, he shovels wood into the firebox, making his escape in super-fast motion. Then the engine and the tender come uncoupled. As on the day before, but now more dangerously and spectacularly, he is forced to use the train as a traveling gymnasium for the performance of athletic feats. Straddling the widening gap, he makes a mighty leap back onto the tender and is momentarily safe. Then, when the engine goes around a curve, the tender goes off the track, falling down the bank and into the water. In one of the best of the punlike quick visual changes undergone by people and objects in Keaton films, the tender's box instantly becomes a boat, the shovel an oar, and without blinking an eye at this sudden conversion and also complete change in direction, Willie rows and floats downstream.

Up to now there has been a chase, but after this second plunge into the water, Willie is no longer bothered by the Canfield men, who do not show up again until the film's seventh and final sequence. Now he is alone and battling nature, for the river he has fallen into propels him to a falls of Niagaran proportions. In a comedy of natural danger, he is soon tipped from the boat, while standing backward with his hand raised to see where he is or at least has just been. Thereafter, he is moved directly by the water as he is driven and swims along, belly-sliding over one semi-submerged rock, somersaulting over a second, shooting out of the water like a leaping fish, always speeding out of control as he nears destruction. What he has become is an existential comic hero, beleaguered by existential cosmic, comic threat, fighting to survive against the blows of nature itself, a world of drowning water. Temporarily, the plot of feud and frustrated love is forgotten. Only the filmic present exists, and in that present he is one small man pitted against the whole natural world, the most under of underdogs, and no one could resist empathizing with the lone man in his contest with the screen full of water. After he successfully survives, it will also be impossible for anyone to think of him as ineffectual or to be surprised by his athletic daring as he rescues the heroine. The Keaton hero is how he moves and what he moves upon, and this last journey through the rapids transforms Willie completely from the inauspicious and childish dandy of the introductory bicycle ride. It also washes away the last of his white face, the porcelain fragileness that had weakened his now determined features during the previous day's train trip to Rockville. Preserving only laughter, for his heroic moves are still funny ones, his river journey reveals him as a man of courage, resourcefulness, endurance, and also acceleration, which somehow has become for him an odd but integral virtue. From the beginning to this point, his moves have become faster and faster as a seeming combination of inner will and necessity propels him ineluctably, more and more quickly, to his final ordeal and triumph. Baptized as well as transported by the rapids, he has become the complete kinetic hero, the embodiment of adventurous action.

The triumph he unknowingly races toward is the rescue of the girl, who has been shown in several cutaway shots running through the woods and then resting by the river. Now as she sits there, she watches Willie bob by. As always, a needed prop is handy, and she leaps into a nearby boat and sets out to save him. Going through the rapids, however, the boat tips and she falls from it, which leaves her in Willie's predicament, swimming and floundering in the rushing water. Her parallel movements here, like her facial resemblance to him in the train, create a strong visual impression of mutual affinity. Even more than their few actual gestures of love, their sharing of the same watery dangers sets them apart from others and unites them, necessitating their final marital union.

Willie, meanwhile, as he is swept along, struggles unsuccessfully to escape. He grabs an overhanging vine and pulls himself up into a seated position, his legs braced against the steep river bank, but following this perfect setup for a pratfall, the vine snaps and he drops back into the water. Next he grabs a partially submerged log and ties his rope, still fastened around his waist, to it. No sooner is this managed, however, than the log breaks loose, and he is again swept downstream in a threatening tandem with it. When he soon reaches an immense waterfall, he goes over, but the log, which shifted from refuge to danger, now shifts roles once more to become his salvation. It jams in some rocks at the edge of the falls, and Willie's plunge is abruptly halted in midair. Scrambling painfully up the rope and onto the log, he reaches the safety of the rocks and there starts to untie himself. But when he notices the boat rush past and plunge over to the abyss below and then sees the girl following it, he stops. Having slowly climbed up the rope to the rocks, he now instantly reverses himself and leaps down over the falls. As the girl plummets by, Willie, like the weight on a pendulum, swings across the face of the falls in a giant arc and grabs her. Briefly the two dangle there, and then, at the end of a swing, he drops her on a ledge. Once again, he climbs the rope, and once again is threatened by an instant reversal and descent, for the log starts to move. Quickly wrapping the rope around a rock, Willie watches as the log goes over and the rope breaks. Now, finally safe, he clambers down the rocks and reaches the girl. On the second day as on the fishing excursion of the first, and with as many comic reversals, he has exerted himself among rocks and water, but where he was comically inept and ironically ignorant and victimized before, he has now with comic heroism repeated and transformed himself and achieved his glory.

On the ledge, he first kneels by the girl and then holds her tightly against him. It is a shot appropriate to a serious drama, the one real embrace in the film, the first completely unmannered and unfunny gesture of their courtship. Employing a technique that will be used in several later films, most remarkably in *Battling Butler*, Keaton's hero has achieved his final transcendence by moving out of the genre of stylized comedy into a world of real people, of real emotions and real physicality. Revealing a genuine and deep passion, the embrace is an immensely effective one, but then the film returns to its comic mode. The kindly village parson passes by, hears the commotion at the falls, and climbs down the rocks just in time to help Willie raise and escort the girl to the parson's carriage, in which the three drive off.

The film's final sequence, the seventh, like the opening prologue takes place at night. The exterior of the Canfield mansion is shown, its windows glowing in the dark and recalling the lightning-lit windows at the beginning. Joe and his sons enter, giving up the search till morning. Then, upstairs, Joe knocks on the girl's door and, hearing no response, softly pushes it open. Inside, he sees Willie and the girl, standing in a close embrace. The brothers see too, and the three men push their way into the room. But as the door is again closed, there is revealed behind it the parson, who walks over to Willie and the girl, their diminutive ally. Turning to the three large Canfield men, he asks, "Won't you kiss the bride?" The girl approaches Joe, pleading with him as she had done earlier and as his wife had done in the prologue. Looking over her head, he sees on the wall, again as in the prologue, the sampler with the message "Love thy neighbor as thyself." With that reminder, the world of the prologue is overcome. Joe kisses his daughter and then shakes hands with his new son-in-law. Laying his gun on the table, he also orders the brothers to do the same. Willie, watching, lets slip the parson's shawl draped over his shoulders, revealing six guns, which he in turn drops on the table, stooping at the disarming's apparent conclusion for one last weapon concealed in his boot. Then, in safety, he and the girl once more embrace and kiss.

That ends the film, a film that has been beautifully and thoroughly planned. In fact, most of its seven major divisions have been given such a carefully organized comic and dramatic structure that if excerpted, they could stand by themselves as complete entertainments. At the same time, however, each is also carefully fitted into

the charmingly simple, complexly coordinated whole. The counterpoint of melodrama in the prologue is used to enhance the pastoral
charm of the world that follows. Thereafter, first- and second-day
parallels and contrasts in situation and action are deftly and continuously managed, and further, such a pervasive unity of comic tone is
maintained within and among the various parts, that they and their
components continually echo and reinforce one another. The train
and the hero, the train's journey and the hero's total journey, the
fishing episode and the final chase sequence—if all are different, all
are also closely related elements in a single cheerful comic vision,
one of constant surprises and successive reversals and final triumphs.

The hero, too, is both a simple and a complex creation. He is, with
his white face and his slapstick falls, part clown, he is part
adolescent fantasy figure, and he is part existential man who creates
himself through action. He is a character, moreover, whose development as adventurer and lover is worked out in great detail, even
though the rapidity and the seeming spontaneity with which he
moves from one scene to another often conceal the great order and
purpose which underlie all of the film's visual statements about him,
all designed to shape and then to change the impression he makes, to
both comically surprise and convince us with his growth into heroic
glory. A changing hero, Willie is also a composite hero, the seeming
simplicity of his characterization being expressive of a wider range
of qualities and interests—first comically innocent, then comically
experienced, first civilized, polished, and polite, then elemental,
assertive, and courageous—than is usually found in the leading
figure of American movies. He is a Woody Allen hero who is also a
Clint Eastwood hero, an Ashley Wilkes who is simultaneously a
Rhett Butler, a fine, foppish, farcical clown who is also a mountain-
climbing, rapids-shooting, ceaselessly moving adventurer.

All of the film's major effects, all of its plot and character progressions certainly, are obviously intended and carefully assembled.
Though the adjectives in current criticism are generally pejorative
ones, *Our Hospitality* would have to be described as well-made and
even excessively linear. Each sequence, each scene, each gag, each
shot, economically performs its necessary function within the harmonious unity of the film, a unity whose rigorously shaped form has

been fully controlled from beginning through middle to end. The glory of Keaton's achievement, however, is that the control never shows. If always there for a purpose within the larger patterns of the film, what happens at any moment is also so unpredictable that the film itself almost seems free and unplanned, a continuous improvisation—as in places it probably is. There is nothing random in the selection and placing of any particular scene, whether a fishing excursion or a leave taking, and everything in it is also related to the scene's reasons for being in the film. At the same time, however, Keaton and his crew—his gagmen, his cameramen, his technical director—were so professionally knowledgeable about comedy that they needed no written scenario to guide them. Their customary method of developing any particular scene, comically repeating a theme action or devising a series of startling comic changes, allowed for improvisation, an on-the-spot invention of whatever gags the setting and situation allowed.

The impression of improvisation so created is, in fact, so strong that few people watching the film are likely to see through it to the organizational principles—the parallelisms and contrasts and meaningful repetitions—that control the free-floating comic spontaneity. Concealed by the overwhelming rush of events and the stunning proliferation of laughs, the architectonics of *Our Hospitality* are almost invisible at a first or casual viewing. It is the solidity of the film's construction, however, the efficient and economical craftsmanship with which it is built, that helps raise it to the heights of a classic and perfectly formed pastoral ideal. Popular entertainment, a farcical melodrama, it is also high comic art. And most of the remaining silent features are as good.

4.

Sherlock Junior

THE FANTASIZING OF REALITY

$\mathcal{S}$END YOUNG PEOPLE out today to make a movie, some young people anyway, and they might easily come up with a film that resembles *Sherlock Junior*. Being young and imitative, they will decide to produce a parody of one of their favorite Hollywood action features—a silent parody, one improvised on location, since their super-eight equipment has no sound and they cannot afford sets. They will shoot on neighborhood streets and lawns, which will be animated with chases and fights and much energetic arm waving. The leading roles, of course, will be taken by themselves and their friends, though maybe a parent will have to be recruited for a minor part.

What this description reveals is that adolescents today in making their home movies are likely to recapitulate the early history of the cinema. Reciprocally, the many parallels to Keaton's production methods also suggest that his features could have been made by (very gifted) adolescents. A similarly youthful spirit is at work in them. They are the creations of a relatively young man, who was only twenty-seven when he started *Our Hospitality* and thirty-three when he finished *Steamboat Bill Jr.* And of all his films, *Sherlock Junior* seems the most cheerfully immature. It is a movie world as it might be visualized by the youngest possible adult.

If it resembles today adolescent parody, almost a Keaton home movie, it is, however, not that at all. It is something more adult,

75

more professional, and more successfully comic. It is less an adolescent parody of movies and more an irreverent parody of movie
adolescents in its satiric comments on then current Hollywood conventions for depicting the young. Further, it aims a few satiric jabs at
young movie fans who attempt to imitate their idols of the silver
screen. Finally, and this is the most interesting aspect of the film, it
is a sophisticated and intelligent playing with the toys of fantasy and
reality, of an actual world and a dream world, of a movie and a
movie within a movie. It is structured as a real life comedy, in which
the adolescent hero ignominiously suffers, followed by a wish-
fulfillment dream, in which he stars in a dream movie, followed by
his awakening into real life and also into a happy ending. While
ostensibly the two worlds, real and dream, are neatly separated into
the self-contained divisions characteristic of a Keaton feature, they
are actually and deliberately so merged, so intentionally mixed up
with each other, that they cannot be separated at all. They have so
many similarities that by the end they are indistinguishable, both
parts of a single highly stylized, highly comic, highly real unreality.
Whether presented as real or dream, the film's world throughout is a
unified vision of a fantastic reality, or of a realistic fantasy, seen by a
creative and transforming comic eye.

The description in the *American Film Institute Catalog* provides
an entry into the film and also demonstrates that no written description of a film in no matter how scholarly a book is apt to be accurate.
The catalog synopsis: ''Sherlock, Jr., who is both the cleanup man
and the projectionist at a local cinema, becomes an amateur detective
through a correspondence course and foils the villain who has stolen
his girl and her watch. He dreams of success on the screen and
awakens to find success in his romance.'' The hero studies a book on
how to be a private detective, but its origin—though a correspondence course would be the most likely cliché of the time—is never
explicitly indicated. Further, he does not foil the villain, his girl does
that, and the stolen watch is not hers but her father's.

With these exceptions, the Institute's summary, what there is left
of it, is accurate. The hero of the film is identified in the opening
titles as ''a boy,'' who is ''employed as a moving picture operator in
a small town theater'' while ''also studying to be a detective.'' Like

another fictional juvenile of the period, Booth Tarkington's Penrod, who fantasized himself as Penrod Jasper, world-renowned detective, this boy, too, has criminological dreams of glory. First shown as he sits in the theater, he wears a fake mustache, and with the aid of a magnifying glass and a detective's instruction book, he studies a fingerprint, his own. Since he is supposed to be cleaning up, however, the theater manager soon enters and angrily orders him back to work. Proceeding with what seems an artlessly explicit introduction of the principals, "the girl in the case" is next presented in a shot of her along with a large dog, a frequent appurtenance of Keaton heroines. Then the introductions rapidly include brief close-ups of her father and his hired man, who will be important later in the dream but now functions only as a laugh in a title: "The girl's father had nothing to do, so he got a hired man to help him." Following these two men, in this illustrated listing, is the villain, "the local sheik," heavily built, thinly mustached, and totally broke. He stands outside a candy store but cannot afford to go in and make a purchase.

Pausing in his work, the boy had gone to the same candy store window that the sheik stands by and also looked at the boxes of chocolates there, particularly a three-dollar box of extravagant dimensions. Checking his pockets, however, he found that he too could not afford a purchase, for he had only two dollars. With his need for another dollar established, there soon follows a carefully polished comic routine, one involving the rapid reversals of fortune and the rapid play with props that provide many of the best moments in Keaton's work. Back in the lobby, the boy sweeps up a mountainous pile of litter, and casually poking through it, he finds a dollar. As he is about to take off for the candy store, however, a pert lady, dressed in fur-trimmed black and carrying a beaded bag, immediately appears, saying, "I lost a dollar—did you find it?" Honest but reluctant, the boy replies, "Describe it." She does; he checks the appearance of the found bill, realizes the description is unquestionably accurate, and sadly returns it. Now he is back to two dollars. Worse, an impoverished elderly lady enters, with the same plaint, "I lost a dollar." What can the boy do with an old lady in distress but give her one of his, so that in a rapid shift from fortune to poverty he has gone from two dollars to three and then down to one. When a

rough-looking customer resembling Black Larsen in *The Gold Rush*
appears next, no titles are necessary. The boy is trapped in a
mechanical routine, a comedy of forced automation. And by now he
knows his move, so without even waiting for a word from the
unshaven, heavy-browed thug, he hands over his last dollar, reduced
to nothing. But the thug shoves it back as too small; it is not what he
has come for. Looking about in the debris, he retrieves instead a
wallet full of bills and leaves with that. Hoping to recover his former
fortune, the boy himself now ploughs through the debris, which had
been as rich as a Klondike lode, but he finds nothing. Still, a modified happy ending for the routine, he has retained one dollar, and
when yet another burly customer approaches, he runs to the candy
store to spend it while it is still his.

Purchasing a very small box of candy, he changes the one dollar
price marked on the back to a more impressive four dollars and skips
enthusiastically but gawkily up the sidewalk to the girl's door. As
gawkily and enthusiastically she runs down the hall stairs to meet
him, and with another gawky adolescent gesture, points the way to
the parlor, where they next appear sitting together on a couch.
Beginning a comedy of restrained and awkward gestures, of adolescent inexperience and hesitation in love, he abruptly hands her the
candy. Then, however, the sheik also comes calling. Standing
unnoticed in the hallway, he observes the young lovers in the parlor.
Preparing for action against his rival, he rifles through a vest hanging
there and steals a pocket watch belonging to the girl's father. In a
short series of crosscuts, the girl first examines a ring the boy has
given her, searching for the stone with his detective's magnifying
glass; and then the sheik comes out of a pawnshop. The girl and the
boy stare dumbly straight ahead, not quite sure what to do next; and
the sheik appears inside the candy store, where the clerk takes the
three-dollar box from the window. The boy timidly holds the girl's
hand, and then his slow courting rapidly ends, for the sheik barges
into the parlor and with his superior chocolates routs his rival. He
leads the acquiescent girl into another room, drawing a curtain across
the doorway after them to shut out the boy.

Worse soon follows. The girl's father, wearing a vest from which
no watch chain dangles, enters, followed by the sheik, the girl, and

her mother. Standing in the doorway, he announces, "Some one has stolen my watch." "It looks like a job for the police," responds the sheik. "I'll take charge of this case and start by searching everybody," cries the boy. He then sits and consults his self-help detective book to see how this should be done, and while he studies, the sheik surreptitiously plants something in his pocket. A conspicuous mirror over a mantel behind the boy is placed where it could reflect the sheik's action, but the boy, preoccupied and unobservant, never glances toward it, a missed opportunity that will be rectified later in his dream. Study finished, the boy searches the most unlikely suspect first, the father, next the sheik, and then he glances decorously in the pinafore and apron pockets of the girl and her mother.

Irritated, the father thereupon turns about and insists on searching the boy. What he finds is a four-dollar pawn ticket for one watch and chain, the object planted by the resourceful sheik. Nearly as damning in the quickly developing chain of circumstantial evidence, is the fact that the boy's box of chocolates is also marked four dollars. "I'm sorry, my boy, but we never want to see you in this house again," says the father, ordering him out. While they are all still in the parlor, the sheik brushes off the boy's porkpie hat, a metonymic visual symbol for the way he has adroitly brushed off his rival, and then hands it back to him. In the hall, the girl returns the boy's ring; and concluding the sequence of ejection, whose shots neatly and symmetrically reverse those in the sequence of entry, the boy is next seen disconsolately standing on the porch outside. When the sheik also leaves the house, the boy again consults his detective's instruction book and sets out to follow him.

The interior scenes so far, in the theater, the candy store, and primarily the girl's home, have been employed for the full exposition of character, situation, and basic conflicts. The outdoor sequence that comes next is in contrast pure action, with no titles needed till it is over. Things have been arranged to start the hero moving, and as usual with a Keaton hero, once the boy is set in motion, he simply moves. That is all there is and it is enough—here a pursuit, a reversal, a momentary entrapment, and an escape.

As his rival strolls in front of him, the boy first follows so closely that he becomes an unconscious impersonator, repeating the other man's movements precisely, though being much shorter on a rather smaller scale. Just a few feet behind, his legs move in unison, he stumbles exactly as the other does, and he halts in exactly the same stance at a curb, an awkward forward lean into which the sheik freezes to avoid stepping in front of a car. As they so proceed, the sheik and his shadow, their performance is essentially a vaudeville routine, one like that more explicitly recreated by Keaton in the two-reeler *The Playhouse*. There playing all the parts in a minstel show, he in one trick shot appeared as a duo dance team, two not surprisingly complete look alikes doing a soft-shoe shuffle with hat and cane, each in movement the precise equivalent of the other. Here, however, the stylized mimicking moves are made on a sidewalk rather than a stage, in what is otherwise a real world. And as the two identically proceed, their comically patterned routine casually undermines the reality of the street, transforming it into a giant backdrop for a duo walking act.

Not only the walk but also the rapid exchange with the dollar bills earlier in the theater lobby is patterned after a standard piece of comic action taken from the stage. They are both examples of Keaton's characteristic depiction of life as a never-ending vaudeville program. But they both fit easily into the film, do not seem staged insertions, in that nearly everything else is as stylized as they are. Though the boy's story purports to be real and is followed by his dream, the real part of *Sherlock Junior* is as fantastic as the dream part and in many ways as far removed from reality. For example, one reason the two vaudeville routines do not disrupt the stylistic decorum of the real part is that throughout the actors are presented as performers playing in a burlesque—clowns all—rather than performers trying to simulate actual people. The boy, though at first sight he seems to be dressed and made up in a realistic way, without the exaggerations of baggy pants and white face that identify and slightly isolate the clowns of the two-reelers, becomes on second sight at least a recognizable relation of theirs. It becomes noticeable very quickly that both Keaton and his father, Joe Keaton, who plays the girl's father, are wearing burlesque slap shoes, clown's size fifteen or so footgear, which turn up strongly in the toe. As they move about the father's house, they seem two strayed vaudevillians, somehow turned up and doing their turn in a nontheatrical setting. And as they walk, the film world moves several steps beyond the photographed reality of naturalistic sets or actual locations into a conceived and comic realm where mimicking shadows also reasonably belong.

The characters do not derive in their actions and dress only from the world of vaudeville. They also have a parodic origin in the world of film. The naive listing of the cast at the beginning—boy, girl, father, handyman, sheik—though conventional for the time, seems deliberately naive, intended to call attention to the fictitiousness of the fiction about to be presented. The generic labeling in the list, this being the only Keaton feature in which absolutely no one is named, further stresses the formulaic qualities of the fiction, that what are being introduced are stock screen characters, the basic ingredients of thousands of movies. Here we go again, the listing implies, with the usual "boy" and "girl" and a "sheik" for a villain, so why even bother further to identify them. They are to be consciously enjoyed as standard movie characters doing standard movie things, not to be taken seriously but as parodic entertainments. Though they and their predictable story are never in doubt, however, the making of that predictability a source of comedy, part of a satire on movie conventions, transforms it into something unpredictable and funny.

In other ways, too, the characters have been oriented toward the world of film as much as to the world of actuality. Mary Pickford's picture is prominently displayed in the theater lobby where the boy sweeps up, and the resemblance between the girl and that picture does not seem accidental. Like the Pickford screen character, she wears her hair in long curls and is dressed in a childish pinafore. Not only does she look like Pickford, she corresponds to the typical Pickford heroine in being small-town, adolescent, vivacious, and wholesomely cute. Like the Pickford heroine, she is even the dynamic force in the real life half of the film. She, it turns out, is the one who will solve the crime, and at the end she will come to break the good news to the boy, though perhaps she should be described as a Pickford heroine in embryo, since her scenes are not long enough to dominate the film. As with most Keaton heroines, hers is a minor part. Certainly, however, she is one of the few Keaton heroines who act, and the only one who saves the day rather than, as in the coming dream sequences, requiring to be saved herself.

In the girl's resemblances to Pickford, there seems to be a double comic thrust. There are elements of satire aimed at the Pickford heroine, a gentle spoofing of the well-known type. There is also, more important, a satire aimed at the movie-going audience, at all the young girls in the country who would model themselves on a screen idol. If the boy's later dream of glory is a transformation and confusion of the characters and events of his real world into a movie adventure, the heroine is already, as an imitative Pickford fan, an embodiment of that confusion, a gawky adolescent actuality comically attempting to look like an agreeable screen illusion. And like her, the two other characters in the central love triangle both seem to aspire to the image of a movie star. The boy is probably a would-be John Barrymore, whose film *Sherlock Holmes* was first released two years before *Sherlock Junior*, and his rival, the sheik, is a would-be Valentino. To the rather limited extent that life in the first part of the film is presented as real, reality aspires to and confuses itself with screen fantasy. The characters all attempt to live in a waking dream of glory, but they comically and continually fall short of the screen ideal they pattern themselves upon.

The most interesting failure in this respect is the sheik. This down-at-the-heels dandified rival of the boy is not an adolescent or even a young man, some variation of the Rudolph Valentino gigolo suggested by his stock label. Instead he is a solid, full-waisted, middle-aged lover, who looks in the film to be about forty. His sheikish aspirations, expressed in cheaply flashy clothing and the pursuit of the girl, markedly contrast with his basic reality, again with a double satiric thrust in the discrepancy that results. Grubby life imitating elegant art is foolish and funny, but the real life parody of the screen ideal also points up the latter as an empty and specious illusion, which is itself fraudulently unreal. Though he is a parodic failure as a sheik, however, neither the boy nor the girl, nor her father and mother, notice the rival's unsuitability. Though he is as old as the girl's father, he is as acceptable a suitor as the boy, and another satiric comment on film conventions results, an unlikely love triangle of confused age groups. It is so casually presented, with such a visual matter-of-factness, that it can almost be taken as real, but it is instead a put-on. Rather than depicting a real love rivalry, even a comic one, the sheik, the boy, and the girl parody movie love rivalry, the standard scenario in which an ingenuous but worthy young hero wins the heroine from an older, more experienced, and probably villainous rival. In the parodic triangle, reality is again confusing itself with the movies and executing a very bad and very unconvincing and therefore very funny imitation of them.

In all these ways, then, actions and characters have so far been so thoroughly and consciously grounded in the conventions of vaude-ville and of film, containing in particular much parodic and two-edged laughter at the expense of the latter and its audience, that there is very little in the real life sequences that is simply and directly presented as real rather than as an oblique commentary upon the movies and their fantasizing effect upon real life. Only perhaps the settings. The interiors are probably all sets, though realistic ones, but the outside shots so far are all taken on actual locations. The girl's house is a slightly shabby lower-middle-class bungalow, with much scraggly grass sprouting about the steps of the lattice-work porch. And as the boy follows the sheik, they proceed along a real residential street of similar small homes. The background at least looks like the "small town" mentioned in the opening titles. But then it becomes apparent that the small town setting is again a film convention that is not being taken very seriously. Behind the houses, a large blank building, evidently a studio stage, impressively looms, and when the boy follows the sheik into a railroad yard, oil wells will tower in the distance. What is being filmed is genuinely a Keaton home movie, shot in the streets of Hollywood and Los Angeles, and no one is making any effort to disguise the fact. The "small town" of the opening titles is simply a comic acknowledgment of the fact that such adolescent heroes and heroines as the boy and the girl, all the Tol'able Davids and Hoodoo Anns of the silent screen, were inevitably placed in a *Saturday Evening Post* never-never land of rural America, of country towns and happy valleys, where innocence and virtue romantically thrive. Though Hollywood at the time was not very large, to use the movie colony itself as a typical movieland small town is just one more casually irreverent comment on screen conventions. Unlike the realistically depicted small towns of *Our Hospitality, Battling Butler, The General,* and *Steamboat Bill, Jr.,* the small town here is deliberately as unreal and parodic as everything else.

Further undermining the reality of the settings, there is at this point, as the mimicking boy tails the sheik, a curious and creative transformation, for the camera soon turns real objects into stylized and comic abstractions. To summarize the action first, after the imitative me-and-my-shadow vaudeville walk the boy and the sheik enter a railroad yard. There the boy is first nearly flattened by a rolling freight car, then blasted by a burst of steam from a locomotive, and next, when the sheik climbs a stairway to a track-side platform, misses the steps and walks into the side of the platform instead. When he does climb the steps, he finds himself walking past the sheik, who has now stopped and stands on the platform, staring at him. With a certain presence of mind, the boy immediately pretends that he just happens to be strolling along and therefore keeps on walking, straight into the open door of a refrigerator car. The sheik instantly closes it behind him, and the train at that moment naturally starts to move. The boy's imprisonment, however, is only temporary, for soon he escapes through a trap door on top of the car. Running along the moving cars, which pass in front of a background watertank, he stays where he is till he runs out of cars, and then he leaps from the last one and grabs onto the watertank's spout. It slowly starts to lower him in a graceful arc, but then, as a flood of water pours forth, sends him plummeting, half-drowned in the deluge, to the track below.

While the action, with its many instant reversals, is exaggeratedly comic, the setting of this railroad-yard episode is real. To match the stylized performance taking place within it, its reality must therefore be undermined, and camera placement effectively fantasizes it. It is such that trains or more accurately and significantly parts of trains fill the screen, dwarfing the boy and the sheik, who carry on now in a context of giant machinery and pure geometrical shapes. The best of these shots comes first. The left half of the screen is almost entirely filled by the end of a boxcar, and then the sheik walks in frame from the right and passes in front of the car. The boy, still following him, also enters but walks only up to the car and then steps behind it to conceal himself. Immediately, another car end rolls in from the right, like the stationary car filling most of its half of the screen as it approaches the boy. For a moment all we see is one small human about to be squashed between two implacable rectangular threats, a symmetrical abstraction of comic doom. Then the coupling units stop the cars from slamming together, leaving a narrow vertical gap of almost abstract comic safety. It is certainly a shot that transcends realism, like the shot of the giant and threatening locomotive that follows, its side filling most of the screen as it hisses steam at the passing boy. And there is the final shot of the boy running across the tops of the four moving boxcars, each seen only from the side, reduced to a two-dimensional racing rectangle on wheels, a cartoon-like abstraction of the dangerous surface of things upon which the human figure has nimbly to run in order to survive, in order not to be carried off into a filmic nonexistence beyond the screen.

Because the train shapes are so large that they create the screen world we see, and because even then not all of an engine or a car appears on the screen but only an abstraction derived from it, an immense and powerful assemblage of wheels and bars and pipes, existing solely to spout steam at the hero, or a moving rectangle that threatens to crush or to carry the hero entirely out of the movie—because of these stylizations, the sensation created by the episode is of a fantastic vision, a dream world where familiar objects have acquired a hallucinatory strangeness, are different from what they formerly, really, were. Throughout the film reality has been casually treated or disregarded, but here it is transformed, in a very filmic way, into a comic abstraction of danger. In the one episode of the film's real life part that is not indebted to vaudeville routines or colored by parodic jokes on the movies, reality is still changed, manipulated for comic ends. Seen through a creative eye, it becomes unreal, dreamlike, and supremely funny, as fantastic certainly as anything in the boy's subsequent dream.

With the boy damply dumped to the ground, the railroad sequence ends as two linemen on a handcart propel themselves underneath the waterspout waterfall. Splashed into a tumble, they retaliate by angrily chasing after the boy. Threatened by them, changed from man following to man pursued, he runs into the background. And only at this point, with the action of the outdoor sequence over, is there need for a transitional title to move the film also in a new direction: "As a detective he was all wet, so he went back to see what he could do to his other job." Once again at the theater, evidently for the afternoon performance, he is now not janitor but projectionist. He is shown preparing for his work in his booth, the audience gathers in the small auditorium, and then there is a cutaway to the pawn shop, where the girl hands the proprietor the pawn ticket. As they talk, the sheik passes outside, pausing to light a cigarette, whereupon the pawn broker points him out to the girl, who has solved the crime. Unaware of this, however, the boy starts projecting the afternoon's film, *Hearts and Pearls* or *The Lounge Lizard's Lost Love*. Possibly because it is a Veronal Pictures production, Veronal being a popular but dangrous soporific of the period (two younger sisters of the novelist Ivy Compton-Burnett committed suicide by taking overdoses), he soon tires of it and yawns. A title states, "A projectionist's job is tedious . . . and the monotony makes him fall asleep." Soon, "he dreams."

In his dream, as a transparent double-exposed apparition standing beside his sleeping real self, he first sees the characters in the movie being replaced by those from real life. An actor and actress, for example, after looking at the camera, turn their backs to it, and when they once more face it, they are the sheik and the girl. Startled, the boy hurries down to the auditorium for a closer view. Then, no longer a transparent dream figure but solid and real, he climbs onto the stage and from there, when the sheik and the girl enter her bedroom and begin kissing, he excitedly steps into the screen. Thrown back out by the sheik, he tries again, once more stepping into the screen, which now shows the exterior of the girl's house. This time he stays there but also remains a real person in the film world, which has not yet assimilated him, leaving him unaffected by cuts to new settings. Such cuts instantly proliferate, and the result is a typical Keaton comedy of actions that are funny because performed in inappropriate contexts, here uniquely inappropriate. Sitting on a garden bench, the boy suddenly falls when the setting instantly cuts to a busy street. Leaping away from that, he nearly jumps off a cliff.

Peering over that, after another instant cut he is staring into a lion's mouth. The settings continue rapidly to shift, from desert to ocean to the snow-covered north, but following a dive into the water that becomes in midair a header into a snowbank, the disconcerting cuts end. The boy is finally a part of the movie. In fact, he is now the leading character in *Hearts and Pearls*.

Though the cutting episode is in no way integrated into the plot of the dream movie, still it is neatly done, and in its alienating of the boy from his context, it is an impressive demonstration of film's ability because of its two-dimensional surface to confuse and merge different kinds of visual impressions. When he steps into the small screen, the boy changes from a seemingly three-dimensional person in a three-dimensional world into a seemingly flat image, though actually Keaton is walking into another stage setting placed behind the screen's cutout frame. The subsequent rapid cutting among the widely disparate settings, cutting that fails to affect the boy, also points up how easily editing can create a convincing impression of something that does not exist. The boy's seemingly continuous motion throughout the cuts, which makes him appear a real person in the imaged settings, is an illusion, produced by juxtaposing shots in which his final position in one is adopted as his initial position in the next, making Keaton's discrete actions seem continuous.

In these ways, the episode comically proves how easily film falsifies things. It is as natural for the medium to fool the eye through editing or dimensional deceptions as it is for it simply to record what is real. As a master of film illusion, Keaton would have been appalled or amused by a single-minded realist critic like Siegfried Kracauer and his much quoted *Theory of Film: The Redemption of Physical Reality*. This episode alone pragmatically refutes any dogmatic definition that, like Kracauer's, attempts to limit film to the truthful reproduction or even redemption of what is real. It is just as basic to the medium to create illusions and to deal in dreams. To take the movies as somehow real, like the boy, the girl, and the sheik in their imitative aspirations to glorified movie roles, is naive, a comic and quixotic abandoning of the real world in favor of a fantasy replacement that they mistake for reality.

And that, in his dream, is exactly what the boy does, for now his

whole bungled real day is repeated on a plane of transcendent movie
success. Following the customary Keaton pattern of repetition in
which a novice hero replaces an initial disastrous attempt with a later
successful performance, the boy is now transformed from an inept
amateur into the world's most competent detective. His glorification,
in fact, charitably extends to nearly everyone. Most of the people
from his real life are similarly exalted in order to provide a context
worthy of his dream eminence. The girl exchanges her long curls
and childish pinafore, the emblems of a small-town ingenue, for a
short flapper hairdo and a correspondingly sophisticated dress, slinky
and clinging and black. Her father is elevated from the dowdy lower
classes into the ranks of tuxedoed millionaires, moving from a
bungalow to a mansion. And even his handyman, introduced but
nonfunctional in the real life part, has been introduced there, it turns
out, so that he can reappear higher up in the servants' hierarchy as
the father's butler in the dream. The sheik, from penniless dude is
transformed into a high society lounge lizard with sleeked-back hair,
and from petty thief is also elevated to being head of a criminal gang.
The watch that he stole is similarly aggrandized, becoming a string
of pearls. The only demotions from real life are the girl's mother,
who appears in a few shots as a background maid, and the theater
manager. The latter, a victim of the boy's aspiring ego, is no longer a
complaining and unappreciative boss but becomes instead Sherlock's
devoted assistant, Gillette, "a Gem who is Ever-Ready in a bad
scrape." (Not only a razor blade but an actor is alluded to in the
name. William Gillette was the first to play Sherlock Holmes on the
American stage.)

Dream action begins as the father discovers that his safe has been
robbed. Calling everyone over to a doorway hung with drapes, the
same location in a more elegant version where the theft of the watch
was disclosed, he announces the loss of a pearl necklace to the girl,
the butler, and the sheik. The announcement, it turns out, is not
entirely necessary, for the sheik suavely and secretly slips the pearls
to the butler while the father is talking. When the father next goes to
the phone, however, the sheik's composure shatters, and he exclaims, "We are lost! He is sending for the world's greatest
detective— Sherlock Jr!" The butler, still calm and more resource-

ful, responds by leading the sheik to a pool table and an adjacent window. As it happens, he has two exploding number thirteen billiard balls in his pocket. One is for demonstration purposes; thrown through the window at a tree, it blasts it apart. The second is to be placed on the billiard table. In a game with the sheik, it is to be hit by the unsuspecting detective. Incredibly and comically well prepared for what has only just occurred, the butler also demonstrates another device, a chair whose seat is wired to a large ornamental battle ax hanging on the wall behind it. When pressure is applied, the ax drops, aimed to split the skull of anyone sitting there.

At this point of melodramatic threat, Sherlock Jr. first appears in the movie as an elegant white-gloved hand ringing the doorbell in response to the father's call for help. As dream hero, he is much needed by the girl's family, rather than merely tolerated and then ejected. Inside, everyone moves expectantly toward the door, and then Sherlock, the cynosure of the waiting audience, enters, impeccably attired in formal evening dress. As they all assemble before him, with the mother turned maid briefly present in the background, he again starts an investigation by in a way searching everybody. Father, sheik, and the girl are lined up, and Sherlock stares closely into the face of each, leaving them all satisfactorily discomposed by his steely, probing gaze. After next examining the rifled safe with the father, he omnisciently understands everything, observing, "Don't bother to explain—this is a simple case for me."

With the crime already more or less solved, Sherlock devotes the remainder of his stay to thwarting the villains' efforts to do him in, a thwarting easily managed, for where in real life the boy was inept, in his dream it is his rivals who are the comically clumsy bunglers. Sensibly suspicious of them, Sherlock easily avoids their booby-trapped chair and next declines a poisoned drink offered by the butler. When the friendly game of dynamite pool is proposed, he also detects, in a mirror reflection, the butler's stealthy substitution of the explosive billiard ball. It is a sharp-eyed observation that makes up for the real-life missed opportunity, when the boy failed to see in a similarly placed mirror the planting of the pawn ticket in his pocket by the sheik.

As the game proceeds, the sheik and the butler run into another room and wait nervously whenever it is Sherlock's turn. He, however, composedly plays on, and finally he clears the table of all the balls except number thirteen. Then he hits that one too, and nothing happens. Strolling out, he passes his trembling opponents in the adjacent room, and they immediately rush back in to see what went wrong. Both are so flustered as they examine the table that the sheik unthinkingly rests his foot on the death chair, nearly losing it when the ax swings down. This in turn so upsets the butler that he grabs a drink to steady himself, the poisoned drink declined by Sherlock, naturally, which he then rapidly spits back out. In the last shot of the sequence, a strong contrast to the chaotic discomposure within, Sherlock leaves the house, still cool and unflappable, his determined face retaining the unfathomable and blank expression it has held throughout, making this the one extended sequence in the film where Keaton's sobriquet of the great stone face would precisely fit. He checks in his pocket, and there is the explosive number thirteen ball, a comic prop too useful to be discarded after only one joke. Exiting, he takes it with him.

In the interior sequence, the millionaire's house is obviously a stage set, a parody of a low-budget movie's unconvincing fabrication of reality, and also a parody of the sort of stage-bound production, a photoplay, that characterized film's early years. *Hearts and Pearls* was advertised in its opening titles as being "in five acts," and the few shots of it that were shown before the boy's dream replaced them were presented as a stilted and stagey carryover from the theater, a carryover that Keaton, one of the first makers of fully filmic films, could easily afford to laugh at. And so the movie house, and after it the dream house, is not only obviously but also intentionally a set, an unsuccessful imitation of the real world intended to fool no one. At this point, however, as in the real life portion of the film, with the initial exposition of the dramatic situation accomplished action again moves outdoors, where it will proceed with a minimum of titles. And once outdoors, the settings it takes place in will again mostly be real, the streets of Hollywood or Los Angeles and the surrounding countryside.

The transition to the chase sequence begins with a debunking title: "By the next day the master mind had completely solved the mystery—with the exception of locating the pearls and finding the thief." Following this, Sherlock first appears in his fool-the-eye home. Dressing before a mirror, which reflects the contents of the room, he suddenly steps through it, for the mirror is a door leading to a second room, which is furnished exactly like the one he has just left. Next, he goes to and unlocks a bank-vault door. Surprisingly, it opens directly onto the street, where a passing trolley car momentarily fills the entire door frame, a surreal image of a moving vehicle that in the context is both acceptably real and hallucinatorily implausible.

Once outside, Sherlock prepares to tail the sheik. When the latter parks his car and walks into a building, the detective, like the boy before, closely shadows him, only a few steps to the rear. As the boy's clumsiness momentarily undermines his dream of glory, the detective even walks into the edge of a door that the sheik leaves open behind him, just as the boy had bumped into the wall by the steps to the railroad platform. Steps, too, reappear, for now the sheik climbs a stairway inside the building, and once on the second-floor landing, as on the platform before, he discovers his pursuer. After looking down behind him, he quickly drops his hat at the base of a ladder leading up to the roof, and then from a closet hiding place he watches as Sherlock mounts the ladder and exits through a trap door. Once again the sheik has an opportunity to lock a door behind his rival, and having done so, he leaves. Stuck again on the top of something, the detective quickly escapes in a manner paralleling the boy's escape from the boxcars. In one of the best comic movements of the film, he leaps from the roof of the two-story building onto the end of an upright railroad crossing guard, which provides a surer descent than the treacherous watertank spout, slowly lowering him in a giant graceful arc into the back seat of the sheik's open car. As the sheik drives away, the inexorable detective is therefore still closely shadowing him, only one seat behind.

At this point the chase in the real world had ended, as the boy, all wet and with no sheik in sight, went off to work. In the dream version, it has only begun and will soon build, as the final sequences in Keaton movies generally do, to a maximum amount of comic action and confusion—here a capture, an escape, a race, and a rescue.

Comic confusion starts immediately with Gillette, who is disclosed clinging to the car's rear-mounted spare tire. Once the sheik has reached and entered the gang's hideout, Gillette mysteriously hands Sherlock a large flat round paper box with a dress folded inside. Leaving the audience to wonder about this, a cutaway to the interior of the gang's shack reveals the sheik, who displays the stolen pearls to three gang members. Outside again, Sherlock sends Gillette away, wedges the box into a window of the shack, and then stands whistling in the doorway, till he is quickly yanked within. Inside, he is frisked, threatened, and leeringly told that the millionaire's daughter has been kidnapped by the butler. Then an extreme long shot shows the shack from outside. One of its walls fades out, so that the audience can now simultaneously see the room inside, the wall with the window and its round box, and the area beyond it. Next, in a medium shot, the sheik triumphantly dangles the pearls in front of Sherlock, whereupon, in another extreme long shot, which is held for the rest of the action, the latter grabs the pearls and leaps headfirst through the window and the box, landing on his feet outside, covered in the dress and instantly disguised as a little old lady, who sedately walks away.

In this transformation, following the double exposure which produces the fading wall, the camera has been deliberately used as a mere recording device. In particular, the final extreme long shot made with an unmoving camera simply photographs the actors and setting, and the illusions created through false perspectives or editing that occur elsewhere in the film have been temporarily laid aside. What you are seeing, the shot announces, is real, even though it seems impossible, a total change as quickly produced as a deceptive cut or a camera trick could manage. But in this film, even a straightforward recording of reality by a sincere camera looks and is illusionary.

Though disguised, Sherlock is soon followed by a suspicious thug, and when scrutinized too closely throws the dress at him and runs off, into what turns out to be a blind alley, with buildings on both sides and a large shed blocking the end. Standing in front of the shed, however, is the faithful Gillette, dressed as a lady salesman, with a tray of neckties hanging at his waist, its lid raised in front of him. When the hero stops, seemingly trapped, Gillette gestures that he should leap into the tray lid. In another long shot that is merely recording reality, Sherlock does, instantly disappearing. (The lid is a trapdoor, and the elaborate setup, which is not explained in the movie, involves suspending Gillette inside the shed, with only his head and arms protruding through the wall and seemingly attached to the fake female body outside.) Confused, several pursuers who have run up watch as Gillette (necessarily after a cut to a new shot) walks away from the blank wall. When they next enter the shed, Sherlock simultaneously slips out and fastens the door, locking them inside and reversing the trick played on him and earlier on the boy by the sheik. But then once again he must run for cover when he nearly bumps into another thug.

As much magicians as detectives, Sherlock and Gillette are masters of fool-the-eye tricks, and the quick-change and trap-door routines just completed are both magician's routines, remembered by Keaton from his vaudeville years and adapted for the film. Like the comic stage business of the rapid dollar exchange and the mimicking walk in the earlier real life portion, the new vaudeville routines again fit naturally into the film, which, whether real or dream, is a contrived and stylized comedy throughout. In the dream, particularly in the continuation of the chase coming up, the more filmic hair-breadth escapes and instantaneous changes and reversals will easily assimilate with these, their vaudeville counterparts; they will seem equally real and fantastic, comic equivocations that the audience can neither quite accept nor reject.

If in its vaudeville borrowings the ingredients of the dream are the same and are casually inserted in the same matter-of-fact way as in the real life part of the film, so, too, the dream is like the first part presented as a parody, both of the movies and of the wishful tendency of life to imitate them. It is again a satire on real young people who would fantasize themselves as movie stars playing movie roles. The parody of movies is aimed both at high society films, the typical Cecil B. DeMille romantic drama of the very rich crudely conceived for a mass audience of the averagely poor, and at the detective film, as suggested earlier, perhaps at John Barrymore's *Sherlock Holmes*. The parody of adolescent fantasy is aimed at the adolescent hero, and results from the fact that the boy's point of view is not shared by the film, which instead presents his dream like his real life from the point of view of an objective and detached ironist. Even in what is his own dream of glory, his glory is undermined and the dream mocked. The boy is the comic target of ironic and debunking titles; parallels between his day and his dream, which he himself could not be aware of, like the revealing mirrors in the parlor and the billiard room, are casually inserted to explode the authenticity of the dream; and finally, some unwanted parallels are introduced to undercut him, to reveal the awkward boy within the world's most famous detective, as when the boy first walks into the side of a platform and then as detective into the side of an open door. His dream is in these ways made more burlesque than actual, a comic spoof of the real thing. Like the movies it parodies, a genuine movie-going adolescent's dream of glory lies behind it only as a grandiose illusion, self-serving, self-deceiving, and therefore ripe for comic debunking and exploitation.

The vaudevillian, the parodic, the ironically detached—all these approaches help, too, to continue in the dream the impression of an entertainment, as in the real life portion a sense of actors comically playing parts rather than impersonating characters. In the dream the girl does become the society lady, but also one is encouraged to see the actress, Kathryn McGuire, as playing both, for both are consciously presented as parodies of conventional film types. And in fact, if one of the two roles is to be viewed as more real than the other, it is the dream role, for in the dream a curious and apparently deliberate confusion of dream and reality has begun. Initially the dream repeated the events of the real day, an egoistic and comic glorification of them, but at the point where the detective starts following the sheik in the back seat of the car, the dream ceases to imitate and begins to take off on its own. And as it does so, it becomes the movie rather than a dream movie within a movie. Lasting longer than the real life portion, which begins to seem a mere prologue to it, and which in its vaudevillian and parodic touches is indistinguishable from it anyway, the dream portion acquires its own filmic immediacy and reality.

Film is a medium of the present tense. What we see at any given moment is what totally occupies us and alone exists. The long chase that follows, therefore, partly because it is long, partly because it is shot on real locations, and partly because it is the best and most engrossing sequence in the film, soon no longer impresses us as a dream. It is as immediate and real and actual as anything else, and its real life antecedents are apt to be so completely forgotten by the viewer that the ending of the total film, which returns to them, is likely to be as much a shock for him as it is for the suddenly deheroized and awakened boy. In the chase, the film is playing with what is a combined strength and weakness of the medium, that it makes everything seem real, that in any shot what is shown exists, so that what begins for the audience as a clearly understood subjective dream has by its end forgotten its beginning and deliberately become an objective reality. Then suddenly the audience will be jolted with the reminder that what it is unreflectively accepting as real, as the movie, is actually still a fantasy, visualizations of the images in the boy's dreaming mind rather than a sequence of purportedly actual events.

Following the magician's routines, the chase in the dream accelerates, acquiring the autonomous momentum that fully liberates it from its bondage to the boy's real life. After the quick change and sudden escape, the detective runs from the dead-end alley and whips out of frame to the right. In a beautifully executed transition, an elliptical cut that is Keaton's trademark filmic equivalent of the vaudevillian quick change, he then instantly runs on screen from the left, entering a broad boulevard lined with palm trees and expensive homes. The sensation created is of his running so fast that in a continuous movement he has in seconds reached a far different part of town.

Running along the boulevard, however, he is stopped for speeding by a motorcycle cop, who then turns out to be the ubiquitous Gillette in his third disguise. Leaping on the handlebars of the cycle, the detective is carried away to rescue the kidnapped girl, carried at least till Gillette falls off while bouncing through a puddle. After this, Sherlock is alone on the handlebars of the driverless cycle, even if composedly under the impression that Gillette is still there behind him. He is therefore no longer actually going anywhere, nor for that matter is he any longer being pursued. There is neither chase nor rescue, only a random race. Having been set in comic motion, however, he has acquired enough momentum that no cause is needed to keep him going. His movement is now pure comic movement, existing for its own sake.

This development is the same as the one in *Our Hospitality* when Willie McKay falls from the locomotive tender into the river and is rapidly carried along by it. In *Sherlock Junior* the river is replaced by a road and water propellant by a motorcycle, but otherwise the situation is the same—pure, unmotivated motion with many comic near-disasters and bare recoveries, with a stoic figure given up to the forces of fate, just sitting or floating as he is carried to his destiny. It is the Griffith last-minute race and rescue made absurd because unmotivated, though still at least remaining in a way heroic. The hero's disciplined endurance, his surviving of the motorcycle or river test, is a considerable feat and will be appropriately rewarded. Where chance carries him is the same place purpose always carries the heroes of melodrama, to a union with the imperilled heroine.

As he is so carried along, guided only by comic fate, Sherlock survives several near-collisions in city traffic and then more emphatically encounters several people, or rather several ethnic jokes. He hits a black laundress, he himself is hit by a shovelful of dirt from each of twelve precision ditch diggers, and then he collides with an outing of comic Irishmen, most of whom are enjoying a tug of war. The cycle naturally runs into the center of the rope, pulling the contestants along with it, through picnic tables, over rocks, and finally into a stream, where the last two survivors are dunked.

From upsettable people the cycle proceeds to encounter obstructive things. First it scoots up a long wooden causeway, the central section of which turns out to be missing, leaving a twenty-foot gap. Just as the cycle is about to fly and fall into space, however, two trucks pass below, and their tops provide a momentary roadway, across which the detective safely travels. When the causeway suddenly sags, he is back on the road and meeting more obstructions, a fallen tree, a construction crew's sawhorse, and then a giant construction machine. When illusionistically seen from a side view, the last seems to block the entire road, but then from a frontal view it is revealed as hollow, letting the cycle pass inside it.

As the climax of the wild ride approaches, Sherlock heads straight for a bend in the road. As he reaches it, there is a cutaway to a rural cabin, where the girl on one side of a table is confronted by the butler on the other. He leers in an evil grin and undoes his tie, a comically understated threat of the fate worse than death. With this melodramatic signal that the last possible moment for rescue has come, the detective is thereupon carried over the bend by the nonturning motorcycle and propelled into the cabin. As the cycle hits it and stops, Sherlock is thrown through a window, slides across the table inside, and slams into the butler, who is knocked through the opposite wall and collapses outdoors. In another symmetrical if not quite so instantaneous exchange of positions, the rest of the gang soon pull up, and as they enter the cabin through the door, Sherlock and the girl exit through a window, leaping and falling into the car just parked there and driving away.

Racing along again, still pursued by the gang, who quickly follow in the butler's car, Sherlock pulls forth the explosive number thirteen billiard ball, which he has carried since he left the girl's house the day before. He throws it, the explosion knocks the gang's car off the road, and the adventure is over. But then the girl exclaims, "Oh, we forgot Gillette. Shouldn't we go back for him?" Approaching another curve, Sherlock slams on the brakes, preparing to turn around. Since conspicuously large letters on the rear-mounted spare tire have proclaimed "four wheel brakes," a customary warning of the time used to alert motorists behind to a car equipped with what was then a new and major improvement in braking ability, an instantaneous stop is plausibly produced. The newfangled device, in fact, grinds the wheels to so quick a halt that the car's chassis detaches from them and keeps moving. It flies off the wheels, across the bend, and into a lake below. Still the complete hero, however, Sherlock turns the car into a boat and its convertible top into a sail. While steering for shore, he also hands the girl her pearls. Then as they hold onto each other in a final embrace, the car sinks. Soon both flounder in the water, and with this damp jolt the dream ends. Though deliberately developing a filmic reality that makes its termination surprising, the dream has remained a dream. In a crossfade the swimming detective becomes the sleeping boy, floundering on his projectionist's stool till he falls off and wakes up.

No sooner is he awake than the girl enters, with what seems a happy ending to a continuing dream. In a loving closeup, she says, "My father asked me to come and apologize for the terrible mistake we made." Cleared of the crime and reunited with his girl, the boy stands beside her, the two together in a happy end as *Hearts and Pearls* on the small theater screen also reaches its conclusion. In a remarkable visual conceit, carried through the final shots, the two endings, of the movie and of the movie within a movie, are thereupon maximally confused and merged. In the last shots of the pair, the camera always looks at the faces of the boy and girl from the auditorium, so that they are framed in the upper center of the screen by the window of the projection booth. So framed, they appear in a space the same size as the small theater screen on which *Hearts and Pearls* is shown, with the stage around it and the audience in front. In this way, the real film and the film within the film are equated. Both are films, the visual parallel implies; neither is more real or unreal than the other. The parallel also helps emphasize one last comic joke on young people who learn about life from watching the movies and who in dream or in earnest aspire to imitate what they see. The boy and the girl, in their small frame, are made to seem more than ever imitators of the silver screen, representatives of real life so assiduously mimicking the movies that they acquire their own screenlike space in which to perform.

In the final series of parallel shots, the boy first turns from the girl and looks at *Hearts and Pearls*. On the small theater screen, the hero takes the heroine's hand. In the next shot, the boy takes the girl's hand, and then stares through the window again to see what comes next. The screen lover kisses the hand he holds, and the boy timidly kisses the girl's. The screen lover gives the heroine a ring, and the boy gives his ring to the girl. The screen lover kisses the heroine, and the boy somewhat obliquely, his face slightly averted as he looks out of the corners of his eyes at her, kisses the girl. Then finally the screen lovers clinch, and there is a fadeout and a fadein to the two of them as husband and wife, she sewing and he holding a pair of twins. After this sudden and not immediately imitable development, the boy can only look on and scratch his head in puzzled uncertainty. And that is the last shot, for *Sherlock Junior* is also over, cheerfully ending with its most comic joke on the adolescent hero's confusion between life and the movies.

It is a confusion that is also one last demonstration of the deceptiveness of film, of how what the boy accepts as an easily aped reality in *Hearts and Pearls* is really a time-compressing illusion produced by editing, a mind-boggling trick that at least momentarily stuns its naive copyist. But then in this Chinese box of a movie, with its pervasive stress on the comic conflation of movies and reality, the boy himself is an illusion, a mocking comment on the stereotyped small-town adolescent hero of many other movies. In *Sherlock Junior* there have been nothing but illusions within illusions within illusions, even if many of them have looked deceptively real.

The film throughout is a realistic fantasy or a fantastic reality in that its often seemingly real world, its pictures of actual people and events, is never naively filmed, though the frames often have a deliberately naive home-movie look of reality to them. Rather, the film's world is the creation of a comic eye, an eye always at work distorting reality, endowing it with comic forms, meanings, references, continually transforming the real into the visionary, a radically new world conceived as funny. At moments, too, when the comic eye is most creative, producing laughs through the most striking, most sudden, most confusing confrontations of seeming real with seeming filmed or dreamt, the creations of comedy even reach the surreal. At these points, the viewer is apt to be not startled into laughter but instead, like the boy in the film, wonderfully boggled, stunned by an illusion that seems, impossibly and simultaneously, both real and dream.

5.

The Navigator

SYMMETRY AS COMIC FATE

THE STRUCTURING of movement into symmetrical patterns, as the opening essay pointed out, is for Keaton a major source of laughter. Like the king of France in the nursery rhyme, who with all his men marched up a hill and down again, Keaton characters frequently expend much energy going one way only to encounter a reversal that sends them back to their starting place. Absurdly because logically, there generally being a good reason for the reversal, the hero's final steps will retrace and cancel his first steps, and like the retreating French army he will have combined motion and stasis in a comic and paradoxical union. An unmoving mover, the Keaton hero often frenetically acts, but at the end of his activity little is apt to have changed. His purposively directed moves will have been reduced to play, accomplishing nothing but their own performance, though that, for the audience at least, is enough. For the viewers of the films anyway, if not for the performer, the Keaton hero's mirror-reversed, nonproductive, symmetrical journeys have such an aesthetic unity in their balanced structure and provide so much delight in their ironic absurdity that they sufficiently justify themselves. They exist and entertain as comically choreographed dances, as precisely patterned drill-like exercises in which physical movements are skillfully shaped into the visible forms of laughter.

If symmetrical motions are basic to all the films, in *The Navigator* they and other symmetries are so dominant that symmetry itself is almost what the film is about. Carefully balanced oppositions, reversed repetitions—ways of structuring things into mirror images of each other—are present not only in movement but also in characters, plot, and settings. All develop, echo, and reinforce each other in this way, composing an elaborate visual exercise in the theme of symmetry and its many variations. If a concern for character psychology or for thematic ideas in the film is lacking, this is not because of a failure in intelligence on the part of its maker, but rather because in this instance that intelligence is concentrated almost solely in creating patterns on the film's visual surface, in symmetrically structuring the movements and objects shown there. The intelligence behind the film is a visual intelligence, an intelligence of motion, and at its most effective and interesting level the film is simply and comically about easily reversible people moving left and then right, up and then down, toward the camera and away from it. And these simple, linear, and alternating moves traverse similarly symmetrical backgrounds. Mise-en-scène managed with a mirror, that is the visual impulse behind much of what the audience sees, so much so that the forms of symmetry eventually create an impression of comic necessity, an effect similar to the sense of fate in tragedy. There seems to be a universal design working with and upon the hero, who is distinguished as hero because of it. It is a design that leads him, however, not to a tragic fall and death, but playfully and absurdly, through circles and reversals, onward and backward to exactly where he started, leaving him a little wiser but otherwise no worse for his experience.

The film begins with the customary long explanatory titles of the early Keaton features, three of them: "Our story deals with one of those queer tricks that fate sometimes plays. Nobody would believe, for instance, that the entire lives of a peaceful American boy and girl could be changed by a funny little war between two small countries far across the sea. And yet it came to pass. The spies of the two little nations were at a Pacific seaport, each trying to prevent the other getting ships and supplies."

The cast of characters is then introduced in the same straight-forward way as in *Sherlock Junior*. First, a roomful of spies. Their leader outlines a sabotage plot—the rival country has just purchased a supply ship, The Navigator, which must be unmoored and set adrift before the new crew embarks in the morning. While speaking, the leader walks to a rear window, through whose curtains a harbor and a ship can dimly be seen. As the other spies gather around him, momentarily blocking the view, he opens the window, and then they all in a balanced and symmetrical division step back and to the sides of the screen, unveiling in the center a neatly framed image of the distant Navigator. Having dramatically displayed the ship, and having also developed an element of dramatic irony (the audience, in fact, now knows something the hero and heroine will never learn), the leader and his spy crew fade out.

Next introduced are "the wealthy shipowner who has just sold the Navigator and his daughter." This is done economically in a single shot held just long enough to establish the faces of the two characters. They appear in the library of their home, he reading a legal paper in the left foreground, she standing in the right background. She then steps forward, as a moving figure the main center of interest, until parallel with him, forming a balanced pair and fulfilling a symmetrical pattern implicit from the beginning, whereupon the shot fades out.

The final introductory title presents "Rollo Treadway—heir to the Treadway family fortune—a living proof that every family tree must have its sap." As with the spies, an establishing long shot discloses both the hero and the entire room he is in, his bedroom, an immense space filled with spindly furniture and framed by elegant swag draperies. The hero himself, served breakfast in bed by a butler, long after everyone else in the film is up and about, is a small, distant, and therefore ineffectual-looking figure in the far background. Rising, he saunters past a window, does a modified doubletake, and reverses his direction to peer again through it. In closeup he stares, and a cutaway shot shows what he sees. On the street a comic jalopy, front wheels much smaller than rear wheels, stops. It is decorated in white, has two "Just Married" signs on it, and is driven by a chauffeur. In the back seat a black bride and groom, formally dressed, smile fantastically white wide smiles and enthusiastically hug each other, a low-life parody of a rich man's wedding.

In walking to and looking through a window, Rollo has repeated the spies' introductory movements, a parallelism in action that seems deliberate, intended to associate his future with theirs, to recall their viewing of the ship, for what he sees will soon place him upon it. Working in this way, the repetition is typical of the rigorous restriction of action in Keaton films, where a meaningfully unified world of movement is created by repeating with variations a small number of basic acts, related to and echoing one another, and carefully excluding any extraneous gestures. The sight of the black bride and groom also is used as a visual way of showing the workings of Rollo's mind and helps establish an absurd incongruity in his character. Seeing the happy pair provokes in him an instantaneous decision, which in turn leads to a comic contrast between the languid, heavy-lidded, and somnambulistic air with which he habitually proceeds and the actual resolution and speed with which he casually carries out his intentions. Looking from the bridal couple to a strategically placed photograph of the girl who was introduced earlier, he thinks, and then he instantly voices his thoughts to the butler in three punchline titles, each separated from the others by a cut back to Rollo, to provide a pause for the building of comic expectation. He says, "I think I'll get married." He adds, "Today." He concludes, "We'll sail for Honolulu tomorrow on our honeymoon—get two tickets."

Having acted or at least having sent his butler into action, Rollo moves to his bathroom, again an immense space, with a sunken tub, almost a pool, in the center, and at the extreme right a shower enclosure with a large parachute-like canopy over it. What is most striking in the room's arrangement is the canopy, for in size and shape and in its scalloped edge and decorated surface, it exactly duplicates the canopy that hung over Rollo's bed in the adjacent room. There the large shape was on the extreme left of the screen, and the reversed repetition makes the two rooms in part mirror images of each other. Here the mirror effect is minor and almost seems gratuitous, but it designedly points the way to the rest of the film, where such symmetries in the settings will become more obviously intentional and obtrusive and will function symmetrically to shape the action performed within them. At present, however, Rollo simply steps through the paces of a single gag, doing something reasonable in an unreasonable way. With the singleness of mind that distinguishes all Keaton heroes, he is so engrossed in the thought of marriage that he submerges nearly waist deep into the tub, still in robe and pajamas, before he realizes that he has forgotten to undress.

A title introduces the next sequence: "He had completed all arrangements—except to notify the girl." What follows is the first major and also perfect example of mirror reversals, so totally realized in the sequence's mise-en-scène that it achieves the kind of completeness that makes it a self-contained and self-sufficient work of visual art, a study in comic symmetry. A long shot reveals the door of Rollo's home, centered between and framed by two foreground hedges, solid rectangular shapes rising from the bottom to the top of the screen. Rollo comes through the door, armed with a load of Keaton comic props—hat, cane, orchid corsage—and walks toward the camera. Then with angular precision he makes a surprising and instantaneous ninety-degree turn, now moving in a plane parallel to the camera as he seems about to bump into the hedge at the left. Instead of colliding, however, he disappears behind it, proceeding down a concealed walk.

In the following shot Rollo's house, a solid stone box, dominates the right two-thirds of the screen. His Rolls Royce open limousine is parked uphill on the street, facing away from the camera and occupying the lower left corner of the screen. At the extreme lower right there is an iron gate to Rollo's yard, and Rollo walks through it and steps into the back of his car. A footman, standing on the sidewalk beside the car, instantly closes the door and himself sits in the front seat as the chauffeur drives off, the transition from Rollo's walking to riding being so quickly made that there is no cessation in his movement, movement whose final effect of comic necessity arises from its uninterrupted continuity. The camera then pans with the car as it makes an unexpected and instant U-turn to the left, stopping just across the street in a reversal of its original position, now pointing toward the camera and downhill. As the pan ends, the girl's house and two others dominate the left two-thirds of the screen, with the car in the lower right corner—a mirror reversal of the shot's initial composition. Again with no impression of a break in his continuous movement, Rollo gets out of the car just as it stops and climbs most of the long stairs to the girl's front door.

There is next a cut to the third shot, a deep-focus presentation of the girl's library. She stands in the background at the right, the same screen position in which she stood in her introductory shot, repeating her father's previous action of reading a paper. As before she walks forward, continuing to read, this time to the left foreground, becoming one-half of a visually preordained pair, which requires Rollo for its symmetrical completion. As she is ending this movement, Rollo, not surprisingly, enters at the rear right, followed by a butler, to whom he hands his hat and cane. Noticing this, the girl lays her paper on a table to her left and then turns around to face Rollo as he walks to the foreground toward her, both thus performing simultaneous actions of approach. Meeting, they shake hands, he gives her the corsage, and he immediately asks, in a title, "Will you marry me?" A brief cut back to the shot shows her lips decisively forming the words of the next title, "Certainly not!" As the shot then continues, there is only now a noticeable pause in Rollo's movement, which has reached one of its limits and is about to reverse itself, for the point of his matrimonial defeat has also brought him as far to the left and as far toward the camera as he will go. The pause, however, does not stop all motion, for if Rollo stands stunned, the butler in the right background still fiddles with his hat and cane, which he will not have time to set down. Quickly if only partially recovering, Rollo draws away from the girl, faces the camera with a look of blank stupefaction, then instantly turns and reverses his direction, walking back to the butler, retrieving his hat and cane, and exiting to the right through the door that he had entered.

Outside, a long shot displays the sidewalk, which occupies the left two-thirds of the screen, while the Rolls Royce, seen only in part, occupies the right third, the footman again standing beside it. Dragging his cane behind him and drooping a little himself, Rollo approaches but does not enter the car, explaining, "I think a long walk would do me good." In a reversal of the previous pan, the camera follows the now dejectedly walking Rollo across the street, trailed by the car, which makes a U-turn to the right and toward the camera, parking where it was before just as Rollo goes back through the gate.

The fifth and final shot is the same as the first, the evergreen-framed door of Rollo's house. He enters the screen from the hidden walk at the left, absorbed in his dejection walks all the way across, nearly bumping into the shrubbery at the right, which conceals no third path, and then pulls back and abruptly turns, heading away from the camera toward his door.

Throughout this sequence, the moves, all of them, are carefully planned, and most of them are precisely parallel to the camera or directly into or away from it. It is, in short, an exercise in horizontals and perpendiculars, two basic linear movements transformed into creative and comic action. It is also an action that achieves much of its effect from its containment. The shrubs of the opening and closing shots form symmetrical boundaries, rectangularly precise shapes that both imitate and confine the movement and help give it form, as do also the similar rectangular shapes of the houses which border the performing space of the street. The editing of the five shots in the sequence further contributes to the symmetry, with the reversed pairings, first of the walk and street and then of street and walk, enclosing the single central shot in the library, where Rollo's movement itself climaxes and reverses.

In the sequence it is therefore the movement, the symmetrical walk, rather than Rollo, the performer of it, that holds the audience's attention. Because the walk is so strongly shaped, propelled by setting, editing, and comic necessity to its inevitable conclusion, it exists as an entity in itself, something to be attended to for its own entertainment value. Like similar assertively visible moves in an athletic contest or an exhibition dance, it further impresses itself upon the viewer by virtue of being a basic unit in a limited but meaningful context composed almost entirely of similar simplified moves. The world of *The Navigator,* like the world of a game or dance, is an abstraction from the real world, a simplification of it to precisely formulated actions performed under arbitrary but meaningful rules. In other words, within Keaton's silent-screen comedy, action dominates, all actions are required to be funny, and also, because of this, all actions are no longer real. Detached from the complexities of sound or noncomic motivation, they become instead meta-actions, commentaries on action. They are pure, powerful, visual revelations, concentrated expressions of a comic view of life.

That view, as conveyed in Rollo's walk, even though it moves in angles and lines, presents the activities of life as a circle. His symmetrical journey back to where he started is, in fact, the classic comic move, a circular progression going nowhere, and the circle itself is so symbolic of comedy that it has often been explicitly used in comic titles, as Max Ophuls's *La Ronde* most succinctly demonstrates. In Ophuls's film a dominant image is the merry-go-round, on which the characters are all reduced to easily replaceable riders, each making his or her spin in the continuing and unchanging whirligig of love. The first loves a second, the second soon longs for a third, the third then meets a fourth, who meets a fifth, who meets a sixth, who meets and falls in love with the first, closing the circle and bringing love back to its starting point, without, however, necessarily stopping it from further nonprogressive whirls.

Provided with a distant and encompassing view of the lovers in which the circular pattern is clearly discernible, dominating the characters just as Rollo's walk dominates him, the audience sees life as essentially being that circular pattern, a sequence of infinitely repeatable actions performed by mechanical merry-go-ground figures. Reduced to replaceable puppets by the comic design, their brief loves seem both fated and inconsequential, less important than the subsuming design, which is what life is all about. It is simply a pattern, a dance, an exhilarating and repeatable activity, one that like a dance is enjoyable for its own cheerfully animated sake and needs no other justification.

Such a view of life as a ceaseless circular dance is agreeable, at least as an occasional vision, because it is deliberately inconsequential. A dance is an amusement, movement meant only to be enjoyed while it exists, and to convert all of human activities, even serious ones like loving, into a dance, a diversion, a form of play, a patterned game, is a pleasant philosophical illusion. It makes life seem far more enjoyable than it actually is. So viewed, it does not progress toward age, decline, and death, but rather seems an eternal and infinitely repeatable entertainment. That agreeable illusion is a basic comic illusion, the illusion of *La Ronde* and the illusion projected by Rollo's round-trip walk and his other moves throughout *The Navigator*. Rollo is an engaging personality, but he is also often a human being presented to the audience solely as a player, a dancer, performing moves that within the film's many circular designs are seen to exist only for their own comic sake, infinitely repeatable and incapable of progressing toward anything less pleasant and amusing than themselves. Trapped in a symmetrically patterned world, Rollo is reduced to an automaton, wound up and turned loose but never going far. Whatever his intentions, as in the proposal walk, his simplified, reversing moves continually fall in step to the basic comic dance. Serious motions made static and inconsequential, they are fated to be circular, trivial, and funny.

All that need be added is that the early proposal sequence on land is the equivalent in its editing and in its movement and reversed movement performed within a contained space to what will appear on the steamship Navigator. An actual ship bought by Keaton's company, The Navigator is also a perfectly constructed set for this kind of pure play motion—a single, continuous, inevitable, dance-like action, which necessarily and symmetrically leads the non-progressive hero nowhere but back to where he started.

At this point, following and despite the failure of his proposal, a short bridging sequence places Rollo and the never-named girl on the ship. As a title proclaims, "Going on a honeymoon without a bride is like singing the words of 'Kiss Me Again' to the music of 'Alice Where Art Thou,' " but Rollo decides to go anyway. Informed by the butler that his boat sails at ten, his response combines his customary decisiveness and indolence, "I don't get up that early—so I'll go aboard tonight." His boat is at pier two, The Navigator at pier twelve, but when the sabotaging spies sneak onto The Navigator's pier just before Rollo's arrival, the half-open gate they leave covers the crucial numeral one. He therefore proceeds onto the wrong pier and then onto the wrong ship. Once on board, after first losing his ticket and hat to a whipping wind (the first installment of a continuing gag), he innocently and ignorantly enters the wrong cabin and prepares to settle down for the night. Next the girl and her father arrive at the pier, he to pick up some papers concerning his just sold ship, and soon a watchman and the father are grabbed and bound by the spies. The struggling father calls for help, the girl runs onto The Navigator, where she thinks he is, and then the spies cast off the two mooring ropes. As the steamship drifts from the pier, the girl now calls for help, and then she collapses in despair on the deck. Meanwhile, Rollo in his cabin sleeps steadily through all the turmoil, the photo of the girl beside his bunk.

Comes the morning, the first of the film's two remaining days, and both soon learn they are on a deserted ship, neither, of course, knowing of the other's presence. After losing two more hats to the whipping wind and also after a solitary visit to the ship's dining salon has failed to produce a breakfast, Rollo strolls to the edge of the second-level deck, coincidentally stopping just above the girl, who stands on the deck below. Moving away, he discards a cigarette from its long holder, and when a little later the girl looks down, she sees it burning in front of her. She cries out, Rollo hears her (as does the audience, for this is a Keaton audible silent sound), and the two begin looking for whoever else is on the ship.

The search that follows, one of the film's highlights, repeats the choreography developed in the earlier proposal walk. It is performed on the forward superstructure of the ship, which greatly limits movement, primarily restricting it to horizontals and perpendiculars, though also providing three levels on its three decks and the possibility of vertical movement between them. At first the two characters simply run round and round the second-level deck, always just far enough apart to be concealed by a cabin corner from each other. The shots depicting this chase, all taken from the middle of the ship, alternately look down the narrow promenades on the two sides of the central cabin block, and are therefore alternately mirror images of each other, with cabins and water exchanging positions on the edges of the screen. This restriction in the point of view also simplifies movement to the purely perpendicular, to mechanical and comically repeatable runs away from and toward the camera; and when combined with a lens of long focal length, it results in a delightful, almost magical, effect. In rhythmic and regular alternation, the two characters change from miniature figures in the distance to giant closeups as they rush forward, and then, in the next shot, they reverse themselves as they rush away and shrink in size again. Adding to the comic effect of this transformation is the acceleration of pace, for motion becomes progressively faster, reaching a speed at which the reversal is almost instantaneous. And equally comic is the contradiction in the fact that the faster the both of them run, the less likely it is that one of them will catch up with the other. At the end of all their frantic oscillations, they will still be relatively speaking in the same place, still separated and unseen, victims of pure comic motion, which, like Rollo's proposal walk, involves much exercise but finally gets you nowhere.

For the record, the shots of the episode will be described, though a verbal description slows them down to a point where their comic charm totally disappears. In compensation, however, the retardation, the verbal freezing of action, makes visible some of the editing decisions that produce the charm. First of all, then, the camera looks down the right promenade, where Rollo walks away from it. Next, the far deck at the prow of the boat, which Rollo approaches, is shown, and the girl climbs up to it and runs toward the camera and the left promenade. This is followed by a cut back to the right promenade, with Rollo, now a small figure, walking far down it, and with the next shot the alternation of promenades begins. It reveals the left promenade, with the girl in the distance loping toward the camera, swerving out of frame to the right just before reaching it. After a second of empty set, Rollo runs around the far corner and toward the camera. A cut to the right promenade shows the girl already running along it and out of sight around the far corner, whereupon Rollo in closeup runs into the frame from the left and continues away from the camera along the promenade. Another cut and it is the left promenade again, with the girl running around the far corner and all the way to the camera, whipping around the near corner as Rollo comes around the far one, the shot holding on him until he has almost reached the camera. The last shot is then of the right promenade, beginning with the girl just entering the frame in closeup, following her till she disappears around that far corner again, and continuing until Rollo has also run into frame, raced along the entire promenade, and also sped around the corner. The last shot, it is also the first where the complete run of both has been shown, the first where both are moving fast enough that this could be done without slowing the pace of the editing.

This segment of the search ends with a ninety-degree change of camera angle, a head-on shot of a doorway facing the left promenade, through which can be seen a cabin interior with a stairway going down to the lower level and directly opposite another door facing the right promenade. The girl, still running, comes into frame from the left but then shifts direction, suddenly walking away from the camera into the near door and then going down the interior stairs. Rollo next immediately enters the far door from the right, walks toward the camera all the way through the cabin, looks about, and moves down the near promenade to the right and off the screen, thus comically concluding the girl's original but then interrupted and diverted linear progression. Even in this shot, though the camera angle has been shifted ninety degrees, the movement is still mainly away from and toward the camera, preserving the unity of direction so far developed. Only briefly do the characters move across the screen, she at the beginning and then both at the end, as she descends the stairs and he proceeds along the promenade, a change of direction that concludes and introduces, for the next segment of the chase is all action left and right, up and down, all in a plane parallel to the camera.

The second installment of the search, an exercise in rectangular movement, is performed all in a single prolonged shot. The camera from the stern is pointed directly down the center of the ship, whose forward superstructure is now shown in its entirety, from rail to rail and from the first-level deck up through the third. At the back of the first-level deck two symmetrically arranged doors open into the cabin block, and just beyond them, at the edges of the screen, two ladder-like stairs lead to the second-level deck and its promenades. There, in about the same position, two more stairs lead to the third-level deck. In the center foreground, directly in front of the camera, a crane rises from the bottom to the top of the screen, dividing the balanced composition of the superstructure into image and mirror image.

For the record again, even if what can easily be seen can only be described in very hard reading, the action in the shot is this: Rollo walks from the promenade around the left corner of the second-level cabin block, just as the girl, having gone down the interior stairs, comes out of the righthand door onto the first deck. He walks right as she walks left, till she reaches the left stairs connecting decks one and two and he reaches the right stairs connecting decks two and three. They simultaneously climb, and then he on the third deck runs left as she on the second deck runs right. Simultaneously reaching the stairs again, he descends the left stairway to the second deck as she climbs the right stairway to the third. She then runs left on the third deck as he now runs right on the second. They then both climb down stairways, she the left stairway between decks three and two, he the right stairway between decks two and one. Moving ever faster, she runs right on the second deck and he runs left on the first, he climbs the left stairway to the second deck as she descends the right stairway to the first, and then predictably she begins racing left as he begins racing right.

At this point, without ever meeting the other, each has made an orderly and complete tour of the playing space, providing as it were the absurdly comic answer to the topographical puzzle of how such a maneuver might be managed. The demonstration completed, a demonstration that is convincing as well as comic because performed in silence, the only way for the relentless mechanical motion to end is as it began, though now in reversed order from the original starting positions. Running left on the first deck, she passes the righthand door, from which she had originally come, but stops at the lefthand door and walks through this back into a cabin. He on the second deck meanwhile proceeds right, to the corner opposite the one he entered by. He then climbs to the third-level deck, one level higher than where he started, and stops to look over the railing. She, in turn, climbs down an interior stairway, ending one level lower than where she started, in a workroom used by the ship's carpenter. With this pause, the two are now at a maximum vertical distance from each other, he on the highest deck in the open and she inside in the lowest recesses of the ship. And once again much symmetrically arranged running has necessarily led neither of them anywhere.

Their meeting, when it occurs, occurs by chance and through an instantaneous reversal of his position. As he leans on an air vent, his hat, a high silk one, is first blown down it and then he himself follows, dropping on top of the hat and also upon a bench, where the girl now rests. The bench collapses, the two fall in sitting positions, their backs touching each other, and after a momentary delay as they wonder and fear who this newly met shipmate is, they simultaneously turn in a symmetrical pairing that makes them mirror images of each other. When they are face to face, his first words, both comically predictable and comically unexpected, are "Will you marry me?" Her response is an emphatically heard "No," though her title reads "Certainly not." A second title adds, "This is a fine time to ask me that. I'm cold and hungry and . . . ," which prepares for the next sequences of the film, the unsuccessful attempts on the first day to secure food, rescue, and shelter in an alien and uncooperative environment.

In the food sequence, the sources of comedy are two of Keaton's staples, the beginner who bungles his way through a situation calling for professional knowledge and the adult who resembles a child. Rollo and the girl will move into the ship's galley, a large room equipped to prepare food for hundreds, with outsize utensils and working spaces. Struggling with the giant apparatus, the two will become diminutive, like children playing house, spoiled children, in fact, so used to being waited upon that they are ignorant of how to do the easiest things for themselves. Because the kitchen outfit is so large, it also at times helps create another effect, becomes part of a Keaton exercise in realistic fantasy. Though what is shown is a real ship's galley, its objects have a dreamlike strangeness to them. Because of their size and because the childish and bungling hero and heroine seem to be encountering all these familiar things for the first time, they are endowed for the audience, too, with newness and wonder.

The cooking activities, which are spatially restricted and provide a relatively static interlude before the next action sequence of massive symmetrical motion, begin with a deep-focus shot of the galley. In the right corner in the extreme foreground, a box filled with large chunks of coal dominates the screen, preparing us for the opening action, a perpendicularly linear progression that, as is frequently the case in this film, seems preordained to complete some partially constructed visual pattern. When Rollo and the girl enter the rear door, therefore, Rollo immediately walks toward the camera and straight to the coal box, grabbing the largest lump and dropping it into an adjacent stove's fire pit. He then ignorantly and unsuccessfully tries to ignite it with a single match.

In a similarly ignorant way, the girl tries to make coffee, placing four unground coffee beans in a giant pot, which she fills with sea water fetched by Rollo, since the faucet on the galley's sink is dry. While she next mangles bacon, arranging a thick slice into an attractive but unfryable bow, Rollo attempts to unseal the band on a can of asparagus, first with its key, then with a knife, and last with a cleaver. The final cleaver blow sends the can flying, breaking all of a large stack of dishes held by the girl. She therefore sets the table with large metal trays and correspondingly outsize cutlery for cooking, two-foot-long prongs and spoons and carving knives; it is while doing this that she most appears a child playing house. Rollo meanwhile opens a can of milk by drilling through it, accidentally drilling all the way through and losing its contents in the process. He also attempts to cook four eggs in a giant cauldron able to hold hundreds, a cauldron so big that in clumsily retrieving his eggs from its murky boiling depths, he breaks all of them.

The girl's cooking having produced something, Rollo and she next sit down to eat it. The giant pronged fork he holds when stabbed at the bacon she fried goes right through the metal tray, the bacon itself is rubbery and inedible, and a taste of four-bean sea-water coffee sends him urgently out on deck, from which he returns with an unconvincing pantomimic apology of having had to make a sudden telephone call. An outsize spoonful of sugar, about half a cupful, is added to the coffee to make it drinkable, but fortunately it is never drunk. The kitchen debacles end as Rollo through a small porthole sees an approaching ship, and thoughts of food give way to thoughts of rescue. From relatively stationary action exploiting the comic possibilities of objects in the galley, the film will now return to larger spaces and the further symmetrical possibilities of a choreographic comedy of reversing linear motion.

Out on deck the two raise a signal flag to attract the passing ship, a naval patrol boat, number 262. But the girl's feminine sensibility, which prompted her to tie bacon into bows, now makes her select a bright flag, and what seems good luck quickly turns bad. The flag unintentionally signals "quarantine," and the patrol boat on seeing it immediately does a turnabout and rapidly sails away, the wisps of white smoke drifting from its stacks replaced by a geyser of boiling black billows.

Quickly responding, the girl suggests that Rollo give chase, and he sets out to do so in the only vehicle available, a lifeboat. She begins to lower it and him over the side, but when the supporting rope burns her hands, she lets go. In the rapid vertical plunge, he is dunked and the boat half-filled with water, but once back aboard, he furiously rows, while above the girl runs forward to watch. Passing the prow, however, he unexpectedly pauses to attach a line from The Navigator and only then rows on, towing the steamship behind him. As Rollo proceeds, the water-filled rowboat naturally sinks from under him. Where before in parallel horizontal lines he had rowed on screen to the right as the girl had followed above on deck, now he must swim to the left and she must also reverse herself and return to midship. Once again they are involved in a necessarily symmetrical journey, whose only possible end is back where it started. In a further variation on this choreographic theme, reversing horizontal movement is next replaced by reversing vertical movement. First the girl throws a lifesaver to Rollo, hitting him on the head. Then she drops a rope, which passes over a pulley, and as he hangs from a hook at its end, she from the second-level deck begins hauling him up, painfully and slowly at first and then instantaneously as she slips overboard and like counterweights they exchange positions. Suddenly finding himself on the first-level deck, he looks about for the girl, then sees her in the water below, and quickly unrolls a shipside ladder to her. But she is too weak to climb, so he must dive overboard to assist her, once again instantaneously reversing his position. The movement of the next reversal, however, decelerates from fast to slow motion, for as he helps her up the ladder, she faints, and he must then laboriously climb with her uncooperative dead weight slung over his shoulder. At this point vertical motion, which has followed horizontal motion, is itself exchanged for perpendicular. An overhead shot looking straight down into the water presents Rollo moving on screen directly toward the camera, and with this final change in direction, the rescue sequence ends. As in the search sequence, all the possibilities of basic linear movement—horizontal, vertical, perpendicular—have been orchestrated into a comically symmetrical triumph, here even more astonishing in the quickness with which the characters have moved, falling or rising, upon an established line of action as they rapidly go nowhere.

Once on board, Rollo places the unconscious girl on a folding deck chair, which immediately folds beneath her. A resting place that provides no rest, it introduces the final activity of the first day. The abortive escape attempt over, settling in for the night now begins, and thoughts of food or rescue give way to the need for shelter. Predictably, it is a need not filled. As in the galley sequence, the childish and ignorant incapacity of the couple constantly defeats their search for a place to sleep, and they are instead terrorized and kept awake by ghosts in sheets, eerily opening doors, fireworks—all the puerile paraphernalia of a Halloween party in a haunted house.

A title introduces this sequence of unquiet rest and also temporarily dries off Rollo and the girl: "By the time they were ready to say 'good-night' they had found a couple of sea-going tuxedos." These are sailor costumes, hers in white, his in blue, both outsize, emphasizing the smallness of their wearers, their roles as miniature misfits in a world of nautical giants. He also is now wearing a porkpie hat, slap shoes, and heavy white face, still Rollo but suddenly made up as the classic Keaton clown, an arbitrary but reasonable adaptation for a sequence stressing slapstick humor and multiple pratfalls. The two stand outside their adjoining cabin doors, and in the background their shadows seem to hug each other and kiss, even if Rollo and the girl do not. Still, the umbrageous embrace suggests what they would like to do if the puritanical conventions of their comic world did not make them behave like funny children instead.

After the good-nights are said, the frights immediately begin. Upset by an ugly picture of an ugly sailor in her cabin, the girl throws it overboard. Catching on the side of the ship, however, it swings repeatedly past the porthole of Rollo's cabin, glaring in at him each time. Soon he is running, tangled in his sheet, a speeding apparition that sends the girl, too, scurrying in fright. Momentarily resting in a storeroom filled with fireworks, they mistake a box of giant firecrackers for candles. These and a roman-candle candle produce more explosively vigorous responses and another run for safety. Recomposed in the ship's lounge, they settle on adjoining chairs to sleep, but the rolling of the ship starts a nearby phonograph, and on a record the bass voice of Wilfred Glenn sings "Asleep in the Deep." Frightened again, Rollo runs to the promenade, where a long row of cabin doors are shown, simultaneously opening and closing with the rolling of the ship. By now a comic mask of timorous fear—his face heavily whitened, with the eyes black-rimmed and popping—Rollo responds to a ghostly greeting from the waving doors by racing once more for the lounge.

After this, he and the girl return to the deck, and there, as he had done earlier, he settles her on a folding deck chair. Like the self-starting phonograph and cabin doors, however, it is an object easily animated by the ship. As Rollo selects his own resting place, the chair slides back and forth to the very edge of the deck. Just as it is finally going over, he looks up and in a desperate lunge grabs the girl's feet and pulls her back to safety. So treated, she first angrily slaps him and then in delayed shock clings in an embrace so tight that it is even more painful than the slap. Abandoning chairs, the two then bundle down in blankets on the deck. It rains, and like many Keaton sequences, this one ends with the hero and the heroine all wet. Returning for the last time to the lounge, they sit damply and disconsolately at a table. Then the exhausted girl falls asleep, her head resting on Rollo's shoulder. In a shot emphasizing the symmetry of the two, his head also falls against hers and his eyes close. As in *Our Hospitality* and *The General*, when a Keaton hero and heroine sleep together, they chastely do so sitting up. So resting here, they also look like two tired children who have stayed up too long after a remarkably strenuous day.

The voyage's first day over and rest finally achieved, it might as well be noted that it took a little too much time to reach. The searching-for-shelter sequence, though a lengthy one, is not the high point of the film, and its relative weakness is in part related to its lack of symmetrically structured action. As a whole, the sequence is fitted into the film's basic symmetry, the conventional Keaton first-day failure reversed by a second-day success, for its imaginary terrors and childish fears will be replaced on the coming day by real dangers, which are courageously and capably resisted, just as all the inadequate resting places will then be contrasted to two ingeniously improvised, totally safe, and agreeably comfortable cabins. Within the sequence itself, however, there is no strong symmetrical impulse. Though there is a regular and rapid alternation between the poles of rest and flight, barely achieved stasis regularly giving way to rabbity runs in which frightened feet instinctively set themselves to work, the only other structural principle behind it is the simple listing of examples, some half dozen ways of being frightened or frustrated. But there is no necessity to a list, as there was earlier to the two major symmetrically shaped chases on the ship or to the earlier proposal walk on land. There is no larger formal pattern to organize the individual comic actions and to create a narrative thrust that drives inexorably onward to a fated and satisfying conclusion. Where Keaton is at his best in the film, there is such an irresistible narrative, most typically created through simplifying and orderly symmetries, a classical order that effectively carries the hero and the audience into the future, even if it turns out to be a replica of the past.

In the searching-for-shelter sequence, however, there is only a gathering of gags, some funny, some feeble, eventually too many of them to continue holding the audience's total interest. Such a list of gags could be longer or preferably shorter and it would make no difference, for though in their search the hero and the heroine run fast and then faster when frightened, their movements do not develop a corresponding narrative momentum. The gags exist in isolation, as just one joke told after another, and when the jokes include such clownish clichés as ghostlike figures in sheets and exploding fire-crackers, the laughs produced may not be very loud (as loud, however, as the laughs created by the similar fireworks jokes in *Duck Soup* and *Mr. Hulot's Holiday*).

Significantly, because Keaton's comic imagination seems to thrive on the absurdly combined dynamism and stasis inherent in any kind of continuous symmetrical activity, the best jokes in the search and fright sequence are those which are themselves based on symmetrical and regularly repeated motion. They are the ones whose generally triadic repetitions—presentation, reinforcement, and climactic variation of an action—are necessary and propulsive as well as funny, carrying the hero to a moment of comic crisis implicit from the beginning and rhythmically, ineluctably achieved. The swinging picture, the self-opening cabin doors, the sliding deck chair—all imitate the symmetrical swaying of the ship in their regular and visibly fated progression toward laughter. Moving with the rocking ship, the cabin doors, for example, first opened behind the apprehensive hero, then opened once more as he turned too late to see them, and thereupon for the third inevitable time opened again before his frightened eyes. He ran; an audience always roars.

At this point, with the hero and the heroine uncomfortably sitting and asleep, the overall structure of the film reveals its own mirror reversal, introduced by a title and a monumental elliptical cut: "Weeks later—still drifting. We now find the crew with a safe and quiet place to sleep." Last seen was the problem of shelter for the night, and this is now first shown as solved. In a curious tunnel-like cabin, Rollo combs his hair. Then an extreme long shot shows most of the ship's engine room, and Rollo emerges from the door of a giant boiler. He knocks with a hammer on an adjacent boiler and inside the girl quickly finishes dressing. Her boiler cabin is decorated with white bows (reminiscent of the bow she tied with the bacon) and is also a mirror image of his. In particular, her bunk attached to the left wall mirrors his bunk attached to the right, which also, as David Robinson points out, makes the two a near double bed, with only a sheet of iron dividing it in the middle. Even with the iron wall, however, the arrangement implies a growing intimacy, an advancement over the earlier cabin bunks, whose heads alone were contiguous.

Next, the problem of food is also shown to be solved. The earlier cooking activities are now exactly repeated, but in much shorter time and with complete success, for the alien objects in the galley have all been domesticated, and the abortive attempts at preparing food have been transformed into a rapidly executed and carefully planned routine. The galley has been turned into an assembly line, full of ropes and pulleys, weights and counterweights, a mechanized food factory. As such, it is just as strange a place as before, but now strange because a Rube Goldberg mind has assembled its parts into an incredibly complicated and unlikely-looking contraption for the equally incredibly efficient and successful production of breakfast.

The preparations start with a reprise of the earlier introductory long shot of the galley, now with its added pulleys and levers, ropes and weights. Again the stove in the foreground occupies the right portion of the screen; in the extreme right foreground the open fire pit is conspicuously filled with paper. Rollo once more enters from the rear, walks toward the camera and stove, and upon reaching the latter this time pulls down a weighted rope. In closeup, the rope in turn tugs a lever, a match at the end of the lever scratches against the wall and is ignited, and then, as the camera tilts downward, the match is lowered into the fire pit, where the paper is instantly ablaze. A shot of the sink follows, as the girl enters from the right. The coffee pot sits under the formerly dry faucet, now connected by a hose to a bottle reservoir. She turns on the water and exits to the left, and then Rollo enters to make his move, pulling a cord, which releases ground coffee down a spout into the pot. When enough has fallen, he releases the cord, turns off the water, and carries the pot to the stove. There another pulled cord drops a lid on the fire pit, and the coffee is left to boil.

A tin of meat, echoing the earlier can of asparagus, next appears, and, as often in Keaton, the hero's mastery of a situation is expressed by his elegantly economical ability to do two things at once. Now a large foot-driven whetstone is attached to a hacksaw, and its rotary motion, as Rollo peddles and casually files his fingernails on its whirling rim, drives the saw, which slices the top off the tin. The meat is deftly transferred to a plate, and in the following shot Rollo is back at the cauldron. Here he pulls a rope and up come the nicely boiled eggs in a large wire cage, from which they are tipped into waiting sieve, fastened to the cauldron's edge. In the final shot of the preparations, the girl lowers some condiments, stored above the table at the ends of long counterweighted cords, and then Rollo approaches and breakfast is about to begin.

In the sequence, the mechanized routines of the galley have been as totally and efficiently managed as the earlier abortive preparations there were totally and ineffectually bumbled—a complete and comic and symmetrical reversal. The success has also involved multiple balanced motions, generally in straight and orderly lines. Things have been pulled this way so that other things may move that way, all appropriate movements within the larger film world, where the same order and balance have been imposed on everything. Here, however, the imposition has been consciously created by the hero and heroine, who have temporarily adapted to the symmetrical necessity that controls all action in their world and are now demonstrating some useful extrapolations of it, rather than, as on the day before with the similar countermovements of the two around a pulley themselves, unwillingly serving as its victims. Though the mechanized kitchen first seems strange, it finally impresses as a logical response to an illogically but precisely patterned world, one where all movement must be reciprocal. Though efficiently produced, the assembly-line breakfast is never eaten. As they sit at the table, the two are interrupted, just as they were during their first meal. Looking out of the porthole again, Rollo cries "Land," and they run on deck. The land sighted, unfortunately, turns out to be a tropical island, and binoculars further reveal a beach full of cannibals, toward whom the boat is steadily drifting. With their seeming salvation turned into a danger, Rollo and the girl run to the prow, where he dubiously attempts to stop the ship by lowering an inadequate anchor, a miniature model evidently belonging to a lifeboat, the first of several small-scale devices that will incongruously appear on the second day. In contrast to the massively outsize equipment of the previous day, it visually suggests a sudden growth in the hero, who in scenes like this becomes a relative giant, forced to make do with the objects of a Lilliputian world. As objects shrink (now an anchor, later a cannon) into toys, the childishly small couple grow into adults, a symmetrical reversal that helps expansively to heroize the hero.

The miniature anchor naturally does not halt the drift to the cannibal isle, but running into a sand reef does. Horizontal movement replaced by vertical, stopping is also combined with sinking. Checking below, Rollo and the girl discover a leak by the propeller shaft, a leak that can only be repaired outside. Following the girl's excited discovery of a deep-sea-diver's suit, Rollo is soon reluctantly going over the side, while above she mans an air pump for him. In a symmetrical reversal of an earlier overhead shot, in which he climbed toward the camera as he carried the girl up the ship's side, now he slowly recedes, waving a sad farewell.

Below, in a comic sequence stressing conventional activities performed in an unlikely place, he labors at the repairs. He also manages several visual puns, turning a lobster into a pair of shears and a swordfish into a fencing foil, with which he duels a second swordfish opponent. Then there is a cut to the surface. The cannibals invade the boat, kidnap the girl, and slash through Rollo's air hose as she desperately clings to it. Below again, Rollo stares at the severed end of the hose and, there being nothing else to do, starts walking. A fight with an octopus hinders progress, but he doggedly continues on his way.

On the island, the girl in closeup comes out of her second faint of the film to discover herself surrounded by cannibal feet. She cries, and in immediate response, though he has not heard her, Rollo steps out of the water, a typically unintentional Keaton hero inadvertently come to the rescue accidentally at the most crucial moment. Shaking himself in his strange suit and waving his gun, he stands there like some terrifying creature from a black lagoon, frightening the natives first into mimicry as they ape his awkward wiggles and then into flight. With the cannibals hiding in the woods, Rollo and the girl are alone and together again. In reward for his courage, she nearly kisses him, or more exactly kisses the glass front of his helmet, one more of the film's many comic obstacles to intimacy. Then Rollo instructs her to grab a handy native oar, and he lies in the water, transforming himself and his air-filled suit into a raft. The girl climbs aboard, energetically begins paddling, and the two head back toward The Navigator. They are, however, observed by the cannibal chief, who peers from behind a tree and now learns that the sea monster is only human. (The chief is played by the great Noble Johnson. Frequently typecast in such parts, he also appears as the warrior chieftain of Skull Island in *King Kong*. He it is who utters there the terrifying chant, "Kara Ta ni, Kong. O Taro Vey, Rama Kong.")

Inexorable necessity having forced both hero and heroine down the ship's side, inexorable necessity drives them back up, though only after Rollo first moves in the wrong direction. When they reach the gangway he pauses, semisubmerged, while the girl removes his diving helmet, whereupon his open-necked suit predictably fills with water and he quickly sinks from view. Re-emerging, he laboriously lifts himself onto the gangway, clinging there unable to ascend further, when his weighty problem is elegantly solved. With a single sudden slash of his knife, a hara-kari ripping open of the suit's rubber belly, he vents the flood that had pulled him down. Now he and the girl climb, and once on deck, with a little final splashing, he removes the burdensome suit. The combined dive and rescue are over, and again much activity has simply brought the hero and the heroine back to where they started, wet and exhausted, but otherwise unchanged.

A break of about two seconds gives them time to dry and recuperate, and then a new round of adventures is signaled, a climactic battle on the boat. As they watch, the rope holding the gangway is suddenly yanked taut, and, sure enough, when they check the situation, they find the gangway weighted by climbing cannibals. Looking about for one of those Keaton props, like the oar, that always turn up when needed, Rollo grabs a handy ax and with one efficient blow cuts the rope. The cannibals, who have been steadily going up, now suffer the customary reversal and instantly drop down. In a further defensive action, somewhat ineffectual given that the swimming cannibals are all wet anyway, Rollo and the girl then pour buckets of water on them. They each empty a bucket, they each empty a second one, and for the comic variation, he slips and falls and drenches himself with a third.

On shore, in a shot worthy of an epic battle, the chief urges on the rest of his savage horde, and a great flotilla of outriggers and canoes sets forth. Rollo and the girl, forced to defend the ship with toys, counter by bringing out the fireworks, which work. A rocket barrage drives most of the attackers away, and another earlier episode of ignorance and bungling, the mistaking of firecrackers for candles, has been repeated and transformed into success. In the most satisfactory of the rocket blows, four men standing together in a canoe are simultaneously bowled over, in precision formation all flipping over backward into the water. On the other hand, what was formerly a successful rescue aid now becomes a source of danger, for other natives climb the rope ladder that Rollo had earlier rolled down to the floundering girl. Detecting them, he once more wields the ax, though this time he first strikes too hard, missing the support rope and burying the ax head in the deck. Then, overcompensating, he aims too high, the ax swinging above the rope and its momentum propelling him into a pratfall. Only on the third swing does he strike home, and another cannibal pile descends with a mighty splash.

The natives, good Keaton aborigines, now prove as resourceful at adaptation as Rollo ever was. They push a palm tree turned ladder against the side of the boat and climb that. The tree itself, however, provides Rollo with defensive weapons, and he pelts them with coconuts, hitting the top man as his head comes into view over the deck. Stunned, that fellow slides back down, dislodging everyone below him, while Rollo, for good measure, lobs a few more coconuts down at them. The tables are briefly turned when an imitative monkey in the palm branches throws a coconut and beans Rollo, but then the episode climaxes in victory. Rollo pushes the entire tree over on an approaching canoe, scoring a direct hit on the cannibal chief, who fortunately in this shot is an obvious dummy substitute.

One native now finds yet another way on board, climbing a line from his boat to the prow, evidently the same line Rollo had used when trying to tow the ship. Rollo, meanwhile, discovers another toylike piece of miniature equipment, a tiny cannon, perhaps used for salutes. He ignites it, aims it toward the side, and starts to walk off, only to discover that his foot is entangled in its rope and that no matter how much he twists and runs to escape, this way, that way, around in circles, it follows him, always pointed in a lethal direction. But then near disaster is reversed. Rollo stumbles and falls just as the cannon fires, and its ball hits instead that climbing native, now at the edge of the deck and about to spear him from behind. With a mighty back flip the native dives into the water, and Rollo safely moves on, thankfully patting the little cannon as he goes.

At this point the girl, who is preparing another rocket barrage, accidentally sets off all the remaining fireworks with a mispointed roman candle. As she and Rollo are distracted by this, the remaining natives, still a small army, successfully invade the ship, Using an unexpected final way up, they ascend its giant anchor, which stretches from deck to water level. After a few more shots of hiding and hunting, as Rollo and the girl cower in a doorway while the natives rush past them, the decision is made to abandon ship. He places a lifesaver around the line that still extends to the native boat at the prow, and the girl slides down on that. He then follows in his own slide for life, but when his feet slam into the edge of the little boat at the end of the line, the girl, now standing in it, is jolted out.

Naturally, he must leap into the water after her, and the great battle ends with the two of them suspended in the life preserver as hundreds of cannibals dive from The Navigator and swim and paddle toward them. Rollo in despair throws the preserver away and clutches the girl to him, and together they sink. And then together they rise, standing on the top of a submarine. Entering the conning tower hatch just ahead of the natives, they reverse direction for the last time and sink again.

Inside the submarine, the girl for the first time actually kisses Rollo, though in keeping with the decorously puritanical and comic tone of the film, it is a timid peck and she immediately looks embarrassed at having committed it. Still, it is enough to make him fall over backward and bump into a control lever that starts the submarine spinning. For a while Rollo, the girl, and a sailor are subjected to the film's final symmetrical motion, as they are whirled about in a circle that carries them nowhere, just as the entire film has done. Then the sailor pulls the lever, and the submarine stabilizes. In the last shot, Rollo and the girl sit on the floor huddled together, again reduced to two small childlike figures, as the captain enters and stands angrily above them on the right. Predictably a cook, holding a flattened coffee pot, fills the gap in the visual pattern required by symmetry. He enters and stands complaining on the left.

It is a good ending, though Keaton himself, at least in a conversation reported in Rudi Blesh's biography (p. 256), was dissatisfied with it. As he and probably the best of his writers, Clyde Bruckman, once reminisced about the film, they agreed that the real end should have been the drowning of the boy and the girl. In Blesh's words:

"The story really ended when you two dove in and sank," said Bruckman.
"Oh," said Buster, "it was in the books for us to die all right. But not in the jokebooks. We were making a comedy, remember?"
Bruckman nodded. As he sat opposite the comedian, his dour face and Keaton's tragic mask were twin portraits of the spirit of comedy.

It is hard to understand how a tragic mask or even a less intensively dour face can express the spirit of comedy, except for Blesh's apparent feeling that comedy is profound only to the extent that it corresponds to the more obvious characteristics of tragedy. If you want a meaningful or deep comedy, you must drown your hero and heroine at the end.

Keaton's classical comedy, *The Navigator* in particular, does have affinities with classical tragedy, but they are not those suggested in the conversation just cited. As does tragedy, to repeat an earlier generalization, the Keaton comedy conveys a strongly felt sense of fate, a complicity between the universe and the hero, who is inexorably led through the pattern of his plot. The comic pattern, however, is not the tragic pattern. If anything, it is a parody of the tragic pattern, expressive of an absurd fatalism that contrives a series of forced moves for the hero, sets him mightily acting, but at the end of all his exertions leaves him unmoved. Tragedy proceeds in one direction, but all the lines of Keaton's classically pure comedy reverse themselves, or else they bend in a symmetrical circle that must finally stop where it started. If the king of France marched up a hill and down again, Rollo's comic fate in the film requires only that he first get on The Navigator and then get off, more competent and self-reliant for the experience, closer to and once kissed by his girl, but with all the other circumstances of his life left undisturbed. It is in the books that he live, for the comic spirit resists anything so long-lasting and irreversible as death. Though its circular patterns are eternal, its vision of an individual life subjected to them is likely to be a short one, here as often in Keaton a two-day view, during which fate takes something like a weekend holiday, stirring up a mighty commotion that turns out to be no more than a leisure-time activity. The nonconsequential interlude continually jolts the hero but leaves him finally unshaken.

To describe the comic-tragic correspondence in another way, where tragic fate has a moral and cosmological element, where it implies something about the ultimate relation between man and the gods, comic necessity is deliberately amoral and explains nothing. Or if the gods are behind its actions, they are gods with a strong sense of the absurd, for in *The Navigator* necessity is simply the result of an arbitrarily and loonily imposed principle of balance, of symmetry, rigorously applied to all aspects of the film. A motion once made will require a similar or opposing motion to follow. An object in one place will require a corresponding object in another.

Everything seems governed by a fixed and mechanical law, which once put in operation, like a swinging pendulum, does not allow of any rest, of any possibility of resisting the pattern, until the end. By the logic of symmetry, one thing must succeed another, even if there is no meaning behind or reason for these symmetrical demands. And that, of course, is what makes the film's air of necessity a merely playful, a purely comic, one, a constant source of amusement for the gods. Viewed in terms of its individual actions and overall structure, *The Navigator* seems finally like a great wind-up toy, which keeps repeating its mechanical motions till the last unwinding of its comic spring. And so it goes left and right, back and forth, up and down, and around in circles, until its spring runs down and suddenly it stops.

6.

Seven Chances

SOCIAL COMMENTARY

SEVEN CHANCES, the credits tell us, is adapted from David Belasco's "famous" comedy by Roi Cooper Megrue. Whatever its origin, on screen the film is all Keaton, a vehicle for his customary continuous and accelerating motion. There is the usual simple linear plot, which moves rapidly in one direction for the first half, then elegantly reverses itself and moves even more rapidly in the other direction for the second. The plot, in fact, is even more simple and thinly linear than usual, reducing Keaton's performance in each half to a single basic comic action, one repeated with increasingly ingenious and desperate variations. First, to propose marriage. Second, to avoid it.

Though *Seven Chances* proceeds as a simple, almost simple-minded, farce, and though Keaton and his crew had comic minds so fine that it seems no idea could penetrate them, still there is a surprising amount of meaning to the film. Of all the features, it perhaps comes closest to a social commitment, to a modest engagement with a major social and behavioral theme, one that still preoccupies us today. As always, however, its meanings are stated visually. If a commentary is made, it is a commentary never spoken. Nor, though it is consciously present, is it a commentary intended as a commentary, a message to be read out of the film. Rather the statement is implicitly there as an informing point of view, controlling the elements that have been selected from the real social world and simplified into a coherent and comprehensible film world. Though the

128

selection and simplification are governed largely by a practical laugh-maker's desire for a laugh, they also of necessity express an attitude toward society and an interpretation of it. What is expressed is a long way from a rigorous, reforming analysis that would turn an entertaining movie into a film of ideas; still a commentary of sorts is present, and it is present in sufficient strength to make *Seven Chances* susceptible, even amenable, to latter-day sociological investigation. It contains ideas about society, even if they are expressed only in visual images, even if much magnification is required to bring them into view, and even if for their time (and even more so for ours) they are essentially complacent and conservative, an unfeeling expression of a then-dominant male chauvinism.

With these reservations expressed, the major social theme, the serious issue of continuing and contemporary importance implicitly developed behind the farcically frantic surface comedy of the film, can be announced. It is the relations between the sexes, or rather, a little in advance of James Thurber and far behind Aristophanes, the war between them, a war waged primarily by a massive women's liberation front. Always in Keaton's features there is a love story and often an ending in marriage, but neither love nor marriage seems the major subject of the films. The heroines exist primarily as objects, as prizes the hero must win by surviving an endurance contest against the hostile forces of man or nature. They are late Victorian hangovers in the long tradition of medieval courtly romance, of the ideal woman as a goddess on a pedestal, someone of whom the man must prove himself worthy by performing valorous deeds. The result in medieval romance and in Keaton is that the girls are apt to be introduced early and then shelved until the end. With the real interest centering on the hero's endurance contest, the heroines, desirable though they may be, exist only as pretexts for initiating his adventures. In *Seven Chances,* however, women are always there, as attractive presences and as active forces. They do not initiate the adventures, they are the adventures. They become the obstacles in the customary Keaton obstacle course, and they are so persistently shown on the screen that finally they dominate the film. It is filled with them, beautiful women and ugly women, around a dozen of the first and hundreds of the second, the first cheerful prisoners of sex, held captive by the sexual roles their society has assigned them, the second of necessity liberated, running amuck in a man's world and enacting a man's role. It is thus also a film about sex roles and their chaotic and comic reversal, a reversal which releases such a fiercely destructive force that the film ends as a comic equivalent of Euripides' *The Bacchae*. In the film as in the play, the primacy and power of sexual drives break through the restraints imposed by civilization, tearing apart everyone and everything that stand in their way. If that is too grandiose a description and comparison, the film finally is also, in the simplifying Keaton manner, about movement and stasis, walking and running as contrasted to sitting and standing, which it schematically presents as sexually and socially segregated states. Men actively do; women passively do not.

It begins with a brief four-part prologue, a year-long romance, whose unromantic constancy contrasts to the alterations of the seasons. The introductory title sets the pattern: "One beautiful summer day, when fragrant flowers were in bloom, Jimmie Shannon met Mary Jones, and he wanted to tell her he loved her." The pattern is repeated through fall and winter and despite a promise of progression continues unaltered in the spring: "However, when nature had changed again, bringing forth spring time with its beautiful buds and blossoms—he still wanted to tell her he loved her." Each of the four scenes following the titles, except for seasonal variations in foliage and dress, is the same. Jimmie and Mary stand in the open gate of the white picket fence in front of her house, and that is all they do. As they talk, he decorously holds his hat instead of her, and his only real action in each scene, comically lacking all other action, is to bend over and pat her dog. A Dalmation, it begins as a puppy and grows from season to season until spring, when Jimmie can pat it without even the slightest lean.

In the four scenes certain elements of costume and setting, which seem inconsequentially realistic, are actually important for defining the roles and places of the sexes, and they will be much repeated, gaining in meaning, throughout the film. The chivalrously held hat is one of them, and so is the picket fence. Fences are associated with most Keaton heroines, who keep appearing behind them, and in this film they will be intensively used to mark off and limit the world of women and to visually and literally express the barriers between the sexes. Mary, as the ideal woman in the film, will never advance any farther outside the picket fence than in the prologue. Her world is entirely bound by it, restricted to her house and yard, and her role is simply to wait, passively if apprehensively, till Jimmie comes to her. One other element, placed in the background, is also significant. As the two characters stand talking, the most prominent feature of the house behind them is the gabled roof of the porch, a gable whose underside is a semicircular arch, positioned just above their heads. Here and again at the end of the film, it is a sign of sexual harmony and unity, a connecting arc embracing the lovers who stand beneath it. Like the fence, it is also a protective and enclosing shape and a restrictive one. And it, too, in the film's first half, will be associated with women, delimiting and characterizing their world.

Following the prologue, the main action of the film, tightly compacted into a period of about seven hours, begins with a title: "Jimmie was the junior partner of the firm of Meeker and Shannon, brokers, that had been tricked into a financial deal that meant disgrace—and possibly prison—unless they raised money quickly." In their office, the two partners glumly read a tickertape, and then another title shifts the scene to their outer office, where "a lawyer, unknown to the firm," waits "with good news for Jimmie." The lawyer, played by the diminutive, prune-faced Snitz Edwards, sits on a bench in front of a waist-high railing, and behind it, set off in a cage-like compound that protects her from clients, is the firm's attractive secretary. The good news he waits with is a will from Jimmie's grandfather, a will whose seventh codicil leaves the balance of his estate to Jimmie. Refused admission to the inner office because the partners fear he might be serving a summons, the lawyer thereupon stages a one man sit-in just beyond the secretary's railing, much to her irritation. Then when Jimmie and Meeker leave for their country club, he chases after them, following Jimmie's Stutz Bearcat in a taxi.

At the club, he manages to hold the will up to a window, and seeing it, Jimmie and Meeker are now eager to meet with him. The three borrow a clubhouse office for a conference, like that of the brokerage firm a double office. As they walk through the outer

portion, another good-looking secretary sits there, as before immured in a small corral behind a protective railing. In the inner
office, a young girl's legs dangle from a large chair to one side, but
the three men are too intent on business to notice. Sitting at the desk,
with Meeker and Jimmie hovering over him, the lawyer reads. The
estate amounts to seven million dollars, but there is one condition
attached. To inherit it Jimmie must be married before seven P.M. on
his twenty-seventh birthday. Looking at a calendar, Jimmie realizes
that today is his twenty-seventh birthday, which leaves him only
seven hours to find a wife. Alliteratively he decides, "Maybe Mary
might marry me," and sets off to make the first of what will be
seventeen proposals.

In a symmetrically arranged sequence, reminiscent of the proposal
in *The Navigator,* Jimmie in the first shot walks past the secretary in
the outer office. In the next shot he sits in his car, while the background dissolves from country club to Mary's house. Mary is in the
backyard, and her answer is yes, which leads to about five seconds of
cuddling and kissing. Then he consults his watch and announces, "I
must hurry back to the country club and tell Billy it's all fixed and
we'll be married today." "Why today?" she asks. He replies, "My
grandfather left me a lot of money provided I marry *some* girl today." Sensing the unromantic implications of that statement, he
adds, "I don't mean *some* girl! I mean, it don't matter *who* I marry,
but I must wed someone!" After a short argument, Mary angrily
breaks the brief engagement and goes inside. Jimmie, finishing the
sequence as he began it, climbs back into his car, as the background
dissolves from Mary's house to country club. Then, the last shot of
the sequence reversing the first shot, he sadly retraces his steps
through the outer office, though he distractedly misses the inner
office door and walks through the gate of the secretary's enclosure
instead, from which, as she stares at him, he must hastily retreat.

Back in the inner office, Jimmie's partner convinces him that he
must marry to obtain the inheritance—everything, even their liberty,
depends on it. Mary, meanwhile, has changed her mind about the
proposal. Unable to reach Jimmie on the telephone, she sends a
message with her hired man, a slow-moving, stereotyped, comic
darkie, played by a white actor in blackface. Following her injunc-

tion to "ride for your life," he bounces away on a spastic, stiff-legged old horse. Though their matrimonial future has already been settled, and though Mary will wait by her phone for the rest of the film to receive her reply, Jimmie now sets out to find another wife. Accompanied by Meeker and the lawyer, he walks to the arched doorway of the country club dining room. There his search will begin, a self-contained play interlude of multiplying mock proposals and accelerating chaos that fortunately circles to an autodestructive end, leading to nothing before his actual wedding.

The first eleven of his proposals will be made in the country club, and the women proposed to, with one deliberately outrageous exception, will all be presented in a visual context that unites and defines them. Two are working women, a telephone operator and a hatcheck girl, and like the two secretaries seen so far, though they labor in a man's world they are strictly sequestered from it, fenced inside small areas reserved for women and women's work. Like the secretaries, the telephone operator sits in a railed-in rectangle, a restrictive and protective pen, and the hatcheck girl is even more secluded. The space in which she stands is a little cave, with a counter in front and above that an arched opening, one of the many visually emphasized arches at the club. Though the railings and arches, as in the prologue, are all realistic, they are also metaphoric, expressive of a society in which the sexes are separate and unequal, where working women are carefully segregated from men and relegated to jobs of passive immobility, where they sit or stand but otherwise are allowed scant freedom or opportunity to move about.

There are also eight nonworking women who are proposed to, country club members or guests, and they, too, are consistently presented as separated from the men, confined and protected by omnipresent arches and railings. The clubhouse, in fact, is a stage set deliberately designed as a social arena for preliminary bouts leading to matrimony, an architectural assemblage of small enclosed cells in which the women are imprisoned. Held in them, they cannot escape a masculine approach, but, a decided advantage in the sexual battle, they also cannot be approached too closely. An unwanted suitor like Jimmie can easily be rejected, kept outside the protective fences and feminine enclosures. The total image of the clubhouse suggests a

male-dominated but decorously puritanical society, where women in
their social and occupational roles are treated as secular nuns,
cloistered and restricted. So immured, they are approachable only up
to clearly defined and chastely distant limits, the boundaries, often
marked by actual railings, created by strong and strongly repressive
social conventions. The catch in the system, however, is that it
works, as far as matrimony is concerned, because the women so
segregated are beautiful and desirable and need do no more than
confidently wait for the amatory advances of gentlemen callers.

At this point, as the three men stand in the arched doorway of the
dining room, they survey the scene, and a slow pan discloses seven
women who sit there. Eating, drinking, talking, putting on makeup,
they are all, with one complex quasi-exception to be discussed later,
very beautiful and sexually alluring, a stationary parade of fashion
models, fashionably dressed. Meeker lists their names in a note-
book—Eugenia Gilbert, Doris Deane, Juddy (*sic*) King, Hazel
Deane, Bartine Buckett, Bonnie Evans, and Pauline Taller. He then
concludes "You have seven chances," and Jimmie, after handing
his hat to the lawyer, is pushed into the room toward prospective
bride number one. She sits by herself at a wall table, and he, preserving a polite distance, decorously sits across the table from her.
Abruptly shattering decorum, however, he next instantly proposes
marriage. First she is startled, but then she laughs, so loudly that all
the other diners notice. Decisively and derisively rebuffed, Jimmie
stumbles back to the archway, the embarrassed focal point of a
roomful of staring eyes.

Retreating outside to the terrace, he receives some needed encouragement and a quick lesson in the art of proposing from his partner
and the lawyer. Then he is pushed after a second beauty, who walks
by and stands in a sylphlike pose at the edge of the golf course. For a
second time he approaches, again he proposes, kneeling and extravagantly gesturing his plea, and again he performs before an unwanted
audience, as a party of four golfers and three caddies walk on screen
behind him. The lady laughs, they laugh, and he once more uncomfortably stumbles away. Reluctantly forced back inside, he next sees
the third girl. She sits on a balcony overlooking the entrance hall,
framed by a protective arch above her and a railing in front,

immobile and only distantly approachable. Standing below, at the hatcheck counter, Jimmie writes a note, "Will you marry me?", and tosses it up, receiving his answer when a small snowstorm of shredded paper coldly descends upon him.

The fourth proposal begins with a long shot, looking through a large arched doorway whose confining shape frames a girl in the next room, where she sits on a couch and reads a paper. In the foreground, to the right of the arch, Jimmie, Meeker, and the lawyer stand, planning strategy. "I'll propose to this one for you," says Meeker. He then adjusts Jimmie's profile, so it will look good from a distance, and walks through the arch up to the waiting girl. Seated beside her, he asks, "Have you ever thought of getting married?" The encouraging reply is "Constantly." The couch affair proceeds rapidly, and there is a cut to Jimmie standing in the arched doorway, watching, while behind him the lawyer stands, his back to the camera, looking through another arch into the dining room. But then Jimmie and the lawyer exchange positions, just before Meeker, freeing himself from the girl's welcoming arms, exclaims "Wait a minute—I'm proposing for him." He points to the spot where Jimmie had been standing, but what in a closeup shot the girl now sees is the grotesquely wrinkled, comically ugly lawyer. She is immediately irate, and yet another move toward marriage has dead-ended.

Proposals five and six are joint affairs and center on a symmetrically comic reversal of movement. They take place on a stairway, whose curve dominates the screen and echoes the arches of the balcony. Jimmie follows a girl walking up, proposing on the way, is rejected at the top, and instantly, without breaking step, turns around and follows another down, still proposing and still being rejected. All this action takes place on the stair's curved steps and is further confined by and seen through its waist-high railings, so that it becomes another protected enclosure, a feminine enclave from which the unwanted man is quickly rejected. At the bottom, mechanically carrying through an established pattern, Jimmie starts to follow a third girl up, but she turns out to be proposal number one, and now as then she starts laughing, driving him away. Finally, back by the large arch that framed the fourth proposal, girl number seven, in a black dress and long white scarf, walks into a phone booth and is followed into that enclosure by Jimmie. Quickly thrown out, he announces "Wrong party." His seven chances are over, and his partner, who has been keeping track of the failures, crosses the last name off the list.

Beautiful, laughing, desirable, and under the circumstances sensibly unobtainable, the seven have all been passive, unmoving, unliberated women, existing in an appropriate architectural context of seductive, confining curves and of restrictive, protective railings, a purdah-like retreat of small enclosures where they can be approached but do not themselves much move. In the conventional routines of social and sexual encounter at the country club, routines decorously analagous to a very decorous sex act, their only options, neither involving much physical motion, are to accept or reject. When the active and intrusive male approaches the often confined and often arched spaces assigned to them, they can let him in or shut him out, but the initial advances are all his. The rituals of social intercourse, however, as Jimmie has quickly learned, are designed to keep him from advancing very far, and serve to protect as well as to imprison the women.

Still determined and undaunted after the seven lost chances, Meeker now says to Jimmie, "Meet me at the Broad Street Church at five o'clock—I'll have a bride there if it's the last act of my life." Speaking to Jimmie, the lawyer adds, "You try and have one there too in case he fails." They then go their way and Jimmie goes his, doggedly progressing through nine more attempted proposals, though by now his situation is so desperate that most of his attempts do not even reach the point of asking the question. There are four more at the country club, three out on the streets, which follow the country club pattern, and two, ending the search in climactic confusion, that are so unlikely they verge on the surreal and the absurd.

The first approached is the country club telephone operator. She sits in her enclosure reading a sensational novel, Elinor Glyn's *Three Weeks,* which looks promising, as does the sign reading "on duty" and "Miss Smith." Proposed to from across the railing, however, she smiles the customary rejecting smile and displays an engagement

ring. Next is an older, more matronly looking woman than any seen
so far. She sits in a large wing chair whose back forms a shallow arch
over her, and reads a paper. Lowering her paper when Jimmie
speaks, she reveals the baby in her lap. The hatcheck girl, a spectator
for all of this, does not even need to be asked. When Jimmie walks
her way, she instantly silences him with a firm and negative shake of
her head.

The last proposal at the club, the first indication of impending
chaos and role confusion, occurs as a perversely baby-faced girl in a
long black coat and currently fashionable cloche steps forward to
make the initial and up-to-now masculine advance, asking with a
petulant, provocative, wide-eyed look, "Do you think anybody
would marry me?" Triumphant, Jimmie leads her out to the
clubhouse terrace, another rectangular and railed space, beside
which the original seven beautiful chances stand in a compact,
grinning group. When he with a supercilious sneer produces the
would-be bride, they stop grinning, but then her angry mother comes
along, pulls off her hat and coat, and reveals a nymphet of about
thirteen, in child's dress and with a child's long Mary Pickford curls.
Her adult disguise removed, she is disclosed as the immature adolescent who had overheard the reading of the will in the clubhouse
office. Two proposals earlier, the last shot in the encounter was of
the matron holding her baby; now the last shot of the little girl shows
her with her doll. And Jimmie, having played the range from the too
old to the too young, abandons the humiliations of the club and
hastily drives away, as usual accompanied by the laughter of a
derisive audience.

Ignorantly passing Mary's hired man, who is still slowly racing
for his life with the message from Mary, Jimmie suddenly draws up
in his Stutz Bearcat beside another Stutz Bearcat, this one driven by
a lady. Seizing the opportunity, he tips his hat and proposes, but
even before she has had time to consider and refuse, his car smashes
into a tree growing in the center of the road. The collision instantly
stops both his vehicular and his amatory advances.

The next lady encountered sits on a street corner bench. Now
walking but still searching, Jimmie halts beside her, sits, removes
his hat, and proposes. In response, she unfolds a newspaper,

revealing it to be in Yiddish and revealing also that his proposal has not come through. Moving on, he then admires the attractively swaying rear view of a lady strolling in front of him and hastens to her side. There he discovers, in another of the movie's many unfortunate racial jokes, that she is black. Veering away, he abandons the pursuit.

So far the women at the country club and on the streets have all been genuine women, if variously single, engaged, married, too young, speaking the wrong language, and belonging to the wrong race. Eight of them have been completely stationary, passively female. And even the six that have moved did so generally in a limited way, like the woman overtaken in her car, who was still sitting and approachable even if driving. The last two recipients of Jimmie's proposals, however, while retaining the characteristic feminine immurement of the earlier ones, provide desperate variations to end the sequence. First, passing a beauty salon, Jimmie sees through the door a seated girl. A large cloth covers her body and an attendant arranges her hair. Proposed to, however, she makes no response, for she is a hairdresser's wooden dummy.

Passing a second doorway, the stage entrance to a theater, he then sees a sign advertising a lady performer in a tight-fitting costume. Bribing the guard stationed there, he goes in. Soon after, another man comes out—comes out and removes a large trunk covering the bottom portion of the sign. This reveals the lady's name—Julian Eltinge, an actual stage performer and one of the best known female impersonators of the period. Shortly, Jimmie also comes out, hat smashed, left eye blackened, collar half torn off. He glares at the guard, retrieves his bribe (all this has happened so quickly that the guard has not pocketed the money yet), and stalks off. It is the end of the first half, the seventeenth proposal; and appropriately enough, being made unknowingly to a female impersonator, it prepares the way for the comically nightmarish confusion of sexual roles that will follow. One man mistaken for a woman will be replaced by hundreds of women actively carrying on like angry, powerful men.

Before moving to the second half, however, we must first pause to consider several aspects of the first half. The first involves a hat. Keaton generally works with props, and the film before this, *The*

Navigator, is characterized by a maximum density of them. In it, the hero's hands are constantly filled with suitcases, flowers, hats, canes, chairs, candles, fireworks, axes, buckets, a miniature cannon, and more. In the first half of *Seven Chances* only one prop, Jimmie's hat, is extensively employed, or rather there are three props, for Meeker and the lawyer are each equipped with a hat, too. In *The Navigator* the hero's hats were employed in a continuing gag routine; one after another they were all blown away. In this film, also, there is one gag with the hero's hat. He briefly leaves it with the clubhouse hatcheck girl. When he comes back to retrieve it, she ignores his outstretched hand until he fishes in his pocket and drops a tip on the counter. Then she hands him the hat, but before she can pick up the tip, he notices another prospective bride, the matron with the baby, tosses the hat back on the counter, reclaims the tip, and walks off. At his next appearance, just before he proposes to her, the hatcheck girl is prepared for the tip as well as the proposal. Placing the hat on the counter, she holds onto it. When Jimmie drops a tip on the counter, she places her other hand over that. Only then, as the two distrustfully eye each other, does she allow Jimmie to pull his hat toward him as she pulls the tip toward her—nicely balanced and mutually mimicking motions of the sort Keaton can always get a laugh with.

Otherwise, though the hats are always there, they are not much used for gag purposes. They are, however, the objects of much manipulation, always being employed in some kind of business. They are taken off and put on, picked up or set down, held onto and gestured with, to such a surprising extent, once one is aware of it and starts looking for it, that much of the actual movement on the screen is that of someone's hat. In fact, such extensive repetition, which is one of the basic principles of humor, as the proposals of this film also clearly demonstrate, finally makes even unfunny motions of the hat amusing. Jimmie has tipped his hat to so many ladies that when he does it once again in only slightly unlikely circumstances, as he pulls up in his Stutz Bearcat to prospective proposal number thirteen in hers, the gesture, so charged with comic intention, produces one of the film's certain laughs.

More important, however, than its use in a gag routine or the development of its comic potential through repeated usage, is the

hat's role as a major visual means of defining male-female relationships. It is one of the forms of a highly formalized society, where
behavior is regulated and restrained by the conventions of etiquette.
Raising or removing the hat is a basic example of good manners in a
world in which public actions must conform to artificial patterns of
behavior. The world of the hat is also a decorously inhibited world,
because these artificial patterns, the gestures required of a male, are
surrogates for more instinctive actions, surrogates that are expected
and safe. Finally, this world is one of clearly distinguished and
unequal sexual roles. It is always the man who performs the actions
required by etiquette, always the woman who is the passive recipient
of them. And it is because she is regarded as the weaker sex that the
stronger male honors her. The gesture of removing the hat, while it
asserts his masculine prerogative of action, also announces his
temporary obeissance and harmlessness. It is a signal promising safe
conduct, a promise that need only be made by the dominant to the
subservient sex. Early in the film, when Jimmie and his partner leave
their office and enter an elevator with a lady in it, they politely and
simultaneously doff their hats to show respect for her, and such
respect is indicated many times thereafter.

So regarded, the frequent business with hats performed by Jimmie
and also by Meeker and the lawyer becomes a major visual means of
establishing the norms of sexual conduct, the roles of men and
women in a civilized, patterned, and restrained society. When
Jimmie meets a woman, he removes his hat, and it is the hat he then
holds instead of her. Like the railings and enclosures, the hat inhibits
action, though of course Jimmie violates the reassurances of polite
restraint that the hat signals when, hat decorously in hand, he
immediately proposes marriage. The proposals are all the funnier
because they are incongruous actions in a world where all actions
should be regulated by the same code that makes a man hold his hat.
Reasonably enough, the final violation of the code, proposal number
seventeen to Julian Eltinge, results in the destruction of the hat.
When the film's first half ends, it has been pulled down over
Jimmie's ears, the crown half torn off and the brim encircling his
neck, a visual symbol proclaiming the end of social propriety and
prefiguring the devastating explosion of repressed feminine energy

that is now to come. In the second half, Jimmie's tidily structured society with its inhibiting manners and its sexual segregation will be torn apart and nearly destroyed by a violently liberated surge of primitive and instinctive action. In it, men's hats and women's chains will be thrown off, and the high ironic humor of drawing room restraint, which has so far held in check the farcical antics of the film, will give way to uncontrolled and wildly bacchantic farce. Women will now act, reversing established sexual roles, emerging from the walls of their cloistered recesses and soon breaking through a new set of walls that rise to define and protect the world of men. In such a catastrophic sexual revolution, hats no longer politely function, and Jimmie's new one, a formal black silk hat, will almost instantly be lost.

Before we examine the second half of the film, it should also be stressed that though certain sexually assigned roles will be totally reversed in it, sexuality itself, basic maleness and femaleness, remains reasonably fixed and certain. It is in fact because sexual differences are seen by the film as certain that the role breakdowns are so comic. It is the comedy of incongruity, of the right behavior performed by the wrong person. In the limited context of role-differentiating action in the film, women suddenly moving about like men or a man forced by them into the subservient role of a woman would not be funny in the way they are intended to be unless basic sexual identities were so certain that they could be taken for granted. Only in a few peripheral instances does the film include something sexually ambiguous or aberrant. The first is the female impersonator, Julian Eltinge, who is present as no more than a picture on a poster. A second, in the forthcoming sequence at the Broad Street Church, is the most visible of the would-be brides who turn up there, a giant mannish-looking woman, possibly played by a man, strikingly dressed in a turban and a man's coat, shirt, and tie.

There is also a mysterious third, who appears in the long panning shot of the country club dining room, when the seven beautiful chances are introduced. Exactly seven girls are shown as Meeker writes their names on an envelope, and subsequently there are seven proposals and the seven names are all crossed out. One of the original seven girls, however, is not proposed to. The second one seen is plump-faced, solidly built, short-haired, and like the later giant mannishly dressed in a suit coat and tie. In the final clubhouse scene, where the seven appear by the terrace to laugh at the departing hero, she is again one of the group, but at the point where she should be proposed to, the slim willowy beauty who poses by the golf course is introduced instead. Though not in the original dining room shot, this new girl does turn up again in the final shot of the group by the terrace, where she now replaces one of the women proposed to on the stairway. The juggling, which in a fool-the-eye way makes eight women appear to be seven, allows for the introduction, exclusion, and final reappearance of the mannish woman. She is a subtle joke on the genuinely aberrant, though a joke so quickly and casually inserted that it can almost pass unnoticed. A case of actual sexual confusion, she is, however, like the other two figures mentioned, present only in a marginal way. The three represent a sexual area that the film acknowledges but does not otherwise enter into, something quite distinct from the comic role confusion of the second half, the turning about of the courtship and occupational patterns that have been assigned to men and women, patterns constructed as much to peaceably separate the mutually hostile sexes as to romantically unite them.

The second half begins as Jimmie's partner and the lawyer, who were earlier shown going into a newspaper building, now are shown reading the afternoon paper, the *Daily News*. Its front-page, head-lined story proclaims: "Wanted, a bride. James Shannon, prominent young broker, falls heir to $7,000,000 if he is married today. All he needs is a bride. Girl who appears at Broad Street Church in bridal costume by 5 o'clock will be the lucky winner." (For those interested in minutiae, the article also names Jimmie's grandfather, Jabez Shannon, and the lawyer, Caleb Pettibone.) A title next reads, "By the time Jimmie had reached the church, he had proposed to everything in skirts, including a Scotchman"; and then, at nearly the exact midpoint of the film, shot 216 out of a total of 424, Jimmie enters the appropriately labeled church. Dressed in top hat and tails, carrying a corsage, and armed with two railroad tickets, the bride's for Niagara Falls and his for Reno, he proceeds all the way down the long aisle and sits in the front pew. There, exhausted from his labors, he soon tumbles over into a troubled sleep, still unconsciously making gestures of proposal and cringing at their rejection. Then he merely lies there, hidden by the pew from anyone in the church behind him, a beautifully still figure, who has moved as far as the plot will allow him in one direction and now waits unknowingly for the reversal that will send him frantically fleeing in the opposite. As he rests, all the visual details that have so far defined and characterized the world of women are again in evidence, but now turned about and applied to him. A waist-high altar railing in front of him and the high, straight pew back behind seem a restrictive fence imprisoning him in a small rectangular pen, and the church interior itself is yet another sequestered space, its entrance, visible in the center background, crowned with a low arch. Railing, arch, enclosures, and held within them a stationary figure who passively waits, but now a man rather than a woman—all the elements proclaim that a great reversal has come.

It and the brides arrive together, not one of them, as the partner promised, not two of them, as the lawyer anticipated, but a multitude. The story placed by the partner in the paper has been read by every old maid and every unprepossessing young maid in the city, all the unapproachables in the conventional social scheme, all who of necessity must do more than merely wait for a gentleman caller to make the first advances. Dressed for a wedding, each at least wearing a hastily and horribly contrived parody of a bridal headdress, they hasten to the church—in a car, on a bike, on a horse, on roller skates, in a trolley, walking, running, trucking their way to the wedding. In the social and sexual context of the film, the norm so firmly established in the first half, it is actually startling to see them actively moving through the streets, a female revolutionary force exploding from its segregated confines. Within the church, first one arrives and sits in the back pew, then three more, then nine, then a crowd, then an ocean, wave upon wave that visibly crest at the entrance as they all squeeze inside, cramming every pew except the one in front where Jimmie sleeps, oblivious of the hydra-headed doom that swells the screen behind him. Then he awakens. Sitting up, he is instantly joined by a fat bride and a skinny bride, who enter and sit beside him. Gradually, he becomes aware of his oppressive predicament, just as the two brides become aware of him, the fat one sidling coyly closer and the skinny one holding and stroking his hand. Each encroaching on what the other believes is her private territory, they next begin fighting over him, literally over, for he is at least a head shorter than either. Then a gorgon in the pew behind (the giant mannish woman) grabs him, and he is quickly dragged into the center aisle, where unintentional dismemberment is imminently threatened.

Fortunately, at this crisis the minister enters from the front of the church and everyone calms down. Then, however, with a mild remonstrance, he provokes even greater chaos. "Ladies," he says, "you are evidently the victims of some practical joker—I must ask you to leave the church as quickly as possible." In the Keaton comic universe, where sudden change is the natural law governing most events, this remark triggers the supreme comic change. Woman-kind's repeated "no," which had turned into a multivoiced "yes," now instantly becomes a single roar of rage as it dawns on the brides that everyone is apt to be left waiting at the altar. Determined to marry or demolish him, or possibly both at once, they all descend with hostile intent on Jimmie. Momentarily it seems he must have been crushed beneath them, but then he crawls from behind a pew, hatless but otherwise intact, and escapes by leaping through a window. In determined pursuit, some seven hundred brides simul-taneously push their way through the door after him.

Outside, the lawyer, Meeker, and the handyman have all reached the church. As the brides flood through the door, the lawyer and Meeker sit trembling on the entrance steps. Terrified by the streaming women who surge around them, they huddle together in a defensive and frozen cringe, the helplessness of which contrasts to their former assertive activity. The handyman, however, reaches Jimmie, and the two of them hide in the church basement, while the brides mis-takenly hurry away to search for their groom on the streets, ending the first part of what is structured as a three-part pursuit—in the church, out in the city, and finally through the country.

Having at last received her message, Jimmie sets forth for Mary. In a sequence of three episodes, a brideless interval that will make the brides' reappearance at an unexpected moment all the funnier, he also tries to find out what time it is, how long he has till seven. Stopping first at Nall's Barber Shop, he asks a black shoeshine man, who pulls out his watch fob. But at the end of it there is only a bottle opener. Seated on a high chair and reading a copy of *Redbook* magazine, his customer conspicuously displays a wristwatch, even if she is a lady and it is strapped to her ankle. (Apparently this was a current fashion fad, perhaps a liberated way of calling attention to a shapely leg. When pretending to be a vamp in *Exit Smiling,* released in 1925, Beatrice Lillie also sports an ankle watch.) Jimmie leans over to check her leg for the time, but she instantly and assertively kicks out at him, driving him off. An omen pointing the way to the reappearance of the brides, she is in addition the first of several women who unexpectedly turn up in places customarily reserved for men. It is as if not only the brides but all women were staging a revolution, moving from behind their railings and into the larger masculine world. Her presence and her aggressive response, therefore, are genuinely disconcerting for Jimmie, as was the original unexpected aggressiveness of the brides. So thoroughly has woman's proper place been defined in the first half of the film that her surprising appearance on the street, like the appearance of the would-be brides, is disconcerting and comic for the viewer as well.

After checking in a clock shop, where all the clocks show different times except the proprietor's watch, which is not running at all, Jimmie is finally informed of the hour. Awakened by his alarm clock after what must have been an incredibly long night on the town, a late sleeper angrily responds by throwing it through a window. Passing by outside, Jimmie is naturally beaned by it, but he also accidentally learns the time, 6:15, and hastens on toward Mary. And now, just when they have almost been forgotten, the brides return. From dominating and active seekers of a mate in the church, the usurpers of the masculine courtship role, the horde of women outside become first destroyers of men and their activities and then the usurpers of men's occupational roles, for the chase after Jimmie now escalates into a full-scale feminine revolt. It begins with a beautifully managed scene in which the camera tracks away from Jimmie, who hastily strides down the street. Then behind him, from side streets, horizontal lines of brides race onto the screen to coalesce into a solid

white mass that slowly sinks down from the top, about to engulf the
solitary black-dressed man at the bottom. Still unsuspecting he walks
faster; they walk faster, too, the gap narrows, and then he becomes
aware of their hovering presence. He runs, they pursue, and what
was a sexual cold war turns hot. Let loose and liberated en masse,
the women take over the streets and in their determined chase soon
do in all the men they meet, men who, in another of the visual
reversals of the film's second half, are now the sex seen within
enclosed spaces, their work areas, which are separated and protected
from the world of women by many supposedly unbreachable walls.
However, where in the first half, Jimmie was always stopped by the
railings guarding and segregating women, in the second half the fury
of the scorned brides easily leads them across all masculine barricades.

The first victim encountered is a bricklayer, who stands on a
trestle in front of a completed building wall—a man at a man's work
in a man's proper place, laboring on another wall and building
himself, as it were, a solid and protective masculine fortess. Then
Jimmie dashes by, followed by a bride, who suddenly stops, grabs a
brick from the unfinished wall, and resumes pursuit. The bricklayer
looks on in momentary wonder, and then he and his wall are surrounded. Brides fill the screen, and after a closeup of his dumbfounded face, they race off and the entire wall goes with them,
carried away to be thrown at Jimmie. Disgusted and temporarily out
of work, all the man can do is throw in his trowel and leave.

Followed by the brick-heaving contingent, Jimmie runs into
another pack of brides, who quickly augment the throng behind him.
He also runs into the lawyer and Meeker, and as the latter runs
alongside him, Jimmie tells him that he should bring a minister to
Mary's house and that he himself will try to reach it before seven.
Having got the message, Meeker stops, whereupon he and also the
lawyer are immediately knocked over and trampled on by the
pursuing women. Jimmie, however, races on. An extreme long shot
then shows a football field, an enclosed area neatly defined by its
yardage and boundary lines, all suggestions of fences that also
delimit a rectangular work space reserved for men and off limits to
others. A play is gone through, but as the teams take positions for the
next play, Jimmie zooms by, vaulting through them, followed by the

field-filling bridal stampede. With absurd enthusiasm, the crowd in the background bleachers waves its pennants and cheers at this new steamroller play, and then the brides are gone, leaving behind them no one and nothing standing, with both hapless teams stomped into the turf.

From destroying men and disrupting their occupational activities, the brides advance to complete usurpation. Pursuing Jimmie, they stop and commandeer a streetcar, chaotically shoving their way into the orderly rectangular enclosure. The driver, not about to submit to their directions, is thrown out and tumbled down the stairs even as a last few brides still clamber up. With an uncertain but determined bride at the controls, the trolley moves on, leaving the driver seated on the street and revealing, about twenty feet farther back, the conductor in a similar position. Jimmie, meanwhile, also adds wheels to his flight, leaping onto the rear-mounted spare tire of a passing car, but it soon stops when hit by the trolley full of brides. As Jimmie woozily wanders away, they sight him and once more pursue on foot, forcing him into an immediate recovery and another prodigious dash. His run ends as he comes to a sliding stop in front of the Omar Turkish Baths. Here there should be safety, and he quickly ducks inside, but a man standing by the entrance moves on, uncovering a sign that reads "Ladies Day." Once again women have unexpectedly turned up in a customary male preserve, and Jimmie, having rushed in, now races out and hurries off screen to the right, just in time to elude the brides, who come running on from the left.

A brigade of eight policemen, of all men those most likely to be able to handle the situation, appears next. A compact, rectangular group, a peripatetic masculine fortress whose walls they themselves form, they march down the street with a regular, orderly step. Jimmie, running up, walks with them, hoping for protection. One by one, however, they look behind them, and what they see causes them to break formation and scatter for cover. This happens so quickly that Jimmie does not immediately notice, but when another policeman, a patrolman, comes running by and past him, he first looks around for his vanished protection and then behind. He, too, must run again, and he soon catches up with the patrolman and in turn whizzes by him.

He then comes to a car, which a chauffeur is about to start, and leaps into the back seat, only to leap out the other side with a particularly large bride holding onto his coattails. He struggles forward, jumping over a ditch being dug across the road, where more men work within a small, enclosed, and protected space of rectangular regularity. As he does so, the bride hanging on behind, falls in. Instantly picks and shovels and then ditchdiggers come flying out, the victims of abused and irate womanhood. Most of them exit by running up a hill toward the rear. Jimmie, who has fallen, runs off to the right, just behind the ditch, and for the sake of balanced motion, one of the diggers runs off left in front of it.

The final episode of the city chase occurs in a factory railroad yard. Another masculine working place, it is set off by the highest wall yet, with the section shown on screen being covered by three billboard-size signs: "Mining and Pumping Machines," "Gray Iron Castings," and "Electrical Steel Castings." The first sign segment has a small door in it, through which Jimmie runs into the protection of the work area. The other two signs, it turns out, are actually immense doors, which the brides, again a giant thundering horde, easily swing open as they all follow him in. Once more a wall has been breached and women have perversely penetrated a man's world. Inside, in one of the best comic action shots of the film, Jimmie stands in the center of the screen, trapped as two groups of brides converge on him. But then, with seemingly no place to go, he goes up, grabbing onto the hook at the end of a crane. Jerked into the air, he dangles above the women, two solid white masses, which collide beneath him with a satisfactory and decisive bump. Again, a man's occupational role is usurped as the crane driver is thrown out of his cab by a determined bride, then set upon by the others, and finally driven away. And again, as with the trolley, the women do badly with men's machines, for the usurping bride, ignorantly pulling levers, first sends Jimmie swinging in an immense spiraling circle and then lowers him onto a track, where he is seemingly smashed by an oncoming train. Lowered behind a fence, however, where the women cannot see him, he leaps out of the train's path just in time, momentarily safe until shortly afterward he is once again discovered by his sadly mourning followers. Instantly undergoing an emotional reversal from grief to rage, they heave rocks and chase after.

At this point, there is a cut to a small church near Mary's house, where the clock in the steeple reads 6:45. Inside the house, Mary, who plays the right feminine role, sits on the couch, still waiting. Her mother, the Broad Street minister, Meeker, and the lawyer wait, too. And this being the world of propriety and conventional gestures, hats are involved in the principal action. Having apparently just come in, Meeker tosses his on a chair to the right, and the lawyer, balancing the movement, tosses his to the left.

When the chase resumes, it has entered its third phase and moved into the country. First the brides pursue Jimmie through a field of corn, whose straight rows form a growing barricade. Like all the other barricades, it gives way, with the stalks being completely flattened and a wide path beaten through it. A beekeeper and his four orderly, fencelike rows of beehives, again a rectangularly precise masculine working space, are next upset. Jimmie, momentarily freed of the brides, who are occupied with the bees, himself runs into a barbed-wire fence, knocking it down and entangling himself in the wire. Encouraged by a threatening bull to quickly extract himself, he then runs to a stream, a natural barrier, and jumps into a boat, just as several brides race up to the shore behind him. Sarcastically throwing them a farewell kiss, he draws away, but they leap into the water and vigorously swim, soon catching up and forcing him to dive from the boat and swim, too. On the other side he once more runs, a motion now so thoroughly established that it no longer needs pursuing brides to keep it going, and for a few shots they are absent. He vaults into and out of a water-filled trench, goes through a marsh, where duck hunters twice fire at him, and finally dashes in front of a narrow gate-like pass between two tall, wall-like cliffs. After their disappearance, which as before makes their unexpected reappearance comic, the brides are seen standing in the pass and watching as he whips by. They start to follow but the leader cries, "I know a short cut—we'll head him off." Until a final climactic appearance, they again are gone, though Jimmie's flight, still in full momentum, continues nicely without them.

As this description has suggested, the settings of the rural and natural world have so far provided visual parallels for the many gates, doors, and walls of the urban world, the dividers that separated the sexes and visually defined their differing roles. And now the natural world also provides a substitute for the rampaging women. At the end of Jimmie's run, which has included a jump over a wide ravine, a leap from a tall cliff into a possibly Freudian pine tree, which is immediately chopped down, and a quadruple somersault across a sandy slope, he stumbles down a long, long hill and kicks some rocks into motion. Little rocks roll into big rocks, big rocks slam into boulders, some of them six feet or more in diameter, and soon Jimmie is being chased by a landslide as fiercely as he ever was by the brides. Leaping into a tree for safey, he watches as the rocks go by, but then a giant rock snaps the tree like a twig, and he is running again. Firmly wedged into the slope is the biggest rock of them all, a boulder at least eight feet in diameter, and he stops and crouches for shelter behind it. One by one a massive pile of rocks smashes into it from above, and it begins to shake loose. Bracing himself, he first tries to hold it in place, then gives up an obviously losing battle and runs again, while it and all the other rocks roll after him.

Fifteen hundred specially made rocks were used for this sequence, and every one of them is an accomplished performer, as determinedly intent on smashing the hero as the brides were on marrying him. Indeed, the sequence is so good that for a while everything else in the film is easily forgotten. It demands to be watched as a purely self-contained adventure, and because the pursuers are just rocks, they develop as something like an abstraction, an ideal of the comic chase. They become the perfect visual symbols of pure, idealized comic threat, just large chunks of abstract hostility doing their best to flatten the hero, whose nimble, dancelike movements among them become also an ideal, an abstraction, an ultimate symbol of all the evasions and runnings and bare survivals of all comic heroes. The sequence is that perfect, that rare, that good.

A cutaway provides a reminder of the time, now 6:50 by the steeple clock, and of Mary, still waiting as she looks through the window for Jimmie. Then the rocky chase ends, and with its climax there is also a conclusion to Jimmie's nightmare of role reversals. In a rapid shift, what seems destruction suddenly turns into salvation, for where football teams, policemen, and assorted male workers could not stop the rampaging women, the rocks do. Racing down the hill, Jimmie abruptly grinds to a halt, for below him, charging up, are the brides. Behind him, though, hurtling down, are the rocks. He makes his choice, turns, and in the most nimble of his dancelike evasions, he successfully avoids the rocks. They crash on down, and below the women throw up their hands and clubs and run. They are last seen as a distant fleeing throng with the rocks in close pursuit. Jimmie, finally safe, walks calmly away, though for comic surprise and anticlimax, one last small rock comes rolling down and bowls him over.

Although a genuine thematic intention is probably lacking in the rocky denouement, which was added as an afterthought to provide a new climax for a previewed version of the film that ended weakly, still it not only adds a magnificently comic conclusion for the chase but also works to reinforce a sexual attitude implicit in the film. The social and occupational roles assigned to men and women in the first half, the sexes neatly and peaceably separated into contrasting divisions of feminine subordination and passivity as opposed to masculine dominance and exertion, are made to seem not only conventional but natural. When they are disrupted in the revolt of the brides, not only are Jimmie and the human realm thrown into a state of chaos, but so is nature. When the chase moves into the countryside, the natural world, whose forms reinforce and parallel those of the city, is at first also swayed by the disruption and becomes as chaotic and dangerous and threatening as the women. But then the natural chaos suddenly turns upon the human instigators of chaos, and the rocks drive the women away. It is as if the universal harmony of things, in this case a harmony obviously established by a Father rather than a Mother Nature, is rebuking the destructively liberated women, sending them back to their proper roles and places, however unsatisfactory they may be. And with the proper social and natural order reasserted and re-established, Jimmie can at last rush to Mary, who, as good women should, still sits and waits, though by now a little nervously.

In a race to beat the seven o'clock deadline, Jimmie hurries to her house, leaping over or sliding under a few last obstacles, dashing across a track in front of a speeding train, and finally sliding to a stop at the gate to her front yard. The gate, still functioning as a sex-separating barrier, is closed, so with great force and determination, he shoves it open. When he catches his coat on it, he even tears the gate off its hinges, dragging it behind him as he runs onto Mary's porch and literally falls through her door and into the house. A few moments of last-minute suspense are provided when it seems he has arrived just too late, at least according to Meeker's pocket watch. Desolately stepping back outside, however, Jimmie looks and sees something and then once more hastens in, directing the lawyer and Meeker to the porch. Standing there, they see what he saw, the church steeple, whose clock now reaches seven. The steeple bell rings the hour and also serves as wedding chimes, for when the two men hurry back in, they are just in time to observe the conclusion of the wedding ceremony.

Following the ceremony, there is one last joke. Jimmie wants to kiss Mary, but is thwarted by the minister, then by Mary's mother, and then by Meeker, who all kiss her first. When the lawyer next prepares to take his turn, Jimmie suddenly grabs Mary's hand, and the two of them run out. The last shot is of a vine-covered arch, placed in the center of a garden wall. Within it is a bench, and Jimmie and Mary enter and walk to it. Standing beneath the arch, now as with the arched gable in the prologue a form suggestive of union, they momentarily resemble a miniature bride and groom on top of a wedding cake. Then they sit, situated in a visual context that for the last time repeats the elements so often repeated from the film's opening shots on, the many fences and enclosures, but now these embrace both bride and groom, uniting them and assuring that normalcy has been restored.

The chaotic conflict between the sexes has ended, for these two at least, in the presumed peace of marriage, where the right roles are again being played by the right people. Of all the Keaton films that end in marriage, this is the one in which it is most essential, where it seems the only possible termination for the action, the only possible solution for all the problems that have preceded it. To keep things from winding up too neatly and sentimentally, however, the joke of the delayed kiss is played for one final laugh. As Jimmie and Mary happily sit beneath the arch, her dog, last seen in the film's prologue and now grown into a nearly horse-size monster, climbs between them, for the moment still effectively frustrating the groom's attempt to kiss his bride.

This joke ends the film, a film unusual for Keaton in that its comic actions establish a social world, a world which points beyond itself to the actual world, the real American society of his day with its real limitations, among them restrictive and sexually segregated social and occupational roles. The film does not question these limitations, as they are questioned today or were questioned by some even then. Though one can try to claim him as such, it is obvious by now that Keaton is not our contemporary; even if *Seven Chances* is in its own curious way his movie about women's liberation, few liberated women are likely to enjoy it. Rather than being concerned with their rights or the development of their full potential in careers outside the home, his approach to the problem of women in the film is instead a more Olympian and also a more traditionally farcical one. He looks down upon the social situation of his day with comic detachment, interested in it only because it provides new opportunities for one more round in the centuries-old and always funny battle of the sexes. Except for the marginal cases marginally introduced to heighten the chaos, men in the film are men and women are women, and almost never are the twain allowed to meet. Instead, they are eternal opponents, waging war across the many sex-separating barricades. Like Punch and Judy, they are joined only through combat, as the man is initially defeated in his matrimonial attack on a near army of beautiful women, and as the siege of the would-be brides in turn fails to capture the embattled male. And it is the continuous battle that the film celebrates, developing from it a hard-hearted comedy whose laughs are equitably gained first at the expense of a consistently rejected and therefore increasingly foolish masculine suitor and then of desperately man-hungry old maids.

If a serious sexual message for the twenties was meant to arise from the film's cheerful staging of a farcical war between men and women, it is a message suggested in the appearance and behavior of Mary. An old-fashioned girl who belongs behind a white picket fence, she is close in style to the country club beauties but not quite one of them. She is merely pretty rather than stunning, slightly plump rather than sveltely slim, plainly dressed rather than a fashion plate, and the inhabitant of a modest bungalow rather than a country club. In short, she is obviously intended as the Hollywood ideal, an unadventurous and attainable ideal aimed at the expectations of a lower-class audience—the girl next door, who herself aims at nothing better than marriage with her neighbor. She is, therefore, the girl the hero inevitably and happily weds.

Still, if the film consciously and complacently flatters the unliberated women in the audience, with homebody Mary held up for unaspiring masculine admiration as a merely pretty heroine who knows and accepts her restricted place, it also unintentionally demonstrates what is wrong with that place. If consciously a reactionary, Keaton can perhaps, though with some critical strain, be claimed as our unconscious contemporary and socially redeemed ally. In the society mirrored in *Seven Chances*, where feminine occupations other than housewife are few and subordinate, where most jobs are reserved to men and literally walled off to women, those who are not easily salable commodities in the marital market, all the ugly would-be brides, are disastrously disadvantaged. If their revolt violates the social and natural order of things in the film, it is because for them that order is clearly a deadening weight, which denies them a life outside the marriage they cannot obtain. And even those with better prospects, the girls with "it," all the Clara Bows at the country club, are reduced to attractive sexual objects who seem to exist only to be wooed. Happier in their sexual prisons, they are still behind bars.

Moreover, when the women's comic liberation comes, it is one of the most wonderful explosions of repressed energy ever shown on screen. As the women invade the streets, they are such an unbeatable and formidable crew that it is no wonder mere men are unable to stop them. In the film, during the final chase anyway, they are obviously the stronger sex, and with only a little effort their breakthrough can easily be seen as a joyous revelation of their triumphant strength. Like a good many Keaton heroes in other films, they have been held down and penned in so long that their final leap into activity is for the viewer a much desired and much enjoyed event.

Because of these redeeming aspects, present-day women's liberationists might even claim the film for their own, much as (though the analogy is perhaps not an entirely happy one) present-day political spokesmen in Russia have claimed Chekhov as a prophet of the Communist revolution and therefore an approved and watchable playwright, even if he was a bourgeois writing in tsarist times. Though perhaps unconsciously, he endowed his humane comedies with such a sense of a collapsing and stagnant society, one shot through with intimations of a new order, that it is easy to see them as testaments to the need for revolution and a better social and political arrangement. Keaton's film might be received in somewhat the same way. Though the work of a male chauvinist creating in a male-dominated culture, the film not only farcically exaggerates the sexist repressions of that culture but exposes them, comically demonstrating how badly an explosive change was needed.

Without quite meaning to do so, *Seven Chances* thus indicts its age as one of women's suppression. And for this reason, some women's liberationists today might actually enjoy it after all, if only for what is a somewhat tangential reason, as proof of how genuinely far they have come and how necessary it was that they make the journey. Conversely, of course, unreconstructed male chauvinists can view the film with nostalgic pleasure over the way things used to be.

7.

Go West

THE USES AND ABUSES
OF SENTIMENTALITY

THOUGH recognizably a Keaton film, employing many of the customary Keaton formulas, *Go West* is the least typical of all his works, aiming for a different kind of audience response. Diminished in it is the earlier films' tough-minded comic intelligence, the tendency to see people and events as machines and patterns designed for the production of laughter. The design of both has now been altered to produce a few tears as well.

The film released just before this, *Seven Chances*, demonstrates in an extreme way what is more typical. It is a characteristic and remarkably unsentimental Keaton comedy, a mocking farce that for much of its course laughs at rather than with its victims, whom we are encouraged to look upon with a superior and ironic amusement, and certainly are never asked to feel sorry for. A classically oriented comedy, it ministers to our needs in a way antithetical to classical tragedy. The latter makes its audience feel the awful presence of a superior hero, whose greater stature reminds them of their own less lofty state, continually reprimanding and curbing their egos. Classical comedy, however, at least as Aristotle distinguishes it, gratifies the egos of the audience, granting them a flattering superiority to a hero and other characters who are less than they are. Its appeal is not to the altruistic or sympathetic or worshipful potentialities in the viewer, but rather to his need to glorify himself in relation to others, whom he can see and laugh at as his inferiors. *Seven Chances* is not quite a pure classical comedy in this respect for, as the hardened survivor of a rocky ordeal, the hero as always in Keaton is transformed and genuinely heroized by the end, though less so than is usually the case. Still, for much of the film, he and the other characters classically exist just to be laughed at with comic condescension. The pint-size, unlucky, and unsuccessful Jimmie, the large ugly women, and, for good measure, stereotyped benighted blacks and a funny-looking lawyer with a caricature of a face—all of them carry on in a film that seems almost an animated comic strip full of Chester Gould grotesques.

Although the result of such a cast of characters is cheerfully ego-gratifying for good-looking, white, or not-too-short viewers, and can even be justified as psychologically therapeutic, helping to reinforce their sense of self-worth, it is obvious that such an approach to laughter is somewhat deficient in feeling, and works by encouraging us to exclude others from our emotional concern rather than to embrace them. In extenuation, however, it must be added that the laughter so obtained seems if not exactly genial at least harmless rather than cruel. Its major victims, the brides and the hero, cannot be injured by it and do not require the sympathy that real people or even more real characters in a more complex fiction would deserve. They themselves do not feel, and neither the mockery of physical ugliness nor the comedy of humiliation and derision bothers them. Both the hero and the brides are presented as monomaniacs, characters so concentrated on a single activity that they are nothing more than that activity. They are people so simplified, so restricted in their behavior, that temporarily at least they become comic machines programmed to repeat comic patterns, and as machines they feel no pain, either physical or mental. Almost one-dimensional characters, at the most two-dimensional cartoons come to life, they inhabit an idyllic if chaotic world of laughter, where the sort of thing that is not at all funny if it happens to real people in real life can for a short time be turned into pure and painless comic pleasure. They do not really feel, they single-mindedly act; and watching, the viewer is excused from feeling sorry for them and can instead harmlessly laugh at their outlandish appearance and behavior, cheerfully cradled in the comfortably sustained illusion of his own superiority.

Unlike *Seven Chances*, however, *Go West* demands from the

beginning an emotional involvement with the hero, a sympathetic response that includes a measure of sadness. Untypical of Keaton, it resembles and is probably indebted to the sentimental comedy of Charlie Chaplin, which engages the audience in an emotionally more complex way. The sentimental comedy stresses character as much as event and asks us to feel sorry for the pathetic and funny hero even as we laugh at him. In Chaplin, the Tramp's situation in a world that ignores or mistreats him is of as much concern as what he does, and the establishment of a tender or sorrowful mood is as important as the development of comic action. We cannot just look down in laughter at the Tramp, for often we are required to experience the film through him and to share his feelings, particularly at painful moments of exclusion or loss. Where the piano rags of Scott Joplin, with their regular player-piano rhythms and syncopated melodies, provide an excellent musical background for most Keaton movies, propelling the films mechanically and lightly forward without ever pausing for a rest, Chaplin's films need violins, a musical accompaniment that moves in varying tempi, that can sustain a mood as well as accelerate an action, pausing to hold and cherish a poignant note rather than steadily progressing along the facile but relentless beat of a ragtime score. And *Go West* is the one Keaton movie whose accompaniment could be played by a Chaplin violin.

At the same time, in *Go West* Keaton's approach to the comedy of pathos and sentiment is very much his own and not Chaplin's. Keaton demonstrates, as no doubt he wanted to, that he is versatile enough to succeed in something different from his usual role. The film's pathos, however, though effective, is deliberately absurd, almost but not quite parodic instead of real. What we are given is a love situation whose pathetic and touching elements are genuinely there. For apparently the first time in his life, the hero, Friendless, is admired by someone who is also in need of his help, and he responds with a devotion and concern that are the height of sentimental love. In these ways the situation is similar to that of most Chaplin features, such as *City Lights*, where the blind girl falls in love with the funny-looking, lonely Tramp, who dedicates himself to protecting her and restoring her sight. But the Keaton love affair is also deliberately a nonsensical one, a parody of the sentimental, for the female lead is Brown Eyes, a Jersey cow. There is a girl in the film, who also admires the hero, but he foolishly prefers the cow to her, and at the end as the girl, her father, the hero, and the cow ride off together in an open touring car, it is hero and cow who share the back seat.

What the film is, then, is an intelligent comic exercise in the sentimental. It follows the sentimental rules and conventions, and it plays them fairly and effectively. But in a satiric spirit, the same spirit that debunked melodrama and the detective story in *Our Hospitality* and *Sherlock Junior*, it also debunks the sentimental by approaching it in as extreme and unlikely a way as possible. We as audience are required both to feel the film's sentimental appeal and to laugh at its essentially nonsensical nature. We are to see the film as a flatteringly imitative joke on Chaplin. We are also meant to see it as a totally disrespectful joke on the sentimentality of D. W. Griffith, for the cow is named after one of the heroines in *Intolerance*, and the hero's name, Friendless, also recalls the Friendless One in that movie. But as usual in Keaton, the parodic references are not so thoroughgoing as to destroy what they satirize. If the Keaton hero is often a parodic one, he is always still a hero, and if in this film he is often deliberately presented as a sentimental absurdity, a satiric criticism of the silent screen's overindulgence in lachrymose feelings, he is also at the same time basically and seriously sentimental, a sad-eyed figure who is himself genuinely pathetic. The pathos and the absurdity are in fact indistinguishable, for while the film wins many laughs from the comic absurdity of the hero's love for his cow, it also presents that love as a convincing and affecting one, accomplishing this by means of a fantastic duality in the character of Friendless. The strangest of the Keaton heroes, he is almost more animal than human, as much stray dog or wild deer as civilized man. And that affinity with the animal world, it turns out, makes him and his bovine love potently pathetic, guaranteed to touch the hearts of everyone except perhaps a heartless vivisectionist. In Keaton's delicately but surely balanced art, one can laugh at a cow and love her, too. Friendless is a hero who is both sentimental and a comic comment on the extremes of sentimentality. The latter aspect of his character does not contradict or negate the former, but rather makes it more effective, certainly more bearable for a modern audience, by keeping its possible excesses under a firm comic control.

The film begins with an epigraphical shot, a statue of Horace Greeley inscribed with his admonition, "Go west, young man. Go west." Then two titles (out of a total of thirty-nine, the second smallest number in a Keaton feature) introduce the hero. First, "Some people travel through life making friends where ever they go, while others—Just travel through life." Second, "In a little town in Indiana, the social standing of a certain young man had kept him continuously on the move." Following these, Friendless emerges from a small cabin, piles all his belongings on an iron bed—dresser, wash basin and pitcher, rocking chair, stove, and carpet—and begins pulling it down the road. He enters a general store and there is offered and accepts $1.65 for the lot. In this exchange as later, he is characterized by a sad-faced expression, stands with a slight stoop, and looks generally downward—appearing small and vulnerable. He also appears in about the heaviest white-face makeup since *Our Hospitality*, which combined with heavily rimmed eyes makes him seem a mask of sorrow, a crying clown, an alien face among all the more naturally made-up others.

Insufficiently paid for his belongings, Friendless then asks if he can ask for work, "I've tried every place in town for a job, do you suppose there's any use asking you?" In contrast to a later inquiry for work out west, his question receives a negative answer, so he begins bundling up personal articles from the top drawer of the dresser, several of which, introduced here, will become important props in later gag routines—a red bandana, a white handkerchief, a shaving brush, and a safety razor. The proprietor of the store watches, appraises the items, and, since he has just purchased all of Friendless's belongings, charges him for them. When Friendless finally takes from the drawer a small oval portrait of his mother, another item that will reappear, he has learned his economic lesson and pays for the treasured memento before the hard-nosed Hoosier even asks for his money. At the counter, Friendless then buys a long loaf of bread and an equally long sausage, and having paid for these is reduced to a single nickel. Looking down sadly, he holds it in his outstretched hand, just as a girl collecting for charity comes in, scoops it up, and fastens a donor's tag to his lapel in return. Taking his bread and sausage, he presents the proprietor with the tag, which the latter sensibly puts on to avoid making a donation. Next, upon leaving the store, Friendless sees a small dog outside and sitting down begins to pet it. The dog, an animal counterpart of the proprietor and a contrast to the later Brown Eyes, will have no part of this and walks off to the left. Rebuffed, Friendless also walks off, exiting right. He has thus been introduced, a pathetic figure reduced from cabinful to bedful to two small bundles of worldly goods—penniless, jobless, unappreciated by man or beast, loved only, as a sentimental hero should be, by his presumably departed and sainted mother (which would, of course, make him an orphan). It is all too true to type to be quite true, but then it is not quite not true, either.

The unwanted hero is next seen walking by and considering three railroad freight cars, all labeled with their line and destination—Southern R. R., Canadian Pacific, and New York Central. In preparation for his later reversal of direction, he enters the third, a young man first going as far east as possible, to the biggest of big cities. Sitting on a pile of boxes that resembles a throne, he holds his bread in one hand like a scepter and his bandana bundle in the other like an orb, an ironic pose that stresses his pathetic and penniless state.

Once he reaches New York, his adventures are dramatized in a single scene of sidewalk shots, in which Friendless struggles to go right through a throng of people, most of whom are hurrying left. Spun about, pushed off screen, knocked over, stepped upon, he crawls to the curb and the safety of the street. There he is hit by an outsize car, whose hood is nearly as tall as he is.

Besides developing the pathos and comedy of Friendless's alienated state, displaying him as small and insignificant, almost lost in the masses that simultaneously surround and ignore him, the New York episode has also, as is usual in a well-made Keaton movie, prepared for the film's concluding action sequence. The failure to survive in New York will be followed by an astonishing success in Los Angeles. Entering that city, Friendless will control the streets and send mobs of people and automobiles flying, a typical Keaton hero, who first bumbles at something and then makes good. Further, the New York episode helps to establish an affinity between hero and heroine. Similarities in gestures, size, and appearance in previous features were used to unite the hero and the heroine, to make them seem visually and naturally destined for each other. In this film the heroine, Brown Eyes, will soon be shown in a similar situation to that of the hero in New York. She will be introduced as a small lonely figure, rejected by her human owners and alienated from her bovine counterparts, all much larger cattle, who ignore her and generally keep her at the edge of their herd. The fact, too, that the crowd in New York is easily describable in animal terms, as a stampeding herd of milling cattle, reinforces the affinity. It is one of the many casual but emphatic parallels between human and animal in the film, parallels that help relate Friendless to both realms.

Back at a New York railroad yard, the hero and the film next repeat an established pattern. Before, he had removed his personal belongings from the dresser. Now, he finds a woman's purse and empties it of its contents, including two items that again will figure as important props later in the film—a grease pencil (something at least that looks like one) and a miniature pearl-handled revolver. Following a cut to a medium shot of an Atcheson, Topeka, and Santa Fe freight car, the statue of Horace Greeley forms in double exposure over the hero, a visualization of what he is thinking. The statue points left, and Friendless goes left, entering the car. This time it is filled with barrels of potatoes, destined for Arizona, and as he before sat on the boxes, now he climbs to the top of the barrel pile and sits on one of them. The barrels, however, roll. Eventually, he must crawl into an emptied barrel for safety, and then five barrels bounce out the open door of the car. Expectation developed, another pattern established, Friendless's barrel bounces, too, rolling out the door and down a hill. Then its staves suddenly fly apart, leaving him unpacked and seated on the ground in Arizona. Frightened by a horse, his tender feet pricked by cactus, unperturbed by a rattlesnake but terrified by some jumping jack rabbits, he is soon wildly running, still a lost soul, for whom the western prairie is as alien as a midwestern small town or an eastern big city.

Title five introduces the heroine, Brown Eyes. An iris shot of her head opens out to full screen. She stands at the center. The ranch foreman, seated left, attempts to milk her, and the ranch owner stands right, watching. Brown Eyes is a failure at her work, however, for the foreman displays an empty bucket. In the next shot, therefore, she is fired. The foreman leads her to a gate in the background and boots her through it, while a reaction shot reveals the owner again, still watching and now shaking his head. The final introductory shot of Brown Eyes presents her standing and looking right in the direction of the two men. The camera, after initially showing her alone on the screen, then pans upward to reveal the cattle herd, a compact mass of bovine togetherness, in the background. Like Friendless, she exists at a distance from both humans and animals, a failure and an outcast.

Friendless then reappears, now in the ranch yard. Frightened by the people there, he runs behind a corner of the bunkhouse, where a departing hand discards his equipment, dropping it just in front of the unseen hero, who in hiding seems a timid wild animal, though one about to impersonate a human being. When the cowboy is paid off by the rancher and prepares to leave, Friendless quickly sorts through his abandoned paraphernalia. Like some of the items in the dresser drawer and the woman's purse earlier, these are identity-producing articles, now masculine and appropriate for western work instead of sentimentally pathetic or, following the Victorian sexual conventions accepted by the film, femininely small and ineffectual, the human side of Friendless's character being a comic and incongruous mixture of all three types. Rummaging, he puts on chaps and a gun belt but rejects a ten-gallon hat in favor of his own customary Keaton porkpie. He also ties around his neck the red bandana, salvaged from the dresser drawer, and drops the miniature pistol he found in the purse into the capacious holster of the belt. So rigged out, he ambles up to the rancher, falling once as he tries to walk bowlegged in imitation of the ranch hand he wishes to replace, with his outer ankles almost touching the ground. "Do you need any cowboys today?" he asks. The rancher first answers no, but then he looks down at the bucket and stool he holds, objects handed to him by the foreman after the unsuccessful milking of Brown Eyes, and these visually explain his change of mind. He calls to the departing Friendless, who runs back, bowlegged and again stumbling. Handed a bucket and stool, he is hired and sent off to milk another cow. The last major character to be introduced is the rancher's daughter, now shown standing by a well and sipping water from a dipper. She looks sultry, moody, and aggressive, a Clara Bow type of western firebrand, just waiting to be lit. Walking by her, Friendless circles around the well and stops to explain his presence. He says "I'm working here." After a cool, deflating look, she observes "You don't seem to be," whereupon, blasted into wide-eyed silence, he stumbles away. The exchange is not promising, but her staring after him in closeup is—that being the forceful but decorous way in which Keaton heroines often reveal their liking for Keaton heroes.

As the film progresses the daughter will become a second, a potential and implied, heroine, and a nebulous love triangle will develop with her, Friendless, and the foreman as its corners. All the elements for either dramatic or comic love rivalry between the two men will carefully be introduced; however, they will also carefully be kept from cohering in the usual tight Keaton manner. What is introduced as potential proceeds as nebulous, and is still unresolved by the end. If the daughter alternates with Brown Eyes as the romantic lead, the hero's romance with her remains resolutely undeveloped and vague. It is always suggested, never firmly stated, throughout the film. In part, this shadowy second romance seems intended to make Friendless more human and more normal, providing him a real as well as a fantastic object for his love. But at the same time it also helps separate him from the real or merely human world, for the girl remains obviously secondary to his main bovine romance. Even more alarming, possibly, is that, following the customary structuring of a Keaton film about the repetition of similar or parallel scenes, the hero's winning of the girl will be shown to be exactly like his winning of the cow. In this film the emotions of human and animal are so alike, their love so similarly aroused, that it is no wonder poor Friendless remains confused and incapable of distinguishing between them or of deciding to which group he belongs. And that confusion pathetically alienates him from both groups and from his two loves, even though girl and cow are his by the end. Of all the Keaton heroes he is the one absolute loner, a Chaplinesque mystery who seems almost a visitor from another planet, never quite an inhabitant of this one, or if he is an earthly creature, a strange mythological mix—half animal, half human.

After an unsuccessful confrontation with a brindle cow, which he ignorantly expects to produce milk unaided, Friendless leaves his empty bucket and prepares to assist the other hands on the prairie. Frightened by the stampeding horses in a corral, he selects instead the world's largest mule as a safer mount. Tethered nearby, it is so grotesquely large that its bulk recalls the earlier outsize car that knocked him over in New York. Both forms of conveyance emphasize the smallness of the hero, part of whose alien and pathetic condition arises from the fact that he is very little in the world of the monstrously big (a much used contrast of Keaton comedy but elsewhere rarely so strongly and never so seriously stressed). After climbing a fence to reach muletop height, Friendless rides away, but then his saddle, placed too far back, slips back still farther. He and it soon topple over to the ground.

Brown Eyes is now reintroduced, just in front of a background herd of longhorns, one of which is butting her away. Friendless appears, grounded and walking in front of a similar background herd. Nervously aware of it, he responds with a characteristic action, a run in search of shelter, a place to hide and look on in safety. This time shelter is a meager but possibly protective Joshua tree, whose angular shape and leftward lean he imitates, in an animal-like way concealing himself by assimilation to his surroundings. And then Brown Eyes hobbles by, favoring her left foreleg.

Rapidly, with minimal and repeated actions, the love of man and cow is established. In a western variation of the story of Androcles and the lion, Friendless removes a rock from Brown Eyes's hoof. Tipping his hat and thinking the incident closed, he then strolls away and immediately steps knee-deep into a gopher hole, where he is trapped by a spur. While he struggles, an angry longhorn charges the defenseless hero, but at the last moment Brown Eyes steps in front of him and pushes it back. Again tipping his hat, now in acknowledgment of the returned favor, Friendless again strolls away. However, this time Brown Eyes follows, heeling behind him like a well-trained dog, an incongruously large but obedient and affectionate pet. And love flowers, for when Friendless stops to confront her, he holds out his hand and she twice licks it. In a closeup over Brown Eyes's head, he looks in wonder at his hand and at her, and then timidly, slowly, but persistently, he pets her. It is a shot filled with genuine emotion, rare in Keaton, and it works. The clown's sad white face seems its saddest of the entire film, as if Friendless, after being rejected by everyone else, is so touched by the cow's affection that he is close to tears.

Parallel editing now ends the scene, preparing a transition from pathos and love to the next joke. The last two shots of Friendless and Brown Eyes show them strolling slowly into the distance back toward the ranch yard. Preceding each of these shots is one of the cook ringing a triangle by the ranch house porch as he summons the hands to dinner. The cook rings vigorously, but though Friendless must hear him, he and Brown Eyes stroll slowly, and the juxtaposition emphasizes the strangeness and power of his new-found love. In a comic climax to this action, he finally enters the dining room and sits, just as the others have completed their meal and rise, and just as the cook comes in and clears off the table, naturally driving him away.

Friendless, accompanied by Brown Eyes, who waited for him outside the dining room, next enters the bunkhouse. There, two cowboys and the foreman play cards, till Brown Eyes nudges the foreman, who chases her off. He also sends Friendless off when the latter tries to bring the cow back in, first providing him with a blanket and then directing him to a distant shed, where he and Brown Eyes can spend the night together. In this ostracism, though the foreman comes across very slightly as a villain and enemy, in addition to being elsewhere a rival for the rancher's daughter, there is basically no real persecution, just as basically there is no real love rivalry. It is present in embryo to provide a semblance of dramatic conflict, which endows Friendless with a quasi-human status, but the conflict never actually develops and Friendless never becomes fully human. In later scenes, though the foreman will again serve as a kind of antagonist to Friendless and the cow, there as here his possible antagonism will always be so underplayed as to be almost subliminal. At the conclusion of the bunkhouse scene, however, a real and major threat is prepared for. Immediately after Friendless leaves, the rancher enters, and his remarks to the foreman point toward a major crisis: "I'm shipping a thousand head, Thursday. I can't hold out any longer."

Ironically ignorant of this, Friendless meanwhile stations Brown Eyes outside the distant shed, draped with a blanket and provided with a basin of water. Inside, he himself settles down for the night, first staring sadly at the oval portrait of his mother and then dining on the last of the bread and sausage he bought in Indiana, now two small scraps and a meager substitute for the missed meal. Both the portrait and the food, in this their final appearance, are dwelt upon and used to stress the sentimental pathos of Friendless's friendless state. They provide a poignant still moment, a long-held note on a Chaplin violin, till they and their mood are replaced by a return to comedy and action.

Coyotes cry in the distance, Brown Eyes moos in distress, and Friendless, after ineffectually reaching for his miniature pistol, which is lost somewhere in its large holster, grabs a rifle. Outside, he sits at guard, in a posture of resolute watchfulness beside the defenseless cow. When morning breaks, he is still sitting but fast asleep, and Brown Eyes is placidly watching as two unthreatening coyotes drink water from her basin. Friendless wakes when the cook rings the triangle to announce breakfast, but after being frightened by the coyotes and attending to Brown Eyes, he is once again too late for a meal.

Though he has missed his breakfast, however, his luck will soon change. This being the second day of the two-day central section of the film, Friendless, as a typical Keaton loser who wins, will soon achieve success where earlier he had seemed doomed to lasting failure. A series of comic bumbling routines begun the day before will proceed, generally with a total of three enactments of each routine, till the final variation eccentrically but convincingly ends in achievement. Alternating with these routines, in the rather static midsection of the film, which is constructed of many short set pieces rather than being a single continuous motion like the journeys that open and close it, there are also a series of equally eccentric and successful rescues of Brown Eyes and a repetition of the encounter with the rancher's daughter at the well. This repetition, too, replaces the rebuff of the first day with success and acceptance on the second.

Success of a sort begins immediately after Friendless has left the dining room. Passing through a corral on his way to some ranch yard chores, he allows two steers inside to escape. Ordered to return them and told that they will respond to something red, he removes his red bandana and casually waves that behind him as he walks toward the corral gate. The steers charge by into the corral, and without even having been aware of his danger, Friendless continues on his way.

After this, in what becomes a pattern of regular alternation, there is a rescue of Brown Eyes. Performing a woman's chores, Friendless is first shown gathering eggs. Meanwhile, the other hands work at a man's task of branding, and Brown Eyes, at the end of a lasso, is next in line to be burned. She moos, facing right, and Friendless, now standing in the chicken run, hears and sets down the eggs he has collected. She moos again, and he runs left in speeded-up motion, arriving just in time for the rescue. Unnoticed, he removes the noose from her neck and leads her away. When the foreman steps on the now empty noose, he is the one who is yanked off his feet instead and dragged to the fire, where with goodnatured outdoors humor, he is branded, at least on his chaps. As an almost villain, he is an almost victim of his almost plot against Brown Eyes. Friendless, meanwhile, even after being seen by the rancher and ordered to "get a brand on that cow," successfully concludes his rescue. Employing the supply of props from his dresser in Indiana, he lathers and shaves a diamond-bar on Brown Eyes's flank and then, apparently using the grease pencil from the lady's purse in New York, painlessly darkens it.

With the rescue accomplished, the cook now rings his triangle for the third time, announcing the last installment of the dining room joke. As Brown Eyes starts to eat grass, demonstrating an affinity and also predicting success in so paralleling the gourmandizing ambitions of Friendless, he races by the cook, who is still ringing, and inside rapidly gulps down a large plate of food. This time he is the one who is finished and rising just as the others enter and sit. After two failures, he has on the second day triumphed, though as he leaves he is immediately faced with a new difficulty. In the progression of alternating scenes it is now time for a rescue, and outside he discovers Brown Eyes being butted by a long-horned steer. First he grabs a rock, but when she escapes and comes over to him, he examines her head and has a better idea. Going back into the dining room, he removes a pair of decorative deer antlers from the wall and ties these over Brown Eyes's ears. Now armed like the longhorn, she is no longer picked on by him.

In the eating and rescue episodes just completed, the dining room activities of Friendless provide the best examples of a curious alienation effect that runs throughout the film. In both, Friendless is so entirely ignored by the others that he seems temporarily not to exist for them. Though they should notice him eating and later removing the deer horns, just as the cowboys earlier should have seen him leading Brown Eyes away from the branding fire, they do not, for he moves among them like an invisible man. This ignoring of him is basically a necessary condition for such jokes, but as it is presented it is so total, so strange, that it goes beyond the needs of comedy to create a dreamlike impression of almost schizoid withdrawal, as if Friendless, at such moments as these, does not inhabit the real world of the others but a solipsistic universe of his own. He seems to live apart in the alien realm of a madman or simpleton or, what may not be too different, in the subhuman realm of a ranch or household animal. As such, he is an accepted presence in the human community but at the same time not quite one of them and therefore easily and often ignored.

The pathos of Friendless's alienation in such scenes, it might be added, is possible because achieved in silence. In an unreal world without noise, it does not seem in any way implausible that Friendless passes by unnoticed, as it would in a sound film. If not directly looked at, neither he nor anyone else on the silent screen gives any indication of his presence. As often, Keaton is thus deliberately using a major limitation of his medium to create an impressive effect that it alone can produce.

In another way, too, the silence of such scenes makes their pathos viable. As D. W. Griffith discovered earlier, emotions are easily evoked and presented in silent pictures. The affinity between feelings and images is so close that the latter can powerfully and consistently trigger the former. Griffith's films, therefore, often proceed like a series of Victorian narrative paintings, as tableaux expressive of some dominant single feeling: "Childhood Innocence," "The Homecoming," "A Death in the Family." Such favorite Griffith emotions as suggested in these titles, when verbally described, are apt to sound mawkish or insincere or overdone, but in silent pictures, which evidently bypass the verbal and conceptual areas of the brain and appeal directly to its more primitive, more imagistic loci of feeling, emotions are realizable. As effectively as music, a rhythmic progression of images can convey a changing series of moods, even sentimental moods, none of which could adequately be conceived or experienced through words. Another master of silent-screen pathos, Chaplin rarely strikes a wrong emotional note when working in pure silent images. When the same feelings are spoken, however, often in long ranting speeches, in his later sound films, they never seem natural. The viewer no longer sees them and therefore experiences them directly. He is merely told about them and therefore remains unaffected.

The evocations of feelings on the silent screen have ceased to work for us only when the emotions conveyed have ceased to be part of our sensibility. Fortunate in having few orphans among us these days, for example, we are no longer culturally conditioned to feel sad when we see one, a fact that occasionally undermines the sincere pathos of Chaplin's *The Kid*, making its sentiments (all firmly based in the horror of Chaplin's own childhood) seem overproduced into a specious sentimentality. In *Go West*, however, when Keaton aims at pathos, he aims, as of course Chaplin also often does, at what is a more enduring and more general source of sadness. The alienation of Friendless, his seclusion and apartness, stress a major and continuing cause of modern melancholy, what is in fact almost a cliché of contemporary art. In such scenes, as Friendless moves about unnoticed, alone even in a crowd, Keaton projects what are still powerful and disturbing images. Complexly comic and pathetic, they speak, like the emotional visions of his own dreams, to the feeling mind of the viewer. In their silence, they communicate sadness.

As the other diners step outside, Friendless, still alien to them, next runs like a timid animal to the bunkhouse, hiding as usual behind a corner, where he can observe their activities in safety. Economically, old patterns of mise-en-scène repeat themselves. The foreman enters in front of the bunkhouse and lays down some gear, not noticing the concealed Friendless. Then the rancher's daughter is shown, again standing by the well, this time examining her hand. Looking toward Friendless and the foreman, she beckons one of them to come forward. Proceeding from opposite sides of the corner, they both do, but though the foreman reaches her first, it is Friendless she wants and she moves closer to him. Several closeups of the foreman's angry face suggest a potential love rivalry as he looks on while Friendless removes with a large knife a small splinter from the girl's hand, in this film a foolproof method for winning a girl as well as a cow.

The foreman and the girl having left separately, Friendless stares after her, sitting down next to the well and accidentally knocking over the bucket that rests on its rim. The bucket falls, and this turns the crank its rope is wound on. As the crank turns, its protruding handle spins, and the handle, completing a machinelike and circular pattern of comic cause and effect, hits Friendless on the head. Getting up, he woozily exits, having concluded an incipient love scene with an undercutting joke, which, though it does not destroy the sentiment, does keep it from becoming too strong for Keaton comedy.

Title fifteen announces "The day of the shipment." When an angry neighbor, who like the rancher has been holding his herd back for higher prices, rides up, the day begins badly. Summarizing their argument, the rancher explains afterward to his daughter and the listening Friendless, "He threatens to stop the cattle. And if they don't reach the stockyards, I'm ruined." Despite the threat, however, the ruin-preventing shipment proceeds. Out on the range Friendless does his bit, ineptly falling from his mule when he attempts to lasso the most amenable of cattle, a stationary calf. But then he at least improves on an earlier ineptitude. Having learned the art of climbing a mountainous mule, he lowers a rope ladder from the side of its saddle and easily scales its formerly formidable heights.

After this, in a continuation of the alternating ranch hand routines and bovine rescues established on the film's second day, Brown Eyes is for the last time endangered, and this time the rescue takes the remainder of the film to accomplish. The rancher orders her shipped with the longhorns to the slaughterhouse. Neither drawing his miniature pistol on the unperturbed foreman nor offering to pay the rancher all of his wages for her leads Friendless to success. In the first instance, another hand takes Brown Eyes away while he is absorbed in the confrontation, and in the second his wages are far below the purchase price.

As the cattle and Brown Eyes are loaded on a train, the rancher's daughter, who has been watching his desperate endeavors, searches for Friendless to give him money. He himself, meanwhile, has stepped into a track-side shed, where he seeks to win funds by joining the foreman and another cowboy in a game of poker. Very quickly, however, the foreman deals himself an ace from the bottom of the deck. When Friendless notices and complains, the foreman now pulls a gun on him and speaks the famous line from Owen Wister's *The Virginian*, "When you say that—SMILE."

Friendless's response is one of the classic moments of Keaton parody, a shot in which his genuinely sentimental appeal is cheerfully and temporarily overshadowed by a satirical takeoff on sentimentality. In it he pays dubious homage to Lillian Gish and D. W. Griffith, both grand masters of pathos, by stealing her most famous closeup from *Broken Blossoms*. In that Griffith film, she played a young London girl who is woefully mistreated by her foster father, a brutalized and alcoholic boxer. When he comes home one night, drunk, rampaging, and violent, he frightens her into near hysteria. This accomplished, he then unreasonably complains that she never smiles anymore and orders her to do so. Fearing that she will be beaten to death if she does not obey, she pathetically raises her hand and with her middle and forefinger pushes up the edges of her mouth, achieving a ghastly rictus superimposed upon a face otherwise occupied with twitches and tears. It is one of the most remarkable closeups in silent film, remarkable because in context it works exactly as a great actress wants it to. It is also so extreme in its stylization that it comes close to comic excess, and therefore in his parody Keaton need only repeat rather than exaggerate it. Friendless, too, forces a smile, a fantastically fearful Gish grin.

Though the Griffith parody dominates here, it is not exclusive. The Gish grin is not just a parodic insertion, for the human side of Friendless's character throughout has consistently had effeminate overtones. His finding of the lady's purse, his mule mount, the woman's ranch yard chores he performed, his miniature gun as contrasted to larger, more potent, and more masculine ones—all have made him seem at times comically emasculate.

The reasons for his femininity are the same as those for Chaplin's Tramp, who also at times is given a strongly feminine or effeminate characterization. Part of the comic and pathetic appeal of Friendless and the Tramp lies in their being equivocal characters in an otherwise sexually unequivocal world. They are laughable misfits in it, and also sad misfits. Just as important, too, their occasional lapses into sexual dubiety make them superior to their world. The fictional society in which both exist is one divided along the simplistic and restrictive lines of what was then still popular Victorian sexual psychology, much mirrored in the formulas of mass art, where women alone were assigned all feeling and sensitivity and men were supposed to be practical and unfeeling. The Griffith ladies, typically, are little more than easily frightened bundles of quivering animal nerves, while the more rational men calmly monopolize the action. In *Go West,* because of this customary sexual division neither the Hoosier storekeeper's demands for money early in the film nor the rancher's adamant refusals to spare Brown Eyes make them seem cruel. Rather, their completely masculine characters have no capacity for finer feelings. They are all business and economic activity, in a world where that is all men are expected to be and capable of being. In such a strictly divided world, to be credibly pathetic, to be capable of sadness and fear and bovine devotion, requires a sensitive feminine soul. Friendless, like Chaplin's sentimental Tramp, needs and therefore has a woman's attributes in his character. To be a complete sentimental hero, a center of pathetic feeling in the film, he must be a sentimental heroine as well.

With Friendless, too, the feminine characterization is used as part of the standard Keaton transformation. Where before the Keaton hero was often initially presented as childish, a comic spoiled child who dramatically grows up, here he is initially presented as effeminate. Keaton's diminutive size is equally suited to both possibilities. Representing the feminine high point of Friendless's initial characterization, the Gish grin is therefore also a signal that the customary Keaton transformation is at hand, a comic and surprising change to more masculine action.

Such action begins immediately. The foreman's gun being directly before him, Friendless slips a finger behind its trigger so that it cannot be fired, while at the same time he jerks out his own miniature pistol and points it across the table. Having lost the confrontation, the foreman lays down his gun, and Friendless starts to gather in the money. The third player, however, who has been quietly watching, interrupts, laying down his hand, which beats both the others. He then claims the pot, and the game is over. As the foreman leaves the shed, still a potential rather than an actual villain, he sees a holster on the wall and removes a large revolver from it. For a moment his intentions are uncertain, but then he presents this real gun to Friendless, snapping the string of the miniature pistol and disgustedly throwing the toy through the window. Friendless keeps the gift, which he will later effectively use, now tying it to the string, but he also retrieves the miniature.

After this, for a few shots he disappears, as the girl continues to look for him and as the foreman and others climb as guards onto the top of the cattle train. The train begins moving, car after car of cattle passing across the screen. Then, Friendless and Brown Eyes, still inseparable, also go by, standing together behind the gate in one of the cars. Friendless, for the moment, looks as contentedly bovine as anyone not actually a cow could, the full equal in wide-eyed placidity to Brown Eyes. The girl, humanly surprised, stares after them in amazement.

The threat to stop the cattle shipment is soon carried out. Somewhere in the countryside the train is ambushed, and Friendless finds himself in a no-man's-land between the ambushers and the ranch crew, who fire at each other from opposite sides of the cars. Jumping down, Friendless joins the foreman, who is leading the defense, but then one of the ambushers forces the engineer to start the locomotive and leap off. With no humans on board, the train rolls away. Seeing it move, Friendless runs forward again and scrambles onto the last car. He then returns to Brown Eyes, and he and she stand together, watching the landscape zoom by. Since the crewless train is out of control, the landscape zooms by very fast. Realizing after several near collisions that something is wrong, Friendless sets out to investigate. In a beautiful and sustained long shot, taken from the back of the train, he walks along the tops of the cars toward the engine, nimbly progressing as they twist around curves and race through Los Angeles. Running the length of the last car, he leaps down into the locomotive cabin just in time to pull a lever and stop the train at a siding.

After helping Brown Eyes out he looks around, discovering an address tag, which informs him that the cattle are destined for the Union Stockyards in Los Angeles. After reading, he thinks, bowing his head to do so, and a rapid fadein and fadeout frame the scene he recalls. It is that in which the rancher says to his daughter, ". . . and if they don't reach the stockyards, I'm ruined." The excerpt is not quite as originally presented, however, for following this title, there is a closeup of the daughter that was not there before. An image introduced to further motivate Friendless, it is also, in his underplayed second romance, the film's major demonstration of his love for the girl. Having reached his decision, he opens the doors of all the cars, and the cattle come out.

In a cutaway scene, the foreman reports the ambush, and the rancher and his daughter drive away in an open touring car. Meanwhile, back in Los Angeles, Friendless and Brown Eyes lead an army of steers from the siding into the streets. As they march, Friendless's earlier total rejection in New York is replaced by an equally total conquest, for now he temporarily controls the city, and its inhabitants are forced to flee. In carefully organized pandemonium, which like the pursuit of the brides in *Seven Chances* builds to two minor climaxes before reaching its final and major peak, he and his steers take over the streets and buildings, upsetting everyone. Though the streets at least look and are real, most of the people upset on them are stock comic figures—a policeman, a drunk, and three ethnic stereotypes. (For good measure, in a later interior scene there is also a grotesquely fat fat girl, another comic staple of the period.)

The policeman is the initial target of the chaos, which begins with individual victims and then builds to crowds. Directing traffic at an intersection, he is approached by Friendless, who stops to ask the way to the stockyards and then proceeds, immediately followed by the cattle, which drive the policeman from the street. The ethnic stereotypes are next. First, a Jewish pushcart peddler, along with a few pedestrians, sees the approaching cattle and in about two seconds folds up his cart and runs into a door. Then the herd comes up behind a black street entertainer, nattily dressed and mightily tapping his toes on the pavement as he dances before a small crowd. His audience runs, and when he spins about and discovers they have been replaced by long-horned cattle, he also takes off, leaping through the window of a clothing store. On the street, the dancer's presumably Italian organ-grinder accompanist runs, too, and when the clothing store manager opens his door to see what is happening, he quickly does the same.

After individuals, the masses. Friendless and the cattle invade another street corner and there cause a three-car collision. Wrecked cars, fleeing crowds, a frightened policeman, and a thundering herd of cattle soon fill the screen. The Los Angeles cattle drive has reached its first and very satisfactory climax.

From many cattle to none. After two shots of steers, the first of them moving left, the second of them milling about in front of a large store, Friendless and Brown Eyes appear, walking right. When he looks about, he discovers that he has lost his herd. Leading Brown Eyes into a parking lot, he parks her there. For the sake of a later plot development, he also leaves with her his red bandana, wetting it in a handy bucket and laying it over her apparently fevered brow. Then he sets off to find his missing cattle, orienting his search by the crowds of running people. After a quiet cattleless interlude, the drive will start again, building up in comic intensity and magnitude to its second climax.

From outside to inside. The lost steers have all wandered indoors. First, in an underplayed scene, Friendless merely shoos four of them out of a small candy store. Then, out on the street, he watches four men in towels run from a Turkish bath, followed by a steer. Next, more chaotically, the steers enter a barber shop. In the confusion, one barber lathers a customer's eyes, and another shaves a swathe all the way across a man's head. A black shoeshine attendant, leaping for safety over a partition, lands on a longhorn's back and is carried off like a rodeo rider on a brahma bull, grabbing his bowler hat from a rack as he passes by. A last well-lathered customer in a chair, abandoned by his barber, is licked by a steer, and being the agile-

legged Joe Keaton responds by clambering up on top of another hat
rack.

When Friendless enters to drive the cattle out, he proceeds, as
always in these chaotic chase scenes, with a poker-faced or more
exactly cow-faced calm, comically oblivious to the oddity and
danger of the situation. Though he has taken over the city, it is
obvious that he is not winning a place in a society that had formerly
rejected him, as Keaton heroes generally do. Instead, responding
like his cattle, he visually remains an alien presence in the urban
setting, not as out of place as King Kong in New York but as
unlikely ever to fit in.

In a few transitional street shots, the shoeshine man bounces by
still on his steer, and Joe Keaton, seen through the window, climbs
from his hat rack and runs out of the barber shop. Then in a department store display window, Friendless sees a calf standing among
the dummies. For the third time he enters a store (the same set used
for the country club interior in *Seven Chances*), and climactic chaos
abounds.

First, a man with arms full of packages is nudged by a steer,
throws the packages into the air, and jumps on a counter. There he
grabs a money basket whizzing by on a wire, and, a one-man cable
car, is carried precariously just over the horns of the cattle. Given a
helpful shove by a clerk, another man trying out a pair of roller
skates rolls helplessly into a waiting herd and disappears from view.
Friendless starts shooing cattle but stops when a man comes up to
complain, and the two of them are then knocked down by the skater,
rolling again and still out of control. Rising, a three-man target, they
are all immediately hit by the human missile, who whizzes by on his
overhead wire and drops. In a reaction shot, a mother and her
immensely fat daughter, the kind of physical grotesque the period
found funny, see the confusion and respond by shoving their way
into a crowded elevator to escape. The elevator goes up, the outer
door remains open, and the skater, rolling once more into disaster,
slips over the edge and down the shaft. Pulled out by the complaining man and Friendless, he emerges just as the overloaded elevator,
done in by the fat girl, crashes down, the people inside sprawling out
and tangled in its broken cables. In a farewell appearance, a curtain

call for a featured player, the skater climbs onto a counter, loses his balance, and topples over backward, for the last time disappearing from view. Also climbing onto a counter, a large central one, Friendless stands there and directs the now obedient cattle out. But as they all docilely leave they are replaced by hostile customers and clerks, who begin creeping back from far corners, closing in on Friendless and throwing things. He retaliates by firing his gun, the gift from the foreman, which successfully scatters them but also brings down a light globe on his head.

The interior scenes climaxed, the city roundup pauses for a few preparations before building to its third and major climax. First, where it will not disrupt the rhythm of a comic crescendo, the rancher and his daughter are shown, driving down a country road. Next, back on the street with his recovered herd, Friendless notes that they still will not follow him. Since his red bandana, which worked earlier at the corral, is with Brown Eyes at the parking lot, he waves a white handkerchief, the last of the dresser props introduced in the film's ninth shot. When this is ignored, he enters a costume shop and asks for something red. A steer enters, too, and the clerk and customers run for cover, so he receives no reply. By himself, therefore, he finds a devil's outfit. Even though shown in black and white, it is obviously all red.

While he dresses, a cutaway to a police station prepares for later action. A captain gives orders to arrest the man responsible for the invasion, and he also calls out the fire department. Then he and his troops scramble when the shoeshine man unexpectedly rides into the station on his steer.

Back at the shop, Friendless is now dressed and a devil, though after some struggle he must abandon his porkpie hat, which will not fit over his steerlike horns. Reluctantly, it is dropped on the floor (except for one shot it will never appear again in a Keaton feature), and he exits. As he goes, wagging his tail behind him, he moves even further from the realm of the merely human. In an untypical final action sequence for a Keaton hero, his adventures continue to distance him from the social world that had formerly rebuffed him rather than to unite him triumphantly with it. With its horns and tail, his devil's suit visually merges him with the cattle instead. As the chase and the film near their conclusions, he has been transformed most completely into an animal presence.

Not surprisingly, therefore, when he now confronts the herd and beckons, they follow, as much because he is one of them as because he is dressed in red. In accelerating tempo, he walks but they walk faster, he runs and they pursue, and finally he races, while they stampede right behind him. Whipping around a corner, he races into a squad of police, who, after their introduction at the station, now turn up to add to the grand final confusion. Last seen scrambling and sprawling, they reappear marching in orderly ranks, which instantly disintegrate as they turn and run away from the cattle and after the man or devil evidently responsible for the invasion. Then, flight proving more imperative than pursuit, they run past him. Putting on more speed, he joins their ranks but trips and is trampled on by dozens of heavily falling feet. Getting up, however, he again runs faster than they, one by one passing them by till he becomes the leader of the group. Then, as all the police join hands, the man behind him grabs his tail. Devil and police in a weird running line, pursued by cattle, they speed down the street together till their way is blocked by a fire truck, the presence of which was also prepared for in the police station scene. As the firemen turn on their hoses, Friendless grabs a pole, instantly stopping, while the police, in crack-the-whip fashion, are thrown into the jets of water. The police, four girls watching from a balcony, and two top-hatted dignitaries in a car are all hosed. The herd and Friendless remain dry. In fact, having turned a corner back by the pole, they are gone. Then, after this climax, a comic anticlimax. One last calf chases a few customers from a store, and the cattle storm is over.

Brown Eyes is now shown back at the parking lot, and when Friendless runs by, she breaks her rope and races after him. When she has caught up, he mounts her and, a devil on cowback, leads his herd down the street, past a bulbous-nosed drunk, who like a traffic cop directs them on their way. The drunk stands in the protective lee of a parked car as the stream of cattle, in the street and on the sidewalk, pours by on both sides of him. He is one last stock comic type in a totally unique comic situation, epitomizing both the heavy reliance on the clichés of vaudeville humor in the Los Angeles sequence and its radically original and inventive exploitation of them.

In conclusion of the two earlier scenes of their journey, the rancher and his daughter next drive into the stockyards. He looks about, that having been his major and almost only characterizing action for the entire film, and a long shot reveals what he sees, empty cattle pens. A cigar-smoking employee is questioned, but he has received no cattle. The rancher just has time to sadly say "I guess we're through," when he and his daughter see Friendless on Brown Eyes gallop by, followed by the herd. He stops and dismounts at the gate to the pens, opens it, and all the cattle charge through. With the last one in and the gate closed, the formerly empty pens are now shown filled, and the rancher, happily saved from ruin, is given his check.

Friendless, after some difficulty, removes his devil's costume by jamming its tail in the gate and running away from it. Then he walks to the stockyards office, where the rancher greets his benefactor with a line appropriate to the ending of a sentimental melodrama, "My home and anything I have is yours for the asking." First looking down, his usual way of thinking, Friendless points and says, "I want her." He points toward the girl but walks past her off screen and returns with Brown Eyes. The rancher laughs, the girl looks amazed for the last time, and then all four enter the touring car and drive off together. The rancher and his daughter sit in the front seat, and Friendless and Brown Eyes share the back.

The shadowy secondary romance concludes in a shadowy way. Friendless leans far over to talk with the girl, his head next to hers, which suggests the customary Keaton hero who, in a climactic display of courage and athleticism, has proved his worth and won the heroine. But in this film there is still Brown Eyes, who sits next to him and remains his first and highly sentimental love. And that keeps him, right up to the final fadeout, far removed from the Keaton norm—in part a deliberately ridiculous relation of Chaplin's sentimental Tramp and a comic debunking of sentimental extremes, but also in part a genuinely sentimental and affecting character.

Viewed another way in the final shots, he is also, as he has been throughout, the fantastic hero of a fantasy film, one that has played on a breakdown of the divisions between the human and animal worlds. So thoroughly, in fact, has the film mixed the two that by the end it is hard to tell which is which, just as in *Sherlock Junior* dream and reality were so persistently mixed that at last they merged. Sitting in the back seat of the car, Brown Eyes finally seems as human as Friendless and the others, and he, at least, as animal as she—a strange not-quite-animal, not-quite-human, being. But then that is just another way of saying that he is the perfect sentimental hero as well as a parody on sentimentality. As a character who is both stray dog and wandering waif, he is doubly vulnerable and touching as well as mockingly and absurdly funny.

8.

＄Battling Butler

OVERCOMING THE LIMITATIONS OF FARCE

THE HERO of *Battling Butler* is a repetition of Rollo Treadway, the hero of *The Navigator*. Both Rollo and Alfred Butler progress through a peculiarly American film fantasy, that of an idle rich boy who through forced labor turns into something like the poor working-class man who is watching the movie (though the hero remains, of course, enviably rich). If both heroes are essentially the same simple democratic character, in the second film Alfred is presented in a much more complex and dramatic context. Where *The Navigator* concentrated on only two characters, whose relationship and personalities were uncomplicated and obvious, this film has one of the largest casts of major figures in any Keaton feature, and they are, moreover, characters whose personalities and wonderfully complicated and confused relationships are developed with considerable subtlety and depth.

Alfred himself quickly develops an internal emotional life of a sort denied to Rollo. Where the latter, typically for Keaton, was a character of pure comic surface, whose love for the heroine was farcically and conventionally exploited for laughs, Alfred's love for his girl is eventually given a much more convincing interior existence, one that transforms him from a stylized farcical type into a credibly real human being. So revealed to the audience, his love efficaciously works as a powerful emotional drive, propelling him and the film to the most intense and unfunny of Keaton climaxes. As with the semisentimental *Go West*, though in a very different way,

182

the film Alfred is the hero of is untypical of Keaton. If it is a Keaton comedy still, it is a comedy that aspires to the fullness of drama. It seems, in fact, a deliberate experiment in the mixing of genres, a light farce that slowly gains in weight, heavily ending in a real battle fought in a context of dramatic and psychological seriousness. The Keaton hero always changes, but here the most interesting aspect of the change and of the film is the unique way in which the change is effected. It intentionally and self-consciously involves the very conventions and limitations of Keaton farcical comedy, for the hero's transformation is presented as a transformation of these, as a transcending move from stylized vaudeville turns to a simulation of real action and its concomitancies, real emotions and real pain.

The comedy begins with a customary prologue. Alfred, doted on by his mother and spoiled by his valet, who goes so far as even to flick the ashes off his cigarette for him, is told by his angry father to head for the country: "Yes—get a camping outfit—go out and rough it. Maybe it will make a man out of you if you have to take care of yourself for a while." Alfred, from beginning to near end incredibly acquiescent and susceptible to suggestion, simultaneously accepts and defeats his father's intentions. Turning to his valet, he instructs "Arrange it." While the mother weeps and the father frowns, master and man then depart in a Rolls Royce with a large trailer full of necessities. A title ends the sequence: "And so Alfred went out to rough it, leaving the city behind—there was no other place to leave it."

In the prologue, the introductory shot of Alfred recalls the introductory shot of Rollo. Both heroes are dramatically presented as the camera looks into a room through a wide double door, theatrically hung with swag draperies, as though a curtain has just gone up. In the second film, however, the following shot is a closeup of Alfred's father, situated just outside the door and watching with a troubled expression the scene inside the room, where Alfred is being waited upon by his mother, valet, and butler. We have not, therefore, been initially presented with a distant and detached audience's view of the hero, as in *The Navigator*, but rather the camera has been used subjectively, first to show us what the father sees, and then, as it turns one hundred and eighty degrees, to show us his response, one of intensely pained irritation. Such a subjective technique is commonly used, of course, but till now it has not been common in Keaton's films. In them the hero most characteristically performed in solitude and was seen from an omniscient distance. Only in this film will he almost always be performing before other characters, either provoking a reaction in them or himself responding to their presence. And as this happens, the hundred-and-eighty-degree camera turn will become the film's characteristic means of shot progression, for we will continually be seeing things alternately through the opposing eyes of confronting characters. The characters will as a result be strongly endowed with a perceived interior life, a dramatic psychological depth generally lacking in the earlier external and surface comedies, where characters tend to exist for us in their movements only. Also, as a result, we as audience will be invited to identify more fully than before with them, particularly the hero, who, though one of the most extreme fools of the Keaton lot, is also one of the most likable. Since we will often be seeing the film's world through his eyes, most significantly in three emotionally charged closeups, we must empathize with him; and sharing many of his responses, we are made to believe in them and to give them our approval.

The prologue is followed by a section devoted to camping, courting, deception, and marriage. In the camping portions, which begin immediately, humor develops from the incongruity of roughing it in the world's most luxurious tent, complete with brass bed, running water, folding bathtub, radio, phonograph, lawn swing, iceman, paperboy, and, of course, the valet who arranges everything. As hunter and fisherman, Alfred disports himself as novice and bungler, and this further adds to the comedy, establishing also an initial athletic ineptitude to be overcome in the boxing match that concludes the film.

In the first of two sporting excursions from the camp, Alfred sets out to hunt, carrying only a cane seat, while the valet handles a golf bag full of guns. Once in the field, Alfred naturally opens the seat and sits, his hands patiently folded in his lap. This gesture with the hands is a typifying one, frequently repeated, and displays in Alfred both a feeble incapacity and a composed assurance. So seated, he may appear inert to the point of vegetable imbecility, but at the same time there is something enviably secure in his position, for only someone completely and justifiably confident that all things will be done for him could so calmly sit with folded hands whenever action of any sort is required. The gesture is also central to the development of the hero, who, in typical Keaton fashion, will progress from the relatively stationary to the mightily active. Alfred will move, in a purely visual way, from childish and spoiled idleness through reluctant activity to urgently willed and decisively effective motion. And along the way, in one of the film's major images and contrasts, his folded hands will be transformed into boxing fists.

In the hunting episode, his hands finally unfolded and a shotgun selected, Alfred rises, stalking forward and ready to shoot. The valet, who closely follows him, now carries the cane seat, handling it as if it, too, were a gun and mimicking Alfred's movements as he does so. In a film of ever-present observers, a host of wildlife— quail, raccoon, fox, and doe—watch the hunters but are in turn unnoticed. Finally, Alfred does spot a chicken and, raising the gun to his shoulder, excitedly fires. Unfortunately, he is holding it backward, and the shot, flying behind him, aerates a handkerchief held by the "mountain girl" heroine, who is walking nearby. Hunting immediately gives way to courting, for on Alfred's part it is love at first sight, love displayed with a comically imperturbable intensity. The girl approaches, complaining strongly, but Alfred simply stares entranced at her, and when her denunciation is finished and she stomps off, he says only "Isn't she pretty?" He then sits on his cane seat to admire her departing form, the cane plunges all the way into the soft earth, and Alfred's tumble causes the valet to drop the shotgun, how held by him, which fires its second round, once more in the direction of the mountain girl. Angered again, this time she throws rocks, and Alfred and the valet must drop everything and run.

Hunting having proved a disaster, Alfred next tries fishing, after changing from a beautiful hunting costume to an even spiffier fisherman's outfit. The two costumes, as it turns out, are only two among many, for the film develops at greatest length the customary Keaton equation of adolescent foppishness with immaturity. Throughout the first half and well into the second, Alfred sports a rich man's wardrobe, a fashionable collection of elegant clothes so exquisitely tailored that they absurdly inhibit the activities they are designed for. Like a fashion model, Alfred visually impresses us as capable of little more than strolling and standing in poses that show off his attire. Though Alfred's clothing in a way makes the man, if only because like his valet it keeps him from acting like one, it is emphatically not the man himself, and the latter portion of the film will develop as a progressive striptease, until Alfred in the last scenes is reduced to boxing trunks, at which point he must be himself.

At present, however, emerging from the tent in his new outfit, he is merely a fashionplate fisherman pretending to a knowledge of the sport, and his bumbling actions continually belie the fashionable fraudulence of his clothing. This second sporting sequence also culminates in a meeting with the mountain girl, and the whole routine leading to the encounter is so well presented that it deserves a detailed record as one of Keaton's classic comic turns. Beautifully structured, it is the kind of farcically mechanized exercise which is consistently used throughout *The Navigator,* but which in this film characterizes Alfred only initially, for he is a hero who at the very end will develop not only in the customary Keaton ways but uniquely, by breaking free of the limitations imposed upon a farcical character who exists only as the enactor of such comically repetitive routines as this.

Seated on a bank and facing upstream, Alfred fruitlessly fishes, not noticing all the fish that leap in the water downstream behind him. He does see, though, a swimming duck, and dropping reel and basket, he climbs into a small canoe and paddles toward it. In a single sustained shot, one of the longest of any Keaton movie, he floats onto the screen from the left, heading toward the duck, which swims in the lower right corner. Stopping, he sets his paddle across the prow, stands, picks up his shotgun from the keel, points it at the duck, some five feet away, and pulls the trigger. The gun is empty, however, so he must load and re-aim, reaching the trigger-pulling point just as the duck dives and disappears. Alfred stares for a few moments of slowly developing awareness at the duckless water, then sits, lays aside his gun, and resumes paddling. Simultaneously, the camera pans slightly left, and a duck comes to the surface in the lower left corner. Alfred, now on the right of the screen, soon sees it. In his haste to bag the bird, he drops his paddle and grabs his gun, stands, and aims, but despite his clumsy speed is again too late. Once more the duck elusively dives.

In what is now a regular and mechanical routine, a pendulum swing developing a kind of comic necessity, the camera again pans slightly, this time to the right, as Alfred, moved by the pan back to the left half of the screen, tries to retrieve the now floating paddle with his gun, which is not quite long enough. Meanwhile, meeting its obligation to its own pattern of up-down, left-right movement, a duck again surfaces in the lower right corner of the screen. Alfred sees it, excitedly he tries to hit it with the stock of the gun, but like the paddle it is just out of reach. So he aims the gun, and for the third time a duck dives. Alfred stands again, lays the gun across the prow, and leans far over the boat. One hand braced on the prow and the other shading his eyes, he peers deep into the water to see where the duck has gone. He discovers nothing, but his forward lean is just enough to push the prow under, and the boat slowly sinks, while he struggles, too late, to remain afloat. He stands but still descends, until he is submerged neck-deep in the stream.

Alfred turns, facing rearward, which is a cue for another boat to enter, continuing the alternating pattern, from the right. In it rows the mountain girl, and as she passes, Alfred, with a greater sense of decorum than the situation demands, raises his fine, white, and still remarkably dry panama hat to her. She stops surprised at the left, he points downward to explain the mishap, raises his hat again, and walks toward her boat. Suddenly he sinks entirely, the beautifully dry hat in his upraised hand being the last and most satisfactory thing to go under. There is a splash by her boat, and (only now is there a new shot) Alfred emerges, hat and arm first, then head, as two ducks emerge with him and scoot off to the right. He grabs onto the stern, and the mountain girl rows off to the left, her oar clouting him on the head—his face shows it hurts—as he is towed off screen.

Back at camp, Alfred invites the girl to stay for dinner. As he changes into formal evening clothes, she watches the valet's dinner preparations. In a sequence emphasizing closeups of his irritated and her amused face, the incongruities of citified camping are made more

amusing by being viewed through her rural eyes. First she quizzi-
cally watches as he sets the outdoor table with seven pieces of cutlery
per plate. She is so amused when he next attaches paper frills to the
ends of two lamp chops that she satirically imitates him, tying a bow
on a third herself and then inviting him to admire the effect. Seated at
the table with Alfred, however, she is slowly assimilated into her
surroundings and is transformed from an amused outsider to a young
lady romantically dining with a young man. Additional alien and
therefore comically perceptive eyes are introduced, as her redneck
father and brother, both outsize louts, come by, dubiously survey the
situation, and leave, their hostility provoking Alfred to ask worriedly, "Have you any more fathers or brothers?" Fortunately she has
not, and love progresses. The two quickly acquire a visual similarity
in the customary Keaton manner of establishing a convincingly irresistible affinity between hero and heroine. In identical poses, they
stare raptly across the table at each other, not noticing that like
Alfred's cane seat earlier it is slowly sinking into the ground. By the
time it is dark, the table is legless and they are romantically prone,
still eyeing each other across it. Alfred then escorts her home, cannot
find his way back, is returned to his tent by her, and the first day's
camping and courting are over.

The second day begins with a closeup of the valet's hands, placing
cans under the legs of the disinterred table. An iceman and a
paperboy make their morning deliveries, and when the valet brings
the paper into the tent, he notices an article. The headline reads
"champion big favorite over Battling Butler," and under a picture,
which seems to be a touched-up photo of Keaton in a boxing pose,
there is the caption "Alfred 'Battling' Butler." The valet points this
out, observing "Some prize fighter has taken your name, sir."
Alfred looks and orders "Arrange to stop it," and then he himself
notices an "Advice to the Lovesick" column by Beatrice Faircatch.
Her topic is how to propose marriage, and Alfred responds instantly
to the suggestion, just as Rollo in *The Navigator* responded to the
sight of a passing bride and groom. He says, "I'd like to marry that
pretty little mountain girl." The valet asks "Shall I arrange it?"
Alfred answers Yes, without a title, since at this point everyone can
correctly read his lips. The valet sets out to arrange, and in a last joke

on luxury camping, Alfred checks the temperature of the water in his portable bathtub, adds a bubble bath solution to it, and prepares to bathe.

In a film of double identity, where all things come in twos, the two debacles of sportsmanship, initially followed by two meetings with the girl, are now necessarily followed by two proposals. The first is made by the valet, who as usual is the agent of Alfred's wishes. Played by the diminutive Snitz Edwards (previously the lawyer in *Seven Chances*), the valet, while never expressing any particular liking for his master, performs the duties of a servant with such dedication that Alfred is totally exempted from all exertion. The valet is invariably by Alfred's side, in fact so constantly there that Keaton for the first time seems a partner in a comedy team rather than a solo performer. Waiting tirelessly on his master, performing all menial and most mental labor for him, the valet is a total security blanket, another of the film's many blocks to self-assertion, one that Alfred by the end will have to cast aside if he is to stand and fight for himself. Till then, however, and that will take a considerable time to reach, the valet so closely attends to Alfred that frequently he seems an extension of him, a slightly miniaturized double, whose imitative actions become a kind of unconscious mimicry, one of the basic sources of the film's comedy.

The valet's proposal scene begins with a long shot of the mountain girl cleaning leaves from her front lawn. Behind her, on the porch steps of her house, her brother whittles, and on the porch behind him, seated on a rocker, her father reads a paper. So placed, the two men provide the background audience for foreground action characteristic of the film, and their responses must immediately be given as close attention as the movements of the girl and valet, for soon they will move to the front and dominate the scene. For a few shots, however, they keep their seats, as the valet enters the yard, approaches the girl, and speaks directly to the point of his visit: "Mr. Butler would like to marry you."

Father and brother, who have been listening and looking more and more perturbed, now move forward, surround the little valley of a valet, and thunder down at him from their stormy heights: "That jelly fish couldn't take care of himself—let alone a wife," and "We don't want any weaklings in our family.'' The valet, wrinkling his already well-wrinkled face in thought, replies "Weakling! You don't know who he is.'' Having brought the newspaper with him, he shows them the boxing article and picture and then displays Alfred's calling card with his (and the boxer's) name on it. The camp is transformed into a training site, and gradually the two are convinced that Alfred is Battling Butler. The girl, who in earlier scenes had been roughly clothed to help develop the contrast between her outdoors expertise and Alfred's conspicuously garbed ignorance, is in this and later scenes always dressed as a suitably elegant consort for him, for if the film first makes fun of his sartorial splendor, it also, somewhat snobbishly, later contrasts the lovers' expensive and tasteful clothing with the cheap and gaudy outfits of the real Battling Butler and his wife. The girl therefore is now wearing a finely frilled apron, and she removes it, revealing an attractive dress, before docilely leaving with the valet to receive proposal number two.

Alfred, meanwhile, turned out for the morning in a knickered tweed suit, reads Beatrice Faircatch's advice to one H. H. R., which he has clipped and placed inside his cap. "I have outlined the following proposal, with the answers you may expect," she says, and a dialogue follows:

He — "Do you think you could learn to love me?"
She — "Why—what do you mean?"
He — "I'm crazy about you."
She — "This is so sudden."
He — "You're the only girl I ever loved."
She — "Give me time to think."

The dialogue continues till she says Yes, whereupon Beatrice advises "Then use your own judgment." Alfred begins memorizing the lines and then steps outside, waiting in a pose of patient abstraction for the girl to arrive. She enters, and the camera pans with them as they move to a lawn swing, the last luxurious necessity of a rough camp equipped even for this eventuality. Soon seated by her, he recites the first Faircatch line, "Do you think you could learn to love me?" Her newly acquired domestic and demure appearance and also several earlier closeups showing her smiling affectionately at Alfred even though amused or angered by his behavior, are sufficient motivation in this film for her response. Not being up on her Faircatch, she immediately replies "I have." After thinking for a moment, he rips up the article and hugs her, his eyes closed in bliss. With her eyes open, however, she asks "When are you going to fight again?" It takes him a long while to comprehend this unexpected question, but eventually his eyes also open and he says "When I'm drafted." She continues, "I mean, who do you fight next?" Now his eyes open wide, and he sees before him the valet, who tries to explain the situation by pointing to the boxing article in the paper. When the message is not comprehended, the valet then pantomimes boxing, and Alfred, aware at least that he is being instructed about something, in a questioning gesture asks if he should hit the girl. The valet ends the predicament by coming up, announcing "Sir, it's time to take your liniment," and leading Alfred off to the tent.

Inside, the imposture explained, Alfred reacts dubiously, despite the valet's reassurance, "These people will never know the difference—the champion will win and no one will ever hear of Battling Butler again." Walking out of the tent, however, he is given no chance to tell the truth. The girl's brother and father wait, left and right, by the door, and as they grab his shoulders and shake his hand, their congratulations physically force him to maintain the deception. The father, who is the film's official timekeeper, then checks his pocket watch and observes, "If you're going to fight tomorrow, you'll have to hurry to catch the train." All Alfred can do is pass the news on to the valet: "Arrange the train." Just engaged and wanting to tell the truth, he as usual acquiesces to the demands of others and is immediately separated from his fiancée as a result.

The real Battling Butler is now introduced, standing in a boxing ring and ready for the first of the film's two championship fights. In the audience, his trainer and his manager are shown in closeup, whereupon the camera pans left to reveal the valet and Alfred coincidentally sitting next to them. Before the fight begins, there is also a cutaway to the mountain girl and her family, gathered around a period radio with a horn speaker. In the ring the Alabama Murderer then briefly appears to take a bow. Announced as the next contender for the title, he is scheduled to fight the winner of this match.

Once the fight begins, it proceeds with intercut shots of the action in the ring and of the valet, Alfred, Butler's trainer, and his manager, all together and disparately responding in the audience. While the first two express a politely restrained approval when the champion is doing well, the trainer, a large blubbery man, goes berserk with enthusiasm whenever Butler scores a blow. Soon he becomes so excited that he begins unconsciously imitating Butler's movements, first hitting Alfred and then usurping his seat, driving him for refuge into the lap of the valet. The real fight and the parody fight both continue into a second round, when Butler, who had started badly, comes through. After being knocked down, he angrily rises and with a single jolting rabbit punch, which is his trademark blow, he downs the champion and ends the fight.

While everyone else stands and cheers and files out, and while at home the mountain girl's family smiles around the radio, Alfred and the valet sit, stunned and still. A long shot discloses them alone in the now empty arena, and Alfred finally speaks, saying "I'm champion." The valet advises, "That means you cannot go back to the mountains, sir." But Alfred, in a rare assertion of independence, says, "You're wrong. I'm going back and tell the truth. I'd rather lose her that way." He then removes a ring from his pocket, and supposing that he will no longer have a use for it, turns it over to the valet. As the two continue to sit in dejected contemplation, they are suddenly surprised as the lights of the arena begin to dim, dimming in fact all the way to total darkness for a naturalistic fadeout of the boxing scene.

As happened when he first learned of the deception, Alfred will once more have no opportunity to tell the truth; for the second time, congratulations will overpower him into silence. Returning with good intentions to the mountain girl's home in Glen Falls, he sits on the observation deck at the rear of the train, where Butler and his manager, also returning somewhere from the fight, come out and sit unknowingly with him. As the train approaches Glen Falls, Alfred goes inside, and it is therefore the boxer and his manager who first see the large crowd bearing the large sign, "Welcome Battling Butler." In response, Butler begins bowing from the deck but is completely ignored. To his surprise, everyone rushes instead to the door from which Alfred descends. From his background position, the last thing the puzzled boxer sees as the train pulls out is the imposter marching off behind a band, walking between the girl's father and brother, followed by admiring children and townspeople. The parade proceeds down the main street, where chickens scatter and a photographer is accidentally knocked over by Alfred, who is preoccupied with looking up at his tall escorts. As before, ouside the tent, their looming presence on either side of him is a beautiful visualization of comic necessity, of the powerful forces of circumstance and redneck character that impose on the easily overwhelmed hero an assumed identity.

Alfred having been brought to the mountain girl's home, everyone marches inside, where he is further congratulated. Then the brother suddenly leads him over to a window, while the father immediately signals the band to play and goes into another room, where a few ominous decorations can be seen through the doorway. He returns with the mountain girl in bridal dress, and in what is a single continuous activity, allowing no pause or resistance, she is led up to Alfred just as a man behind them turns around, is revealed to be a preacher, and starts to conduct a marriage ceremony. The valet provides the ring, the father and brother at the sides of the screen provide more comic compulsion, and the ceremony is swiftly concluded. Doing what he wanted but not quite as he wanted to do it, Alfred is married, still an unwilling deceiver.

No sooner was he engaged than he was sent away from his fiancée, and in the usual double pattern, no sooner is he married than it happens again. A Keaton hero, he is also the victim of a mathematical, mechanical fate that relentlessly forces him to keep repeating the same movements, like a never-ending sine curve. Someone therefore now runs in with a newspaper, and in it, over the by-line Demon Onion (a parody of Damon Runyon), large headlines proclaim: "Battling Butler to fight Alabama Murderer. New champ to defend title Thanksgiving. Starts training at Silver Hot Springs tomorrow." The father says to Alfred, "That means you have to leave right away." Alfred says to the valet "Arrange it." The bride says "I'll hurry and pack my things," and Alfred, again fearing disclosure, stops her, explaining, "I'm sorry, but you can't go. I want you to know me as I am—not as the brutal, blood-thirsty beast that I am when fighting. Promise me you will never come near the training camp or to see me fight.''

Outside, Alfred kisses his bride good-bye, in front of a large background crowd of watching band and wedding guests. As the valet then drives him off in his Rolls Royce, he looks back, and a subjective shot shows us what he sees. Through the small oval rear window, which functions as a natural iris, blocking out everything from his sight except her, the face of the mountain girl first appears in closeup and then slowly and sadly recedes behind the departing car. In a visually striking and memorable way, the shot conveys the concentration of his attention, the unusual iris effect isolating her face in a lasting image of love and loss; and subjectively seeing her this way through his blinkered eyes, which at such a key moment can see nothing else, we are obliged to believe in and to share his emotion. It is a sharing, moreover, that will be significantly repeated in two further subjective uses of a similar natural iris. Like this one, they will be important shots in establishing Alfred's single-minded and single-hearted love as a genuine and major motivating force, a force which becomes through the cumulative impact of the three shots powerful enough finally to bring him to independent life and impel him to dramatically real rather than farcically stylized action.

As they drive off, reluctantly exiled and uncertain where to go, the valet observes that Alfred could best write to the girl from the actual Butler's address in Silver Hot Springs. That becomes their destination, and in the film's second half, therefore, the fraudulent training camp of the first half will be replaced by the real thing. As before, too, the depiction of Alfred's activities at the new camp will concentrate on a two-day period, the major events of which, continuing the pervasive doubling of things, occur twice. There will be two episodes of practice boxing in the training camp ring, each followed by an episode of cross-country running. Within this continuation of the film's orderly and repetitive structure, moreover, character confusions will become in an equally orderly way more and more disastrous and complicated. Alfred's boxing identity, casually assumed on the second day of the first half, will on the second day of the second half be fully forced upon him. Just as the fraudulent training camp becomes the real one, so he, too, will wake up to find that he actually is Battling Butler.

The first shot in the second half is of the Silver Hot Springs Hotel register, as a pen signs in "Alfred Battling Butler & wife." In the scene that follows, Butler and wife, both more realistic characters than is usual in a Keaton film, are shown as vulgar and brassy, she as a flirt and he as a jealous and belligerent husband. She makes eyes at the hotel clerk, who ogles back. Butler notices and elbows her, and she responds by jabbing him with a pin. Their marriage is further typified in the following shot, which begins with Butler's manager and trainer standing outside the door of the training shed. Butler and his wife arrive, and he opens the door in his wife's face, leaving her cut off behind it as he and the others go in. Entering last, the trainer closes the door, revealing the wife abandoned outside. Evidently used to being so ignored, at least raising no protest, she sets off walking, to turn up a little later.

Alfred and the valet are now reintroduced in their car, and the comedy of a road sequence begins with Alfred's supercilious admonition, "Drive carefully. These country folk may not be used to city speed." Country cars immediately begin violating in superfast motion all the rules of safe driving, repeatedly threatening to collide with the sedately progressing urban intruders. A final shot discloses a road running toward the camera, and then a chastened Alfred timidly walks onto it from a cross road. Peering cautiously up and down, he signals that it is safe to proceed, and the limousine slowly follows him out onto the screen. Still walking, he next drops his gloves, and the valet must stop to wait for him, braking next to Battling Butler's wife, who stands beside the road, a bouquet in one hand and a shoe with a broken heel in the other. She asks the valet for a lift, he agrees, and she steps into the back of the car. A moment later Alfred gets in from the other side and then, surprised by her sudden presence, immediately bounces back out. In a reprise of the country driving comedy, a final rural racer immediately hurtles by, nearly hits him, and sends him leaping once more into the limousine. Having vigorously moved one way, Alfred has then instantaneously reversed himself, a typical Keaton exercise in play motion, existing for its own sake and getting him nowhere but back where he started. Inside, after the surprising passenger has explained her presence, Alfred pulls down a window shade because the sun is in his eyes. Butler's wife, who misinterprets the gesture, quickly and reprovingly pulls it up again. The sun then hitting her eyes, however, she understands his true intentions and herself once more pulls it down. Alfred, now misinterpreting her, prissily pulls it up a final time, so that at the conclusion of the routine, the shade, after much movement, is also back where it was at the start.

Since the shade's movements have immediately followed the similarly arranged leaps of Alfred, the juxtaposition of shade and man suggests that at this point both are being treated alike, as objects equally amenable to the mechanizations of farcically repetitive action. The reciprocations of both are controlled by the needs of comedy and restricted by the limitations of its conventions, which in such a pairing seem as inhibiting to the development of Alfred's autonomous self as his fashionable clothing or incessantly arranging valet. Like the last two, such farcically patterned movements will have to be discarded or transcended if he is to become a person instead of a comically moving thing. Meanwhile, however, the stylizations of comedy continue, and the car now reaches the hotel porch, just in time for Battling Butler, walking around a background corner, to see Alfred assist his wife out, hand her the flowers she had picked, and then follow her inside. The boxer also follows, and watches, still not understanding the situation, as Alfred signs the register "Alfred Butler and man," just below the earlier "Alfred Battling Butler & wife."

After the arrival, there is an immediate cut to the training shed, where the first of two practice boxing episodes begins with a shot of Battling Butler slugging a dummy. His trainer is then shown checking the time, a gesture that he occasionally repeats and one that pairs him with the mountain girl's father, who on three occasions did the same in the film's first half. The boxer's manager is also present, here and elsewhere an otherwise dramatically unnecessary figure who is on hand solely to equate with the girl's brother. On the coming day in particular, he and the trainer, both tall men, will appear with Alfred in shots posed similarly to ones with the father and brother before, two new visualizations of continuing comic compulsion and further examples of the pervasive pairings in the film, all designed to double Alfred's identity, making inevitable his assumption of the boxer's role.

Having polished off the dummy, Battling Butler next, in a long shot, spars in the ring with a partner, while his wife in the left foreground leans on an exercise horse and watches him. Alfred, walking through the shed door, past a ''no admittance'' sign, joins her, and in closeup the two talk. ''How's your heel?'' he inquires. ''He's all right,'' she replies, and gestures toward the boxers. As they speak, Alfred accidentally rests his hand on hers, and Battling Butler sees this from the ring, almost incidentally knocking out his sparring partner so that the latter's blows will not distract him from the fascinating sight. Alfred, oblivious to the jealousy he has aroused, escorts the wife out. At the door she continues walking, but he unexpectedly stops, for he sees his own wife, the mountain girl, strolling up the road with a suitcase in her hand.

She goes to the hotel and sits on the porch, one of the Silver Hot Springs hot springs appearing in the foreground just in front of her. Alfred sidles back into the shed to avoid being seen, but inside the training routine has progressed from sparring to road work, and the trainees pick up weights and don exercise sweaters, preparing to go out. Soon, while the manager stands by the open door, the trainer, Battling Butler, and the sparring partner leave the shed, already running. After a moment's pause, to set up the manager's doubletake, Alfred follows, also carrying weights, or rather a pair of hairbrushes he has picked up, and dressed in borrowed and oversize sweater and cap, looking like a strange child imitating an adult in adult's clothing. His ruse, however, works. From the porch, the mountain girl waves as the four runners jog by her, Alfred a little to the rear and unnoticed by the others. The four continue down the road, around a corner, and past a chicken. Then, as they run by a house, out of sight of the hotel, Alfred does a U-turn and stops. The valet, meanwhile, having also discovered the girl and observed the runners, soon adds his imitation to Alfred's, chasing after the four, going around the same corner, scaring the same chicken, and finally, when he sees only three figures ahead of him, pulling up to a stop by the same house where Alfred sits. There the valet joins him, adopting the same pose of wearied dejection as his master, until ''eight miles later'' the runners return, and master and man once again fall into place behind them.

As they pass the hotel porch for the second time, however, Alfred's wife runs down and blocks his way. Having to speak to her, but like a wound-up toy unable to break out of his jogging routine, he combines both activities by running in a circle around her as she turns to keep him in view, and as the valet, in the very center of the circle, wildly spins to keep up with them both. The three of them are thus briefly caught up in a meaningless but neatly geometrical motion, the kind of patterned lunacy which is comedy's equivalent of tragedy's fate and in which on a larger scale Alfred is trapped for most of the film. At present, the circling continues till the mountain girl, who refuses to leave, goes into the hotel with the valet, allowing Alfred to straighten his path and run on to the training shed. There, as the others watch in wonder, he lays down his weights, doffs his cap and sweater, picks up his hat and cane, and walks out, for them still a mysterious and unexplained figure.

Two scenes featuring the wives now follow, one in the evening and one on the morning after, the two marking, in repetition of the time scheme of the first half, the passage of a single night. The first is set in the hotel, as Alfred climbs the stairs to his room, located to the left of a central hallway. Battling Butler's room by dramatically necessary chance is directly to the right, and the boxer's wife steps out and asks Alfred in just as Butler naturally appears on the background stairway to observe. The wife wants Alfred to unscrew a ceiling light bulb so that she can use the socket to plug in a curling iron. What Butler in the hallway sees through the transom is the light going out as Alfred, standing on a dresser, begins to unscrew it. He barges in, knocking Alfred over, though fortunately in the dark Alfred is able to grab his hat and cane and scoot out the door. On all fours he crawls across the hall to the safety of his own room, just as the valet, filling the need for an always occupied background, comes up the stairs and discovers him. When Battling Butler soon after emerges, looking for his rival, he sees the valet, and as he approaches menacingly, the latter expeditiously slides down the stairs and out of sight. Butler then goes back into his room, his wife explains, and he begins to remove the bulb for her. When it falls and breaks, Alfred, across the hall, hears the explosion and faints into the arms of the mountain girl. And a night passes.

In the morning, Battling Butler's wife is introduced outside, sitting by a lawn table and reading in the *Saturday Evening Post* an article entitled "Bed Cases." Besides the world's ugliest dress, she also sports a nasty black eye, Butler's final jealous comment on the events of the night before. A comic shiner, it is also obviously the result of a blow that hurt, unlike most violence in Keaton, which is farcically incapable of producing real pain, and therefore it points the way to the even more potently painful blows the boxer will finally deliver. The mountain girl next appears and sits with some sewing on the opposite side of the table. A hotel employee immediately steps up between them, sets a box of candy on the table, ambiguously announces "Compliments of Mr. Butler," opens it, and, having established another farcical situation, quickly leaves. Battling Butler's wife gets to the box first, samples a piece, throws it away, tastes a second, discards that too, and reaches for a third, as the girl watches, fuming. Noticing her, the wife offers a piece. The girl, looking mean, grabs the entire box and pulls it over. The wife pulls it back, and the girl yanks it away from her. As they both stand, tugging and tearing at the box, there is a cutaway to a gate, where the valet watches and where boxer, trainer, and manager walk up behind him and watch, too. In long shot, the women continue their struggle. Then, in the background, Alfred steps out of the hotel, walks off the porch, and observes the row. Reversing his direction, he noisily stumbles on the steps, which attracts the girl's attention and brings her running to him.

Shots now cut between two dialogues. There is first Alfred and the girl, as he tries to evade the situation by going back in, and as she angrily detains him: "That woman says she is married to you, too." Second, the valet, seeing the need to arrange, explains things to Battling Butler: "—so you see, sir, it would wreck his home if she knew the truth. Won't you be a good fellow and fix it for him?" Butler, a feisty little fellow pugnaciously at ease in his profession, is obviously not one to do anybody a good turn. Nonetheless he agrees, for what will turn out to be his own unpleasant reasons, and walks forward. The girl simultaneously drags Alfred to the table, where the wife remains seated, and all four now meet for the first time. There is, however, no exposure, for Butler seemingly obliges Alfred by supporting his deception. With a threatening look to his wife to keep quiet, he says, "My dear, we are not the only Butlers here. This is the Lightweight Champion, Mr. Battling Butler, and his wife." The two depart as Alfred and the girl sit down, though Butler partially reveals his intentions in his closing statements. "Don't forget your date Thanksgiving," he advises. Alfred asks "What date?" Butler replies "With the Alabama Murderer."

Back at the gate, the jealous and belligerent Butler explodes, saying to his trainer and manager, "If he wants to be Battling Butler, let him fight the Alabama Murderer, and he'll never flirt with anybody else's wife. I'm through—get him in shape the best you can." He leaves, and Alfred's impersonation now becomes a transformation, for he has officially become Battling Butler. The manager and trainer come over to where he sits, and in a repetition of the pose outside the tent, when the girl's father and brother had first admired him on mistakenly learning who he was, they now stand on either side of him, two large specimens of continuing comic compulsion. They easily pick up the small Alfred, feel his biceps, squeeze his leg muscles, and test his jaw, while he, acquiescent and puzzled, the passive victim of a repetitive comic pattern and the valet's arranging, wonders what is going on.

What goes on next is the second training workout in the ring, this time featuring the bungler Alfred instead of the expert Butler. The scene proceeds with four basic gag routines, interlocking and repeated with variations throughout. These are the putting on of boxing gloves, getting into the ring, sparring, and getting out of the ring. All of them are learned procedures, requiring training, and all represent disaster for the novice in a typical Keaton farce of the bumbling beginner. The proceedings start outside the ring, as the manager, the trainer, and the valet stand in a group, the trainer in the center with his back to the camera. Boxing gloves are handed across to the valet, and then the other two symmetrically leave, left and right, revealing Alfred, previously hidden by the trainer. Dressed in boxing trunks and a jersey, his hands folded in front of him, he patiently waits. Slowly the valet gloves him, very slowly, for the boxing gloves are incongruously treated like fine kid leather, dampened with spit and carefully stretched over Alfred's fingers in a routine reminiscent of the earlier citified camping. The process is even further slowed by a disregarded thumb that obstinately remains outside, and all this laborious activity is set off by a single shot of expert ease in which the trainer instantly gloves a sparring partner. Finally gloved, Alfred approaches the ring. He climbs its ropes as if they were the steps of a ladder, but when he stands on the top two, they reveal their true nature and give way under him. He falls, flails about, and after a few unlikely but convincingly executed flips winds up with a foot caught between the two of them. Advancing to the rescue, the trainer flips him again, producing a further and neatly predictable intertwining of ropes and Alfred, who is now left with his head twisted between the upper two. In the most striking and comic of his gestures of composed passivity, Alfred, in this predicament, simply sits on the lowest rope and folds his hands on his lap, waiting. The trainer having figured out the entanglement, a single final flip in the right direction unwinds the ropes and drops Alfred where he started, outside the ring. Now he cautiously slides under the ropes, mistrustfully eyeing them as he proceeds.

At last both gloved and in the ring, Alfred spars, with a maximum number of difficulties. Positioned into a boxing stance, he rigidly maintains it till his sparring partner knocks him flat. Running in circles to escape further blows, he leaps into the trainer's arms and is ignominiously dropped to the floor. Trying to leap out of the ring, he trips. Getting back in, he is slapped by the ropes, which the trainer first stretches apart for him and then angrily lets fly together. Seated on a corner stool, his arms stretched out, he is accidentally fastened to a rope by the valet, who is retying his left glove. Attempting to evade the rush of a new sparring partner, he is therefore brought up short and falls. Freed, he is still much punched and only then saved by the trainer, who briefly stops the match. At this point Alfred, now a shade petulant, stands behind the trainer's large protective form and, resembling a small and spoiled child, ineffectually strikes out at his sparring partner and then kicks him.

The trainer has halted the massacre to give boxing instructions, Alfred's debut having revealed no natural gift for the sport, and these quickly turn into a routine of comic imitative action. As the sparring partner boxes, the trainer from a distance demonstrates the appropriate responses, and Alfred, always watching him, precisely imitates them, always a few seconds too late to strike or avoid being struck. Soon this routine develops further into a Keaton comedy of farcically mechanized motion, in which the actors become funny because of their resemblance to objects. Alternately struck in the face and the belly, Alfred protectively moves his hands back and forth between them, again always just too late. When the trainer, who has become more and more irate with his unpromising pupil, starts booting him in the rear, the unsuccessful protective progression of Alfred's hands now has three areas to defend, and he and his assailants seem the automatons of a German clock, curiously and regularly striking the hours on one another. If a few of the hard knocks Alfred has received in the ring were not quite farcical, these last blows are so comically exaggerated in their regularity that they convey no sense of pain. The most extremely stylized in the practice bout, they keep it from becoming too real and from ever more than momentarily hurting.

Returning to his corner, Alfred next gingerly sits on his boxing gloves, only farcically hurt and sorely in need of a padded seat. Then the trainer himself gloves up, and when Alfred notices the preparations for this new ordeal, he bolts, sliding under the ropes out of the ring. Stopped and urged back in by the manager, who grabs the top rope and himself vaults over it, Alfred reluctantly and imitatively does the same. However, his leap becomes a spin and he makes a complete circle, ending back outside, so that once more he must ignominiously crawl underneath the ropes to enter the ring. After the trainer has demonstrated a few blows and after the valet has unsuccessfully tried to arm Alfred with an Indian club, the mountain girl enters the training room. With her appearance, the mise-en-scène is transformed into a double of that in the earlier sparring scene, when Battling Butler from the ring saw his wife talking to Alfred as the two of them leaned against a training horse. Now the girl and the manager lean against it, and it is Alfred, transformed into Battling Butler and almost reliving his experience, who is in the ring and sees them, or rather sees only her.

In the second of the film's important subjective closeups using a natural iris, the girl appears in Alfred's vision framed within a triangle formed by his opponent's bent arm and body, and this sight of the woman he loves, comically but forcefully stressed, propels him into offensive motion. Suddenly mightily active, he swings his arms and spins about, though the only result is that he gets dizzy and must wobble off, for the last time crawling under the ropes, to collapse in the locker room. If the others are dumbfounded by this performance, the girl at least is pleasingly if ignorantly impressed, her smile of pleasure as she watches her husband effectively contrasting to the manager's look of stupefaction.

The next training sequence is again a repetition, this time of the previous day's cross-country running, with the large trainer in the lead, followed by Alfred and the valet. As with the earlier run, Alfred's clothing, though far from his customary elegant attire, is still being comically used to conceal the man. Both he and the valet are now dressed as he was before, in oversize sweaters and caps, and both look like small children on an outing with an angry adult. Running being a regular motion, the first jokes play upon the mechanical continuation of it in situations that reasonably call for a halt. Alfred stumbles and falls, and the valet automatically jogs over him, only noticing and returning to help him up after he has first thoroughly stomped him into the ground. When the trainer next pauses to tie a shoelace, Alfred and the valet, ordered to continue their run but also obliged to stay near him, trot in circles about his kneeling form, just as Alfred earlier circled the mountain girl in front of the hotel.

Following this, in an echo of the country-driving routine, Alfred and the valet leap on the running board of a car, unnoticed by the trainer in front of them. Alfred bribes the driver to allow them inside, and then the car makes a U-turn and carries them away. Reckless rural drivers, however, still terrorize the roads, for at a crossing a truck runs into their car and knocks it over. As they crawl out and stand by the vehicles, the trainer comes back, looking for them, discovers the accident, and chases them into a continuation of their run, though not before Alfred, as usual just too late to prevent a blow from landing, raises a mechanical turn signal, a metal arm on the door of the truck.

After this, to keep an eye on him, the trainer has Alfred run by his side, with the result that when they come to a narrow bridge, Alfred misses it and plunges into a brook. The trainer then grabs him by the collar and scoots him unwillingly along, a shot in which Alfred appears most miniature and childlike, most incapable of survivng in a pugnacious adult world, and therefore also a shot predicting that the turning point for him must be near at hand. Meanwhile, however, the run continues, through fields of mud and water, and in a beautiful panning shot, the three runners struggle on, high-stepping their way through and across the top half of the screen, while in a puddle below their upside-down images imitate them. At the end, as they all appropriately run away from the camera into a fadeout, their shoes are so heavily mud-coated that they can barely be lifted, with the valet, behind the others, having acquired so much mud that he seems to be running in bushel baskets.

Not surprisingly after this exercise, "by dinner time the only thing Alfred had on his mind was his stomach." At the hotel dining table, the comedy is a reversal of the earlier inappropriate application of citified ways to rough country living. Now the rigorous rules of training are incongruously forced upon the pleasant rituals of a formal and elegant meal. Sitting with the mountain girl, Alfred is served a cocktail by the valet, lights a cigarette, and contemplates a steak brought in by the waiter. Then the trainer enters, moves the drink over to his own place, grabs and discards Alfred's cigarette, and finally even commandeers his steak. As a training table substitute, Alfred must settle for milk, crackers, and four dismal prunes, while watching the others enjoy the pleasures of his former good life.

"And so," a title reads, "for three weeks Alfred trained and starved and suffered and ached and bled and groaned and hoped and prayed and—and then came the storm." As the two days of the first half were followed by his unexpected marriage, so now the two days covered in the second are climaxed by an even more formidable event. The time is Thanksgiving night, November 26, 1925; the place is the Olympic Auditorium, an actual boxing arena in Los Angeles; and the film's second championship fight is about to begin.

This final sequence opens with a shot of the locker room, where the trainer paces angrily, looking at his watch and waiting for Alfred, who arrives, formally and thoroughly dressed in top hat and tails, a cane in one hand and a horseshoe in the other. The trainer throws away the horseshoe, and Alfred is subsequently plagued by many bad-luck portents of disaster as he slowly undresses and prepares for the fight, unwillingly divesting himself of his spoiled rich boy's finery to become an elemental man in boxing trunks. Through a sliding partition the trainer first observes in the arena the progress of a preliminary bout between Joe Slattery and One Round Hogan. One of them, presumably Hogan, is badly battered; and returning to Alfred, the trainer graphically describes a smashed nose and rivers of blood. Unhappy about this, Alfred is further unsettled when the Alabama Murderer passes through to his locker room, stopping at the connecting doorway to look murderously at his opponent. Meanwhile, back at the partition, the trainer sees more carnage in the ring and again describes it to Alfred, now with a pantomimed performance of numerous teeth flying. The valet enters and having arranged for the worst leads Alfred to an outside window, through which an ambulance can be seen waiting in the street. The loser of the preliminary bout is then carried in on a stretcher and deposited near Alfred. Seated with his hands still in their customary pose, folded on his lap, he nervously looks away from this sight to the door connecting the locker rooms, where he is instantly entertained by the Alabama Murderer, who knocks a sparring partner into a complete somersault. That is one portent too many, and Alfred crawls under the sheet covering the preliminary victim. For a moment, as the stretcher-bearers start to carry him and the loser out, it looks like he will escape. Both men topple off the unbalanced stretcher, however, and the downed fighter groggily rises, punching away at Alfred, who is thereupon noticed by the trainer and ordered back to his seat.

Catastrophes continue, for the mountain girl, told to stay away, nevertheless enters, announcing that her father and brother have bet all their money on Alfred. Temporarily at least she is kept from the truth, for the valet, instead of escorting her to an auditorium seat, leads her into a storage room and locks the door. And then, before it starts, Alfred's championship fight is over. The arena audience cries out "Butler! Butler!" When Alfred looks through the partition to learn why, he sees the real boxer standing triumphantly in the ring over the Alabama Murderer. Alfred has been the victim of an ill-willed comic hoax. Questioned, the trainer explains, "You didn't think we'd throw away a championship just to get even with you." Outside the locker room, the exact intention of the hoax becomes even clearer. As the trainer, the manager, and a few admirers gather around the victorious Butler, Alfred approaches. Not quite comprehending all that has happened but relieved, he says, "Thanks—for saving me." Putting a gloved hand on Alfred's shoulder in an ironic gesture of friendship, the bullying Butler replies, "I've been saving you for three weeks." He then pushes Alfred back inside, while the trainer and manager, with it's-none-of-our-business shrugs, depart.

In the locker room the final fight, Butler versus Butler, begins. Where the earlier blows in the film were mostly comic, they had at least the potential for becoming real and painful, like a few of the knocks handed Alfred in the practice ring and like the unseen punch that produced a black eye for the boxer's wife. Further, the characters, presented with a visible emotional life created through the use of a subjective camera, had a potential for becoming dramatically real rather than merely comic and two-dimensional figures. In particular, with the two Butlers we were made to feel a strong emotional motivation centering on their wives. With the pugnacious boxer, it was a possessive, jealous, and violent love, easily leading to blows; with Alfred, it was an adolescent and romantic attraction, an urge to prove worthy of the mountain girl's admiration.

When the fight comes, therefore, it is real, not a parody, one that completely breaks through the stylized and generally painfree farcical decorum of the film's comic surface. Alfred genuinely fights. So long incapable, so long victimized, so long idle and incompetent, he finally redeems himself, though the film has been so structured, his character as a farcically childish clown so strongly stressed, that the only way he can convincingly change is for the film to change. In its very form, its stylized comic routines, it is as inhibiting to his development as any of the other obstacles; and having stripped to his boxing trunks, he clearly must also divest himself of the trappings of farcically arranged motion. He and the film therefore deliberately break through the limiting conventions of comedy into the fuller world of naturalistic drama, and the remarkable result is as if an animated cartoon figure had suddenly become a real person, or as if a puppet had come to life. And the potential for such a change from farce to drama having been supplied earlier, the characters having been given more psychological reality and depth than is customary in Keaton, when the change does come, it is not only remarkable but also completely credible and acceptable. It is, in fact, one of the most effective and memorable moments in all the feature films, the most original of the many transformations that Keaton heroes undergo.

Butler first shoves Alfred about in the locker room, and Alfred at first as usual runs, though now it is not funny, trying to escape a demanding situation. He struggles to the door, opens it, and sees standing outside the mountain girl and the valet. As they look on, Butler, however, drags him back and slugs him—the blow is real and painful—across to the opposite wall. The valet, in a last effort to arrange things, rushes in but is knocked back, falling through the door, where the mountain girl kneels and cradles his head in her arms. Then, as Alfred, still purely defensive, goes into a clinch, he sees over Butler's shoulder, first in medium shot the mountain girl holding the fallen valet, and then in closeup, in the third and most important subjective use of a natural iris, her face alone, framed by the door behind her. Unlike the oval car window or the triangular frame of the trainer's bent arm, the iris now has no comic overtones; but again it strikingly and emphatically concentrates his and our vision and discloses how important she is to him. For the third time we see her through his eyes and feel with him, and it is therefore precisely the right shot to signal the dramatic change in Alfred's character, the right shot to make the audience emotionally acquiesce in it.

There is first a remarkable shift in facial expression. Alfred's eyes lose their former mild and vacant gaze of mindless torpor, a heavy-lidded somnambulist's stare appropriate to a politely acquiescent victim whose comic moves are always controlled by others or dictated by the patterns of farce. Instead, they become focused, angry, even vicious. In a uniquely unfunny variation on the Keaton theme of the novice who makes good, Alfred fights back, fights hard, and fights well. After all the comedy, it is a genuine fight, a grudge fight, all of whose blows are obviously painful. As usual in this film,

Alfred performs before an audience, whose responses help give meaning to his actions. In the doorway the girl and the valet are joined by the trainer and two others, and all react in strongly contrasting ways, the first two more and more frequently smiling as the others uneasily frown.

In the prolonged fight's final moments, Alfred lands a right and then a left to Butler's jaw and then a right to his stomach. The effort brings the exhausted Alfred down to his knees, but it also doubles over Butler, who falls. Alfred then picks him up and delivers another right to the jaw, as both a second time collapse. Alfred is still lifting and viciously if now ineffectually striking at the unconscious Butler when the trainer and another man run in to rescue and carry off the flattened champion. It is, for anyone who approves of an occasional fight, anyway, a great victory; and having been forced to the point where it was both necessary and a pleasure to knock another man down, Alfred has splendidly come through, much better if a little battered for the experience.

Left alone with the mountain girl, Alfred in a not quite necessary explanation then explains, "That was Battling Butler. I lied to you—I'm not even a fighter." She replies "I'm glad." Though his boxing gloves provide a comic impediment to an embrace, he holds and kisses her. The valet is next allowed a farewell shot, one of miniature defiance and triumph, as he stands beside the prostrate boxer and then looks up and snaps his fingers in the trainer's face before leaving. After this, in the film's final shot, one that returns us to the genre of farcical comedy, Alfred strolls arm in arm with the mountain girl on the crowded sidewalk in front of the auditorium. She is elegantly dressed. He sports a top hat and cane but is too preoccupied with the girl to have thought of changing out of his boxing trunks and gloves into evening clothes. So attired, he is a last incongruous mixing of incompatible life styles in a film that has gained many of its laughs from such clashes. He is still the rich young fool and clown, but he is also, very satisfactorily, the man of action, a working-class hero who has proved his worth and impressed his girl in a real fight. An unbeatable combination, he is in addition a unique union of differing dramatic styles, both a farcical and a realistic character, another seemingly incompatible but ultimately successful pairing.

To describe the merger in another way, one can also see it as the union of the classical and the romantic, as these terms are conventionally applied to certain antitheses in art. Critics have often labeled Keaton's comedies as classical, and the adjective is accurate. Along with other implications of the term, his films are classical in two ways, in their reliance on tradition, on farcical tradition with its long-established comic actions and characters, and in their sense of form and containment, their striving toward a simplicity and unity that rigidly bounds all the wild moves of the plot within a neat geometrical shape and that equally fixes the characters, however unpredictably they act, as simplified and readily perceptible types. Tumbling through the standard turns of a farcical plot, with its instant reversals and alterations, its multiplying confusions of identity, and its vast misunderstandings, all of which magically and almost mathematically work themselves out by the end, the characters in Keaton's films are apt to be equally standard and equally shaped, classically simplified and traditionally farcical types, rather than complex, shifting, and motivationally untidy persons. They have the graspability and conventionality of form that chess pieces have. They are basic, monomaniacal, and unchanging—reductions of human personality to a few fixed, steadily perceived, and comically exaggerated traits or motivations. Behind them is a long farcical tradition of several millennia of similarly created characters, from Terence through Molière to the present—centuries of swaggering soldiers, misanthropes, newly rich aspirers to culture, flimflam men, bumbling novices, man-eating viragoes, bird-brained blondes, jealous husbands, flirtatious wives, conniving servants, suspicious parents, ardent juveniles, and ingenuous ingenues—all universalized, fixed, and funny, all made up and waiting in the wings or just off camera, all designed to do without fail their few funny things in any play or film that wants to employ them and in a carefully coordinated concert to produce a growing chaos of rigorously shaped laughter.

Battling Butler at least begins as a traditional farce populated with classical farcical types. As mentioned at the beginning, the unchanging comic mold the hero is poured from is that of the upperclass nit—a dim boob obviously unfit to survive any Darwinian social struggle if he were not cocooned in a rich wrap of servants and money. Alfred is a wealthy American equivalent of the titled fool of English and European farce, a simpleton so feebleminded that much of the time he seems unaware of what is going on about him. A similar character is occasionally used by Harold Lloyd, but to take the best known example of the type, Alfred is a near relation to an English literary figure created in the same decade, P. G. Wodehouse's Bertie Wooster, and Alfred's keeper-servant is, of course, another adeptly managing Jeeves.

In Wodehouse's pure and classical farces, Bertie, like the other characters, remains unchanged at the end of each of his many adventures. A comic clown rather than a real person, he is fixed as a simplified if eccentrically personified type, eternally good-natured and eternally vague. By the final page of a Wodehouse novel he has blundered his way, with Jeeves's aid, to some sort of triumph, but he is still the same, set in his dimness and ready to blunder his way through yet another comic plot. Classically conceived, he is evidence of the classical aesthetic and psychological precept that people are limited, fixed, and unchanging, always true to type. It is a belief particularly central, in fact it would seem necessary, to classical farce, where the players almost have to be clear, fixed, simplified chess pieces in order to be easily recognizable as they progress through the complicated moves of their comic game.

In Keaton's two films with a Wooster hero, however, the hero untraditionally, unclassically changes. In *The Navigator*, where the transformation is muted, where circular action dominates over character, Rollo remains fairly close to his origin in a farcical type, though by the end he is certainly more self-reliant, more mature. In *Battling Butler,* on the other hand, the element of change, of transcendence, is so strong that it altogether carries the hero and the film out of the realm of classical into that of romantic art. Of all traditionally identified romantic concerns, transcendence is easily the most romantic, and in a comedy stressing it, the changing hero must be far removed from a closed farcical type. Such a romantically conceived hero must be a formless hero, not a fixity but a process, not a type but an individual, a uniquely growing person, whose development becomes the focus of interest rather than the comic routines he may perform. As a finally unfolding potentiality, Alfred is therefore necessarily in conflict with the simple and stable forms of personality and plot that generally characterize and limit the sort of classically organized farce he is the hero of. Like all Keaton's heroes, though he begins as typecast, he refuses to remain typed. Instead, at the end he carries on in the manner of an unlikely Bertie Wooster, one who suddenly fires his Jeeves and becomes the able manager of his own affairs.

The union of romantically conceived inner character and classical outer farcical form, though it could be a weakness in the film, is instead a major strength. Through the union Keaton endows the traditional farcical plot and hero with a nonclassical humanity, a romantic sense of potential, of youthful striving and achieving, that they do not usually possess. The result, as claimed for all the features in the opening essay, is a film with more weight and seriousness than a conventional farce, a film that has a strong emotional center as well as a brilliant comic surface. What Keaton achieves in *Battling Butler* and elsewhere is what almost seems an impossibility, a farce of character, a personal farce, a transcendent farce, in which the hero is not just a lightweight or stereotyped figure of fun, though he is that, but also someone as real, as fully present, as the hero of serious drama.

9.

The General

THE THEME OF MECHANIZATION

WHAT *The General* is best remembered for, frequently to the exclusion of everything else, is the railroad chase and the eponymous locomotive. Though there is somewhat more to the film than these, the chase is one of Keaton's most impressive sequences, and the locomotive itself is the most brilliantly used of all his many machines. When critics speak, as they invariably do, of Keaton's remarkable affinity for the machine, it is generally their memory of The General that they are generalizing from. They are apt to conclude that the affinity is a direct correspondence, that the Keaton hero works well with machines because he is one, a little wind-up mechanical man who runs through his automated routines as regularly as the many moving parts of a locomotive run through theirs. There is much truth to such a conclusion, and happily it is a very comic truth, but the full scope of the affinity is considerably more subtle and complicated than that. In a film like *The General,* for example, the movements of the locomotive are as often humanized by the presence of the hero—their regularity dramatically varied as they lead him to his triumphs and failures—as he is mechanized by his frequent imitations of them. Moreover, in the customary offhand manner of Keaton's visual fantasy, which comically conflates disparate things, the engine and the engineer are now and then even more curiously merged, the film casually accepting and casually presenting them as exactly alike, even though they are allowed to retain their distinctively mechanical or human identities. Finally, too, con-

212

trasts are as abundant as similarities, and one of the affinities of the machine to the man is that of the perfect foil. The mindless regularity of the locomotive is frequently used to counterpoint the individuality and ingenuity of the intelligently human hero, who often must dexterously manipulate this regularity for his own irregular ends.

Before a discussion of *The General*, a discussion first stressing the importance of the locomotive and the railroad in it (then turning to the hero's second career as a soldier), some further background observations will establish Keaton's basic attitudes toward machines and his characteristic deployment of them. To begin, his response to machines is eminently that of his age, an age in America of mechanical optimism. The first quarter of this century was the time, to go to another of the popular arts, of machine songs—of automobile songs and airplane songs and telephone songs, of "Hello Frisco!" and "He Had to Get Out and Get Under" and "Come Josephine in My Flying Machine." They are all songs of comic delight, in which the machine is both a gadget—something that any man can invent, tinker with, and master—and a source of liberation, possibly of amatory liberation in its provision of a new kind of portable privacy, and certainly of spatial liberation, as distance was conquered by road and air and wire. In the songs, the latest machines are wonderful new toys, and all machines are still admirable and full of promise, with the machines of transportation regarded as the most inspiring of all. These provide an ecstatic and relatively new pleasure, the simple joy of just getting around from place to place, whether on a bicycle built for two or on one of the many trains someone was always taking to his Dixie home or to an Alabama jubilee. The bicycles, the trains, the automobiles, and the planes—all are good, all are part of a craze for travel, and all are associated with love and the ties that bind family and friends together (as was also, in this last respect, the telephone, especially in the many long distance song calls little children kept making to heaven).

Noticeably absent from the songs, as it is absent from Keaton, is the long-standing European reaction, one given in films both a contemporary and a continuing expression, fear of the assembly line, of machines in a factory, where the worker is regimented, dehumanized, and made the mechanical slave of a demanding iron god. That is the one clear vision of Fritz Lang's ideologically muddled *Metropolis,* released in 1926, the same year as *The General.* It is also the vision, to trace a direct line of influence and descent in the next decade, of René Clair's *A Nous la Liberté* and then, when transported to this side of the Atlantic, of Chaplin's *Modern Times.* It is not, however, Keaton's vision. Though there are mobs in his films, of cops and cows and angry brides, there are no anonymous laboring masses. Of the many machines, there is none in a factory.

So far are Keaton's machines from possessing any depersonalizing aspect that the three most impressive of them have names themselves: The Navigator, The General, and The Stonewall Jackson. As their grand names imply, these are important machines, they are glory machines, and they confer an identify, a dignity, and an importance upon the man who operates them. Adept or inadept, whether he is a one-man steamship captain and crew, a railroad engineer, or a pilot on a riverboat, the Keaton hero is employed at an occupation made glowing through tall tales, folk songs, and legends. His are the adventurous and romantic callings of the machine age. They still retain the wonder they had for the century that originated them, when Mark Twain, young and awestruck in Hannibal by the mythic powers of riverboat pilots, determined to become one of their company and did. Like all the callings aspired to by Keaton characters (detective, boxer, athlete, cowboy, and soldier, to list those not associated with machines), these are the ones that small boys then still wanted to join when they grew up. They are the callings in which heroic heroes are made, in which individual men are called upon to control mighty engines, to be alone responsible for the largest and most powerful of the then existent means of transportation. And as Keaton beautifully demonstrates, the smaller the person in such a dynamic context, the funnier is his assumption of responsibility and the greater his glory when he succeeds.

Keaton's choice of machines, then, is an American movie-maker's affirmative choice. It is also the choice of a movie-maker who specializes in comic melodrama. Not only do his major machines provide a basic and continuous motion necessary in film, particularly in silent film, they also lend themselves well to the melodramatic needs of conflict and danger. Races and chases, sinkings and derailments, rescues and escapes—trains and boats are made for these, and in the films they are the means for generating intense emotional experience, even if they themselves as mere mechanisms are necessarily uninvolved emotionally. Usually for Keaton machines are only machines, no matter how exciting they are, and with the major exception of the locomotive in *Our Hospitality*, which is decidedly personified as a little engine that could, there is little anthropomorphism in the films. This does not keep the machines, however, from functioning in his comic adventures as human characters might, as allies or antagonists. As pseudocharacters, they frequently provide in their fundamental operations many of the obstacles the hero must overcome and many of the tests he must pass on his way to triumph and glory. Often he and a boat or he and a train will be alone on the screen together, with his mastery of the machine, or his temporary defeat, creating the dramatic interest.

When not costarring in such situations, Keaton's best-known machines, in their great size, are on occasion transformed from character-replacing dramatic objects into total comic environments, which exist in cheerful kinetic harmony with the hero. Unlike the cars and trains and planes of today, whose dynamics are all concealed, the moving parts of machines then were all on display; and in Keaton, when a busily working locomotive fills the background, it becomes a complete screen world of mechanized motion, of whirling wheels and driving pistons. It is a world whose simplified and regular patterns also correspond to the similar simplifications— the repetitions and reciprocations and linear drives—of the hero's most characteristic and laugh-producing moves. In fact, the comic principles governing human action gags and the mechanical principles governing the activity of the machines that provide the setting for the gags, are so alike, that even when a train or a ship is proving a source of maximum difficulty for the hero, a sense of happy harmony, of symbiotic interdependence, ultimately prevails. In the films men and machines naturally belong together, for both are seen through the same comic eye, an eye always cheerfully alert to the parallels in motion between them. So viewed, both finally seem the inhabitants of a mechanical and human paradise, joined in an affirmative comic union that is one of the distinctive greatnesses of

Keaton. It is a union that is today both a cause of laughter and a revelation of an almost lost charm and grace, attainable only perhaps in his age of mechanical innocence, when the great machines were still new and good and a hero could therefore naturally and gloriously be allied with and even imitative of them.

In such an affirmative context, the Keaton hero's occasional resemblances to a machine are rarely intended to make him seem less than human. Rather, the resemblance is what allows him to become a hero, a near superhuman, someone in whom fallible human qualities—like endurance, persistence, and concentration—have been stoically developed into a machinelike perfection. It is a perfection that is often comic but also often enviable, one needed for his accomplishment of heroic deeds. In the dogged single-mindedness of his pursuits, the nonstop, nontiring way in which he applies himself to any task at hand, the Keaton hero demonstrates that the mechanical in some cases can also be a very desirable, very human, and very necessary attribute. Certainly, a strenuous and orderly rigor, a mechanically trained perfection and application of one's abilities, is necessary for any runner who hopes to move as fast as his rapidly accelerating locomotive, or, when he is trying to catch up with it, even faster.

Of all the innocent and compatible machines he allies himself with, it is the locomotive which is obviously Keaton's favorite. It is easily the most ubiquitous. Trains appear in eight of the nine features and are absent, of watery necessity, in only one, *The Navigator*. Along with *The General*, two of the films, *Our Hospitality* and *Go West*, have extended train sequences; and in three others, *Battling Butler, College,* and *Steamboat Bill Jr.*, the hero travels on a train, in the last two being brought to the scene of his adventures by it. In *Seven Chances* and *Sherlock Junior*, trains are at least incidentally used, racing by in quickly passing jokes, and one of the gags in *Sherlock Junior,* when the hero is locked into and then runs along the top of a moving train, is among the most memorable scenes in the film. With such a background, then, one of the Keaton films had to be fully about trains, and the introduction of *The General* quickly establishes that it is that film, though it is a Civil War film, too.

As in *The Navigator*, the first of the major characters introduced is the leading machine. A lengthy prologue, nearly a fifth of the film, begins with a title, "The Western and Atlantic Flyer speeding into Marietta, Ga. in the Spring of 1861," and then in extreme long shot the entire train is shown as it travels through the country. Only next is the hero, Johnnie Gray, disclosed, standing in the locomotive cab and looking placid, ineffectual, and a shade foolish as he idly taps his hand on the windowsill. This shot continues, panning forward across the front of the engine, ending on a large brass nameplate, which reads "General," and then once more in extreme long shot the train pulls into Marietta.

At the station, Johnnie steps down beside his locomotive, where he is waved at by the departing passengers, and where he is also admired by two small boys, who immediately begin imitating his motions as they raptly stare at him. So presented, approved by passengers and the mimicking boys, he is unique among Keaton heroes in being from the beginning a professional, a competent expert in his work, even though he will soon want to excel in a different line. A title then states in three stages, "There were two loves in his life. / His engine, / And ———." In an elegant combination of word and image, the blank is filled in by the next shot, a closeup of an oval-framed photograph of his girl. A long shot shows the picture to be hanging in the front of the cab, and as Johnnie changes into his street clothes, he slips it into his coat pocket. Following the words and the picture, there is next the reality, Annabelle Lee herself. She stands in front of a white picket fence, a confining object associated with most Keaton heroines. Further to add to the sentimental domesticity of the presentation, there is a trellis of roses behind the fence, and to provide a modicum of action and a reason for her being there, an unseen person hands Annabelle a book.

Johnnie now reappears, walking down the sidewalk followed, though he is unaware of it, by the two boys, a progression that resembles a locomotive and its cars, a way of visually identifying the hero with his career, which he cannot escape, even when away from the railroad. Annabelle again turns up, standing at a corner and concealed by a fence and a tree. When Johnnie and the boys obliviously pass her by, she steps forward and joins the end of the procession, still unseen. What is now a three-car train, one leader and three

mimics, rolls on to a pleasant Greek revival home with another white
picket fence in front, and Johnnie unknowingly steers his followers
through the gate, down the sidewalk, around a flower bed obstacle
(which always produces a laugh), and onto the porch. Standing by
the door, he extensively spruces up, all the while watched from
behind by Annabelle. Then he knocks, turns sideways, and discovers her, his face registering a blank amazement.

She in turn sedately walks forward, opens the door, and invites
him inside. He and the two boys enter into a parlor, and as he and
Annabelle sit on a foreground couch, the boys sit on another by the
door. Watching them watching him, he thinks for a moment and
rises, picks up his hat from the table he had placed it upon, opens the
door, and seems about to leave. The boys, as imitative as ever, also
rise and file out in front of him, whereupon, having deceitfully sent
them rolling back down the line and out of the way, he quickly closes
the door and returns to Annabelle. Reaching into a coat pocket, he
pulls out a rectangular picture, a complement to the earlier oval one.
In it, he stands in the center foreground, while The General occupies
the entire background. Annabelle takes the gift and appreciatively
sets it on the table.

The introduction of the principals completed, a major character
relationship among them has been subtly but decisively defined.
Boy, girl, and machine have been structured into an amiable and
slightly fantastic triangle, one in which differences between the
human and the mechanical, as with the human and the animal in *Go
West,* have been visually erased. In their movements, he, she, and it
have all been equated. They have also been equally treated, each
even getting his, her, or its photographic due in the two still pictures
that were shown, an extension of the technique of an initial visual
affinity created through parallels in appearance, movement, or situation, which in the earlier features united hero and heroine only.

At this point, in a sudden comic reversal the just emptied parlor is
again invaded. Annabelle's brother and father hurry in from opposite
directions, and the brother announces that Fort Sumter has been fired
upon. While the two men set off, wanting to be "the first to enlist,"
Johnnie remains seated, frozen in his pose of interrupted courting.
Then, Annabelle, nervously twisting the ends of her long shawl-like

collar, a gesture that will characterize her throughout, asks a motivating question, "Aren't you going to enlist?" Lightly kissed by her, he is sent away to war, tumbling from the porch as he goes.

Out on the street, he finds himself last in a large crowd of hurrying men and therefore suddenly shifts direction, racing through an alley and popping around a corner in front of the recruiting office door just as the others arrive and fall in line behind him. Inside, this pattern immediately repeats itself. After starting toward the left, he sees the others heading to the right, toward a counter window. In response, he leaps upon and obliquely traverses two large tables, quickly dropping in front of the window, once more first in line, just as the others, more regularly progressing, step in place behind him.

His expertise at moving about, at finding the quickest way of getting from here to there and at keeping ahead of anyone racing with him, like his earlier maneuvers in directing the boys out the parlor door, parallel and predict his later actions during the locomotive chase. They are evidence of a professional railroad man, one knowledgeable in the stratagems of rapid transit. Here, too, as will happen frequently later, the uniform and mechanical movements of the other men provide a military equivalent to the regular motions associated with railroads, a regularity that points up the individuality and ingenuity of the hero, who often irregularly proceeds through what becomes a pervasively mechanized world.

Though successful in being first at the window, however, Johnnie is not first or even last to enlist. On hearing Johnnie's occupation, a white-haired old man, who will turn up as a southern general at the film's end, explains to the recruiting officer that Johnnie would be more valuable to the South as an engineer than as a soldier. Neither of two ruses, assuming a false occupation (bartender) and then grabbing another man's enlistment papers, is of any use. Finally booted out onto the street, all Johnnie can do is yell back, "If you lose the war, don't blame me."

He is, of course, instantly blamed. Ignorant of what has actually happened, Annabelle's father and brother complain at home afterward that he "didn't even get in line" and that he is "a disgrace to the South." As Annabelle hurries away to find Johnnie, her father then begins to sort some mail, brought back from the post office recruiting office. Working in a carefully established triadic rhythm to a neatly patterned climax, he inspects one letter and sets it on the parlor table, does the same with a second letter, and then discards a third, which is tossed to the floor. The routine is repeated as two more letters are tabled and a third is floored, but this flooring in turn initiates a new three-part action, for it is followed by a second floored letter, and then Johnnie's letter-sized photo is picked up and like the two envelopes just before it casually but decisively cast aside.

A cutaway discloses Johnnie uncomfortably seated on the crossbar between his locomotive's two largest wheels, and then Annabelle approaches. He stands and starts to explain that the army refused to take him, but her immediate hypercritical response, accompanied by much angry twisting of her collar, is "Please don't lie—I don't want you to speak to me again until you are in uniform." Effectively having denied him any further chance at an explanation, she leaves. He dejectedly sits again on the bar, so dejected that he does not notice when his fireman starts the engine. The locomotive moves forward, and its wheels make three complete revolutions, lifting him each time some four feet into the air. Immediately upon the third and last elevation, he belatedly notices what is happening to him, looking about in comic surprise just as he is carried out of sight into a railroad shed.

His exit, which ends the prologue, is an eclipse from view that visually corresponds to his rejection by Annabelle and her family. The cycloid described by his movement, with its three peaks culminating in a climactic laugh, even repeats the triadic structure of the discarding of his picture, turning the regular reciprocating motion of the train into the basic triple rhythm of a standard Keaton gag, where an action is presented, precisely re-enacted to establish an expected pattern, and then comically varied, here by means of the hero's discovery and eclipse. In the routine the machine does not, as some writers have observed, mechanize the hero, assimilating him into the regular spinning of its wheels (though it does in comic contrast certainly dominate him and emphasize his smallness). Instead, its motions are humanized. Through the presence of the man, they are made to assume the laugh-producing rhythms of life, of repetition followed by climactic release, and they provide a classic example of

Keaton's incredible ability to endow mechanized regularity with emotional tension and comic surprise.

In one other way, too, the shot is a key one. The original triangular alliance of hero, heroine, and train has here ended in a separation, with the hero and the train deserted by the girl. At the film's end, however, in a recapitulation of this scene, the three will be together again, with both the hero and the girl sitting on the connecting bar.

The prologue finished, the film's main action begins a year later, "in a Union encampment just North of Chattanooga." General Thatcher and his chief spy, Captain Anderson, sit at a table, Anderson in dandified civilian clothing. Expansively gesturing with a cigar, he points to a map of the railroad between Marietta and Chattanooga and outlines his plan. With ten men he will steal a train, bringing it north to meet an advancing Union army under a General Parker.

A slow fadeout is followed by a slow fadein to a station sign, "Marietta," and the two-day period that is the entire rest of the film begins. Beside a passenger car, Annabelle, who is traveling to visit her wounded father, speaks to another family casualty, her uniformed brother, whose arm is cradled in an ostentatious sling. After seeing and snubbing Johnnie, who stands by his tender and appears to her an unharmed and unpatriotic slacker, she steps into the car. Anderson and his men are also in it, and at the first stop, Big Shanty, when all the others go to the station for dinner, they remain by the train. Unnoticed by everyone, Annabelle then returns and enters the first baggage car to retrieve something from her luggage. Immediately, the spies leap on board, she is discovered and held, and the train, reduced by an uncoupling to two baggage cars, pulls out. Johnnie and the passengers rush from the station, and he gestures to them to follow as he races down the track. Briefly they do, but then they halt in what seems to be a futile pursuit. Though he as yet does not realize it, he now runs alone.

The two chase sequences that begin at this point, first the pursuit north and then the flight south, are among Keaton's most remarkable achievements. In them the narrative line of the film is also the spatial line of the film, the distance traveled; and both are none other than the actual railroad line itself. Its rails become a visual embodiment of a comic fatality controlling characters and events. Restricted to them, excluded from other directions and other possibilities of action, the northerners and Johnnie are held in conflict. Theirs becomes a portable battle, one in which, though the armies remain about the same distance from each other, the battlefield moves, regularly providing as it does so surprising new offensive resources and defensive opportunities for both sides. The eventual reversal of the chase is also implicit in the nature of the railroad. Not only is the battle mobile, it comes with a round-trip ticket. Having gone up the line, it must go down the line, destined to do so as much by the necessity of following a regular train schedule as by the demands of military strategy (at the end, of course, everyone, trains and armies, arrive exactly on time for another battle at the Rock River bridge).

What Keaton is doing in the chases is what he often does. As in the human-mechanical love triangle at the beginning of the film, he is merging and comically confusing two different worlds, here that of the railroad and that of war, making each partake so much of the other that there is no telling them apart. Through the merger, as in the gag that ended the prologue (the one with Johnnie sitting on the side of the moving engine), the mechanically mundane operation of the railroad with its reciprocating and automatic movements is dramatized and made to assume the unpredictable human rhythms of conflict and comedy. Conversely, it is the inbuilt order of the railroad that produces the satisfyingly regular progression of striking contrasts and reversals and repeated confrontations for the humans who travel on it. Temporarily it is their entire field of action, and they must fight and win or lose their very peculiar war according to the highly limiting rules of battle it imposes. The result, finally, is that both the railroad and the war are seen in an entirely new way. Both acquire more fanciful identities, and both reveal potentialities never expected. Through the merger, what is ordinary in each becomes extraordinary, continually surprising and continually funny.

The chase north, having started, proceeds with alternating shots of Johnnie and of the northern spies. Generally the emphasis is on him, with the shots of the northerners subordinated. They will be shown briefly creating an obstacle that he can then at length and with much laughter overcome, or else there will simply be a short cutaway to them to allow for an elliptical presentation of an action of his. He will begin some sustained motion, the cutaway will occur, and then he can instantly be shown reaching its usually disastrous conclusion. This manipulation of parallel editing not only produces sudden comic climaxes, but also increases the rapidity with which Johnnie's actions are presented, making their execution incredibly but also convincingly fast, which also means that the sequence itself moves along at express train speed. Despite their subordination to these ends, however, the shots of the northerners are all carefully planned as a coherent series in themselves. They provide necessary information about Anderson and his men, and they proceed in a plausible, dramatic progression.

In the first set of northern shots, Annabelle is bound and gagged by the spies in the baggage car. Then Anderson in the locomotive cab orders the train to halt, and several men leap out, one to cut the telegraph wires beside the track. Following this, there is a return to Johnnie, as the first chase joke reaches its climax. Far into the countryside, he is still running down the track and still gesturing the non-existent others to follow him. Then, looking back, he discovers the absence of a crowd and stumbles to a disconcerted stop. But, in a typical Keaton rapid reversal, dismay is replaced by discovery, for he has pulled up next to a track-side shed, and from it he soon drags a handcart, the first of three machines that will increasingly accelerate his pursuit. Acceleration does not come immediately, however, for success is initially followed by a new (literal) reversal. When he starts to pump on the cart's handle, it rolls backward instead of forward. Further, a worse catastrophe is being arranged; Anderson's men, having cut the telegraph wires, are now shown removing a section of rail.

This second defensive action of the northerners, like other measures they will soon take, gives the chase sequence an additional forward impetus, a kind of dramatic attraction toward the future unusual in film, where action tends to exist in a continual present. As here, however, film action in the chase is always pointing ahead. As Johnnie rolls along on his handcart or later in a locomotive, he is always being carried toward some new disaster, a comic climax that only the audience is always prepared for. Just as a sense of rapid movement in the chase has been created by the elliptical editing of the sequence, so, too, a sense of going somewhere is created through such audience preparation. As is appropriate to a railroad journey, the audience always has the feeling it is approaching a destination, an impression produced by its simultaneous movement both with and a little ahead of the comically underdog hero, who is throughout ironically and laughably ignorant of what lies in front of him.

In blissful ignorance, therefore, Johnnie begins his first forward roll. He pushes the cart, leaps on it, and determinedly brings the weight of his entire body down on the upraised handle. As he does so, his legs fly straight out into the air in imitation of the handle's form, so that while he and it descend together, the urgency of his action momentarily identifies him with the machine he travels upon. In a cutaway, Anderson's train passes the next station at Kingston, where another train rests on a siding, and after this Johnnie's handcart travels, just begun, can be shown immediately reaching their end. Derailed by the missing rail, he falls flat on his back as the cart tumbles down a bank and overturns in a stream below. Again, however, a discovery replaces the loss. He looks ahead and runs, and in the next shot he leaps onto the seat of a high-wheeled bicycle just parked by a gate. Peddling off on it, he now moves more rapidly than before. Another cutaway intrudes upon this journey—showing Anderson being handed a package, its contents undisclosed, while his men cut more telegraph wires—and then, as with the handcart, bicycling instantly ends. Bumping along a rough road, Johnnie falls over.

Following a second cutaway to Anderson, who opens his package and puts on the Confederate officer's coat and cap it contains, Johnnie next appears racing on foot up to the Kingston station and the train shown earlier. There he explains the situation to an army troop: his General has been stolen, he thinks, by three deserters. A flatcar behind the tender of the train is filled with soldiers to aid him in his pursuit. He uncouples the rest of the train behind the flatcar and hurries to the locomotive, The Texas. A shot of Anderson checking his watch provides a minimal anticipatory pause, and then, as the soldiers on the flatcar wave and yell, the camera placed in back of them shows Johnnie's locomotive and tender charging off alone, the victims of another unexpected uncoupling. For the second time he thinks he has acquired a posse, and for the second time he proceeds in ignorance of its dereliction. And as before, when he finally looks back and discovers the loss, he does so next to a trackside shed, which again provides a replacement. In it is a solid, stocky cannon on a small flatcar, and following a cutaway to Anderson's train stopped next to a watertank, Johnnie's train moves ahead with the cannon in tow.

In so repeating his earlier actions in these ways, with the loss of men succeeded by a gain in equipment, Johnnie is also doing what becomes typical of the chase, where many situations receive a double presentation. If its basic structure is simply one long series of comic mishaps, lucky breaks, obstacles, and confrontations, there is within the chase a mechanically consistent substructure built upon a unifying rhythm of twos. During the pursuit north, many of the individual events occur twice, just as the entire chase itself, in keeping with the regular reciprocating rhythms of railroads, will be given a reprise in reverse following its conclusion.

The cannon having introduced a new potentiality for martial action, preparations immediately begin for its comic exploitation in the film's first battle. Anderson's train is again shown by the watertank, with his men still taking on fresh supplies of water and wood, but when Anderson sees The Texas approaching, he orders an instant getaway. Abandoning everything, including the watertank spout, which is left lowered and still spewing water, his men scramble on board, most of them entering the first baggage car. When he reaches the tank, Johnnie natually sticks his head out the window just in time to be drenched by the stream of water. Then, back in the cab of The General, a belligerent northerner asks Anderson to stop and counterattack. Anderson, however, restrains him, fearing they are greatly outnumbered. He does, though, decide to improve the current numerical odds and to take some counteroffensive measures without interrupting the flight. Grabbing an ax, he climbs over the tender and begins chopping through the solid front of the first baggage car to release the eight men who had leaped inside.

So far trains have started and stopped and people have scrambled out of and into them, but this move of Anderson's inaugurates an episode of extensive activity upon the trains themselves, which become traveling stages for the performance of carefully choreographed action. Anderson's concern with the supposed army behind him, which has led him to the top of the tender, where he stands facing rearward while he opens the baggage car, is now symmetrically matched by Johnnie, who climbs onto the roof of his locomotive cabin and stands there in the classic Keaton forward lean, his hand shading his eyes as he stares ahead to learn exactly who it is he is pursuing. The northerners in the baggage car are next shown climbing out through the opening Anderson has made, and then Johnnie climbs back over his tender and down to the cannon, for he, too, is about to take offensive action. Loading the cannon, he drops in one handful of powder and starts to add another. On second thought, he cautiously reduces the amount to a pinch instead, and then the cannon is lit.

A cutaway to the northerners, all out on the tender now, shows them climbing onto the roof of the first baggage car, led by a gun-waving Anderson. Following this, in an extreme long shot taken from the side of the track, Johnnie's cannon fires, the ball in a short neat arc just clearing the tender and landing next to him in the loco-motive. Discovering what has happened, he rolls it out and for a second time returns to the cannon. There is a moment's puzzlement when the discarded ball explodes back down the track, but when he observes its smoke and learns its dangers, he quickly decides to replace the too little with the too much, dropping a whole can full of powder into the cannon before he lights the fuse. This overreaction, however, instantly takes a turn for the catastrophic, for as he climbs back on the tender, his foot catches in the long v-shaped handle of the flat car. He is able to free himself, but when his foot is shaken loose, the handle falls down onto the ties. As it bounces over them, it continuously jolts the cannon. The last link in a mechanically fated chain of cause and effect, the cannon thereupon slowly lowers into a horizontal position, monumentally charged and aimed directly at Johnnie. He starts to scramble for safety, but in another of the chase's doubled actions, his foot is a second time caught, now in a chain hanging from the back of the tender. Eventually yanking it free, he finally succeeds in climbing up, foolishly pauses to throw an ineffectual piece of wood at the cannon, and then runs forward. Completing their last shown action, which has been extensively prolonged to allow the establishment of a comic symmetrical pattern, Anderson and his men are only at this point disclosed still hurrying back across the tops of the baggage cars till they reach the end of the second, guns in hand and ready to do battle with their pursuers. The northerners having moved as close as they can to him, Johnnie continues his forward dash as near as possible to them, climbing down and crouching on the cowcatcher of The Texas, where he awaits the worst. With both sides in position, the cannon now climactically discharges just as Johnnie's train goes around a curve and out of the line of fire. The exploding ball therefore passes by him and nearly hits the end of the car where Anderson and his men stand. Frightened by their enemy's formidable and well-aimed fire power, more convinced than ever of being outnumbered, they quickly reverse themselves and having just finished running toward the back of the train turn about and start to run forward, away from danger. Though he does not know it, Johnnie has won his first confrontation. Further, what he accomplished through dumb luck here he will on the second day of the film consciously repeat as the final victorious action in a major battle, a repetition that will, in keeping with the customary learning pattern of Keaton films, demonstrate his second-day development in military skill.

After this confrontation, with their counterattack having quickly aborted, the northerners make only purely defensive efforts, which involve only minimal stoppings of their train. The first effort is the immediate uncoupling of the second baggage car, to increase their speed and to create an obstacle. Still seated on his cowcatcher, Johnnie looks up, almost too late, to see the uncoupled car slowly rolling just ahead. Quickly clambering back to his cabin, he rapidly decelerates but still bumps into the car, pushing it along in front of him. A cut to Anderson's men shows them chopping through the end of the remaining car for an as yet undisclosed new defense, and then Johnnie stops at a switch and pushes the obstructive car down a sidetrack. This obstacle seemingly out of the way, a new one immediately replaces it, for now the northerners, through the opening they have made in their car, drop a log across the track. Moreover, the detached car is only seemingly out of the way, for while Johnnie is preoccupied with gathering wood from the tender, the vagrant car crosses a second switch and rolls back onto the main track, once more in front of him. When he next looks ahead (in a studio shot with a moving panorama of painted pine trees in the background), he is nonplussed by its surprising reappearance. Then a spurt of steam from the boiler distracts him, and as he searches for something to handle a hot lever with, the obstructive car runs into the just dropped log. With an elegant and ironic economy, the two dangers proceed to cancel each other. The log derails the car and the car in turn bumps the log off the track, so that when Johnnie, having curtailed the steam, for a second time looks forward, the track is mysteriously clear. He stares ahead, he blinks, he looks back, he stares ahead again, his eyes roll suspiciously left, then right, then center once more. Of his many doubletakes in the chase, this one is easily the most impressive, an epically sustained expression of totally unbelieving recognition.

For the second time, the northerners drop logs, two of them, and for the second time one danger will be used to cancel another, though now instead of merely being the ignorant beneficiary of the cancellation, Johnnie is the creator of it. Approaching the first log, he slows his train to a crawl and then climbs down and runs ahead of the engine. Standing in the center of the track, he furiously and single-mindedly struggles with the log, which is tightly wedged under a rail. So monomaniacally does he wrestle with it that he is oblivious of the approaching train, drawing nearer and nearer and filling the screen behind him; but fortunately just as he is about to be crushed between it and the log, he pulls the log free and is swept up onto the precarious safety of the cowcatcher. Twisting about to stabilize his position, he holds onto the log like a tightrope walker to his balancing pole, and then log number two, obliquely angled over the right rail, looms ahead. Instantly raising the log he holds, he decisively throws it down on the other, bouncing both of them off the track, and two more obstacles are simultaneously overcome.

By now, however, the railroad line has become an obstacle course, obstructions turning up almost as regularly and frequently as ties. Preparing the next boobytrap, the northerners stop beyond a switch and reset it behind them. In preparation for his response, which will be another monumental doubletake, Johnnie is then shown gathering wood from the tender. On the northern train again, Annabelle, still bound and gagged, is carried out of the baggage car, and following this suspenseful pause, the film returns to Johnnie's train as it crosses the reset switch and heads down a deadend sidetrack. Straightening up with a huge pile of wood in his arms, Johnnie as usual at the comic last moment discovers what lies ahead. Having laboriously hefted the wood, now with a neatly self-canceling reciprocity he immediately drops all of it, leaping forward to brake the train just before its wheels run out of rails.

Another cut to the northerners shows them smashing the contents of the baggage car, and then Johnnie's train backs beyond the switch, which he resets for the main track. When he attempts to start forward again, however, the locomotive wheels lose traction and spin. To create friction, he scatters sand under them, facing the camera as he stoops beside the track and tosses several handfuls behind him. Then, while he is engrossed in kicking away a rock that hinders his labor, the wheels catch hold, and the train, unnoticed by him, rolls away. Once again there is a belated discovery, precipitating the abrupt termination of one action and the sudden substitution of another. Throwing sand gives way to running, and, rapidly racing, Johnnie just manages to leap onto the back of the receding tender. After this self-caused difficulty, the northerners' current maneuvers, till now obscure, are revealed and climaxed. Reduced to tinder, the interior of the smashed baggage car is set on fire, and it is uncoupled and left within a covered wooden bridge. Running into the bridge, Johnnie for the second time acquires an obstructive car, this time a flaming one. Soon the smoke drives him from his cab to the end of the tender, where he sits, fanning himself with a piece of wood.

The final and major event of the chase, again a double one, is now prepared for. Anderson's men, all crowded into their tender, which is the only remaining car behind the locomotive, first simultaneously stand up to view the results of their latest action. Johnnie is next shown switching away the burning car. Then a title announces the

retreat of the southern army facing Chattanooga, and an officer on
horseback orders his men to the right. Anderson, in The General's
cab, sees them coming, and he and his men, having just stood,
immediately reverse themselves and crouch out of sight. Johnnie,
busy chopping wood, once again is shown so monomaniacally occupied, so characteristically absorbed in the mechanical regularity of
his activity, that he does not notice the entire army retreating behind
him as he and his train pass in front of it. In the initial and best shot
of this undiscovered meeting, the army retreats, a moving mass of
men and wagons, on the far side of the track. Then the smokestack
and the top of the locomotive move before the camera, followed by
Johnnie, chopping as he stands on the tender, with the fleeing army
visible behind him. The train gone, the camera lingers, as through a
battle-like veil of smoke drifting back from the engine the southern
army continues on its way.

Having risen and fallen, the northern spies now stand again, with
Rockette-like precision popping up in a row from the tender. And in
the last of the pursuit's doublings, a second title introduces a second
army, one that advances, the victorious northerners under General
Parker. And once again, still chopping wood, Johnnie misses the
mass of men moving behind him. Anderson's spies, however,
see and wave, and Anderson triumphantly discards his southern
officer's cap and coat. Only when the army proceeds on both
sides of the track does Johnnie also notice it. Looking in front of
him he sees northerners, looking behind him he sees northerners,
and it is now his turn, in one more of the carefully choreographed
parallels of action between the two trains, to crouch for cover.
Leaping down into the cab, he huddles there, head on hand,
wondering what next.

The chase ends as the northern train goes under an immensely high
wooden trestle and then, after what must have been a very tight
curve, enters the screen on top of the trestle, where it stops. When
Johnnie approaches from below, the spies drop logs on him, and as
he steps back out of the cab to see what is happening, his solitary
state is discovered. "There is only one man on that engine," Anderson cries. Braking his train, Johnnie leaps off. In the last of the
chase's parallel movements, Anderson's men leap from the tender

and run after him. In a sudden and total reversal, the sequence ends as the man pursuing becomes the man pursued.

With the chase north ended, a final word about it. As unique and fresh today as when it was filmed, it still impresses as a one-of-a-kind performance. Not even elsewhere in Keaton is there anything quite like it, though it is demonstrably a characteristic Keaton sequence. Typically, it stresses the comic and frustrating repetition of a single basic activity, and the hero's confronting of obstacles in it obviously comes from the same sequential mold as the multitudinous marriage proposals to obstructive women in *Seven Chances*. Further, the individual gags in it are produced in the usual Keaton way, by the mechanical shaping of action through sudden reversals or through unexpected parallelisms or repetitions into the classic comic patterns that result in laughter. But neither the overall structure of the sequence nor the individual gags seem in any way formulaic. It is hard to think of them even as detachable from the chase, so thoroughly are they integrated into it. What has happened, and something like this does not always happen in the other features, is that Keaton has allied his customary comic forms with two areas of activity—railroads and warfare—that are themselves already characterized by simplifying formalizations. The many shots of the locomotives' wheels, with the ceaseless repetitive movement of the driving bar, visually summarize both the railroad and the chase, expressing an idea of not quite eternal but still impressively sustained recurrence. The track with its double parallelisms of endless rails and countless ties further typifies the patterned repetitions both of the chase and of the railroad, where obstacles and stations regularly appear and on the coming return trip will reappear, neatly and comically reversed.

Warfare, too, possesses an inherent form amenable to Keaton's characteristic gags and to his standard deployment of them in a great gag chain. Some of the repetitions belonging to it are visually emphasized later in the film, when parallel lines of tents and horses and cannons and marching men will be shown. And in both the chase battles and in the final fixed battle at Rock River, there is a strong awareness in the film of the reciprocations that constitute military movements, of advance and retreat, of victory and loss, of the mirror images created when two opponents proceed against each, whether they are maneuvering on trains or on the opposite sides of a valley. Such martial symmetries resemble those both of the railroad and of basic Keaton comic action.

To state the same point itself reciprocally, the stylized patterns of Keaton comedy find their perfect equivalent and locus in the equally stylized patterns of the railroad and of war. In all three there is a need to reduce the complexities of motion into a regular and classic simplicity, to impose a formal restraint upon the divergencies of action. The result, throughout the film but most beautifully within the first chase, is a perfect realization of Keaton's ideal of silent-screen comedy. In the chase, the possibilities for his characteristic and by now supremely skillful shaping of comic action are so abundant and yet in the context of locomotive warfare so natural that the constructions of comedy seem spontaneous and uncontrived as well as irresistibly funny. Highly polished comic art appears almost the naive and unaffected capturing on film of a real but intrinsically comic event, whose humor arises out of the very nature of railroads and war.

As the film continues, there is now a sequence behind northern lines. Like nearly everything else, it is plotted around a precisely symmetrical round-trip reversal. First, Johnnie races into the woods, where he is much frightened and rained upon. Next, he runs up to a house and seeks shelter within, crawling through a dining room window. Soon he is cowering under the dining room table, for several northern officers not surprisingly enter. Though a victim of their unintentional hostility, bumped and kicked and even burned when a cigar is accidentally held against the tablecloth, Johnnie also learns their plans. Thatcher with two supply trains will meet General Parker's army at the Rock River bridge, and once across it, he claims, "nobody on earth can stop us."

Next, the inadvertently captured Annabelle is led into the room. In a repeat of the iris effect so brilliantly used in *Battling Butler*, Johnnie for the first time discovers her presence as he sees her face framed in the round hole just burnt in the tablecloth. She is led away, the others also depart, and after that Johnnie escapes. Grabbing a piece of firewood, he clobbers a sentry by the door. Then, in Union uniform, he walks up to another sentry outside, downing him by swinging his shouldered gun in a well-aimed arc that ends on the northerner's head. The blow is one more ingenious execution of a mechanical military motion.

Locating Annabelle's room, Johnnie enters through a window and awakens her. His northern journey having reached its far point, he and she quickly race back into the woods, to exactly the same spot from which he earlier had emerged. Once in the woods, however, as happened to him before, they are much frightened and also much rained upon. Finally, wet and exhausted and lost, they crouch and cling to each other. Protected by his arms, Annabelle lovingly thanks him for having come to her resue, and while he deprecates his heroism, he sensibly does not deny it or explain the true object of his ignorant pursuit.

The two sleep, and in the morning they wake to discover they have accidentally (and symmetrically) run all the way back to the railroad, where the northern supply trains, one of them headed by The General, are being loaded. Observing this, his eyes heavily rimmed and popping in a comic stare expressive of deep mental activity, Johnnie reaches a decision, one disclosed to Annabelle but not the audience. Stealthily grabbing a bag from a supply pile, he empties the boots in it and Annabelle crawls inside. Joining a long line of marching men, he then proceeds behind the first baggage car of The General's train, where he stands while the concealed Annabelle removes a coupling pin. Ordered by an officer, he next walks forward and gently deposits his bag inside the car, recoiling in horror as other soldiers casually throw heavy boxes and barrels on top of it. With Annabelle disposed of, perhaps permanently, he joins a second line of soldiers, carrying wood to the tender. Stepping up to the locomotive cab, he swings his log and knocks out General Thatcher, who stands there. Another officer is pushed out to the left, and a wood-carrying soldier behind Johnnie is kicked back out to the right. Then Johnnie starts the engine, and his return trip begins. Behind him, Anderson quickly gives chase in The Texas. And behind Anderson, a lengthy supply train soon follows, with three officers, one of them Joe Keaton, conspicuously seated around a makeshift table on a flat-car, where they plan their campaign.

This marks the beginning of the film's major reversal, and as is customary in a happily transformational two-day Keaton comedy, the hero, subjected to greater dangers on the second day, radically improves on his earlier performance. Such improvements have, in fact, already started. As he maneuvered in his highly individual way through the mechanized lines of soldiers who loaded the supply train, Johnnie's movements visually recalled his earlier maneuvers through the recruiting line in the prologue; but where then they failed to lead to enlistment, they now have successfully ended in the recapturing of The General. With the start of the chase, his former underdog position as the victim of the northerners' booby traps also changes. What he had before innocently and ignorantly run into, he now diabolically leaves behind him, recreating all the former obstacles and doing so more effectively than the northerners had first managed. Moreover, where before the audience was always one up on him, knowingly anticipating one stunned doubletake after another as he made his many anguished discoveries, now he is often ahead of them, constantly beginning ruses whose surprising climaxes are only later revealed, both to their victims and to the viewers.

In addition, if all this were not enough to elevate the hero and make the audience now look up to rather than down on him, to turn him from an Ichabod Mudd into a Captain Midnight, Johnnie's display of continued railroad and newly acquired martial expertise is contrasted to the bumbling of several others. First, there is Annabelle. In a series of comic progressions, which make her the most lifelike and likable of the Keaton heroines, she develops rather like a typical Keaton hero. She slowly learns her way around the train, proceeding in knowledge from totally incompetent novice to at least adequate engineer, and in movements from a fearfully frozen immobility to a fleet-footed dexterity, which turns the locomotive and car into as feminine a promenade as a garden path. By the end, the love triangle of boy-girl-train has been firmly re-established. Annabelle, too, has learned to run the locomotive, and all three obviously belong together in happy harmony. In the meantime, however, Annabelle's progression is slow enough so that on most occasions her ignorance comically points up Johnnie's skill. He is the expert, she the novice, and her earlier scorn of his supposed martial cowardice is now replaced by his sorely tried patience at her engineering ineptitude.

A second such contrast is also provided by the northern officers, particularly Joe Keaton and the two others on the flatcar of the supply train, who demonstrate an ignorance of railroads as great as Annabelle's. They soon prove that a master in one profession is likely to be an apprentice in any other, and as they stumble and fall and are continually unseated by the jolting progression of their train, they point up the sure-footed and accustomed ease with which Johnnie races about on his. Annabelle and the officers, amateurs all, together mightily increase our pleasure in watching a real professional at work, one thoroughly proficient in handling the many machines of a railroad, and one who has by now also learned the hard way much about applying them to the needs of war—an accomplished soldier-engineer.

It is the soldier half of the compound, undervalued by other commentators on the film, that now becomes more important. Untypically expert for a Keaton hero, a professional railroad man, Johnnie is at least typical in his first-day novice bungling and second-day proficient success as a soldier. Though lacking the initial catatonic incompetence of many Keaton fools and clowns, like them he changes for the better by mastering a new career. The ignorant victim of military maneuvering the day before, he now proves he has learned from the experience and himself become an adept military strategist. As a comic military hero, he of course does not progress with uninterrupted proficiency to his final triumph as a soldier. There are many reversals along the way. But then, as a comic hero, he is also the beneficiary of lots and lots of military luck.

As the flight south begins, so do the now altered repetitions of events from the chase north. As Anderson chopped a hole through a baggage car to release his men inside, so Johnnie must now chop a hole to release Annabelle. While readily removed from her bag, however, she is only with extreme difficulty extracted from the car. As Johnnie stands outside on the coupling links, she timidly sidles out to a seated position on his shoulders, where she suddenly freezes and clutches and threatens to topple both of them until he manages at last to tip her over onto the tender.

Once Annabelle is safely in the locomotive cab, the problem of the pursuers is addressed. Expertly and economically, Johnnie first repeats two of the northerners' initial defensive maneuvers as a single elegant action. The ideal hero of his age, he demonstrates a mechanical adeptness that will continue to be much in evidence, as he triumphs through his mastery of maximally productive and mechanically ingenious labor. Throwing a rope around the track-side telegraph line and tying its ends to the top of the baggage car, he pulls down the line and with it also a telegraph pole. Then, while the train is still moving, he grabs an ax and cuts the rope, leaving the pole stretched across the track, which simultaneously provides an obstacle for his pursuers and severs their communications.

A comic hero, he does not enjoy continuous success, and an immediate contrast is provided when he and Annabelle next must stop for firewood. While she, in the first display of her increasing agility, runs back over the tops of the tender and baggage car, he walks to a track-side fence and begins throwing its loosely stacked rails onto the train, efficiently demonstrating three variations on how to load wood in a maximally unproductive way. First a board too weakly thrown up falls back down and nearly hits him, then thrown a little more vigorously it knocks off several other boards, and finally hurled mightily it flies all the way over the tender and hits the ground on the other side.

Annabelle, meanwhile, has been shown untying what is left of the rope used to topple the telegraph pole, and now she proudly reveals to him and the audience what she has managed with it. Tied to two small pine trees, it stretches across the track behind the train. With a visually displayed sarcasm, he plucks the feeble barrier as if it were a guitar string, but before he can comment further, The Texas approaches. Racing ahead with Annabelle to the locomotive, he kneels by its steps, one hand outstretched to assist her up to them. Having acquired a little railroad expertise by now, however, she ignores him, easily leaping up the first high step by herself and quickly ascending into the cab. Caught by surprise, he momentarily holds his pointlessly chivalrous pose. Then, ignoring the steps, he scrambles directly up the engine's side, falling through the window and onto the throttle, a move that allows him instantly to start the train as he enters it, yet another example of his expert and comic ability to do two things at once. As they pull away, behind them The Texas runs into Annabelle's rope and is unexpectedly stopped by it, if not quite in the way she intended. When hit, the rope does not break; instead, the small trees it is tied to are uprooted and pulled along the sides of the locomotive, threatening to dislodge several soldiers stationed there and forcing a brief stop for the trees' removal.

Still imitating and bettering his predecessors in flight, Johnnie next wields the ax again, knocking out the entire back of the baggage car, rather than merely chopping a small hole through it. Where the northerners had then dropped only three logs from the back of their train to stop him, he proceeds to shove out a long line of boxes and barrels, which they themselves supplied him when loading the car. In a customary Keaton change of identity through change in function, what had earlier been a threat when tossed on top of Annabelle now becomes a defensive weapon when tumbled out. While Johnnie is occupied in emptying the baggage car, however, a cut discloses General Thatcher, still lying where he had been floored but now beginning to stir, a potential danger to Annabelle, alone in the cab, who does not notice him. But then he is a second time stunned. A board flies down and beans him just as he starts to rise; and soon, Johnnie, who appears as the thrower of it, leaps down into the locomotive, too.

As the northerners, their progression hindered to a crawl, are shown busily clearing the track, Annabelle, momentarily unoccupied, looks for some new way to be of use. Discovering a broom and being a femininely home-oriented Keaton heroine, she tidily starts sweeping the cab in a poorly timed exercise in domesticity, particularly since the pursuers at this point remove the last of the obstacles and accelerate their chase. Noticing Annabelle's unproductive labors, Johnnie therefore throws away her broom and orders her to stoke the fire instead. She obediently throws in a small board, and in sarcarcastic comment he picks up and hands her a minuscule chip. Ignorantly impervious to irony, she obligingly throws this in, too. Provoked, he begins to shake her by the throat, but then recovers and instantly converts the gesture into an embrace and a kiss. Following a jump cut, the next shot reveals a more reasonable and more peace-able division of labor. Annabelle is now the one sitting at the con-trols, a useful job that she will slowly learn to handle, and Johnnie expertly stokes the fire. In preparation for several later events, he also in this shot discovers the Confederate uniform discarded by Anderson when crossing behind northern lines.

In another repetition of the first chase, Johnnie next stops by a watertank, very like the one that earlier had drenched him, but as he and Annabelle struggle with its spout, she is now the victim and is even soaked twice. When, as happened to Anderson before, they are soon forced by the approaching Texas to drop everything and speed away, the watertank spout is also again left lowered, first splashing Anderson in the Texas cab, and then, leaving no possibilities dry, the three officers on the supply train. In the deluge, the three all tumble about, Joe Keaton the most energetically and with the greatest flail-ing of upturned legs.

Back in The General, Annabelle, once more serving as fireman, picks up a suitably large board, but then she discovers a knothole in it, fuelishly judges it defective, and before Johnnie's wondering eyes casts it overboard. On The Texas, meanwhile, a soldier is ordered by Anderson to crawl forward to the cowcatcher, and as The Texas overtakes and bumps into Johnnie's baggage car, the soldier man-ages to couple locomotive and car together. Several more soldiers immediately join him and all leap into the car, but as they do so, the camera pans ahead, revealing Johnnie simultaneously uncoupling the car at the other end. The General quickly pulls away, leaving a new and ever-widening gap, and as in the chase north, the pursuers now have the problem of a loose car in front to contend with. The car is disposed of at a switch, where it is pushed down a sidetrack, but when the locomotive backs onto the main track, it accidentally slams into the supply train behind it. The collision for a second time sends the officers on the flatcar sprawling, Joe as usual tumbling the farthest as he topples backward over a box. After a preparatory pause, a long shot of The Texas moving forward again along the main track, the reseated officers on the flatcar get a third unseating jolt as their train jerks too quickly to a start.

Johnnie now stops The General, and in an improvement over the northerners' earlier ruse of sending him down a deadend sidetrack, he prepares to do the same and also to make certain they will not come back. Again transforming an obstacle of the first day into an aid on the second, he takes the chain at the end of the tender, the chain his foot had caught on when he was trying to escape the super-charged cannon, and attaches it to the switch's movable rail. He then signals to Annabelle, left alone in the cabin, and for the first time she starts the locomotive by herself. The train rolls ahead, and before the chain snaps, the rail is permanently bent into the switch position.

Unfortunately, Annabelle is not yet knowledgeable enough to stop the engine she has started. As Johnnie watches in stunned helpless-ness, The General steadily moves on. Running after it, he then exe-cutes one of the film's most neatly symmetrical and reciprocal move-ments. As the train goes around a hairpin curve down a hill, he takes a shortcut, scrambling straight down a steep bank to the track below. He reaches it before the train, but also just in time to see Annabelle, still learning the routines of an engineer, successfully stop and reverse, so that he must instantly reverse also, energetically scram-bling up the hill to reach his starting point. This time he and the train arrive together, and he leaps onto the front of the backward-moving engine. Scurrying across it to the cab, he brakes the train just a few feet in front of the broken switch, stopping it just as Anderson's train and the supply train cross the switch and roll up onto an elevated and unexpectedly short sidetrack. The second train bumps the first to the very end of the track, where its cowcatcher hangs over empty air; and the first, when its direction is desperately reversed, in turn bumps the second, which for the last time sends the flatcar officers sprawling. Johnnie, meanwhile, smoothly and speedily rolls ahead, and soon in a shot most suggestive of knowledgeable expert ease and mechanical affinity, he is purposefully striding, a determined sol-dier-engineer, to the front of the racing locomotive. When he reaches it, he removes the lantern from its holder, again planning some new booby trap momentarily undisclosed to the audience.

A title next identifies the Rock River bridge, and there are several suspenseful shots of General Parker's northern division, the one that had passed by Johnnie the day before, marching toward the bridge to meet the supply trains in accordance with Thatcher's plans. Then

Johnnie rolls onto the bridge, which is little more than a long track stretched from supports at either end, and he stops directly in its slightly sagging center. His removal of the locomotive's lantern is now explained, for he proceeds to heap wood on the track behind the train, and then he pours the lantern fuel over it, about to recreate the northerners' final obstacle of a burning bridge. The ignition, unfortunately, takes place prematurely, when Annabelle accidentally knocks the ignitor, a small burning board, off the tender. Standing on the far side of the wood pile, Johnnie is suddenly separated from her and the train by a wall of fire. Carefully calculating his risks, however, he gauges the distance and coolly jumps over the flaming barricade, just as Annabelle, once more dubiously assisting but also still increasingly competent at train-handling, responds to the emergency by driving The General forward. Instead of landing on the back of the tender, therefore, he falls through the space left by a conveniently missing rail and splashes into the river below. Crawling up the far bank and bridge side, he is at least at this point more ably assisted by Annabelle, who has by now reversed the train. In one more of their many unplanned but precisely timed meetings, he reaches the track just as the train backs by, and he leaps on board.

In the first of several cutaways to the northerners, the other officers and Anderson are now shown, all gathered about the bent rail of the switch. Continuing to demonstrate their ignorance of railroads and things mechanical, as well as the legendary inability of army officers to do anything, they fiddle about with the switch, give orders and counterorders, stumble over one another, and accomplish nothing. Johnnie's ruse has effectively stopped them, and he and Annabelle therefore placidly roll on and pass into the safety of Confederate territory. Once there, however, when Johnnie waves in greeting to a track-side sentry, the latter immediately and hostilely fires back. After a first response of fright and confusion, Annabelle points to the reason for the attack, Johnnie's northern uniform, and he replaces it with the Confederate officer's coat and cap discarded by Anderson.

The two next reach a small town, site of the southern divisional headquarters, with the locomotive's whistle bellowing visibly in clouds of white steam as they sound the alarm. Hurrying down the

street to the headquarters building, they report to the southern
general there, the same white-haired old man who in the prologue
had decided against Johnnie's enlistment. He orders out the troops,
while Johnnie and Annabelle in turn assist his aide in preparing him,
helping him on with his gloves and hat and coat, an assistance that
implies not only deference to rank but, in another standard army
joke, a certain senility on the part of the aged leader. In a final
cutaway to the broken switch, the Union officers at this point also
continue to receive a comic drubbing. As they still argue and bustle
without success, the civilian engineer from the supply train comes
forward and with one knowledgeable blow from a hammer drives the
bent rail back into position. Having demonstrated his railroad expertise and their incompetence, he then casually strolls back to his
train.

With the way cleared for the northerners to advance, the film
returns to the southern town, where the main street is suddenly filled
with hurrying horses and men, carriages and cannons. Johnnie and
Annabelle, who stand in the street, are several times nearly run over.
Then, Annabelle's wounded father, seated behind a picket fence
(where as a proper Keaton heroine she herself will soon be placed),
is discovered by his daughter. Completing her much interrupted
journey, she races to him. The last of the thundering army also
gallops off, and as the dust and confusion abate, Johnnie finds
himself standing alone in the street. Forgotten but undismayed, still a
military reject but still determined to become a soldier, he picks up a
sword someone has dropped, girds himself for battle, strides
forward, predictably trips over the dangling blade, falls, rises, and
advances to the front.

In a film that has been an almost continuous chase, the climactic
event, in a reversal of the usual Keaton order, is a set piece, the great
battle at Rock River. In it the hero, in continuation of his elevated
status on the second day and in successful fulfillment of his military
ambitions, will impressively display a newly acquired proficiency as
a soldier, though he will also comically bungle. The battle itself
begins before he gets there, as General Parker and his marching men
now reach the Rock River bridge, simultaneously with the northern
trains. Having surveyed the briskly burning span, General Parker, a

plump melon-faced fellow, takes charge and tells Anderson: "That bridge is not burned enough to stop you, and my men will ford the river." Once again the military proves wrong about railroads, and another officer is caught with his incompetence showing. Anderson in The Texas obediently drives onto the bridge, and exactly as the locomotive reaches dead center the span collapses, in a spectacular chaos of falling timbers, billowing steam, and spraying water—a monumental joke, which is also apparently the death of Anderson. Deflated, in an anti-doubletake, a response devoid of any expression, Parker stares at the catastrophe he has created, while his officers with hurt looks stare accusingly at him. Then in subdued silent speech, with a weak wave of his sword, he orders his army forward. On horseback his men start across the river. Immediately, a line of southern cannons fires from the opposite side; and the northerners, as the reciprocations of battle parallel those of railroads, quickly turn around and head back where they started, their retreat symmetrically canceling their advance.

The arthritic old southern general next appears, on horseback, giving orders as he stiffly waves his sword. Johnnie, a typical Keaton imitator, has by now reached the battle and stands beside him, repeating the orders and even attempting a mimicry of the general's gestures. When he tries to draw his sword, however, it obstinately remains stuck in its sheath. As he struggles, more and more preoccupied with it, an incredibly swaybacked officer with an incredibly padded rear strides up to make a report, just in time for Johnnie accidentally to poke him. The walk-on butt of a joke, the officer immediately stalks off, leaving Johnnie, his sword at last unsheathed, to continue his imitation, repeating the general's orders as authoritatively as if they were his own.

Several crosscut shots next alternate between Johnnie waving his sword and a row of firing cannons. He is still somewhat hampered in his gestures, since each time he swings the sword its blade flies off, and the last flight lands it between two of the cannons. When Johnnie approaches and bends to pick it up, the cannon directly behind him naturally fires, effectively demolishing his assumed officerial dignity. Recovering, he proceeds authoritatively to give orders to an adjacent cannon crew. Unfortunately, as soon as he gives an order, the man he is speaking to is shot by a northern sniper. After three men, the entire crew, have fallen, Johnnie reasonably shifts to the cannon behind him and somewhat nervously repeats his orders there, again swinging his sword as he does so. For the last time the blade flies off, and this time it hits the sniper, who lies motionless, with the blade vibrating in his back. Accidentally but still courageously, with an ambiguity that befits a humane but heroic comic hero, Johnnie has confronted and killed his first enemy. He has passed the initiatory test of battle and become a soldier.

As a new series of cutaway shots begins, northern soldiers are shown firing from behind rocks in the river. Then Johnnie mightily pulls the release cord on a cannon, pulling it so hard that he jerks the cannon upright and the ball shoots straight into the air. He looks worriedly upward and cautiously exits, but the ball comes down not by the cannon, but just behind a wooden dam in the river. Exploding, it bursts the dam, sending a visually not quite convincing flood of water toward the Union soldiers. Again accidentally, Johnnie has performed well, and has in fact won the battle. The remaining northerners, their front line destroyed, run back to the supply train in defeat. As the officers clamber on board, however, Johnnie directs another cannon crew, expertly aiming the cannon at the rear of the last car, a tactic that consciously and with no element of luck repeats his unintentional firing at the rear of The General's baggage car during the previous day's chase north. The ball hits, the car is derailed, and the immobilized train and its supplies must be abandoned to the South. The northern officers all leap off and ignominiously foot it as they retreat in a disorganized rout.

The battle is over, and when a southern flag-bearer is hit by a last bullet and falls, Johnnie runs up and grabs the Confederate flag, proceeding to a small hill, where he stands and waves it. He waves it, that is, till the hill turns out to be the back of a prostrate southern officer, who angrily rises and topples the hero. The shot summarizes the film's attitude to the battle and to war, a kind of amiable irony, where the genuine glory suggested by the gesture is there to be admired but also to be debunked, undermined along with one last pompous officer for a laugh. The deflation, however, while it trips the heroic pose with laughter, does not cancel it, for as usual in a

Keaton comedy, the irony is basically approving. The nature of Johnnie's heroism here and elsewhere is such that it is best served by a light touch. The heroism is real as always, but its deadpan dash requires a tongue-in-cheek approach. You can laugh at your military glory and have it, too; and the title that introduces the final sequence is seriously and joyously meant: "Heroes of the day."

After the title, the southern army, with Johnnie walking beside the general's horse, is shown marching in triumph back to town, though as the army moves down the main street and across the railroad track, Johnnie stops, still the military outsider, and begins to check over his train, which remains obviously his first love and his prime concern. As he inspects the cab, General Thatcher, long forgotten but still lying there, opportunely comes to. Johnnie, after an initial surprised start, brushes him off to make him a more presentable prisoner and leads him away at gunpoint. Brought to the southern general, Thatcher surrenders, though the formal motions of the ceremony in which Thatcher surrenders his sword are disrupted briefly by Johnnie's accidental firing of the gun he holds.

With Thatcher escorted away, the southern general turns his attention to Johnnie. "Is that your uniform?" he asks. When Johnnie answers "I had to wear it to get through the lines," he is brusquely ordered "Take it off." As Annabelle and her father, still positioned behind the picket fence where they were before the battle, look on from a distance, Johnnie sadly does so. However, the general's aide immediately supplies another coat and cap, which the general with feigned anger throws to Johnnie. Slowly he puts these on, and rapturously he discovers they are an officer's uniform. Annabelle runs forward just as he finishes dressing, and instantly he assumes a Napoleonic pose for her admiration. The general orders the attendant to "enlist the Lieutenant," and the attendant, the same man who had refused Johnnie in the prologue, asks again the prologue's disconcerting question, "Occupation?" Johnnie's proud answer, that of a young man who has proved himself in a new profession, is "Soldier."

The final scene of the film repeats the final shot of the prologue. Johnnie once again sits on the connecting bar between The General's two largest wheels, though this time Annabelle sits with him.

Perched there, they begin to hug and kiss, but a soldier coming by forces Johnnie to interrupt his wooing and salute instead. Then another walks by, and looking toward some distant tents, Johnnie discovers a vast crowd approaching. Exchanging places with Annabelle, he now holds her with his left arm, which allows him to kiss uninterruptedly as his right arm automatically salutes all the passing men.

The scene provides his last demonstration of ingenious efficiency, of how to do two things at once. Appropriately, it is also one last demonstration of how to remain human and funny even when employed in the highly mechanized and serious professions of railroads and war. Appropriately, too, in the final shot Johnnie, Annabelle, and The General are together again, for if the machine is a machine and the humans are humans, in the affirmatively mechanical world of the film they have also been fantastically and approvingly presented as alike. Girl and train have been equated in their kidnapping and rescue and by the hero's equitably divided love. Hero and train have been equated as Johnnie, a Keaton kinetic hero in an age of admirable machines, acquired some of The General's mechanistic glory through being its expert engineer. Charging down the line with it, he himself became a miniature driving juggernaut, unstoppable and unbeatable. Posed together now—boy, girl, locomotive—they form a romantic and dynamic trio. whose shared adventures have happily united them at the end.

10.

College,

SEXISM, RACISM, AND ESCAPISM

ADVENTUROUS physical feats, comically but athletically performed, are basic to Keaton's screen character, and having already made one film about actual athletics, *Battling Butler*, in *College* he made another. Harold Lloyd's *The Freshman*, released in 1925, featured a brash but weakling hero who nevertheless won glory on a college football field, and this, too, seems to lie behind Keaton's film, if only because its success discouraged downright imitation. In *College*, the weakling hero's bumbling athletic endeavors are a tour de farce of many collegiate sports, with the significant exception of football.

Not surprisingly, it is in the athletic workouts and in several quasi-athletic routines of work and hazing that the film's best moments occur. In fact, there are few other moments at all, the remainder of the footage providing little more than a minimal framework upon which the sporting activities are displayed. The framework is unusual for Keaton in its sparseness. It is sufficiently perfunctory and sufficiently lacking in dramatic tautness and rhythmic drive to make the film the least successful of the silent features. By now it seems the mechanics of a Keaton feature are so well understood by the makers that they can run through them without having fully to bring them to dramatic and comic life. The formulaic thinking behind the films finally results in a formula movie, and for the first time individual Keaton routines look rather better than the film in which they occur.

246

With this flaw admitted at the start, a description and commentary can reasonably go on to acknowledge some other Keaton weak points as well. After so many chapters chorusing praise, it is time, if only for the sake of variety, to plainly speak some critical reservations, to point out his most serious failings, and in a palinodic way to subject even his putative virtues to caustic scrutiny, to imagine how they might look to an unsympathetic eye. The limitations of Keaton's formulaic and personality-based art, for example, are apparent in a certain speciousness about the Keaton hero, who when viewed in the right or perhaps the wrong critical way, an unenchanted way, seems more a manipulative contrivance to engage the audience's emotions with the star than a psychologically or experientially valid character. In one-man shows stressing the hero only, the presentation of the remaining characters is also always superficial. The otherwise shapely Keaton heroines, as has been noted earlier, usually suffer from dramatic thinness, and the more minor characters are often reduced to physical and ethnic stereotypes. Racial humor in particular is something the films frequently resort to for what in their day were certain and easy laughs, and *College* contains one of the most extended of Keaton's many black jokes. If such limitations as these, more evident in *College* than elsewhere, make it the sole Keaton feature that has not yet turned up on somebody's list of favorite movies, this does not mean that it is remarkably bad, only that it is the ninth best of nine good Keaton comedies.

The film begins with a verbal-visual pun. A duplicitous title seems to promise a palm-lined beach: "On the sunkist slopes of the Pacific, where land and water meet . . . California." The first shot, however, discloses a city street in front of Union High School, as people run rapidly and damply toward the building to escape a torrential rain. What brings them out is "High School Graduation Day, where the next step is either to go to college or go to work." The graduation ceremony constitutes the opening sequence, a customary Keaton prologue to the main action of the film. In it are introduced, to identify them as they are namelessly listed in the opening credits and then later described in titles, "the girl," who is Mary Haines, "winner of every popularity contest in which the boys were allowed to vote,'' and ''a rival,'' who is Jeff Brown, a ''star athlete, who believed so much in exercise that he made many a girl walk home.'' There are also ''a mother'' and ''a son,'' Ronald, who is the hero of the film. The last two first appear walking to school in the rain. As they soggily proceed, he pulls a $15 price tag from his brand-new woolen suit and another tag from his hat. Too late to prevent a soaking, he next pauses to buy an umbrella from a stand in front of an old-clothing store. Then they reach the school, where Mary, who is cheerfully talking to Jeff, apologizes to Ronald for a broken date, ''I didn't think you would call for me in the rain.'' Unintentionally speaking a double truth, she adds ''I'm sorry you are all wet.'' The metaphorical side of Ronald's dampness arises from his being the school's ''most brilliant scholar,'' which in the totally sports-oriented world of the film wins him no popularity among his peers or even with his girl.

In the course of the graduation ceremony, Jeff receives his diploma and as athletic hero is wildly applauded, despite the principal's comment, ''Young man, it's time you graduated. You've been here seven years.'' Mary, escorted to the stage by the attentive Jeff, is also enthusiastically congratulated by everyone, even the principal, who says to her, ''I know you are going to be as popular at Clayton College as you were here.'' Only the principal, however, approves of Ronald. Awarded a scholastic honors medal, Ronald delivers a valedictory address on the ''Curse of Athletics'' to an increasingly unappreciative audience. ''Books not sports,'' he proclaims, is the secret of his success. ''The student who wastes his time on athletics rather than study shows only ignorance. Future generations depend upon brains and not upon jumping the discus or hurling the javelin.'' He then asks ''What have Ty Ruth and Babe Dempsey done for science?'' Since shortly thereafter all his audience, except his mother, angrily stomp out, the question is never answered. Another question, ''Where would I be without my books?'', pretty much answers itself. When earlier he sat in the auditorium next to a radiator, his wet wool suit began to steam and shrink, and it continues to diminish as he stands on stage. Legs and sleeves visibly shorten, and after all the buttons on his vest, from top to bottom, pop off, suggesting that a similar progression is about to begin on his pants, he steps behind a table, ingenuously asking the question while he strategically places a book where it will preserve public decency.

After the ceremony, on the steps outside, Mary berates him: "Your speech was ridiculous. Anyone prefers an athlete to a weak-kneed teacher's pet. When you change your mind about athletes, then I'll change my mind about you." She then rides off with Jeff in his jalopy, leaving Ronald with his mother. Though rebuffed and deserted, he immediately announces that he wants to go to college with Mary. His mother observes that they cannot afford it, but he replies, "I can work my way through, other boys do." And so the following term he enrolls at Clayton.

Possibly because *College* is the seventh film to employ one, possibly because it is the eighth film discussed, the prologue produces a slight sense of déjà vue, an awareness of formulas at work, and also an awareness of the limitations of formulas. The prologue itself is formulaic, a standard means of establishing the basic conflicts and struggles to be developed later. To consider one major example within it, also produced to formula and functioning in the accustomed ways, there is the heroine. It is obvious by now that when a Keaton hero's girl, like Annabelle in *The General* or Mary here, complains of his inability in some field, the hero will have to devote himself to mastering it in order to win her love and approval. And after so motivating him, she will usually have little more to do than look on and eventualy approve. In this film, Mary is even more literally than elsewhere reduced to an audience. As a spectator at athletic events, she realizes the ideal that all Keaton heroines aspire to.

So presented and so limited, Mary and the others necessarily exist in a state of preliberation innocence. They have little in common even with the new women of their own day, the heroines of Shavian comedy. To fall a half century further behind, they lack even the modest audacity of the Victorian bloomer girl. The formula they adhere to, in fact, goes all the way back to the days of King Arthur and his Round Table as presented in medieval romances. In them and in the many nineteenth-century reworkings of them from Scott to Tennyson, a chivalric knight would dedicate himself to the service of a pure and beautiful lady. Wearing her emblem and morally, spiritually, and physically ennobled by her love, he would perform great deeds on the fields of tournament and battle. On occasion, if she were a damsel in distress, held captive by an ogre or dragon or un-chivalric baron, he would also have to rescue her, but primarily she existed simply to adore and to inspire, to love him and cause him to seek glory for her sake.

In such a role the chivalric heroine is herself both glorified and demeaned. Clearly she is totally subordinated to the man. A passive being who has only a slight existence of her own, she derives an identity primarily through her relation to him. At the same time, and this is the element in the medieval tradition most emphasized in the popular nineteenth-century revivals, she has to be much better than the man if she is to inspire him. A purer soul, one belonging to a higher spiritual order, she is worshiped as a goddess whose angelic influence can redeem the base animal nature of her human and masculine devotee. To use one of their favorite clichés, the Victorian medievalists like Malory before them placed women, at least good women, on a pedestal. And once there, pedestals not being very large, the women cannot move. They can only look and in turn be looked at.

The Keaton heroines are mostly pedestal girls. Though they seem very real and though they are presented unsentimentally, with their goodness and innocence implied rather than stated, they nevertheless originate in the unreal and sentimental world of Victorian popular art, in the convention of woman as the better half of humanity, as the angel in the house, a saintly Venus or secular madonna, whose love can inspire a man. The transcendence achieved by Ronald, who will doggedly seek to transform himself from weakling bookworm to athletic superstar, a transformation that at the end will be instantly achieved, is motivated and explained solely by his love for Mary, a force in the long tradition of medieval romance easily strong enough to effect his miraculous alteration.

Such a love relationship is good for the hero, making him the center of much comic action and a dramatic change; it is very restric-tive for the heroine. So conceived, Mary's role, like that of most other Keaton heroines, is so limited that it almost does not exist. Of all the Keaton heroines, only two are allowed to expand beyond their initial Victorian constrictions, and they are the two best of the lot, appearing in what are also two of Keaton's finest films, *The Navigator* and *The General*. Alone with the hero on the steamship or the locomotive, they share nearly equal time on the screen. Like him, too, they move about, they act, they even dramatically change in a way that parallels his transformation, from spoiled rich child to self-sufficient adult in the first film, and from a bumbling novice at a demanding new job to a modestly competent worker in the second. In both films, too, though the inspirational power of the women is seriously used to motivate the hero, it is also comically perceived and qualified. Even while invoking it, *The General* expresses an ironic awareness of the unreality of such a sanctified womanly role, and of the laughter likely to be created when it is incongruously assigned not to a female saint but to an average and decidedly nonideal young lady. The comic beauty of Annabelle is that except for her beauty she is eminently uninspiring, no more reasonable or bright or understanding than most other girls, though rather more likable for the audience and no less desirable to the hero because of her deficiencies. In other Keaton films, however, notably *College*, though some comic debunking is engaged in, the romantic convention of the remote and inspiring heroine is not itself consistently viewed as a source of comedy. If it is occasionally exploited for laughs, along with everything else, the convention is still unreflectively used as a replacement for reality rather than an illusion to be tested by it. The heroines who are so conceived and so limited are brought to a semblance of real life, if at all, only by the personalities of the actresses who play them.

In *College*, the actress playing Mary is Ann Cornwall, who is happily and engagingly pretty, animated, and real, an actress so favored that even a critical misogynist like John Simon would be forced to concede her his approval. As she plays Mary, she is so agreeable and makes such a pleasant impression on the screen, that it is only with later reflection that one is apt to realize how minor a part she has actually been given. Reflection suggests, too, that though the part is a romantic and traditional one, it is also in its formulaic sketchiness one defined by then current masculine prejudice. Hollywood has always tended to reduce minority groups to a few restrictive clichés, to deny their members any depth of characterization that would transform them into individuals and dissociate them from their minority status. Instead they remain stereotyped types, restricted to doing their accustomed thing in minor role after minor role. And women in the Keaton films, with the fortunate but incomplete exceptions of the heroines in *The Navigator* and *The General*, are stereotypes—limited, depersonalized, and conceived as interchangeable—all old-fashioned girls, most of them, it seems, named Mary. If the leading ladies in the films have considerable character and individuality, sharing in common only the physical fact of being Hollywood's original Little Women—they are all about five feet tall in order that they not tower over Keaton—what they are given to do is almost always the same. They narrowly enact the very small role of approving viewer in a world of male-dominated action. Mary watches Ronald perform.

Treated in this way, the heroines have much in common with another minority in the films, blacks, who are also presented as similarly unvarying stereotypes, stereotypes which though often funny, at least for audiences of majority people, constitute a most uncomfortable limitation in Keaton's otherwise amiable popular art. Considering the dominant social attitudes of his age, which his mass-audience films unthinkingly accept rather than criticize, it is probably an unavoidable limitation. In what are essentially one-man movies, where the real interest centers on the athletic comedy of the continually cavorting Keaton, everyone but the hero has to be reduced to an extra, a quickly identifiable and efficiently functioning type rather than an individual character. And the laugh-producing types most likely to turn up in silent-screen comedy, when they are not strikingly visual caricatures, ugly faces and monstrous bodies, are apt to be instantly visible ethnic jokes. Like the heroines, however, the ethnic figures are not conceived as real; nor are they necessarily intended to be taken as real. Where the former are merely conventional romantic stereotypes, the latter are only conventional comic stereotypes, stock jokes rather than actual people. In the films, the hero alone is allowed what seems a full and convincing existence. The others are there to motivate him or to provide a laugh, and these functions excepted, as is reasonable in lightweight action comedies decorously devoid of any social concern, there is nothing else to them. Still, having made that half-hearted defense, one must concede that in sexual and racial attitudes, the latter to be demonstrated shortly, the films hold tightly to the repressive beliefs of their time. And this, if not necessarily a major moral flaw in what are socially amoral entertainments, is for later times no strength either. The virtues of the films, certainly, are not those of an art that promotes social understanding and a sympathetic respect for the individuality of all people, the right of each to an unhindered development of her or his potential. But then, of course, not all art should be required to do these things.

Moving on, therefore, to the masculine and socially unredeemed action of *College*, Ronald's freshman year begins as he gets off the train at the Clayton station. The prologue having announced the areas for the hero's struggles, athletics and work, his college experience will proceed through alternating examples of the two fields of endeavor. In what is for Keaton an unusually diffuse and timeless way, through a period that covers most of Ronald's freshman year, he determinedly goes out for two jobs and three sports, and as a novice bungler fails at all but his final effort.

An example of work immediately begins the series when he walks by the Collegian Drug Co. Another man is needed behind the soda fountain, one as good, the manager explains, as the present soda jerk, who obliges with a showy display of his highly entertaining and highly skilled routine. Performing an egg shake, an act that requires practiced dexterity, he tosses a scoop of ice cream far into the air, catching it in the shaker can. He next stylishly adds milk, holding the can far below the bottle and creating a long milk fall, not a drop of which is spilled. Three squirts of soda water from a spigot are authoritatively splashed in, obviously the exact amount needed, and last there is an egg, which is juggled before being cracked on the side of the can and with one-handed expertise emptied into it. While the can is being shaken on a mixing machine, the clerk continues to juggle with a water glass, which he then fills and slides down the counter, so adept that he does not even have to look at what he is doing. At the far end it reaches a callow collegiate customer, who sits there, straw already in his mouth, waiting for his shake. The shake itself is then poured, again with a great flourish and a long descent of liquid from can to glass. This glass, too, is nonchalantly whipped down the counter and stops directly in front of the customer, who bends over, completing the performance, as his straw is submerged in foam.

Nodding his ability to do as well, Ronald gets the job and is told to commence work the next day. After leaving the drugstore, he heads to his dormitory, on the way encountering Mary, who strolls by with a friend. She greets him coldly, "Well, if it isn't the student prince," but afterward she stops and looks pensively back in his direction. He has already entered the dorm and so does not notice, but in a heroine who is no more than a spectator, it is a sure sign as always with Keaton heroines of her interest and love.

Once in his dormitory room, Ronald unpacks his crammed suitcase, which holds a full supply of football, baseball, track, and boxing gear. It also contains a portrait of Mary, the cause of all this anticipated activity, and an ample selection from Spaulding's Athletic Library—*How to Play Baseball, How to Play Football,* and *How to Sprint.* Despite this resolve to enter a new arena with new goals, however, his high school reputation as scholastic outcast survives to make him unpopular, at least with his peers. A formally dressed and elderly academic (played by Snitz Edwards) enters and announces, "I am Dean Edwards. Your principal writes me what an excellent student you are." He adds, "A boy like you can make this athlete-infested college a seat of learning once more." And then, when Ronald's three obviously athletic roommates enter, he delivers the final alienating blow, admonishing them "You boys will do well to follow the example of this young scholar." Reasonably enough, they thereupon all eye Ronald with sarcastic grins and saunter off, leaving him again in the same isolation as on the high school stage, appreciated only by principals and deans.

The next title announces, "Sunday found Ronald taking 'fizzical' exercise." In a comic turn exploiting imitative action and ineptitude, he attempts as novice soda jerk to match the experienced counterman's bravura performance. His predecessor's professional routine of flamboyantly disciplined gestures was a delight to watch, the sort of efficiently organized activity that continually fascinates in Keaton films. Ronald's performance is an equally organized and fascinating parody, an efficiently contrived accumulation of disasters and unexpected recoveries. It begins as the same dude seen the day before walks up and orders another egg shake, patiently sitting as he waits with a straw once again foolishly stuck in his mouth. Decked out in a counterman's professional working clothes, white jacket and cap, Ronald picks up the shaker can and maladroitly twirls it. He then drops in a heaping spoonful of powder, only to discover that after the twirl he is holding the can upside down. After cautiously repeating the action with the nontwirled can carefully held right side up, he next juggles and drops an egg. Once again an unadventurous repetition must follow flubbed flamboyance, and a tightly held substitute is carefully cracked on the side of the can. Not yet defeated, however, still doggedly staging a performance, he now tries tossing a scoop of ice cream into the air. But it refuses to leave the scoop, and he must inefficiently and inelegantly scrape it out as it falls heavily into the can. Picking up an unopened quart of milk, he next attempts a dazzling one-handed operation, pushing the top in with his thumb as he holds and tips the bottle for pouring. His thumb-work lacks finesse, however, and the milk squirts violently. Still, the bottle is opened, and holding it far from the can he manages to pour the milk in a long and visually striking stream. Encouraged to further accomplishment by this modest success, he even twirls the milk bottle very cautiously as he sets it down. While the shake is under the mixer, he then takes time out to improve his art and to practice some of his fumbled motions. He executes three gingerly juggled tosses of an egg, and again made bold by success follows these with a tricky behind-the-back catch. He misses, and at this point he places both hands behind him, the customary Keaton gesture denying responsibility for or even knowledge of some just encountered disaster, though an occasional downward glance undercuts his bluff of non-involvement. The shake is then poured into a glass, with enough trembling to send much of it onto the floor after the egg, but it is at least completed. With something close to nervous exhaustion, Ronald plops it down in front of the dude, who has watched, with increasingly comic stupefaction, the whole astonishing performance.

A second order from a man far down the counter ends in total rather than partial debacle. Again imitating the professional, Ronald slides a badly made soda down the counter, an accelerating disaster that ends in the lap of the customer, who waits for it and gets it. The final loss of face then occurs as Mary, her friend, and Jeff enter, sit at a table, and call for service. Dismayed at the thought of having to wait on his girl and his rival, Ronald slips down behind the counter. When he emerges, he is out of uniform and has on instead his freshman beanie. Sidling over to the counter side, he sits on a stool, impersonating a collegiate customer as he sips at a second soda he has been mixing. When the manager approaches, however, he gives up the show altogether. Dropping a coin on the counter to pay for the drink, he leaves the store and his job.

In a film where one example of ineptitude and ostracism relentlessly follows another, the drugstore failure is immediately succeeded by an athletic counterpart. Stumbling by and discovering Clayton's baseball field, Ronald returns in uniform to join a crowd of would-be players around the coach. Finally selected to play third base for the second team, he launches his baseball career. It will sink after only one inning.

As his three athletic roommates watch from the sidelines, serving like the dude in the drugstore as a chorus of comic response to lead the audience's reaction, they suddenly begin doubling up with laughter. What they see is disclosed. It is Ronald, now standing by third base, cautiously rigged out in complete catcher's attire—face mask, chest protector, and leg guards. One of them obligingly advises him on what the well-dressed, less-dressed third baseman should be wearing, and then the game begins, or at least it begins as soon as Ronald, who has stationed himself directly on top of third base, is ordered off it. Moving to the side he dusts it, and then, inspiration suggesting no further activity, looks about to see what the others are doing. They are all crouched, hands on knees, waiting, so he does the same.

As it turns out, he waits very well, still holding the pose when the first batter hits a grounder that rolls through his legs unstopped till it reaches the left fielder. Yelled at by him and now knowing what is expected, Ronald intently scans the ground as the next batter hits a line drive just over his head. This produces runners on first and second, and again a new move is introduced to confuse Ronald when the man on second attempts to steal third. The catcher throws the ball, Ronald unprepared misses it, and then he is bowled over by the sliding runner, who winds up safely on base. As the runner limberly hops about, prepared to take off again, Ronald dubiously and nervously eyes him. Then the batter hits a grounder toward Ronald, who, ready for this, stops it, picks it up, and then holds it, not knowing what to do next. When the infielder excitedly approaches, Ronald politely hands it to him, while the man on third races home and scores a run for the other side. In triple response to Ronald's ignorance, the infielder angrily throws down the ball and points to the catcher, who angrily throws down his glove, as the coach angrily watches.

With men once again on first and second, the next batter hits a line drive over Ronald, the still focus of much action. The left fielder catches the ball for the first out and throws it to second base, which makes the man advancing from first to second out. The second baseman throws the ball to the catcher, who waits for the one runner left, now racing toward home plate, but when the catcher starts toward him, the runner reverses and heads back to third. Not trusting Ronald to execute a squeeze play, other players hurry up to trap him. Ronald watches as the ball is tossed back and forth among them, but when the runner suddenly makes a desperate lunge for third, Ronald jumps there ahead of him and catches the ball before he is knocked over. The last out is declared.

The three onlookers, ready for more laughs, hand Ronald a bat and wait for new disasters. Awkwardly holding the bat upright, the incredible rookie moves to home plate, where the first batter in the lineup pushes him out of the way, assumes an accomplished stance, and hits a double. Again Ronald advances to the plate, still holding the bat upright, and again he is chased away as the next batter approaches, limbering up with three bats swung simultaneously. Taking his place, he discards two of them, and Ronald picks them up, imitatively trying his own three-bat swing. He whirls them in a successful arc, but like the sliding soda in the drugstore they gain too much momentum, stopping only as they slam against his head. Dropping them, he rubs his skull and dazedly wanders off, looking back at the bats with a hurt and puzzled expression, as if the fault were somehow theirs.

The second batter at this point also hits a double, and as Ronald's turn in the batting order now actually comes up, there are men on second and third. Assuming an awkward stance and facing away from the plate, he is correctly positioned by the catcher. Again, however, not knowing what to do, he watches as two strikes whiz by him. Then, as he turns to the catcher, he is struck on the rear by the third pitch. He leaps into the catcher's arms and topples him, but having been hit by a pitched ball, he also advances to first. He stands there for a while, rubbing his aching backside, another in his rapidly accumulating collection of sore spots. Next, he tries to steal second but immediately trips as he starts off first and therefore quickly thinks better of it. Then the batter hits a pop fly, and Ronald runs, even though the infielder catches it. Racing around the bases, past the runners who stand on second and third, he strenuously reaches home in a combination somersault and slide. Looking up, he sees the umpire, who looks down, wagging three fingers as he declares, "You forced two men out and you're out too." Shoved by the catcher, hit by another player, kicked by the coach, threatened by everyone, Ronald stumbles away defeated, a Charlie Brown of the baseball world.

Such ignominy marking Ronald as a perfect victim, once off the field he is surrounded by his roommates, Jeff, and a boisterous crowd that soon runs up to assist. The Clayton freshman most likely to be hazed, he is dropped in a blanket, carried over by a dormitory, and tossed into the air. When he is tossed, it soon becomes apparent that the dormitory is a women's dorm. Inside a second-story window, just at the apex of Ronald's ascent, an ample-busted lady, perhaps an outsize dean of women, combs her hair, clothed only in a not-very-revealing slip and dressing gown. Detecting Ronald, who keeps bobbing up outside her window, she objects to an aerial Peeping Tom and throws an umbrella at him. When he catches and opens the umbrella, it acts (in beautifully managed slow-motion photography) like a parachute. As he reaches the window, he now noticeably pauses, sitting in the air while he looks inside, and only afterward leisurely descends. Finally he discards the umbrella and

grabs onto a tiny balcony outside the window, whereupon the infuri-
ated lady leans over it and begins lambasting him. The balcony
crumbles, and hazing ends as the two of them plummet into the
blanket below. The tormenters immediately scatter, and then the fat
lady dazedly sits up, recovering just in time to be tipped over and
knocked flat once again, for Ronald crawls from beneath her and
runs like the others.

The episode has helped reinforce Ronald's unathletic and alien
status among his peers, it has provided the one exception to an
otherwise too mechanical alternation of sport and work activities,
and also, as usual with events that occur before the turning point for
a Keaton hero, it has provided an ignominious situation that will
afterward be repeated in a heroic context. At the film's end Ronald
will once again be involved with the second-story window of a lady's
room, but instead of bouncing he will athletically vault up to and
through it in order to rescue Mary.

Immediately following the hazing a restaurant sign, "Wanted
Colored Waiter," introduces Ronald's second occupational turn.
Like clerking at a soda fountain, posing as a colored waiter is a job
that will end in embarrassment and disaster, but till the end he does
very well, adroitly concealing inexperience with imaginative innova-
tion. The first shot is of a dining room, as black waiters truck back
and forth through a pair of swinging doors that lead to the kitchen.
They are doors naturally that continually threaten to smack someone,
particularly whenever Ronald goes through them. The inevitable collision, however, is long delayed, so frequently set up and then
avoided that its repeated failure to occur becomes as funny as the
actual final event. Ronald himself first appears coming out through
the doors. Professionally outfitted in a waiter's uniform of baggy
white and also wearing white gloves and a small white cap that sets
off his vivid black face, he clumsily places a bowl of soup in front of
an instantly complaining customer. Sent back to the kitchen with the
order, "Bring me something you can't stick your thumb in," he
returns with a coconut. Then, after another trip to the kitchen, he
brings an empty bowl with an overturned cup placed in its center.
This is set before the customer, the cup is lifted, and soup pours
forth, guaranteed untouched by a waiter's thumb as it fills the bowl.

Going back to the kitchen, Ronald then takes the coconut with him, holding it in the crook of his arm like a football and charging violently through the doors.

In the kitchen, a pretty black cook smiles at Ronald, while a sullen black dishwasher angrily looks on. Then, when Ronald returns to the dining room, his second pair of customers sit down. In repetition of his drugstore humiliation, they are again Jeff and Mary. At first Ronald pretends not to notice them, but when the manager orders him to do so, he approaches their table and with averted face hands them a menu. When they curiously scrutinize him, he intensifies his disguise, rapidly but shiftlessly ambling away in a loose-jointed, rubber-boned shuffle, a racist cliché of a comic darkie's walk. As he conveys their order to the cook in the kitchen, she again ogles him, while the dishwasher glares. Coming back into the dining room, he carries a bowl of soup, holding it high and elegantly balanced in the palm of his hand. Just outside the door, he drops a napkin, and when he stoops over to retrieve it, he is predictably slapped from behind as another waiter enters. The swinging door knocks him into a complete somersault, but the arm holding the bowl remains straight, the wrist supply twists, and the soup is neither dropped nor even spilled. What he has lost, however, is the blackface on his right cheek, wiped away in the tumble, and when Jeff notices this, Ronald scurries, shuffling for cover.

Back in the kitchen, he steps between the angry dishwasher and the flirtatious cook. They are both occupied at a table full of knives, and when they detect Ronald's underlying whiteness, a minor race riot erupts. Everyone in the kitchen grabs a knife, and led by the cook, who wields a cleaver, they take out after Ronald. Whipping for the last time through the swinging doors, he climaxes the long anticipated but till now generally avoided or at least muted collision, knocking over an entering waiter with a full load of about-to-be-broken dishes. Racing past Mary and Jeff, who laughingly points at him, he reaches the street, slips and falls, and then rises and runs on. His second job has ended in a blaze of failure even more ego-consuming than the first.

The restaurant scene, which has been described with a noncommittal objectivity, is one of the most extended examples of Keaton's use of racial humor, an area, like his use of the passively inspiring Victorian heroine, in which his films have become dated, fortunately for society but less happily for Keaton. However, even if they are socially unregenerate, many of his racial jokes remain funny, and that includes everything in this scene, even the darkie shuffle. The many audiences with whom I have watched the film (admittedly always dominantly white) have always laughed as loud at the black gags as at any of the others. And, as observed earlier, the laughter is defensible, even today. If there is an uncomfortable acceptance of then current clichés and prejudices in the gags, such as the assumed affinity in the kitchen between blacks and knives, there is no malice in them. Rather they result from a formulaic reliance on stock comic types endowed with stock comic traits, who when introduced on the screen could be quickly programmed to do their funny thing and produce unmalicious if socially unredeemed laughter. The black characters in the films are not presented as real people; they are simply ethnic jokes, laughable caricatures, in the same way as the dean of women at her dormitory window was not real but only a fat-lady joke, one of the physical clichés comically popular at the time.

Just as many ethnic jokes today, involving stock comic Irishmen or stock comic Poles or stock comic whomever, seem reasonably harmless, safe outlets for everyone's occasional need to feel superior to someone else and to indulge in the ego-gratifying pleasure of derisive laughter, so, also, the individual black jokes of Keaton seem harmless. In aggregate, however, they do become disturbing. The unsettling fact is not that Keaton's blacks are comic caricatures in ethnic gags, but that they are rarely anything else. A complete summary of their appearances in gags and elsewhere comprises, fortunately, only eighteen items, but that is enough to produce an unpleasant cumulative effect. In addition to the scene in *College,* there is in *Sherlock Junior* a menial black woman, carrying a large basket of laundry, who is bowled over by the hero's speeding motorcycle. In *The Navigator* there is the early gag of the grinning bride and groom in their jalopy limousine, a low black parody of a rich white man's wedding, which inspires the hero to the idea of his own marriage; and then at the end there is the tribe of comic blacks on their cannibal isle, the aborigines who wage war against the white hero and heroine. In *Seven Chances*, the most racially exploitative of the features, just as it was the most exploitative of women and of physical grotesques, there are five examples: the Stepin Fetchit handyman (played by a white actor in blackface), who delivers with molasses slowness the crucial note sent by the heroine to the hero; a black man at the country club, who is dressed like the hero and momentarily mistaken, to the latter's distress, for a mirror image of him; a black woman on the sidewalk, whom the hero first approaches and then when he sees her face decides not to propose to; one of the brides in the church, a fat black woman in a cook's hat, who angrily tweaks the hero's nose; and fifth, a black shoeshine man, who when asked the time has only a bottle opener at the end of his watch fob.

In *Go West*, another black shoeshine man turns up in a Los Angeles barber shop, from which he is soon sent riding on the bouncing back of a bull, a comic rodeo clown who is somehow, like the one black bride or the overturned laundress, supposed to be all the funnier for being black. There is also a black street entertainer, dancing with happy feet before a small audience until first they and then he are frightened off by the hero's threatening herd. Since he dances beside an Italian organ grinder, who plays for him, he may also be intended, in an unpleasantly racist joke, as a comic substitute for the music-maker's traditional monkey. In *Steamboat Bill Jr.*, when the hero's father, who has not seen him for many years, looks for him at a railroad station, he approaches several strangers, including one discovered with a comic recoil to be black. Later there is also a little black boy, sitting on a dock in the dark and singing and strumming his banjo, who is suddenly frightened into a tumble when the hero emerges from the river in front of him. Again, he is a figure supposedly more funny because black and therefore easily frightened by horrors in the night.

Though they are not used for denigrating jokes, black actors also appear in *Our Hospitality* and *Battling Butler,* and like the black actors in the other films, are confined to stereotyped racial roles. In the first, there is a courtly old black butler in the Canfield mansion, and in the second, there is the Alabama Murderer, the boxer whom the hero thinks he must fight. Similarly, in the opening shot of *Steamboat Bill Jr.* black workers are briefly seen laboring in a cotton field to help establish the atmosphere of a southern river town.

The one feature from which blacks are almost entirely absent is *The General,* where they are present in a single shot only, appearing in the prologue as workers unloading boxes from the hero's train, inconspicuous figures who are almost invisible and easily overlooked in the crowd of passengers at the Marietta station. In a Civil War film, even in a Civil War comedy, blacks could not easily be dismissed in Keaton's unintentionally dismissive gags. Their presence would have recalled one reason for the war, and that would have introduced an unfunny element of social concern. In the vaudeville world of the films, seriousness of that sort is always carefully avoided or rather never even remotely contemplated. Stock comic darkies, unreal and laughable ethnic jokes, are entertaining and therefore welcome. Black slaves simply do not and could not exist. The Keaton darkies, like everything else in his films, are necessarily limited by the need to be funny. They are, therefore, a banjo-playing, toe-tapping, knife-waving crew—comic servants, shoeshine boys, waiters, and dishwashers—all outsiders and extras to be brought in for an immediate laugh and then to be passed over quickly as the films move on to their next gag.

As Hollywood continued to do for many decades, until it became profitable to do something else, Keaton's comedies obviously approach oppressed minority groups from the point of view of the ticket-buying majority. With an astonishing exactness, the films conform to all of the then current prejudices. Blacks are always seen as alien and other, as musical, emotional, and inferior, a race of servants and menials, whose existence is separate and decidedly unequal. A fuller sense of their outsider status in the films, though it is something the films themselves discourage our thinking about, can be suggested by a comparison of them to the hero, who himself always begins as an outsider. If he is initially presented as a loner, he is not really alienated and set apart. Instead, he is the classic comic protagonist, who begins as alien but winds up accepted, a hero in the society that had rebuffed him. One of the reasons his rejection by his peers or his girl or her family is so funny, a cause of audience laughter rather than dismay, is that there is never any doubt that basically he belongs and that in the end he will win them over. The average Keaton hero is not a rebel, like Chaplin's Tramp, but rather at best a would-be Republican, a conservative soul who through ignorance, ineptitude, and unlucky circumstance has been ostracized by his girl and her social circle and thereafter fights determinedly to be accepted by them. His acceptance always comes, and after all the humiliations, his final victory is for most audiences a joyous and genuinely enjoyed occasion, a comic triumph of togetherness that all the rest of the film has been emotionally building toward. Excluded earlier, he wins his way in. Disapproved, he is admired by the end.

The blacks, however, are simply accepted throughout as unacceptable, with no chance of ever being included in the hero's world. They and not he are the true outsiders in the films, existing in a segregated state, a state most clearly revealed in the several gags where their being momentarily mistaken for a socially acceptable person is intended to be incongruous, impossible, and wonderfully funny. A more detailed description of these gags, which are also unpleasantly tainted by anti-Semitism, will demonstrate Keaton's almost automatic reliance on repressive ethnic stereotypes to produce what at that time were easy laughs.

In *Seven Chances* and *Steamboat Bill Jr.*, similar episodes occur. In the first, when the hero is finishing his seventeen unsuccessful marriage proposals, the proposals at the end of the sequence are structured to become more and more comically farfetched and implausible, culminating in an absurdly catastrophic climax. The last acceptable woman proposed to is obviously a WASP, driving her Stutz Bearcat. She is followed by a woman reading a Yiddish newspaper, who is followed by a black woman, who is followed by a wooden dummy, which is followed by a female impersonator. The final quartet are all evidently meant to be increasingly unlikely choices, comically existing beyond the fringe of nineteen-twenties' WASP society. Similarly, in *Steamboat Bill Jr.* when the father searches for the hero at the railroad station, he approaches and asks several strangers if they are his son, and this time the series is organized to begin and end with an alienating laugh. It starts with an approach to and startled withdrawal from a man who is revealed to be black, and it ends in the same way with an orthodox Jew when his identifying beard becomes visible. Even where overtones of exclusion are less apparent, an automatic linking of such cultural outsiders is still apparent. In *Go West*, as the hero proceeds through Los

Angeles on his cattle drive, in a sequence emphasizing individual victims of the herd he first frightens a long-bearded Jewish pushcart peddler and then immediately afterward the black street entertainer. Ostracized when he meets these two, the hero will proceed to save the heroine and her father from ruin and be accepted by the WASP ranch society; the street people are the real outsiders in the film, urban exotics briefly encountered and then quickly passed by.

Such a distressing treatment of minorites in the films can be historically explained, even though the explanation does not remove the blemish. What can be said in extenuation is that Keaton once again, as he does in other ways with happier results, reflects his age. It was an ethnic age, one we are apt nostalgically to look back on now as a time of cultural vitality and variety, particularly when compared to our own drab cultural homogenization with its weakened values and traditions. As a strongly ethnic period, however, it was also a time of derisive ethnic stereotyping, of ethnic separatism and mistrust. Irving Howe's *World of Our Fathers* describes a vital first-generation Jewish immigrant culture in New York; it also suggests how isolated that culture was, existing within a closed Christian society that was ignorant and abusive of it. Similarly, in the nineteen-twenties any black much older than sixty had probably been born a slave, and many whites believed and wanted to keep on believing that blacks were only fit for slavelike menial labor.

If the age produced great ethnic popular art, like the classic comic songs of Fanny Brice or the ragtime music of Scott Joplin, it also produced in its popular arts much ethnic and cultural derision, and Keaton's ethnic humor, unfortunately, is of the second very common sort. His numerous black jokes always deride rather than celebrate physical differences; his two Jewish jokes reject rather than appreciate cultural differences. One Irish joke that turns up in the features and that can be mentioned for the sake of completeness is also predictably derogatory. As Sherlock Junior on his motorcycle runs into a tug-of-war at Tom Murphy's picnic, the two anchor men tied to the rope are dragged by the motorcycle until they are dropped in a stream, whereupon, being stereotyped brawl-loving Irish, they immediately begin a violent fight with each other. Like Keaton's other ethnic jokes, this one seems to pander to WASP feelings of cultural superiority.

The only good thing that can be said is that the Irish joke, like the others, at least does not inflame WASP prejudices. In fact, it is only under cumulative analysis that Keaton's ethnic humor seems unpleasant. When individually his ethnic jokes flash by on the screen, existing for only a few seconds in a context of many other jokes, they impress instead as brief and harmless laughs—ignorant, culturally smug, but in the context of their smug, ignorant, ethnically divided age relatively unmalicious. It seems likely, too, that even if WASP-pandering jokes were used in the films, nineteen-twenties' WASP prejudices were not shared by the movie-makers. Keaton himself was of Irish descent, and his producer, Joseph Schenck, without whom there would have been no Keaton Studio, was Jewish, as was the second most memorable performer in the films, Snitz Edwards, who is the lawyer in *Seven Chances,* the supercilious upper-class valet in *Battling Butler,* and the understanding dean in *College.* (To recall one earlier Jewish name indispensable to Keaton's career, there was also the great Harry Houdini, who in his barnstorming days, before he went on to become a hero of *Ragtime*, provided the infant Joseph Francis, and the world, with the immortal nickname—Buster.) Even with the continually denigrated blacks, there is also one partial exception to the customary racist squelching. In *Seven Chances,* dismayed by the rebuff of all the country club beauties, the hero reassuringly checks his appearance in a door mirror, turns aside, and then looks in the mirror once again. While he is turned, however, the door opens, and a black man, elegantly dressed in a suit just like the hero's, steps into the doorway. When the hero looks again, he is therefore stunned by his apparent blackface reflection, a slur, in the days before black was beautiful, on the presumed aesthetic inferiority of black to white. If the joke exists because of the slur, which causes the laugh, it also matter of factly serves to integrate a ritzy nineteen-twenties' country club. The expensively attired black, stepping out of what seems to be a lounge filled with chintz-covered furniture, must be either a member, a guest, or an officer. The integration seems as unintended as it is unlikely, a social inconsistency casually inserted for the sake of the joke, but when a joke demanded it, the film-makers could as easily accept and promote integration as they could elsewhere exploit darkie stereotypes. Admittedly, though, it takes an incredible strain to find and magnify this one momentary shot of redeeming social value. If the films inescapably have racist elements, they are obviously in no meaningful sense racist movies, though that consolation may not be enough to keep a modern admirer of them from feeling some discomfort at their moral failings. A point to repeat and remember, however, is that the only seemingly real person in most of the films is the hero, with nearly everyone else reduced to an extra, a romantic or a comic type or an ethnic joke, and never intended to be viewed as more than that. Taken seriously as real people in a real world, they would not be funny, but in many ways the films are artificial and shallow enough that seriously is not how they need or should be taken. A few moral reservations and an awareness of their humanistic limitations are unavoidable, but after that the films can still be laughed at, even *College* as the black-faced Ronald shuffles his way into an angry crowd of knife-waving blacks in the menial quarters of their kitchen.

Returning to *College* and the by now perhaps muted laughs it contains, the discovery of Ronald's disguise ends his employment as a waiter, and the dash from the restaurant simultaneously parallels and predicts his next athletic endeavor. The alternation of work and sports continues as a title introduces "Clayton's wonder track team training for the intercollegiate meet." Then Ronald enters, dressed in his track suit and determined to make the team. Imitatively chasing after some runners, he begins one of the longest of the great Keaton gag chains, each of whose deliberately weak links is a comically misperformed track event. Though Ronald's tryout is one long humiliation, it also becomes an exemplary demonstration of pluck. Like most Keaton heroes, when Ronald sets out to do something, he does it with a single-minded, almost mindless, determination. He becomes so fixated on the events he performs that he is oblivious of everything else—the laughter of others, his own inadequacies, the obvious impossibility of success. Just as there is a joy in engaging wholeheartedly in anything, so there is a similar and less strenuous joy in watching anybody else engage wholeheartedly in anything, when his whole being becomes absorbed in the action, when he is totally what he is doing and exists only as an illustration of it. And though Ronald does not achieve his goal, he does exist and function beautifully at this basic level. He is what he does, it is a wonder to watch him being and doing it, and the sequence is the visual highlight of the film, the comedy of action conveying as well a beauty of action, an almost mesmerizing grace of action.

Ronald's troubles start as he mimics another runner by limbering up with a stationary run. His clumsily flailing legs first propel him backward before he reverses direction and converts to a forward dash. When he stops, an act rather like braking on a freeway, he is instantly overtaken by other runners and nearly smashed into. Cautiously looking about to make sure there is no more speeding traffic, he then timidly leaves the track.

A large heavy-set athlete next demonstrates a shot put, Mary and her girlfriend are shown in a cutaway entering the stadium, and then Ronald walks up to the shot, ready to try another event. He manages to assume the proper form, holding it in his right hand a little above and behind his right shoulder, ready to exert a strenuous forward shove. The shot's weight, however, unbalances him, and he falls over backward, whereupon he once again walks away from a failed performance.

After the shot put, more running. A sprinter's distance is measured and timed, and while Mary watches, though no one else pays any attention, Ronald also sets out to time a dash of his own. At the starting line, he checks his wristwatch and starts running. At the same moment, two small boys on the field begin to fight, and one chases the other. As Ronald exerts himself, they suddenly follow his course, overtake him, and soon easily leave him behind. Slowing down, he looks after them and then sits dejectedly, his drooping head supported by his hand.

After the running, more throwing, this time the discus. This time, too, Dean Edwards is present, at the side of the stadium, talking to several others and as always formally dressed, even in a perfect-target top hat. After a professional demonstration by someone else, Ronald throws the discus, which flies far and, to the dean's angry surprise, hits its fated target. Not seeing where it went, Ronald meanwhile looks about for it, apprehensively looks up, and then, with his hands behind his back, once again walks away.

The dean, having been inauspiciously introduced, is now added to Ronald's audience, and he watches as the javelin throw is taken up. Facing the camera from the far background, an athlete hurls the javelin into the air; it falls to earth in the near foreground. Starting from the same position, Ronald runs forward to add momentum to his heave, and then he, too, throws the javelin, which lands some fifteen feet in front of him. A mighty try having produced a puny result, Ronald again puts his hands behind his back, and, as if nothing had happened, walks away.

While Ronald performs a series of low variations on the high jump, his audience temporarily increases. Jeff joins Mary, and soon the two quarrel. Though he scorns his rival as a "campus clown," she sympathizes ("At least he is trying"), and when Jeff angrily leaves, she remains to watch. As high jump failure is followed by broad jump failure, by a hurdle race failure, by an uncontrolled dervish's whirl of a hammer throw, she sadly views the world's worst athlete perform. When she finally departs, Ronald is still doggedly attempting to fly into a pole vault after three crash landings, though obviously with no real hope of ever soaring into success.

After two failures at athletics and two failures at work, the final sports sequence and the customary great Keaton reversal are prepared for when Ronald is called into Dean Edwards's office. The dean observes that because of his baseball and track efforts, he is failing in his studies. Ronald explains the need to impress Mary, and the sympathetic dean not only understands but, when the rowing coach enters with a list of men eligible for the crew, orders that Ronald be made coxswain.

Understandably unhappy about this, the coach afterward predicts to the crew that something is likely to happen to the "poor boy," and then a title quickly announces "The day of the race." The remainder of the film takes place on this day, and as usual for the last day of a Keaton film, it is one of change for the hero. Preceding the change, there is even the usual sleep, though in this case it will be that of someone else. When the regular coxswain complains to the coach that "nothing has happened to mama's boy," he is handed two cups of coffee, one with powder in it. The coach explains, "Don't worry, you're coxswain. Give him this and he'll wake up just in time for the football season." In the crew dining room, however, the two cups are accidentally switched, and it is the coxswain who downs the drugged drink. A cutaway to Jeff, meanwhile, shows him entering Mary's room, where, despite her objections, he closes and locks the door and pockets the key, adding, "I'm going to stay here until we are discovered . . . then you might change your mind about marrying me." Back at the boathouse, the regular coxswain soon falls asleep, and when the horrified coach cannot awaken him, Ronald is reluctantly sent off as a replacement.

Eagerly running to the dock, he reaches the water before his crew. When they walk up behind him, therefore, carrying the shell, its tip passes between his legs and he suddenly finds himself uncomfortably lifted into the air and then dropped. As the crew maneuvers the long boat toward the dockside and water, he is next almost flattened by it and must run to escape its threatening sweep. Then, as he watches from a safe distance, the shell is launched. Its name, inauspiciously borrowed from a rapidly sinking predecessor in a Keaton two-reeler, is shown in closeup, "Damfino." Ronald fastens the rudder to its stern, and from the dock orders the crew to shove off, which they do, moving the shell some four feet out into the water. Realizing that he has created a predicament for himself, Ronald responds by leaping to the boat, coming down into it feet first and going right through the keel. After everyone has swum back to the dock, a new shell is brought out, "Old Iron Bottom," and this time Ronald gingerly seats himself in it before the rowers step in. Then the crowd cheers, an official waves, and Ronald and his crew move to the starting line.

The contest begins badly, for Ronald, preoccupied with his sun-shade and also looking back to see where he has been, steers the Clayton shell too close to its rivals. Only after many interlocked oars have been untangled can serious racing begin. Then, Ronald shouts his orders and the crew rows, while on shore the coach and the dean excitedly watch, and occasionally a cutaway discloses the two prin-ciple nonwatchers, Mary and Jeff, both still locked in her room. In spirit, however, Mary is very much present, for a brilliantly comic closeup of Ronald calling through his megaphone superimposes her face within the circle of the megaphone's rim, a reminder of her inspirational presence and a portent that Ronald, so inspired, will at last come through a winner, a modern-day collegiate knight in an aquatic tournament. In the meantime, of course, his difficulties continue, for as he jerks on the control rope, his rudder, inexpertly attached, falls off. After a brief pause for a horrified response, however, he ingeniously and absurdly ties it on behind him, edges his way back to the tip of the shell, kicks himself a handhold, and soon sits there, his rear extended over the water and the rudder once again in operation. While counting time and shouting orders, he holds out his right leg to shift the rudder, steering his shell around a raft full of onlookers, and then holds out his left leg to bring it back on course. Like Willie, who transformed himself into a train's signaling device in *Our Hospitality*, Ronald has made himself a part of the mechanism he is involved with, literally embodying its actions and triumphantly making them his own. As he expertly if unconventionally steers, a combined coxswain and rudder, the Clayton shell overtakes the rival crew. Then, while the spectators shout their approval, it pulls into the lead at the finish line and the race is won.

After a capsizing that comically undercuts his glory, Rollo and the other crew members return to the dock. There they are greeted by their girls and leave in hugging pairs, but after looking for his girl, Ronald stands alone. Mary, however, at this point manages to call for help. Answering the crew house telephone, Ronald hears her cry, "Hurry . . . Jeff has me locked here in my room, and he . . . " The sentence is not completed, for Jeff takes her phone at this point and breaks its wire. However, the message suffices to propel Ronald into action.

Success in rowing is now followed by success in track and successes in other sports as well, though it is success of a curious sort, for on this day of glory, Ronald will demonstrate a determined proficiency at all of them only as he races to Mary's rescue, instantly inspired by the need to save her to accomplishments formerly far beyond him. First there is a high jump as he races and leaps out of the locker room window. Then there is a sprint along the sidewalk, followed by something like a football player's agile evasions as he weaves his rapid way through a large crowd of slower movers. There is next a high jump as he leaps a tall hedge, and his progression then changes into a hurdle race as he runs and leaps over four low hedges, ending with a spectacular leap over one both high and wide. An ornamental pond in his way forces him to execute a broad jump, and as Mary calls from her window, he comes sliding around a fence corner like an expert base stealer and runs the final length of an open yard toward her dormitory. Grabbing a handy pole that supports a clothesline as he passes, he pole-vaults with it up to and through her second-story window, a success that makes up not just for his former track failure, but also for the ignominious blanket bounce to the window of the dean of women. Twisting through a somersault that lands him on his feet inside, without a pause in his movements he starts grabbing china from Mary's dresser and throwing it at Jeff. A bottle is hurled, a plate is heaved like a discus, and Jeff is struck by both. More objects are thrown, including a doll hurled like a javelin, and then when Jeff also starts throwing things, Ronald grabs a paddle from the wall. Using it like a baseball bat, he slams Jeff's missiles back at him, scoring a hit. As Jeff gives up the fight and scrambles toward the door, Ronald downs him with a football tackle, forcing him to run instead to a window, from which he desperately leaps, closely followed by a flying table. A shot outside discloses Jeff descending on a slowly lowering fire escape rather than falling to the ground, but his troubles are still not over. Ronald heaves a floor lamp through the window like a javelin, and traveling far and straight, it nearly hits his fleeing opponent. Looking back to see what else might be hurtling his way, Jeff consequently runs into the clothesline, now drooping without its pole. Hitting it, he is jerked into a pratfall, and that is the last of a thoroughly routed rival.

Jeff's defeat marks Ronald's victory, which is a typical Keaton triumph, even though it has taken far longer than usual for the turning point in the hero's fortunes to come. His day of glory occupies only about the last ten minutes of the film, and till then there has been no real indication on his part that he could ever reach it. The leap from failure to success is a surprising contrast suitable for a comedy but obviously without much psychological validity. Not only the heroine, not only the fat-lady dean and the knife-waving blacks in the film are presented as fictitiously comic stereotypes, but so in many ways is the Keaton hero. Ronald may seem real, but that is only because he is there on the screen most of the time, acquiring a reality for the audience through action. But at the heart of this running, jumping, somersaulting figure, who so engagingly engages our attention with the captivating moves of classic action comedy, there is no real person, only a calculated assault on the viewers' feelings. As is frequent in Hollywood films, the hero is basically no more than a device to attract the audience, skillfully constructed to hold their emotional sympathies and interest. In Keaton's manipulative formula, he is initially an underdog and at least partial misfit in the film's world, someone who is bullied or mistreated or mostly ignored by the society in which he lives. Though rejected by the characters in the film, however, he is made intensely appealing to the viewers— in Ronald's case, in addition to his underdog status, through his ingratiating comic presence, as someone who makes us laugh and whom therefore we are inclined to like, and as someone, too, who energetically and pluckily tries and tries and fails again, building up our desire for his success. The other characters, meanwhile, are reduced to animated cutouts, cardboard presences like the ethnic and physical jokes or the dramatically underdeveloped antagonists or the passively onlooking heroine—all deliberately planned not to become too real, not to develop psychological depth, and not to engage our emotions or interest in challenge to Ronald. Rather they are all just foils to set off the hero, to make him and him alone seem real and worth feeling about. The result, in the somewhat dreamlike ambience of a movie theater, is that the audience is forced to identify with the hero, for like themselves in their own dreams he becomes the only seemingly real presence in a world of images. His victory is theirs, and when after much frustration he finally breaks through and wins, they will vicariously share his triumph. Not only will they share it, they will actively want it, and when they see it happening they will for the moment fully believe in it.

The hero's triumph has been made so pleasant a vicarious experience that it is accepted. Ronald's breakthrough is such a gloriously sustained action sequence that its weight makes it seem real, a desirable and, while it is being watched, obviously actual occurrence and conversion. But in this case, though not always in Keaton, a little post-film reflection quickly leads to the conclusion that the emotional satisfaction is gained at the expense of psychological and experiential realism. Ronald's failures as sadsack athlete are too prolonged. When it comes, the change in his abilities is too formulaically and inadequately explained, with the crucial turning point obviously imposed to provide a stock happy ending. Though the film grants Ronald and the viewers identifying with him an emotional pleasure the latter have been conditioned to want and are eagerly waiting for, it does so at the expense of all credibility. Thought about, which of course it should not be, Ronald's triumph is impossible. In contrast to some of the more extravagantly stylized features such as *Go West,* where the implausibility of the hero's triumph is deliberately part of the fantastic fun, and in contrast to some of the more realistic features such as *The General,* where it develops irresistibly out of the dramatic situation, in *College* the hero's triumph is simply the result of an abrupt character change imposed to meet the needs of formulaic and escapist entertainment. The total athletic failure, the bookworm Ronald, cannot instantly turn into an athletic superstar, even under the impetus of love and danger. The athletic skills he displays in his last dash are not immediately acquired, nor is it likely that such a character as he is assumed to be at the start could easily develop them, except, to recall unfavorably the opening chapter on all the films, in the ego-gratifying realm of wish-fulfillment fantasy. Of the various formulas behind the Keaton features, that is the one most fully in control here, and ultimately it makes Ronald as unreal as any of the other stock comic figures in the film.

But then it is also true that Ronald never really lacked athletic ability. In another of the film's amiable and unreal fraudulences, Keaton's athleticism is as well displayed in the brilliant and deliberate comic misperformance of a sports event as in its successful execution. That is why the baseball and track routines are the highlights of the film, making it a joy to watch despite its dramatic inadequacies. It is doubtful that anyone viewing the earlier parts of the film, certainly not any Keaton fan, actually takes him for the uncoordinated novice he is pretending to be. Rather, and here the personality of the movie star enters into the viewing experience, the knowledgeable audience of Keaton fans is aware from the beginning that it is watching Buster Keaton, engaged in extravagantly athletic comic action and playing a typical Buster Keaton role in a typical Buster Keaton movie. From the beginning, they know the end, even if not the specific ingenious ways in which it will be arranged. As they watch, they are consciously and happily deceived, acquiescing in the experiential and psychological fraudulence of the picture for the pleasure of viewing a favorite entertainer who comically leads them through an agreeable emotional experience. Total failure instantaneously replaced by total victory is rarely encountered in real life, but it still makes a wonderfully appealing illusion as Keaton simulates it for us on the screen.

So analyzed, *College* may seem rather shallow, but then, to extend palinodic comment from this movie to most movies, it is possible that film is in many ways a shallow and escapist medium. What understanding of human nature lies behind it, certainly, does not easily or often lead to the necessarily complex depiction of psychologically credible characters and events. Most often it leads to a manipulation of the audience's psychology, to an effort to draw them into the simple but satisfying dreams of glory that film is best capable of creating.

In fact, so well does it lend itself to a pleasant viewing experience, Keaton's trademark dream of glory is one that is still occasionally revived, though much refurbished to meet a modern movie-goer's expectations. Such a recent film as, say, Sam Peckinpah's *Straw Dogs* is made to the same wish-fulfillment design as *College*; it is just as agreeable and just as fraudulent a dream. In it, the milksop mathematician, played by the diminutive Dustin Hoffman, who is implausibly married to a mindless sex kitten, is humiliated and threatened for most of the film by some comic-strip heavies, who are the sole inhabitants of the unreal little town where he and his wife have settled. After much unlikely torment and torture, during which the audience has been completely won over to the suffering underdog hero (though also, with an emotional inconsistency, encouraged vicariously to enjoy the rape of his wife), the mathematician finally commits mayhem. In the film's last few minutes, he turns into a pint-size Sampson; and in a very satisfying but obviously fraudulent celebration of machismo, he mightily slaughters all his enemies. It is an illusionary slaughter, however, for he, his victory, and everyone and everything else in the film are transparently unreal contrivances, designed emotionally to involve and gratify the viewers and sacrificing all plausibility to this end. Allowing for an escalation in sex and violence, *Straw Dogs* is in the Keaton tradition, a perfect parallel in its emotional patterns and audience manipulation to *College*.

If Keaton's particular success fantasy rarely exists today in its pure form, if it has been replaced by or itself turned into fantasies of sex and violence, still fantasies of some sort remain the movies' prime business. Hollywood is still manufacturing escapism for the masses. There are and have been very few film-makers in America who, like Jean Renoir in France, have the capacity and opportunity to think about the real world in a film, few who have captured some of its reality in a sufficiently large-minded way that they can compel an intellectual viewer's intelligent interest. Most, like Keaton or Peckinpah, turn instead to stock patterns of agreeable emotional fantasy with certified audience appeal, though few have crafted such comic and lasting entertainments from them as Keaton.

Returning to *College*, which is not quite over, back in her room Ronald hugs Mary, just as Dean Edwards and the gorgonesque dean of women enter from the hall. Scandalized, the latter asks, "Young lady, do you know what this means?" Mary's immediate reply is "Yes . . . it means we are going to be married." After a moment's stunned hesitation, Ronald decisively picks her up and leaps through the window, a move that startles the two oldsters into running forward. Outside, just like Jeff, the two young lovers slowly descend on the fire escape. Then, as the elders watch from the window, the two run up the steps of the campus chapel. In a double exposure, they immediately walk back down them, married. For the third time, a Keaton feature ends in an actual wedding.

Except, *College* does not end here. As if in recoil from all the formulas and fraudulences of his unreal screen art, Keaton adds a three-shot epilogue that transcends them. He had already undercut the clichéd romantic endings of popular movies in *Go West* and *The General,* augmenting and therefore undermining the obligatory final shot of boy and girl together by turning it first into boy and girl and cow together and then into boy and girl and locomotive together.

Now, in an emotionally complex revelation, both comic and sad, he shows what happens in real life after the conventional marriages that happily conclude romantic formula films. In the first shot, Ronald and Mary sit in their home several years later. She sews, he reads a paper, and three small children play in the background. In the second shot, they are alone and very old, sitting now in front of a fireplace, and he speaks, a little angrily it seems, to her. The final shot is of two tombstones, side by side. Around both ivy grows, the faintest echo of long-past adventure and love in their ivy-covered college youth. Together, the last three shots compose an ironic realist's deadly comment on the pleasant fantasies that have gone before.

11.

Steamboat Bill Jr.

MYTHIC TRANSCENDENCE

THOUGH it is possible to take a dim view of the Keaton features, and as in the discussion of *College* to dismiss the inevitable transformation of the hero as satisfying but spurious, it is also possible to view his change in more glorified terms. In the last way of nine ways of looking at a Keaton movie, the pattern of change emphasized in all his features—the hero's sudden acquisition of competence and autonomy—need not be described as an abstraction and comic intensification of the adolescent experience of learning and growing, or dismissed as an implausible and escapist dream of mundane glory. Rather, it can be seen as a semisecularization of mystic aspiration, a modern enactment of an age-old and still compelling myth of spiritual rebirth and of a vernal age of grace that follows from it.

The patterns of ancient myth are the patterns of man's most profound spiritual experience. The legends of Greece, for example, provided classical man with an emotionally and intellectually necessary expression for his sense of the universal order of things and the possible implications of this order for himself. As mythic criticism has long pointed out, the traditional forms of tragedy and comedy are also essentially mythological in their origins and over the centuries have retained a deep and ultimately religious significance. Tragedy is a ritualization of death and division, a dramatic means of confronting from a bearable distance the universal fate of all men. Every man dies, alone, and tragedy acknowledges this in its progressive sepa-

278

ration of the hero from all other men, as he moves toward the final and mysterious and total separation of death. Comedy, by contrast, in its mythic mood stresses resurrection and union. It is about the transcendence of death or deathlike states, and it is apt to celebrate the individual's rebirth into a new life and into a new and better world. Where tragedy is about ultimate endings and divisions, comedy is an affirmative rebuke and renunciation of alienation and death. In a seasonal paradigm, which is the basis of much mythology, tragedy posits the approach of eternal winter; comedy counters with the promise of a universal spring. Like many other myths, those of tragedy and comedy express man's sense of the natural world and its progressions, and of his own relation, actual or potential, to them.

All of which leads to *Steamboat Bill Jr.* Of the nine Keaton features, this is the one where the hero's transformation seems most to suggest the patterns of regenerative myth, where his conversion is closest to an April resurrection and heralds the springlike arrival of an almost heavenly kingdom of harmony and grace. It is the feature, too, where the hero, initially a typical Keaton fool or simpleton, seems most curiously spiritual, in the mystic tradition of a simpleton saint or holy fool, an idiot savant or a divinely inspired madman with a message of salvation for a winter world. Rather as a lyric poem might, a lyric poem by Yeats or Keats anyway, the film presents its mythic hero and his resurrection through a series of powerful if comic images, which evoke a slightly disturbing sense of his strangeness and a strongly felt awareness of his transcendent experience, doing this, however, in a slapstick way, from which laughter is never absent.

To speak of *Steamboat Bill Jr.* in such terms as these is, of course, to speak extravagantly, but then the joy of so seeing the film is too great to resist. Though it may remain doubtful whether the application of mythic criticism to the farcical film reveals an actual profundity in the latter or merely a certain speciousness in the former, still, the juxtaposition of the two is so unlikely and so Keatonesque a merging of opposites, that it is worth attempting. It must be stressed, however, that the film in no way knowingly uses mythology. It is not, like *Black Orpheus,* a modern and self-conscious retelling of an ancient myth, nor is it, like *Jonathan Livingston Seagull,* a self-conscious (and ludicrous) effort to create a new myth, to make a deep statement on death or the purpose of life. As always with Keaton, the film avoids thought, and is only concerned with comically telling its eminently secular and realistic story. But as that story is told, it resonates with a universal and spiritual desire whose archetypal patterns of conversion and rebirth lie behind its farcical actions, endowing them with a significance far beyond what is obtained by films that directly and ineptly aim at religious or mythic profundity. Such an assertion is better offered as ingenious speculation rather than as critical fact. Still, it is speculation that provides some not unreasonable insights into the emotional dynamics of the movie.

The last of Keaton's independent productions, it begins by cautiously establishing and repeating the dramatic situation of the first. Again there are two feuding families, reduced now to two quarreling fathers, in a small southern town, River Junction, Mississippi. As in *Our Hospitality,* one of the families is again named Canfield, and finally, too, there is a Romeo and Juliet pair of young lovers, their love crossed by the feud till, as before, the boy rescues the girl from a river. The feud and even the rescue, however, are secondary to a more important conflict and reconciliation, that between the hero and his father, and this is a variation which makes *Steamboat Bill Jr.* an entirely different picture from *Our Hospitality.* Considering that the Keaton hero is almost always a junior, a perennial adolescent, it seems inevitable that in one of the films a parent be an important character, and in this film the comic potentials of having a Keaton hero for a son are at last explored.

The customary expository title is omitted at the beginning in favor of a terser and more cryptic "Muddy Waters." A long slow pan discloses first the tributary river that gives River Junction its name, next a cotton field on the peninsula dividing the rivers, and then, as the camera movement momentarily stops, the Mississippi, on which in the distance a riverboat approaches. Attention having been concentrated on the boat, the pan continues to the opposite bank, revealing the town's waterfront, with bunting-draped buildings, a large crowd on the docks, and a second paddlewheel steamer anchored there. As with the ship in *The Navigator,* the boats have been introduced before the human characters, two of whom are now presented in carefully balanced shots that simultaneously suggest similarity and conflict. "The new steamer, King," pulls up to the dock in front of the stationary steamer, and then we see "J. J. King, owner," a plump, white-haired, formally dressed man, surrounded by his officers and friends. The next shot turns to "the old steamer, Stonewall Jackson," situated in the background behind the crowd that is waving and cheering for the new rival. "The owner, William Canfield, better known as Steamboat Bill," in closeup looks out a window of the steering room, alone on the screen as he holds his pipe and emphatically spits his disgusted comment on the inaugural festivities. Played by the character actor Ernest Torrence, he is a big burly man, whose outsize facial features have an innately comic quality to them, naturally composing a forcefully funny caricature of a face. He contrasts in the following shot to his "first and last mate," a small fat fellow, whose rotund featureless face suggests no character whatever.

After the new boat has docked, King delivers a speech, and while he does so the camera cuts away to the visible signs of his prosperity, literal signs that read "River Junction Bank, J. J. King President," "Hotel King," and finally that on the new steamer, four large letters regally proclaiming "King." When he has concluded to the enthusiastic applause of the bystanders, King turns to his captain, cheerfully observing, "This floating palace should put an end to that 'thing' Steamboat Bill is running." Back on the slumship Stonewall Jackson, the first and last mate agrees, saying to Bill, "Looks like you'll have to look for a new river." Bill, however, angrily and determinedly announces, "I'll run on this river if I'm the only passenger on the boat."

With this conflict established, the film proceeds to the introduction of the hero, an ironic buildup to the deflating comedy of his initial screen appearance. A telegram is delivered, one that has been held in the office for four days. It reads, somewhat ungrammatically and vaguely, "Dear Dad, it was Mother's wish that when I had finished school to pay you a visit. I think I arrive Saturday 10 A.M. You can't mistake me. I'll be wearing a white carnation. Regards, William Canfield Jr." Ambiguously implying a strained family situation that has evidently separated him from his late wife and child for some two decades, Bill explains, "It's from my Willie, I haven't seen him since he was a baby." When the mate responds that Willie must have grown some by now, Bill brags "I'll bet he's bigger'n me." Then the two realize that today is Saturday and that it is already ten o'clock. Quickly they leap into an open and decrepit passenger bus that provides a shuttle service between the depot and The Stonewall Jackson, and drive off to meet the train and Willie.

Across the dockside street, at a little stand in front of his hotel, King reappears as he buys a white carnation for his lapel, and a sign on the stand explains the flower and the occasion: "Mother's Day." Then the film's last major character, his daughter Kitty, drives up in a small convertible. Like Willie, she is also "home from school," and therefore as usual a Keaton heroine who has been given an affiancing similarity to the hero.

At the railroad station, after the train has arrived, Bill follows the telegram's instructions, searching for a white carnation, and it being Mother's Day, what he searches for, he finds—in confusing abundance. Soon desperate, he simultaneously asks several bystanders "Any of you boys looking for a father?" But none is. Finally stymied, he and his mate move to the end of the platform.

In long shot, the train now pulls out, backing away from the station, and its departure serves as a dramatically opening curtain, unveiling the hero, who stands across the track behind it. Facing away from the camera, he reads the River Junction sign. Then, in medium shot, he turns and turns out to be a slightly preposterous adolescent, foppishly attired, like many of the students in *College*, in the extremes of current style—a blazer, wide, wide pants, a sweater of ugly geometric design, and a checked bow tie. He carries a ukelele in one arm and a suitcase in the other, and worst of all, from Bill's working-class point of view anyway, the whole horrible figure is topped off with a beret and a foolishly feeble but then popular pencil-thin mustache. A small but aspiring sophisticate, he is an obviously effete and nonlaboring collegian, as well as the tiniest possible chip from a very large old block.

Unveiled, he is the one who continues the frustrating comic search. Progressing through a long line of waiting passengers, he dubiously displays the flower in his lapel, pushing it forward under many noses and hopefully looking for a response of recognition that never comes. Finally, in desperation, he shoves the flower toward a seated bum, who mistakenly accepts it as a handout and takes it from him. Grabbing it back, Junior is sufficiently upset that he fails to reattach it properly, and unnoticed by him it immediately falls from his coat, brushed off by his ukelele. Almost the only man at the station without a carnation, he walks on, still conspicuously displaying his flowerless lapel to all the bystanders, who are either baffled by him or just as often oblivious to his presence. Rendered unrecognizable, he at last encounters his father, who stares at the pointlessly gesturing twerp. Bill wonders for a moment, but then makes a face of disgusted thankfulness that this idiotic wretch could not be his Willie, and stomps off.

Junior's eccentric wanderings continue. Then, as Bill and the mate, who have been watching, walk up behind him, he deposits his bag by the station and strolls around the corner, where he pauses by an implausibly parked baby buggy. Uneasily frowning in fear of the awful possibility, Bill examines the abandoned bag. In closeup, its label proclaims "Wm Canfield Jr. Boston," and he stares in wide-eyed horror toward the station corner concealing his son. Junior meanwhile has inadvertently leaned against the buggy, awakening the baby inside, who cries, a silent-screen noise heard by him but for the sake of a joke not by his father, a noise, too, that a mere jiggling of the carriage will not stop.

Around the corner where they cannot see or hear the baby, Bill and the mate continue to stand, Bill shaking his head in angry disbelief, the mate stifling a laugh and urging him forward. Then the two are unexpectedly entertained by Junior, for he emerges from the corner, tripping back and forth in front of them through the crazy leaps of a parodic Grecian dance, Isadora Duncanish nonsense, accompanying himself on his uke as he attempts to amuse and pacify the crying baby. Bill responds by warning the mate, "If you say what you're thinking, I'll strangle you," and then, a strong man broken, he pulls out and nervously twists a handkerchief, seeming about to cry himself. The dance having also done in or at least silenced the baby, Junior next tiptoes back around the corner in exaggeratedly high steps, and there reclaims his bag.

There being no help for it, Bill calls to his son. Spinning about and running to the men, Junior mistakenly goes to the mate first, who corrects him by pointing an identifying and accusing finger at Bill. Father and son greet each other with a handshake, though Bill can hardly bring himself to look at his disappointing boy as he does so. Then handing Junior's bag to the mate and taking his ukelele himself, he sullenly strides away, leaving his son to follow. There is some difficulty when they reach the parking lot, for Junior is still misidentifying things and enters the brand-new bus for the steamship King. Bill must yank him out, and when the attendant runs over and complains, thinking a King customer is being stolen, Bill's frustrated feelings break loose. Shoving the man, he knocks him into the King bus and slams the door behind him. He, Junior, and the mate then set off in their own bus for The Stonewall Jackson.

The hero's arrival having been inauspiciously concluded, the misadventures of his first day are ready to begin. As in *Battling Butler*, he has been introduced in a totally undercutting way, made foolish by his foppish clothing, initially limited to eccentric, ineffectual, and here even sissified gestures, and incongruously placed in a small-town setting and among blue-collar, redneck types, both of which provide the strongest possible contrast to his outlandish appearance and behavior. A proletarian reprobate, a rough-and-ready giant, his father in particular has been stunned by his miniature dude of a son, a ukelele-playing idler in River Junction's plain-dressing, hardworking world. Though the film, with Keaton's customary avoidance of sentimental commentary, never idealizes the father or his work, in fact makes a "river tramp" epithet that King will later apply to him seem the most appropriate of labels, it at least conditionally accepts his way of life; and Junior will proceed, if very slowly at first, to assimilate himself into it and to win his father's approval, overcoming the deepest possible of generation and culture gaps.

Moving beyond this realistic assessment of character and situation, it is also possible to make a few transcendental points. One is that the exaggerations of comedy, the strong contrasts and the clownish behavior that mark Junior, have made him a very strange character. As he proceeds in his compulsive and repetitive way about the station, his extravagant gestures, taken as comedy, get their deserved laughs. Viewed differently, however, not just as comic stylizations but as the genuine moves of an actual person, they also seem evidence of someone who is simpleminded or mad. As appropriately as Ed Wynn, Junior could be labeled "the perfect fool." Almost as much as Friendless in *Go West*, he also impresses as a natural and an outsider, the idiot as isolate, a near-mindless being, moving among but not part of the rational mass of humanity, those who animate in normal fashion the railroad station platform.

It is the impression of difference and apartness caused by his clownishness that is important for Junior's later transcendental development. In the tradition of a saintly fool or madman, whose irrationality is compensated for by moral wisdom, the tradition, to take the loftiest example, of Dostoevsky's *Idiot* hero Myshkin, Junior's oblique relation to his society will make him a force for its betterment. A childish Keaton clown, he is not hampered by an adult mind. He is below or above River Junction's concern, demonstrated in the opening sequence, with the practicalities of money-making and business competition, a concern productive of economic and class hatred, the social divisiveness between rich and poor. Instead, in a film where the progeny have more wisdom than the parents, Junior with his carnation seems almost the first of the flower children, someone who is incapable of entering into the pugnacious and competitive world of River Junction, who will become a powerful force within it working for peace and harmony. An impossibly simple son, he is also a saintly one. Like Prince Myshkin, however, he is at first too passive a presence, that being part of his saintliness, to change the world. He must be, and not surprisingly will be, mystically transformed and energized before he can bring this about.

Back in town on the dockside main street, Bill decides to make Junior more presentable by his and River Junction's not very stylish lights. He therefore drags his son by the hand into the Hotel King barber shop, where Junior's minimal mustache is removed with two rapid sweeps of a razor. Kitty is also there, having her fashionably short hair even more severely bobbed, and when she and Junior see each other, it turns out they were college friends in Boston. As Bill dragged Junior into the barber's, now she excitedly drags him out, wanting to introduce her father, whom she inaccurately describes as lovable. While she looks around for King, however, Junior is again grabbed and dragged by his own father, this time to buy an American replacement for his French beret.

Inside a clothing store, the purchase occupies two lengthily sustained shots, which together compose one of Keaton's best comic routines, a vaudevillian turn of thirteen rapidly exchanged hats, all deftly manipulated with a juggler's finesse. In the first shot, a stylishly and loudly checked cap is the basis for a three-part action building to a comic climax. It begins as Bill discards Junior's beret, tossing it on a counter. Junior retrieves and pockets the beret, but he also discovers and is immediately infatuated with the highly visible cap there. Its striking checks soon crown his head, and when Bill turns with a sedate white fedora he has selected, he is struck by them. Recoiling, he grabs and discards the cap, then considers and rejects the fedora, and finally consults with the clerk over another selection. Junior, of course, recovers the cap and dons it again, so that when Bill turns a second time to his son, it is still blazing away on his head, and must for a second time be removed and discarded. The third and climactic round soon follows. This time Junior is most insistent, posing in the cap and urgently pressing its claims, and Bill's response, when he once more confronts the checked horror, escalates from irritation to violence. Ripping the cap from Junior's head, he throws it far beyond retrieval, so vigorously flinging it that the clerk angrily winces at the mistreatment of his merchandise.

Following this, the second shot of the routine is taken from the position of a mirror, as Junior stands facing the camera, his father beside him, with the clerk an unseen presence handing over hats. High-crowned and low-crowned, dark and light, felt and straw, they are tried on and rightly rejected, most of them somehow managing to look even more foolish than the highly foolish hats that have gone before. Even a trademark Keaton porkpie is dropped on Junior's head, though he instantly yanks it off. At last, when it becomes apparent that nothing will improve his son's appearance, Bill settles for a wide-brimmed white hat. Junior thereupon goes into a mad routine of adjusting the angle of its brim, a routine that ends as Bill with a resigned slap knocks the brim into an acutely unstylish downward position and leads his son out of the store.

On the street a strong wind, an omen of the storm to come, blows up a cloud of dust, and also immediately blows the new hat into the river. Junior, unperturbed, responds by reaching into his pocket and putting on his beret, thus absurdly ending the episode in exactly the same condition as when he started it. When Bill, who as usual strides several distancing steps ahead of his booby son, at last turns to look at Junior, he is, in a capping reprise of all his former shocks, mightily upset by the sight. Before he can object, however, he is even more disconcerted, for now Kitty approaches with her father. The banker derisively greets them with ''Is that—Steamboat Bill, Junior?'' Bill must reluctantly admit that it is, and then he once again angrily drags Junior to the clothing store, this time ordering a complete change of appearance: ''Fix him up with some working clothes for the boat.'' King's laughter also soon converts to anger when Kitty runs to the store and stands in the doorway beside Junior. While her father looks on, she holds Junior's hand, intimately speaking in a wide-eyed, little-girlish way, which makes him close his eyes in love-struck blinded bliss.

A title announces ''Working clothes for the boat—with her help.'' Then Junior strides along the dock, in a spiffy captain's uniform, with a swagger stick under his arm. As often in Keaton, the professional clothing points up the amateur ignorance of the man who wears it, and what follows is a sequence emphasizing Junior's incompetence on the boat and the further frustrated progress of the feud-crossed love.

Stepping onto the boat, as Bill recoils from the sight in horror, Junior stumbles his way to the prow, a destination as perilously attained by him as the top of Mount Everest would be for most others. Once there, he sees Kitty and her father, standing on the deck of the new steamer, which is berthed directly in front of the old. Posing for her benefit on a coil of rope, he is instantly jerked into a fantastic neck-twisting front flip when a deckhand pulls it away. Recovering, he pretends to give orders to the now departed hand. Then, as King talks to his captain, Kitty steps across the short gap between stern and prow and stands beside him on The Stonewall Jackson.

In a shot emphasizing symmetry and conflict, the two look up to the right, and as the camera pans in that direction it reveals King, who angrily yells down at his daughter, ordering her back. Panning again, the camera reverses, pausing on the young lovers. Obediently, the girl returns to her father's boat, and Junior naturally follows. Now they look up and to the left, and as the camera swings in that direction, it reaches Bill, who balances and counters King, shouting from the steering room for his son to leave his enemy's deck. Before Junior can do so by himself, however, King orders an officer to evict him, and the latter vigorously shoves Junior back onto The Stonewall Jackson. As Bill angrily responds to this affront, the girl, also angered, defiantly follows Junior; but a born peace-maker, he reasons with her and insistently helps her back onto The King. When she with equal insistence starts forward again, it is her father who provides the next restraint, running up and physically dragging her back. Bill now comes up behind Junior, just in time to be threatened by the banker, "If I find him on this boat again, I'll personally wring his neck." A man whose self-esteem has obviously been formed through many fights, Bill unhesitatingly meets the challenge and risks his son's neck. Shoved by his father, Junior reluctantly steps onto The King. The officer once again pushes him off, and Bill decisively pushes him back. Like a ball in a ping-pong game, Junior is briefly bounced back and forth, ending in mid-bounce as he precariously straddles the gap between the boats. Then the officer shoves him one last time, and the two of them together topple over onto The Stonewall Jackson, legs waving in the air.

When they rise, the officer shakes his fist at Junior and silently but loudly tells him off. Bill urges his son to hit his opponent, but Junior, an eminently small and nonviolent fellow, a properly nonfighting Bostonian, turns away. Reaching another breaking point, Bill thereupon grabs his hand, folds the fingers into a fist, and holds it in front of Junior, silently saying "See that." He then hits the officer with it, knocking him overboard into the river, and explains in a title "That's what that's for." Leaving Junior to hold his painful if conquering fist, Bill now responds to King's last taunt by as usual imitating him, "If anybody else is caught on this boat . . . my son'll handle him." Junior, made bold by victory, steps forward, assertively repeating the boast, but his defiant pose is undercut when Bill abruptly grabs his hand. As he has already done many times before, he drags his miniature son away, inadvertently dragging him into a cable, up which he painfully starts to slide before being extracted and yanked around the cabin corner. Two symmetrical shots conclude the episode by accentuating the reluctant separation of the young lovers. King also drags Kitty off, as she looks back and waves her hand; and Bill continues to drag Junior, who also turns and waves.

Where Junior is dragged to this time, after a pause for Bill to take out his grievances on a deckhand, is the engine room. Here he proceeds to instruct his son, but Junior is inattentive, and two times, first out of idiot curiosity and then accidentally, he pushes the lever that starts the paddlewheel, both times ramming the stern of The King. "I'm trying to teach you to run it—not 'wreck' it," Bill complains, but when he discovers the second collision has tumbled the banker overboard, he cheers up at the sight of his floundering rival. Returning to Junior, he shakes his hand and slaps him happily on the back. Moved to further affability, he takes a bite of chewing tobacco and urges his son to do the same. Junior chaws off a small plug, but then his father, still enthusiastically chortling, claps him on the back once too often. Junior instantly swallows his tobacco and stiffens, falling over backward in a dead faint, still not up to the demands of Bill's rough-and-ready river tramp world.

A title introduces the next and last sequence of the first day, "Eight bells and all is wrong." In his cabin Junior seems to be sleeping, though actually he is wearing his captain's uniform under his nightshirt, in preparation for a visit to Kitty, who has written him, "If you really care for me come tonight." Discovered in the King salon by her father, however, she is sent to her cabin with the angry admonition, "I'll pick the young man for you—and it won't be the son of a river tramp." Also discovered before he can steal away, Junior is ordered back to bed by Bill and his uniform is confiscated. As usual, Bill also provides both a contrast to King and an imitative balance, exclaiming, "I'll pick the young lady for you—and it won't be a girl with a father like that."

Resourcefully if inelegantly dressed in some of Bill's outsize clothing, Junior leaves anyway. In a scene that prepares for some contrasting nimble leaping across the decks the next day, he stumbles and falls down the levels of The Stonewall Jackson and at the prow inevitably plunges into the river. Still unlucky, he is also seen by an angry Bill as he climbs up the shipside ladder of The King. Once on deck, moreover, not only does he not meet Kitty, but an encounter with King and an officer ends with everybody overboard. Swimming to the dock, Junior ends his evening's misadventures as he crawls up its side. A small black boy, sitting there playing his guitar, stares at the emerging fright, tumbles over backward, and runs off, the last of the many upsets on the film's first day.

With the first day over, its contents can again be summarized in both a realistic and a transcendental manner. As usual in Keaton, its events prepare for a series of second-day reversals, and all Junior's failures are the foundations upon which the future and better day will build. Parental disapproval, the frustrated romance, Junior's ignorance of and incapacity for work, his athletic inability, his feebly foppish appearance, and even his effete eastern disinclination to fight—all of these will be reversed or overcome in a realistic and satisfying, if of course not entirely probable, leap to glory, a total change of behavior along the lines then demanded of a mass-culture, popular-art hero.

Viewed less mundanely, however, other elements in his character also assert themselves. They are those often described in the literature of transcendental experience, whether Judeo-Christian or classical or Eastern—the characteristics of someone with a strong potential for mystic communion with whatever divine or universal forces exist beyond the realm of the merely human. He continues, for example, to be presented as a simpleton, a sublime Keaton clown, whose wide-eyed white face as he feverishly tries on hats in the clothing store suggests an intellect so feeble that its owner remains both less and more than human, a being in touch with some subrational but more natural order of things. To repeat and press a point for all it is worth, he resembles a wise fool, a type to be found among Christian saints or Taoist mystics, a man whose childlike irrationality is a necessary concomitant of a more profound wisdom than any attainable by a conventionally thinking adult. His perception of the moral order of things, certainly, is better than that of his ignorantly battling elders.

Like some Christian saints or meditating Taoist monks, he is also, in the most curious aspect of the Keaton hero's characterization, a being so passive that he almost ceases to exist as a self-acting and self-motivating entity. The dominant image of him so far makes him seem less a person than a rag doll, something continually dragged or shoved by all the other characters. In a few of the scenes, of course, he does act; the passivity is by no means total. Still, it is stressed enough to create a sense of disturbing difference, of someone at the fringes of humanity. That someone is the Western saint or the Eastern monk, the practitioner of ego-abasement, the renouncer of his own will for the divine will, which becomes his sole mover. The inert and passive Keaton clown, like a mystic seeking an epiphany, seems to have broken down all the walls of the ego, the sense of self that shuts out the world. He vulnerably exists as a psychic vacuum waiting to be filled by the inspiring forces of a transcendental power, whether that power be conceived as a Judeo-Christian god, as an Eastern world soul, or as a Dyonysiac frenzy, the divine madness that will shake an aspiring bacchant.

The inherent stillness of the Keaton hero, of the rag-doll Junior, also visually suggests a different though related inner state, one described by many mystics and one central to the seasonal myths of regeneration, the change from winter to spring. To take a single mystic example, there is the *Pilgrim's Progress* man, John Bunyan, in the seventeenth century, who existed, before his own mystic experience, in a state like that of Coleridge's Ancient Mariner, of dull passivity, of death-in-life, awaiting and needing a divine revelation. When it came, it produced in him, he said, a sense of vital rebirth and transformation, of being in a state of grace, in harmony with God and man and nature.

To take a single mythic example, from Keaton's time, there is T. S. Eliot's *The Wasteland*. Employing references to many past regenerative myths, Eliot like them makes public and general the would-be mystic's private torments, describing a society, contemporary England, that is fragmented, inert, and dying, and in desperate need of regeneration. The most important of the ancient myths he refers to are those that center around a sick and dying king or god, whose decline is seen as the cause of natural and social decay. In such myths, once the dormant king or god is restored to vernal health, is revitalized or resurrected, his land and his people will similarly be restored. In short, Eliot says, what the present needs is another miraculous savior risen with the spring to save a spiritually dead world. What he fears is that his world is so far beyond the redemptive powers of religious belief that no savior will arise and no salvation will come.

This and the other transcendental elements described can, not too unreasonably, also be detected as elements of *Steamboat Bill Jr.* and its hero. Though the tone of the film, unlike Eliot or Bunyan, is devoid of any neurotic or apocalyptic anxiety, is instead always confidently funny as it approaches its comically and mythically certain climactic transformation, still the transcendental parallels are there. A characteristic Keaton clown, Willie is also almost the mystic seeker in extremis, waiting for and certain to receive a divine seizure and salvation. When in the film the moment of the hero's change comes, his leap to glory, it will be presented as a compelling, mysterious, and in terms of his mystically oriented character inevitable transcendental experience, a startling assertion of superhuman and life-transforming forces, which change not only him but the strife-torn world of River Junction. Much more obviously, of course, he is a mundane, mass-audience, American hero, a realistic underdog in a slightly escapist story of farcically achieved success; but the mystic parallels provoke in the farce some curiously unfarcical stirrings.

Junior's day of change, transcendental or real, now begins and begins badly. First Bill wakes him and sullenly hands his son a one-way ticket back to Boston. Then Bill discovers that he himself has been handed a condemnation notice, that at King's instigation The Stonewall Jackson has been officially declared unsafe. A confrontation with King leads to a fight, and when River Junction's leading citizen complains that "this man not only threatened my life but has defied the law," the river tramp is arrested. Slowly walking toward the railroad station, Junior sees his father driven to the jail and led inside. He decides to stay and help.

The rest of the film is given over to accelerating action and multiple rescues, beginning with an attempted jailbreak. It is preceded by a closeup of a newspaper weather report, promising a day "unsettled, wet and cloudy," and then in a tropical downpour, a solid sheet of rain, Junior walks along the street, again dressed in his father's outsize work clothes. He carries a white parcel and an umbrella, though the latter fails to keep him dry when he strides across a puddle, which soon becomes waist-deep. As he cautiously skirts another puddle, his umbrella is blown inside out by a strong wind. Now thoroughly drenched, from above as well as below, he struggles on, holding its useless form over him.

Still the fool and clown, he reaches the jail, where Bill sits dejectedly behind bars. When he sees his idiot son, he turns away in disgust, but Junior insists on a visit. Unwrapping the parcel, he displays a large loaf, explaining "I've brought my poor father bread." When Bill refuses it, Junior next silently mouths an unreceived message. When Bill still shakes his head in an angry No, Junior then walks back and forth, determinedly thinking, though since he also carries the precious loaf like a baby, patting and jiggling it, he appears more foolish than reflective. Having thought, Junior announces "I'll just wait until he is finished," and then he sits, still protectively cradling the baby loaf in his arms. As Bill stares in disgusted fascination at his demented simpleton son, Junior next looks up and sees, framed on the wall, the verses of a song, appropriately enough "The Prisoner's Song." For lack of anything else to do, he idly starts to sing it, keeping time with his right hand as he taps his fingers on the top of the loaf. Then, still singing, he pantomimes an escape. Stretching out his left thumb like a bar, he saws through it with his right hand and seemingly detaches it. After repeating the trick, he points to the jailer, gestures a knock on the head, and with his fingers walks across the top of the loaf, blowing a farewell kiss as a last signal of escape. Confused and angry, a fighting rather than a thinking man, Bill is not up to the subterfuges of jailbreaks and the decoding of pantomimed messages, and therefore he again moodily turns away.

Desperately driven to a direct statement, Junior now selects a rock paperweight from a table and silently places it on the floor beside him. Then, while the sheriff is attending to other matters, he throws a second rock weight through a window. As the sheriff spins around,

Junior leans over and picks up the rock on the floor, pretending that it has just come crashing into the jail. When the sheriff falls for the trick and leaps to look outside, Junior tears open the end of the loaf, showing Bill a hollow interior filled with carpenter's tools. Now even Bill understands, and therefore when Junior rises and for the benefit of the sheriff seems about to leave, he plays his part in the deception. What follows is an extravagantly overdone parody of melodrama, developing from the earlier suggestion of a baby loaf of bread, a tearjerking scene of anguished pleading, in which the father briefly assimilates himself to Junior's foolish-looking but as it turns out not entirely dumb style. It is his first such unbending, a major sign of the approaching reconciliation with his slight and simple son.

Starting the scene, Bill calls through the bars, ''I've changed my mind—I want the bread.'' As the sheriff looks at the two of them a little suspiciously, Junior with a sad-eyed, broken-hearted expression shakes his head and says, ''No—I don't think you do.'' As he reluctantly turns toward the door, rejected and still cradling his infant loaf, Bill pleads with tearful overacting, ''Come, my boy—I was only foolin'.'' More refusals, more pleading, and Bill finally stretches his arms through the bars, wildly crying ''You talk to him, Sheriff.'' Visibly moved by the emotional scene before him, the sheriff steps forward, grabs Junior's shoulder, and undercuts the highly sentimental melodrama with some realistically phrased advice, ''After all, the old bum is your father.''

Junior is easily convinced, and the sheriff escorts him to Bill's cell. But then the torn end of the bread gives way and the tools fall to the floor. Soon the sheriff is chasing Junior, a chase that ends when the sheriff drops his jail keys and Junior stops running, politely picks them up, and obligingly hands them over. Unthankfully, the sheriff replies by shoving him, an abusive gesture recalling the struggle with the officer on The King the day before. As happened then, Bill reacts with a characteristic cry, ''Don't let him do that to you, Willie, bust him on the jaw.'' The sheriff laughs, unworried by the ''shrimp,'' and then contemptuously juts his jaw out at Junior and orders him to take a poke. Junior replies, ''No, I might hurt you,'' but when the sheriff insists, he responds, not with a jab to the cast-iron jaw but with a hesitant poke at a paunchy stomach. The sheriff instantly falls, implausibly knocked out, while Bill, surprised and happy, mightily approves of his victorious son.

As fights go, it has been a minimal and deliberately unconvincing one, but still it reverses the ignominy of the day before. Further, just as Bill has displayed a new ability to play along with the foolishly clowning Junior, so in the fight his son has made a conciliatory move in his father's pugnacious direction, another indication of a developing reconciliation. He will not, however, move much further, for if a source of fun, his comically saintly pacifism is also something the film does not entirely undercut. Junior's first fight is his last fight, and though he soon changes drastically, at the end he will remain a peaceable peace-maker.

With the way cleared for escape, it is attempted and flubbed. Released from his cell, Bill runs outside and hides, but Junior, his coat accidentally caught by the closing cell door, is trapped. He finally frees himself, but on the jail porch is stopped by two entering deputies and then knocked out by the sheriff, who has come to and angrily steps up behind him. Responding, Bill emerges from his hiding place, stalks up to the sheriff and flattens him, and then goes back to his cell. The unconscious Junior, meanwhile, is driven off to the hospital.

Once again the newspaper's optimistic weather report is shown, this time modestly predicting "storm clouds in the offing." The prediction is followed by a cyclone, the last of Keaton's great nature sequences. As with the river and waterfall in *Our Hospitality* or the rocks and the hill in *Seven Chances,* a Keaton hero will be threatened by the forces of nature; soon Junior will be alone in a deserted town, buffeted by a destructive wind. His stormy trial is the climactic sequence of the film, and like much that has been described so far, it has both a realistic and a transcendental aspect, though with the storm the transcendental will at last be in the ascendent. Realistically, the cyclone is simply an emergency, calling for vigorous action, and the hero rises, often literally, to the occasion, athletically and heroically responding, rescuing those in danger, and coming through with consentaneous approval. But there are also the transcendental parallels and possibilities. The storm is intensely meaningful weather, with such a resonance of effect and with such a significance for the hero that it quickly surpasses normal, even dangerously normal, experience.

For one transcendental parallel, the impact of Junior's trial by the storm is something like that of a primitive maturity rite, a solitary and mystic test of fitness that marks his coming of age in River Junction. Like an aboriginal youth whose entry into manhood is ritualized through an initiatory ordeal, the adolescent Junior, the childish clown and fool, is subjected at the crucial moment to a transforming trial. For most of the storm, he is entirely alone on the screen, as isolated as if he had gone into the wilderness seeking an identifying sign, and his experience in the storm has an almost totemic significance. Threatened by it, he is also accepted by it, wed to the wind as he is blown about. Like the earlier Willie of *Our Hospitality,* he gains his identity through his movements. Commoved by the storm, he becomes man as motion, an embodiment of the energy of the storm, which he retains even after it is over. If he were an Indian youth returned from such a mystic ordeal, he would probably thereafter be known, at least if his tribe had a certain sense of humor, as Willie Big Wind, and be expected to behave with an energetic and restless drive.

Similarly, there is suggested in the storm the transcendental mythic pattern described earlier, comedy's seasonal legend of death and resurrection and an edenic restoration. A saintly fool, Junior has been out of place in the feuding world of River Junction and rejected by it, even if it needs something of his peaceable nature. He has also, in his total passivity, in the much repeated images of his being shoved and knocked and flipped about, been characterized as willless and inanimate, visually more a thing than a person, a dead man rather than a live one. The passivity is climaxed as he is struck by the sheriff and carried unconscious to the hospital, where he will next appear lying in bed. Without cohering into a fully intended pattern, such elements of his presentation all at least suggest something like a legendary dying hero or god, one with the potential to save a wasteland world but obviously without the power. And then the storm comes, a meta-storm, a supernatural breath or spirit, which almost literally blows life back into Willie. From passive inertness as the storm begins, he is mightily moved by the wind, tossed by it into a divine frenzy of action, so animated that it seems natural (and the transforming moment is even likely to pass unnoticed) that when the storm stops he should still keep on moving, now a self-motivated and autonomous actor. It seems natural but it is not, for the visual change from totally passive to totally active is so great, the comic contrast so extreme, that it unrealistically resembles a miraculous rebirth. And so resurrected, a wise fool in harmony with and revived by the forces of the world, Junior can and does change the unnaturally divided society of River Junction and bring it peace.

To suggest two further mystic parallels to Junior's stormy experience, one past and one present, there is first from the English Romantic period Shelley's "Ode to the West Wind." In this poem Shelley, a crucified soul torn by the thorns of life, longs to be revived by the vital forces of nature, forces identified with the west wind, which is nature's breath of life. Speaking to the wind, he utters two lines that could easily be an epigraph for Willie: "Be thou, Spirit fierce, my spirit! Be thou me, impetuous one!" As is customary in such transcendental poems, his own longed-for rejuvenation is also at the end equated with a social regeneration. When and if he is revived by the wind, it will, he hopes, be into a generally revived world, one promised by the optimistic extension of seasonal renewal: "When winter comes, can spring be far behind?"

The second and contemporary parallel is the amiable four-volume fiction of Carlos Castaneda. In his adventures, he searches like Shelley for a transforming force in the natural world, a force inaccessible to a rational and conventionally civilized mind. Led, often comically, by the Indian magician don Juan, rather like Mickey Mouse as the sorcerer's apprentice, he finally breaks through into transcendence, transcendence conceived in a manner very similar to Keaton's. At the end of Volume IV, like Willie at the end of *Steamboat Bill Jr.,* he takes off, flying. In Castaneda's phrase, he at this point becomes "a man of power." And so, when he soars, does Junior.

The great transforming storm begins as soon as Junior has been deposited in the hospital. King and his captain stand in front of King's hotel, where the captain reports "The pier is not strong enough to hold the boat against this wind." On the street, the wind is then displayed, as people, including the banker and captain, run for cover, and much waste paper is blown about. One shelter-seeker hurries to his parked car and starts to crank it. Then its convertible top is blown up, like a sail, and it is propelled down the street by the wind, dragging the man after it until it crashes to a stop against a curb and he runs away. At the river, the dock for the King steamer collapses, as its crew scrambles for shore, and on The Stonewall Jackson the mate worriedly signals its crew to fasten the ship more securely. The destruction of the King property continues, as first a corner and then the entire front of the Hotel King is blown down, following which a small restaurant pavilion, King's Fish Palace, entirely collapses. Next a desperate group of people struggle into a storm cellar, one man rolling across the ground in a wind-driven tangle of vines and weeds. Finally, outside the hospital, the patients run into the street, a comic mob in their white nightshirts, the last of them, a fat bearded man with a leg in a cast, stumbling and falling most comically of all as he makes his awkward exit.

And now, in an astonishing shot, the hospital for a moment sits there, a substantial presence filling the screen, and then it is gone, its roof and walls casually lifted into the air by the cyclonic winds. Inside, the only patient left, Junior is sitting up in bed, an icebag on his head. Looking about, he rises, grabs his coat, puts his hat on over the icebag, and after these delays races toward the rear and the safety of a solid background building. Then its facade moves toward him, leaning forward and collapsing, so that he must instantly reverse direction to avoid being crushed. There being nowhere else to go, he goes back to bed, retreating to the open-air hospital and crawling under the covers. No sooner is he there than the wind-driven bed starts moving, out of the ruins, down the street, and into the open door of a stable, where it finally stops against a far wall. Emerging from the covers, Junior is startled to discover his new location, but before he has time to adjust to the rows of watching horses, he is gone again. The wall behind him is a door, it blows open, and he is once more out on the street, this time rolling to a halt in front of a two-storied house. Suddenly blown out of the bed, he quickly crawls under it, cowering there and waiting for the worst. The worst begins as the front of the house behind him starts to split off. A shot of its upper corner reveals a desperate man in an attic room. Scurrying to an open window, he looks down and sees the bed below. Naturally, he leaps, nearly smashing both bed and Junior, and then he runs off as the bed is blown after him. Uncovered and dazed, Junior stands, groggily weaving, and, in another classic shot of the sequence, the entire front of the house falls over on him. It falls without breaking, flattening a wide area before it, but Junior stands in just the right spot for safety, the small area covered by the open window, which passes around him. Safe or not, he is frightened into running again, in a partially self-propelled and partially wind-driven progression that sends him sliding and tumbling into another collapsing building, which disintegrates a few feet in front of him. Turning and racing away, he next appears sliding down a street, carried by the wind like a scrap of paper. When he manages to stand and tries to run into the wind, he makes no progress, though he is able impressively to lean into it at about a sixty-degree angle without falling over. A few determined leaps into the wind do not advance him either, and then an open truck, its bed filled with boxes, drives by in front of him. The wind instantly blows all the boxes off, right into Junior, and after this he gives up and runs in a wind-approved direction.

The unreal events now become even more unreal, genuinely surreal, as the storm pauses for a theatrical interlude, a dreamlike magical confusion compounded of memories from Keaton's vaudeville childhood. In the ruins of a theater, there stands a fragment of exterior wall surrounding a stage door. Running up to it, searching for shelter, Junior enters and starts to close the door, just as the wall falls over on him and he finds himself standing in the now horizontal entrance. Still, he is or at least may be inside the backstage area, and next he appears on stage, where he runs into a rope and falls. Standing, he untangles his foot from the rope, and a sandbag at the end of it immediately drops and flattens him. Standing again, more groggy than ever, he stares at a painted canvas backdrop of a lake, and then suddenly races toward and dives into the water. After painfully rising once more, he examines the backdrop, lifting and walking under it, and then it falls entirely, changing from illusionistic to nonexistent. Advancing to a dressing room door, Junior looks left at a ventriloquist's dummy resting on a shelf. The shelf sags, and the dummy therefore leans toward him, its head turning as it does so. Frightened into running back on stage, he steps on a horn, the sound of which causes him to leap onto a box. Then glancing up, he sees a canopy above him and a cord attached to it. He pulls the cord, the curtainlike sides of the canopy instantly lower around him, and when they rise again he is gone, the victim of a magician's disappearing trick. But then his head emerges from a trap door in the box, and soon he crawls forth and once more runs. Blindly racing, he encounters the dummy again, bumping the shelf, which causes the apparently animate dummy to fall over into his hands. Dropping it, he runs till he reaches an exit in another fragment of wall and quickly steps outside, escaping from the surreal horrors of the theater. Behind him the wall collapses, and the magical theater itself performs a last disappearing act.

Placed in the center of the storm sequence, the theater interlude has functioned as a rhythmic rest, an aesthetically necessary pause between the two crescendos of outdoor activity that surround it, a rest, too, that seems a natural pause, something like the calm in the eye of a hurricane. It also works, even if unintentionally, in a transcendental way. As there is to the whole storm sequence, there is most intensely in the theater interlude a surreal, time-transcending quality, a dreamlike ambience that places it beyond the real and the temporal. The hero moves into a fantastic realm, where immutable spatial properties are easily revoked, where everything both is and is not, where the most solid is the least substantial, and where all objects are part of a universal disappearing act. It is a realm where so much action and destruction, so many total reversals, are concentrated into a few minutes that the sense of temporal duration is distorted. The events are so many and so strange that the time in which they occur seems much denser than normal time, as though a lifetime's experience has somehow been contracted into a few highly elastic moments. In the theater as throughout the storm, the whole experience is so disorienting, such a fantasizing of reality, that it exists completely apart from the everyday world of River Junction in which Junior has previously lived. When he enters this new realm of irrational and animating energy, of distorted space and time, where both are unsubstantial and plastic, all continuity with his past is effectively canceled. It is a realm where a wooden dummy can come to life (as does the hero), moved like everything else by the animating forces unleashed by the wind. Junior's experience in it is mysterious, mystic, and transforming, and it promises and delivers a new beginning for the radically redeemed hero. The storm becomes for him simultaneously a destruction and a rebirth.

Having left the mysterious sanctum of the theater, the innermost eye of the storm, Junior now runs toward a gate in a tall fence. Leaping on top of it, he is instantly carried in a circle as the impact causes the gate to swing all the way around and to slam against the opposite side of the fence, tumbling him over to his original starting position. After this neatly self-canceling motion, he tries again, walking through the now open gate, which immediately reverses itself and slams shut in his face. Rising, he runs in another direction and next comes on screen sliding into the safety of a doghouse. Predictably, he leaps back out, holding the seat of his pants, and races on into an open field, where he distractedly scurries about in circles till an entire house falls upon him. Opening a door in its side, he walks out and wanders on. Then seeing something in front of him, he turns and races back to the just dropped house, retreating inside through a door. A large outhouse, like a wheelless tank, rolls by, and then Junior once more steps outside, looking back as the entire house behind him instantly disintegrates into a pile of scrap lumber.

In the first of several cutaways to the other characters, Kitty now appears, climbing up on a house porch. Then Junior reappears as a crowd of people near by push their way into a storm cellar. Running up just as the door is closed, Junior knocks on it, then unsuccessfully tries to pull it open. Retreating, he walks across a downed power line, and is suddenly writhing in a shower of animated sparks. For the last time, he runs again, sliding to a stop by a solid-looking tree. Wrapping himself around its trunk, he embraces its rooted safety, which is quickly transformed into anabatic danger. The entire tree rises into the air, and as he desperately clings to it, he soars over the ruins of the town. Like a low-flying balloonist, he is carried along till the tree reaches the river, where it slowly descends and drops into the water.

A cutaway now reveals Bill, still imprisoned in his cell. Then a large tree is blown over, slamming into the riverside jail and pushing it down the bank and into the water. Hurrying to the window, Bill grabs onto its bars, waist-deep in water as the temporarily floating jail sails away. In a last shot, the water around him has become chest-deep and he is calling helplessly for help. As the film next cuts back to Junior, he is climbing up the paddlewheel of The Stonewall Jackson, which has broken loose from its moorings and is floating in the river but otherwise is undamaged by the cyclone. No sooner has he reached the deck than he sees a semisubmerged house floating by, and there is Kitty, clinging to a roof corner and also calling for help. Running forward, to the first of what will be four rescues, he grabs an anchor and throws it like a grappling hook, catching the house corner. Tying the other end of its rope to The Stonewall Jackson, he then swings hand over hand across the rope to the house. When he reaches Kitty, she goes into a thankful and fearful clinch, clutching so tightly to him that they both nearly fall off, but then, as she still hysterically clings, he starts hand over hand to swing his way back. Halfway across, the anchor tears loose, and both are dropped into the water, but soon they come up by the paddlewheel and climb aboard.

Another cutaway to Bill shows him still calling through the bars, with the water around him now nearly neck deep. On the deck of The Stonewall Jackson, Junior deposits Kitty, and then, as the jail instantly floats by, he sees his father and prepares for another nonstop rescue. Racing to the engine room, he displays a nautical expertise totally lacking in his stumbles and bumbles of the day before. After tying two ropes to the forward control level, he next appears in the steering room, where he arranges the other ends of the long ropes for easy grabbing. Pulling the first rope, he drives the ship forward, simultaneously steering it into the jail, which it rams and smashes. Pulling the second rope, an efficient one-man crew, he stops the ship, and as Bill rises from the floating wreckage around him, Junior leaps from the steering room window to the roof below and then to the upper, middle, and lower decks—a continuous, soaring, graceful run that carries him across and down the ship in a few amazing seconds, as if he were still blown by the wind.

After he has helped Bill climb on board, they are approached by Kitty, and Junior looks on approvingly as Bill, following a moment's hesitation, smiles at her and takes her hand. Then, however, he sees something else, and leaps back up the various levels, as quickly almost as he had leaped down them, reaching the steering room and once again starting the engines. What he sees is the sunken wreckage of the steamship King, like all the banker's flaunted possessions destroyed by the leveling storm. Its smokestacks emerge from the water, as does King himself, who clings to a board and calls for help. Jumping to the upper deck, Junior ties a rope to his waist and then dives into the racing waters, soon swimming back with the rescued banker. The two are pulled onto The Stonewall Jackson, Junior unties his rope, and then Kitty kisses him, while the quarreling fathers shake hands, the feud happily over and a new era of cooperation obviously about to begin. But suddenly Junior creates a discord in this harmonious scene. Staring at the water, he grabs a life preserver and once again leaps overboard. As the girl looks on in rejected shock and as the fathers perplexedly watch, he swims away. Then the final shot explains his curious action, for now he swims back, towing in the preserver his last rescue, a placidly floating priest, happily prepared to conduct an instant wedding ceremony.

With Junior fully triumphant, he and his world revived and transformed, both in a state of grace and ready for a ritual blessing of union and peace, the movie ends. As the parallel comments on it have indicated, the film can be viewed realistically, as a comic story of a boob who makes good, and yet it is also the most mysterious of all the features. Willie's magic theater is not quite Steppenwolf's magic theater, and Keaton is not quite another Hermann Hesse, though it would be pleasant if all the mystically inclined young people today could be fooled into thinking he was, but he is also far more than a mere farceur. In a free-floating symbolic way, the images with which he creates and presents his hero—the strong comic contrasts between passivity and action, bumbling and mastery, feeble timidity and athletic courage, clownish simplemindedness and moral wisdom, character contradictions forced into unity by the dislocating transformations of the fantasy storm—all unintentionally relate the film to the literature of transcendental experience. It echoes age-old myths of rebirth and resurrection, of a risen hero who saves a world. It echoes primitive rites of mystic revelation and tribal initiation, of a solitary transforming vigil or test (like the hero's solitary river journey in *Our Hospitality*, his solitary motorcycle ride in *Sherlock Junior*, his solitary run with the rocks in *Seven Chances*, his solitary train ride and cattle drive in *Go West*, his solitary athletic race in *College*). In the film, passing the cyclonic test endows the hero with new energies, energies that closely identify him with nature and the forces of nature and enable him to save his world. In all these ways, though in an unconscious and modest manner, *Steamboat Bill Jr.* is perhaps also one with such modern and conscious longings for transcendence and transformation as Hesse's. Certainly some powerful and enduring desires resonate through the film, providing a psychological depth that makes its farcical success story a compelling, affecting, and finally even transcendent experience.

12.

A Final View

WITH THE LAST of Keaton's independent features discussed, it is time to summarize, to review what has been said about them and why. Encouraged by the high rating accorded Keaton's work by many other film critics, and also aware that in these days of proliferating film talk everyone who ever made a movie is likely to have been acclaimed as a genius by some film critic, I have attempted an objective and close viewing of the nine Keaton features, a description and explanation of what they most basically are, which, I hope, is also a description and explanation of why they are good, a documentation as well as an assertion of their values. A major work of art should have sufficient emotional density and sufficient intellectual density to command continuing interest, and the Keaton features are heavyweight contenders in both ways.

The emotional density resides in the central theme of change and development, of the learning, self-transcending, glory-achieving hero. These patterns of character transformation, it seems to me, are sufficiently important in human, especially youthful, experience, and also well enough executed in the films, to attract and hold the feelings of a large and lasting audience. The features are significant expressions of universally significant experience, and I therefore have stressed the nature of this experience, the ways it is achieved, intensified, and manipulated in the films, and the many joyous variations they play on it. Though the theme of change as Keaton handles it is a cheerfully and farcically comic one, behind the laughter there

305

is an affirmative and valuable understanding of the human condition and its at least temporary victories. The films are powerfully effective celebrations of some of the ways in which it is good to be alive, at their visually most basic celebrations even of a kind of coming to life, as the hero and the film, after an initial comic dormancy and restriction, become increasingly animate and active.

It must be admitted, however, that behind the discussions proclaiming the seriousness and effectiveness of Keaton's developmental theme, there are several doubts. First, a suspicion and a worry that the treatment of the theme is too much characterized by fantasy and escapism, that the films are little more than attractive dreams of glory. By way of critical defense, it has sometimes been assumed that if that is what they are, why then that is a good thing to be, that wish-fulfillment fantasy is as reasonable a subject for art as any other, and perhaps even a subject most suitable for the very real, yet dreamlike, world of silent-screen images. By way of critical caution, as in the dismissive comments on *College*, equally strong reservations have also been asserted. And finally, by way of critical balance, since ultimately my conclusion is that the fantasies of the films are far more than idle ones, I have proclaimed a cosmic profundity for the transformational pattern of *Steamboat Bill Jr*. Perhaps the films function at many levels simultaneously, from the very shallow, if entertaining, to the more intense mythic deep.

A second doubt is that the treatment of youthful character development is not only too escapist but too limited, forced by the inadequacies of a purely visual medium into an exclusive and therefore distortingly narrow stress on action, a constraint which in no way keeps the films from succeeding as farcical comedies and adventurous melodramas but which might perhaps undermine any claim of seriousness, of relevance, for them. If the films are about the maturing of a young hero, they certainly do not provide a model that many young could follow. In fact, it could as well be observed that the kinetic Keaton hero's development into and through action is the opposite of most people's, that maturing is more likely to mean restricting one's physical activities in the pursuit of a non-Keatonian because sedentary career in business, government, education, or wherever else most nonheroes labor. A medium that cannot deal with mind, with the acquiring of any skills or knowledge that are not expressible in a visually striking way, is obviously one that omits a large and, as the philosophers self-servingly tell us, most valuable part of life. The world's need for locomotive engineers, cowboys, boxers, and riverboat pilots is a minor one, and the Keaton hero therefore strives in a romantic realm of glorified labor where few can join him. Even in their own day, the films often nostalgically pictured the past or what was even then a rapidly receding and unpreservable present.

Still, despite this limitation, the films do not seem irrelevant. Since they have no didactic intentions, they do not present the hero and his activities as models for development, as the precise way in which all people should learn and grow. Rather, they simply take a few limited kinds of experience and development, ones that could be visually and amusingly shown, and turn these into such memorable entertainments that they become resonating symbols for all the transformations and triumphs available to or hoped for by all the maturing young. The events of the films are highly particular, unique in time and place and to the cultural expectations of that time and place, and unique, too, to the inimitably comic Keaton characters; but the emotional significance of the events and the characters was and remains central and important and generally accessible. There is an emotional density to the films that is universal and timeless, making them everywhere and forever relevant.

Moving from emotional to intellectual density, to the area in which an informed intelligence seems most on display and most capable of holding the intellectual interest of an audience, this is to be found, it seems to me, in the extraordinary knowledge the features show of the classic principles of comedy and laughter and in the equally extraordinary discoveries they make about the comic potentials newly provided by film. Like much great art in any medium or mode, they are about that medium and that mode, a continuous exploration of film and of comedy, of their nature and their possibilities, of what can be done with them. As supremely successful comedies, they reflect centuries of comic tradition and accomplishment, from the mechanizations of farce to the gentle ironies of pastoral romance. And in the ways they make us grin, giggle, or

guffaw, in their massive exploitation of many traditional gag techniques, they compose an encyclopedia on laughter.

Coming at the beginning of a new art form, the medium of film,
they are also among the first exuberant experiments with that
medium, among the first major achievements and demonstrations of
what it could do and do well. As stressed in several earlier chapters,
one of the most comic film potentials that Keaton discovered and
used well was the medium's ability to merge different objects or
disparate kinds of experience, through parallels of presentation to
equate visually what normally is seen as unlike. The features are in
part about our perception of things, and how in films this perception
may be comically controlled and altered. The punning doublenesses
that make one thing into two things, the deliberate confusions or
conjunctions of human and animal, human and mechanical, adult
and child, stylized and naturalistic, real and dream—all these are
among the most interesting, the most distinctive, and, in this study
anyway, the most discussable of Keaton's filmic accomplishments.

So, too, is his handling of stasis and motion in the films. Though,
as observed, the limitation of the silent-screen world to motion
greatly restricted the areas of life Keaton could work with, what is
astonishing is how much variety of meaning, both comic and
serious, the limited means allowed. With a comedian's eye for contrast, working with the silent-screen polarities of static and active,
stillness and movement, he managed to communicate with these
simple oppositions many complex messages, so many that some lin-
guistically oriented film critic should probably undertake to compare
Keaton's binary visual language with computer languages, all of
whose messages also begin as arrangements of equally simple binary
bits. Less ambitiously, another stress in earlier chapters was Keaton's basic and filmic concern with the bipolar patterns of stationary
and animate: the slow, sudden, or alternating transitions from
stillness to motion, or the contrast between the two. Restricted to
these two simple basics of silent-screen language, he nevertheless
conveyed with them complex character developments and a great
variety of comic sensations, like the sense of joy triggered as marble
serenity explodes into gravelly chaos. In *Seven Chances* he even
managed, through arrangements of stasis and motion, a satiric com-

mentary on the social and sexual divisions of society; and in *Steamboat Bill Jr.*, he enunciated with them a differentiation between the restrictions of the mundane and the liberations of the supernatural.

In all these ways and others, then, my contention has been that the Keaton features, both emotionally and intellectually, can be taken seriously, and I have attempted to demonstrate what a serious discussion of them can and should emphasize, even if I harbor some doubts about the outcome of such a demonstration. If it has been successful, its only result might very well be to promote the inclusion of Keaton's films in more and more university film and literature courses. This trend has already begun, and it is not necessarily the happiest fate that might be anticipated for them. But then again, outside the schools and a few, too few, museums and archives, it is hard to imagine where else the silent film is likely to find a sufficient interest and audience to survive. In the best of all possible worlds, a large and lasting audience would be stampeding into thousands of theaters to munch popcorn and watch Keaton movies. In the world as it is, it will be enough if for the present they are studied and taught and kept alive by a discerning few.

The Collapse

Besides summing up intentions and hoped-for accomplishments, it is also impossible at the end not to speculate on why after *Steamboat Bill Jr.* the laughter for Keaton soon stopped. He made two more silent features under contract to MGM and then some half dozen sound features, the first ones so disappointingly bad that it seems impossible that the later ones could be worse—but they are.

This collapse has been variously explained. There were, though they will not be elaborated on here, marital and personal problems, not the least of which was a growing alcoholism. There was also the difficulty Keaton had with MGM and its assembly-line approach to film production. At MGM he missed, too, his old co-workers, and it is likely that his silent successes owed much to others, that they were the result of a happy and expert collaboration. Though in this study Keaton's is almost the only name that has been used, it has probably

and unintentionally often been used synecdochically, as a part
standing for a whole or for some other element within it, Keaton's
crew or its constituents: writers, directors, cameramen, special-
effects men, actors, whoever was actually responsible for some
particular excellence in a Keaton movie. When these people departed, as his original production team gradually broke up, Keaton's
glory may have gone with them.

The shift from silence to sound was, in itself, also obviously basic
in destroying Keaton. He was not the only one who failed to make
the transition; in fact, few of his major contemporaries really succeeded. Mary Pickford, Douglas Fairbanks, Harold Lloyd, all made
sound films but not very good ones, and their careers soon ended.
Even Chaplin, after his prolonged resistance, when he finally made
an all-sound film in *The Great Dictator,* fell far below his silent
peak, and none of his later sound films ever reached it either. The
silent stars were so formed in silent cinema that they could not
change to meet the demands of a largely new medium.

Except for Chaplin, whose timeless Tramp has no age, the others,
too, like Keaton suffered from a peculiar and still present limitation
of a popular art that aims at a youthful mass audience, namely, that
they were all required to play essentially juvenile roles. Even in the
days of their silent-screen success, they were far older than the characters they represented. Both Keaton and Pickford often enhanced
their actual smallness to create an illusion of exaggeratedly diminutive juvenility, by casting their films with very large actors and using
equally large-scale sets and props. Eventually, however, they all
became too old for the illusion of youth to succeed anymore. Age, in
Keaton's case, already affects his two MGM silent features. In both
there is a necessary abandoning of juvenile status. Keaton no longer
plays the comically changing child-adult but an elderly young man, a
difference that can be reduced to two words. The little hero is no
longer an aspiring young rookie but a sadsack, and that produces in
the films a significant deflation in comic tone to something less
cheerful and expansive than before. Instead of a glorious young fool,
the heroes are now pathetic little men, and in both films for the first
time there is an air of condescension toward them, implicit throughout and explicit in the attitudes of the other characters. The change

greatly diminishes Keaton as a screen presence, depriving him of the heroic assurance, the underlying potential for glory, that even in the course of ludicrous bumbling made him a focus of admiring attention before. In both films, too, there is a blurring of old form, of the dynamically charged narrative of youthful transformation, and sequences are no longer tightly integrated to effect the hero's change. In *The Cameraman* (1928), there is one totally extraneous interlude, as the hero goes to a deserted ball park and pantomimes a baseball game. It is nicely done, but it does not fit in; and in *Spite Marriage* (1929), which is long and sprawling, there is a multiplication of plots and a slack episodic structure. Both films are good, but both are a falling-off. Both suffer from an aging and diminished star, which leads to a weakening in the dramatic form of his formerly supercharged vehicles.

The form and even Keaton may not have been quite exhausted. His second sound film, *Doughboys* (1930), if it could have been made a year or so earlier with his old crew, might have been another classic silent comedy. With sound, however, the comic techniques, perfected for silence, do not work, and Keaton, puffy-faced and strained, is a sad reminder of his former self. A never used idea for a sound film, proposed by Keaton to Irving Thalberg at MGM, also sounds promising, at least if it could have been done in silence—a teaming of him and the great Marie Dressler as a bumbling young man and his formidable old aunt, who together set out in a wagon train to the West. Keaton's sense of history was impeccable. *Our Hospitality* and *The General* are among the most authentic-looking period films made in America. Considering also how well he worked with the character actor Ernest Torrence in *Steamboat Bill Jr.*, it is for a Keaton fan a source of regret that he never costarred with Dressler in such a movie. If somehow things had been a little different, if Keaton had been able to keep his independence a year or two longer, if sound had been delayed a year or so, we might today be able to enjoy a few more classic comedies.

As it was, Keaton's first sound film, *Free and Easy* (1930), prefigures his later sound career. For the first time he is not the youthful romantic lead but instead is turned into a character actor himself, a Fieldsian or Marxian clown, who does not win the leading lady

(Robert Montgomery does that) but rather is paired with her supposedly comic battle-ax of a mother. As a character comedian,
Keaton is not very good. There is no way of retaining and exploiting
his characteristic silent compound of comic fragility and heroic
strength, of diminutive and finely featured vulnerability combined
with physical dexterity and unflappable endurance. To fall back on a
comparison that other Keaton fans may never forgive me for, in the
days of his silent glory he could have been the original for the later
cartoon character Mighty Mouse, a comic combination of smallness
and strength, a muscular mite whose youthful triumphs were as
convincing as they were laughably improbable, as satisfying as they
were surprising. But in a character clown of the sort Keaton became,
all this appeal was discarded, and nothing replaced it. A better new
screen character might have saved him, perhaps something in the
nineteen-thirties' detective vein, a cross between Sherlock Holmes
and Charlie Chan, or, to use two modern figures that seem closer to
Keaton, a combination Columbo-Clouseau. And then again, perhaps
not. In actual life with the occasional supporting roles it offered, it is
only in his final years, when Keaton's lined face acquired a great
strength of character, something old and good and likable, that he
seems once again a commanding screen presence. Our loss is that
there was not then time or opportunity for him to perform more.

Finally, too, the sameness of all his silent features, the fact that
Steamboat Bill Jr. could have been as easily made first as last, helps
explain the early collapse. Perfection was instantly achieved and
firmly held, but it was a static perfection. It led nowhere. It provided
no opportunities for development. If the Keaton comedy was not
necessarily exhausted, even under the best of all possible circumstances it soon would have been. As Keaton grew older, a major
change in his feature films was inevitable, and, so totally do the
silent features resist change, under any circumstances it would have
been difficult. The coming of sound, a marital disaster, a drinking
problem, the repressive factory system at MGM, all combined to
make it insuperable. For what Keaton achieved before the collapse,
however, we can be thankful. His silent work survives, and in it he
survives and triumphs as one of the best of American film- and
laugh-makers.

Bibliographical and Filmographical Comments

Books

In addition to the works mentioned in Chapter 2—the biography of Rudi Blesh, the critical essay of David Robinson, and the chapters in the two books by Gerald Mast—there are many other studies of Keaton. Some of the most recent and interesting of these deserve comment.

Both recent and good, in fact the closest to an indispensable book on Keaton, is Jean-Pierre Coursodon's *Buster Keaton* (Paris, 1973), a massive square volume of some 400 pages, which in an orderly way summarizes the complete and disorderly array of Keaton studies. Following a brief description of each of Keaton's films, from the Arbuckle period through the sound movies, Coursodon proceeds through all the topics that have developed in Keaton criticism, sensibly making his points and in a summary generally allowing each of the many Keaton critics to have his say. The most interesting sections, for one American reader, are those which seem most characteristically French, like a discussion of "la mise-en-scène Keatonienne" (a proclamation of style as content, in which Keaton's handling of the camera, of film space, of characters in space are all analyzed, synthesized, and eulogized into a profound world view). Less illuminating but more fun to read are several sections on "le gag," which has become a source of extensive and angry debate in France, possibly because none of the critics there seems to know what a gag is and thus they can all endlessly theorize about it. Despite much elaborate taking of positions, the most formidable of which is that of one woman who threatens a complete film semiology based on the gag, they never really master the subject, though some worthwhile insights are provided. The final part of Coursodon's book is the best: a lengthy dossier, a compendium of appendices, including the most recent and also the most complete Keaton bibliography that I know of, an equally complete filmography, an excellent and detailed outline of his life, and briefer professional lives and filmographies of his most important co-workers (writers, directors, featured actors, leading ladies).

Biographical, historical, critical—all that is known about Keaton and his films up to 1973 is encyclopedically assembled in a major work; and if the critical knowledge seems to me occasionally inadequate or in customary twentieth-century ways second-rate and cranky (as in a section on "éjection et nostalgie matricielle," where it is asserted that Keaton's fondness for leaping from things and for water reveals a massive birth trauma and an intense desire to return to the womb, a point that could be made with equal illumination about the films of Esther Williams and Donald Duck), why that is rarely Coursodon's fault but instead reflects the crazy critical world in which he is immersed. All in all, his is certainly the one book I would recommend, with only modest reservations, to anyone who wishes to learn more about Keaton's films and what criticism is doing with them.

Another recent and good French contribution is in the issue of *Avant-Scène du Cinéma* for February, 1975 (no. 155), which is largely devoted to a very competently written screenplay for *The General*, breaking the film down into individual scenes and shots, each of which is accurately described. My only complaint is that whoever handled the accompanying illustrations was incompetent. Frame enlargements printed with the screenplay are occasionally keyed to the wrong shots, and of the three stills printed on the opening page of a concluding Keaton filmography, all are attributed to the wrong movies.

Besides this shot log, there are also two recent books that attempt a bindable record of *The General*. The first is a picture-book version, *The General* (New York, 1975), in a series edited by Richard Anobile. It consists of some 2,100 frame enlargements, which provide a complete visual summary. The summary is claimed to reproduce at least one frame from each shot, but unfortunately there is no indication where shots begin and end or how long they are held. There are only the pictures, which by themselves often present a much less intelligible account of the film than do the verbal descriptions in the *Avant-Scène* screenplay. Unfortunately, too, in order that as many frames as possible might be crammed on a page, most of them have been severely cropped, so that the precise look of the movie is seriously compromised. Still, what remains is a useful and attractive record. The book also contains some brief but valuable introductory material, factual and anecdotal comments on the film's production by Raymond Rohauer and Marion Mack, the actress who played Annabelle Lee.

The second book is E. Rubinstein's *Filmguide to The General* (Bloomington, Ind., 1973), which as a more serious work requires longer comment. Like my own film chapters and like the other volumes in the Indiana University Press filmguide series, to which Rubinstein's book belongs, it tries to be both descriptive and explanatory. Its chief merit and limitation is its star-oriented approach. In a celebratory and sometimes confused way in which the fictional character Johnnie Gray, the real person on the screen who is Keaton, and the invisible Keaton who is the film-maker are all merged into one another, Rubinstein concentrates on Keaton, extolling and explaining his genius, his screen presence, what it is that makes him a cinematic star.

Emphasizing Keaton in a short book, Rubinstein necessarily slights almost everything else. Though he provides a complete summary of the film, for example, he does not convey a sense of its narrative structure and the meanings that structure contains. The cannon fired at the rear wheels of the Union train in the flight north is noted, but the repetition of this act as the final and decisive shot of the Rock River battle is omitted altogether. Similarly, the major pairing of the northerners' attempt to set fire to a covered bridge and the hero's subsequent successful firing of the Rock River bridge is insufficiently stressed. In fact, the first bridge (evidently a confusion here with a scene in *Our Hospitality*) is even converted into a tunnel (p. 38).

One thing Rubinstein's commentary does do is develop what has become in French criticism a common topic of Keaton appreciation: his wondrous relationship with the inanimate objects of the world. In his films, all objects are supposedly endowed with life, made the animate inhabitants of a unique, mysterious, Keaton universe. This is an interpretation that I believe is totally wrong, and since Rubinstein provides the most extreme English-language statement of it, I hope he will not mind if I single him out as the individual target of a general attack. One typical excerpt illustrates the anthropomorphic point of view and also reveals its inadequacies. During the flight south, Johnnie Gray must stop in order quickly to replenish his fuel supply, even though the northerners are in close pursuit. Rubinstein describes and comments, "Johnnie's attempt to garner firewood is almost as unbearable as it is delicious. Helping himself to a woodpile near the tracks, he hurls several pieces toward the tender; but there are, he discovers, some wooden objects that elect to come right back down at him, and some that like to dislodge a few of their new companions on the tender, and some that prefer to fly straight to the other side of the train. Time is nothing to independent Things" (p. 48).

My objections are these. First, there is no wood pile; instead Johnnie removes the unfastened, angularly interlaced, carefully balanced railings from a zigzagging wooden fence. Second, in Rubinstein's description, the movements of the railings are divorced from what the hero does with them, even though the actions follow the order of a typically constructed Keaton gag, in which comic cause is always followed by predictable comic effect. In trying to load the tender, Johnnie throws the first rail too lightly, so that it falls back down toward him. Then he compensates and throws the second rail more vigorously, but he also throws it carelessly, so that when it lands on top of the tender, it upsets the precarious balance of several boards already carelessly thrown there. These are piled in an overleaning and disorderly heap, which is in vivid and obviously intentional visual contrast to the stabile fence, enabling the audience to see what is coming and ironically to anticipate and then to enjoy a laugh when the new board hits the others and they all tumble toward the unsuspecting Johnnie. Having learned but not very well from his experience, he then grossly overcompensates with a third board, heaving it so strenuously that it flies all the way across the tender and falls on the other side. That is the comic climax of his triply-presented action. After three self-caused disasters, he gives up.

Rubinstein ignores Johnnie's repeated failures, cutely attributing them to the anthropomorphic antagonism of the railings themselves. He does not call a board a board, he does not call it, as Keaton might, a comic prop. Instead the railings are "Things." They are endowed with characters and wills, and what they do is described as the result of their own capricious election. This, it seems to me, is specious nonsense, an unsuccessful and often repeated attempt to turn Keaton into the sentimental creator of a screen world in which every last object is humanized (especially the trains, which "eat" meals, "drink" water, "die" a sad death, and even, not quite so sentimentally, engage in "unnatural couplings"). To ignore the rigorous logic of Keaton's films, in which comic effect is always the rational result of comic cause, and then to replace that logic by a muddle-headed notion of magically moving Things is a critical crime deserving of capital punishment.

That objection vigorously stated, I should also cautiously admit that it is partly because Rubinstein's approach to the film is so different from my own that I find it unacceptable. A reader less overwhelmingly pleased with his own sensible view of *The General* might find the discussion more valuable. He would certainly find valuable the annotated bibliography Rubinstein provides—the most complete and recent in English.

Of older books on Keaton, two are still worth reading. The first is a French study by Jean-Patrick Lebel, *Buster Keaton* (Paris, 1964), which also is available in an English translation by P. D. Stovin (New York, 1967). A general critical essay, it covers many topics, though its main concern seems to be a dialectical interpretation of Keaton's "world action," a positive philosophical pattern in his films, underlying character, activities, and some gags, which proceeds from affirmation through negation to a final triumphant affirmative negation of negation. This central idea seems to me valid and possibly even heuristic, capable of sustaining an elaborate and significant analysis, but Lebel does not quite succeed with it. He is too free-wheeling and disorganized, and his fanzine prose style occasionally winds up somewhere between gibberish and gush. Still, much that is interesting is said, and the enthusiasm, if it now and then counters meaning, is also happily contagious. For anyone who enjoys the films, it is a delight to read such unreservedly extravagant praise.

The other and better of the older books is Keaton's own autobiography, *My Wonderful World of Slapstick,* written in collaboration with Charles Samuels (New York, 1960). This, it is agreeable to report, is far better than a Hollywood as-told-to life story. What impresses is the honesty and modesty with which Keaton surveys his life. Though there is much reticence, often pained reticence (in the account of his decade-long first marriage, if his wife and her family are often necessarily referred to, neither is ever identified by name), still Keaton calmly reviews and accounts for everything, unpleasant as well as pleasant, that happened to him. Unlike most movie greats, he seems careful to describe himself as no better and no worse than he probably was, emerging by the end as a somewhat limited sensibility and a not entirely agreeable personality, but also as a basically admirable and likable figure. His few comments on his films tend to be technical, those of a craftsman rather than a poet.

Besides these books and others, there are many reviews, articles, and chapters on Keaton. From the period of his rediscovery, the most important is also the first, James Agee's famous essay "Comedy's Greatest Era," in the issue of *Life* for September 5, 1949. In a discussion of silent-screen comedy that includes all the major comedians, his comments on Keaton are only a few paragraphs in length, but the observations are so persuasively and beautifully set forth that they have been much repeated ever since. In fact, of all that has been written on Keaton, it seems likely that only Agee's essay has a permanent literary value rather than a temporary usefulness. His words should survive as long as the films themselves.

After Agee, there were nine years of anticipatory silence. Then, in 1958, *Cahiers du Cinéma* devoted 31 pages of its August issue to Keaton (an interview, a filmography, several articles), and in the United States the fall issue of *Film Quarterly* also printed an interview and an article, both by Christopher Bishop and both very good. After this, a steady stream of material followed, in many American, English, and French film magazines. There were some half dozen further interviews (listed by Coursodon and Rubinstein) until Keaton's death, in 1966. There was also for about ten years a proliferation of critical essays, though the number of these has greatly decreased in the nineteen-seventies. In France, where film commentary tends to be analytic, systematic, and hermetic, the original coterie of critics mutually pursued several topics through the films. Their observations have been summed up in Coursodon's encyclopedic book, and with its appearance French commentary seems to have temporarily concluded. So far no younger group has appeared to renew or continue the critical dialogue. In the English language, the first wave of commentators was less organized, happily writing for a larger audience rather than for one another, and most attempted no more than an introductory survey: general description and comments, a few insights (their own or Agee's), or else repetitions from Keaton's autobiography or his interviews on the technical aspects of his work. This spate of introductory observation, much of it appearing in conjunction with a Keaton retrospective or as a memorial following his death, was also largely a labor of the sixties. In the last several years, very little on Keaton has appeared in the film journals. This book, of course, is an effort to keep the dialogue going, to repeat, enlarge upon, and occasionally refute what has been said and to provide some new topics for discussion.

Besides those already mentioned, four other short essays in English seem to me very good. These are Penelope Houston's "The Great Blank Page," in *Sight and Sound* (Spring, 1968); the section on Keaton, part interview, part commentary, in Kevin Brownlow's *The Parade's Gone By* (New York, 1969); "Self-Help with a Smile," a chapter on Keaton and Lloyd in Raymond Durgnat's study of American comedy, *The Crazy Mirror* (London, 1969); and "Buster Keaton," a recollection of a visit combined with film description, in Penelope Gilliatt's *Unholy Fools* (New York, 1973).

Most recent and also good are the chapters on Keaton in Walter Kerr's excellent *The Silent Clowns* (New York, 1975). These are extensive enough to provide a comprehensive survey of all Keaton's silent work within the book's larger survey of much American silent-screen comedy. They are also, as is the entire book, beautifully illustrated. With this strong recommendation briefly stated, a few modest reservations can be lengthily detailed. To repeat for the last time a customary complaint first voiced in Chapter 2, I find Kerr's commentary, like most commentary on Keaton, inaccurate in its descriptions and unconvincing in the ways in which it attempts to define Keaton's greatness.

First, the inaccuracies. Too often, Kerr states a generalization, usually a sensible one, and then illustrates it with a beautifully supportive example. The support, however, is provided only in the book and not in the original film. In a chapter stressing Keaton's "stillness," his "alert repose," Kerr notes that Keaton is always impressively unmoved in the face of disaster. In *Our Hospitality*, when Keaton, trapped halfway down a cliff, is tied with a long rope to another man above him, he is suddenly intrigued by the rope, which suddenly slackens and starts to slither down. Kerr summarizes: "As he watches it with such interest, the man's body flashes past him, heading for the river far below. This, it turns out, is quite interesting too. Buster contemplates the matter, calmly, until the rope suddenly goes taut again, this time from below, and *he* is yanked from his perch to plunge down with the man he is tied to" (p. 217). In the film there is no such total calm. The hero's response is delayed for a few seconds to make it funnier when it occurs, but it does occur. Seeing the man flash past, the hero soon realizes what is in store for him and in alarm flattens himself against the cliff, braced with comic unsuccess against the approaching pull. This being the case, Kerr's concluding comment that the scene focuses "exclusively on Keaton's repose at the dead-center of things, a man studying a rope that is behaving oddly" (p. 218), is just one more of the many lies that carelessly watching critics tell about films.

Similarly, in a discussion of *The General*, Kerr praises Keaton's total "fidelity" to what is real, favorably contrasting this to Chaplin's disconcertingly casual mixture of studio and documentary shots in *The Gold Rush* (p. 256). What Kerr evidently failed to notice is Keaton's casual inclusion in *The General* of two studio shots during the chase north, both using a moving-diorama background. Or, in the same film, Kerr observes that when Johnnie attempts to assist Annabelle up the steps of The Texas after they have stopped for firewood in the flight south, "she bypasses his palms and hikes herself upward efficiently, accidentally starting the train as she does so, which means that Buster must scramble for his life to get aboard'' (p. 261). Johnnie starts the train, not Annabelle. Scrambling up the engine's side, he simultaneously and efficiently pulls the throttle as he climbs through the window above it. Even the classic Keaton shot, in which Johnnie, angered by Annabelle's ignorance as a fireman, grabs her around the neck, begins to choke her, and then recovers and kisses her instead, is erroneously described by Kerr, who makes Johnnie's "two arms leap forward to her shoulders" (p. 261).

Like other critics I have excessively complained about, Kerr also stakes an unconvincing claim for Keaton's (and his own) profundity. In an increasingly vague way in which words rapidly lose all meaning, he proclaims Keaton's metaphysical "stillness," his "zero" quality, which is illustrated in his mysterious "negation of things." In Keaton's negative film world, Kerr solemnly concludes, even the laws of nature are apt at any moment to be repealed. Kerr's major example of such a profound moment is the scene in *College* where the waiter hero, ordered by an angry customer to bring something he can't stick his thumb in, returns with a cup. Kerr writes, "The cup is upside down on the saucer, its rim unavailable. The cup is perfectly centered, the saucer perfectly dry. Deftly, he removes the cup. The saucer at once fills with coffee. Who suspended gravity while Keaton was turning the full cup upside down?" (p. 219). Rather than being impressed by the mystery of Keaton's "negation of things," I am instead uneasily moved by this example to the conclusion that Kerr is unable to figure out how the very easy trick is managed—except by desperate recourse to the repeal of gravity. It also should be added that the cup is placed not on a saucer but in a bowl and that it is filled not with coffee but soup.

A final word has to be said about the earliest writing on Keaton, from the first decades of the century, which is only now beginning to re-emerge. Of the original reviews of his work, those most accessible are in the *New York Times,* reprinted in its six-volume collection of film reviews and also cross-listed in its one-volume index for those with access only to microfilm files. What the *Times* reviews suggest is that basically much of what is said about Keaton now was said, less amply, then. The nicely named film reviewer, Mordaunt Hall, frequently commented on Keaton's "stone-faced stoicism," though unfortunately he disapproved of it and panned several of the films.

The original reviews in *Variety* are also interesting in the evidence they provide of how Keaton's films struck his contemporaries. Then as now, the critics in *Variety* all impress as wise old hacks who know everything about show business, and a review of *Steamboat Bill Jr.* (May 16, 1928) concludes, "The gags maintain an even tempo of laughs, and are all new to picture house audiences, although several are reminiscent to a vaudevillian." The prime example of a "reminiscent" gag is a shot which modern critics are apt to praise as uniquely, unmistakably, and impressively Keaton's—proof of his comic originality—that in which the house front falls over on Willie, who stands before it in the one spot where an open window will pass around him. The *Variety* reviewer, however, knows better. The gag is a mere, though successful, enlargement upon "the old vaudeville stunt of a falling set with the victim emerging unharmed because it held a center door fancy which framed his body."

From Keaton's childhood there is finally, in the library of the American Film Institute in Beverly Hills, both a xerox and a microfilm copy of a Keaton family scrapbook, kept by Myra Keaton during the first decade of this century. It consists of some 100 very large pages of newspaper clippings: advertisements, reviews of the vaudeville programs the Keatons appeared in (Buster is invariably singled out for particular praise), and many interviews with the family and articles about it. For anyone interested in Keaton's childhood, or in the nature of vaudeville and its impact on his films, the material is all here, more detailed and more revealing than the account of either Blesh or Keaton himself.

Films

Keaton's films survive, but like *The Night Watch,* Michelangelo's *Pietà,* and the Parthenon, they do not survive undamaged. The last word about them must be not a critical appreciation, but a discussion of their state as physical objects, as properties, as prints: of what they were like and how they were shown originally and what they are like and how they are shown now, of their copyright status and how this affects their availability.

To begin, though silent movies, they were originally never shown in silence but with a musical accompaniment (provided, depending on the opulence of the theater, by an orchestra, organ, or piano) and perhaps appropriate sound effects. Presumably, an accompanying musician could play anything he chose, and no doubt some did, but the Keaton features, as was customary in the twenties, were distributed with a thematic music cue sheet. David Shepard, who over the last decade has done much valuable work in the recovery and restoration of early movies, first with the American Film Institute and at present with Blackhawk Films, has obligingly provided me with copies of the cue sheets for *The General* and the first of the Keaton Studio features, *The Three Ages*. They are four and two pages long respectively, and each has the same format. A cue indication, either a title or a piece of action, is followed by a line or two of thematic music and a time indication of how long it is to be played before the shift at a new cue to a new theme. With *The General*, there are forty cues at intervals of from one-half minute to three and three-quarter minutes apart. Since the musical selections are represented only by a brief quotation, they are necessarily limited to works a reasonably proficient musician would know or could easily obtain: standard pieces, both popular and classical, current hits, or mood music of the sort to be found in one of the several collections published for silent-screen accompanists.

The initial cues, selections, playing times, and instructional notes for *The General*, all of which are typical of the whole, are these:

1 AT SCREENING . . . Dixie Queen (Brooks) . . .½ Min.
2 (Title) THE WESTERN AND ATLANTIC FLYER . . . Alabamy Bound (Green) . . . 1 Min. NOTE: Comedy train effects ad lib, whistle, steam, bell, etc.
3 (Title) THERE WERE TWO LOVES . . . I've Been Working on the Railroad . . . 1 Min.
4 (Action) ENTERS HOUSE . . . The Parlor Is a Pleasant Place (Crumit) . . . ½ Min. NOTE: Burlesque by playing on Harmonium—alternate with orchestra.
5 (Title) FORT SUMTER HAS BEEN FIRED UPON . . . Light Cavalry (Suppe) . . . 1¼ Min.
6 (Action) RECRUITING STATION . . . Fantasie Dixie (Mollenhauer) . . . 3¼ Min.

The cue sheet for *The Three Ages,* with its burlesque approach to history, more consistently uses contemporary songs for anachronistically comic effect: "Running Wild," "The Vamp," "Toot-Toot-Tootsie," and "Three O'clock in the Morning."

Though the musical accompaniment on both sheets would probably still work, particularly the one for *The Three Ages,* which has an agreeable comic sound to it, the drawback with both is that too many of the musical selections are too popular. The sheets are the mass-produced compilations of skillful hacks, assembling pieces that an average musician could quickly handle; and since the selections are often so well-known, they insistently call attention to themselves, distracting attention from the film. I, at least, when I hear the melody of "I've Been Working on the Railroad," have a hard time not thinking of the words.

A better accompaniment would be one that matches the rhythm and tempo and mood of the action, but which while thus lending support does not have a strong enough independent identity to compete with the film. At one time, as suggested in the chapter on *Go West,* in running Keaton film series I used the piano rags of Scott Joplin and others, which it seemed to me fulfilled all these requirements, though since Joplin has become a major national musical treasure (largely, I suppose, for lack of any others), it no longer seems altogether appropriate, or even possible, to use him as background music. A recent theatrical showing of *Sherlock Junior* had a soundtrack that was evidently compiled of period phonograph records, dance music of the nineteen-twenties or slightly earlier, snappy fox trots and two steps, a few popular enough to be recognizable, most of them anonymous, and these served very well.

Until such time, if ever, as a gifted arranger or composer brilliantly scores the Keaton films and definitive sound prints are distributed, such improvisation will be necessary. The original cue sheets, while a purist might enjoy using them, have too many limitations to ever become again the standard accompaniment for the films.

Next, there is the matter of projection speed. In these conforming times of fixed-speed projectors, only a silent speed of sixteen or eighteen frames per second and a sound speed of twenty-four frames per second are available. In Keaton's time, an age of variable-speed projectors and also of hand-cranked cameras, there was much more variety. Silent films were shown at anywhere from about sixteen frames per second to something approaching the speed of light. When the addition of a sound track necessitated the standardizing of projection speed, the choice of twenty-four frames per second was in part the choice of an average, with actual projection speeds at the time being more or less than this figure. There is also the further confusion that a creative projectionist could vary his speed, slowing the pace of this sequence, increasing the pace of that, within a single picture. At different times, too, theater managers might call for slower or faster projection, more likely the latter in an effort to maximize the number of programs and audience turnovers in the course of a day.

Still, there was some regularity within the chaos, and the music cue sheets provide an indication of what was probably the most used or at least the recommended projection speed for the films. With *The Three Ages* in 1923, a speedometer setting of eighty-two feet per minute is explicitly called for, which at sixteen frames per foot of 35-mm. film means 21.9 frames per second. Also, since the length of the film, 5,230 feet, and a maximum projection time, sixty-five minutes, are both stated (the individual times for all the musical cues add up to 64½ minutes), the minimum projection speed can be determined from this information and comes out as a rate of 21.6 frames per second.

With *The General* in 1926, the cue sheet states the running times only for individual themes, which add up to a total of 61¾ minutes. Other sources, however, like the *American Film Institute Catalog,* generally give 7,500 feet as the film's length, and assuming that this closely corresponds to its length at the time of its first release, one can compute an astonishing projection speed of 32.3 frames per second. That is one-third faster than sound projection speed today, a fact that might help explain the surprisingly unenthusiastic critical reception the film first received. A contemporary viewing of it might have been a painful exercise in keeping up with the super-fast motion of a mechanical dervish, allowing no time or opportunity to enjoy anything but the most obvious and protracted of the rapidly passing gags.

For the present, then, twenty-four frames per second seems right. That works well and is closest to the original speeds. On the other hand, there is so much visual detail packed into the Keaton films, so many momentary and often subsidiary comic touches, that a naive audience unaccustomed to the attentiveness required by the films might feel more at ease, might even enjoy them more, if they were shown at the slower present-day silent speed. I can foresee the rise of purists, too, who will insist on watching *The General* at exactly 32.3 frames per second, no more, no less.

Third, there is the problem of framing and format. The features were originally made and shown with silent 35mm. equipment, which in framing conformed to what is called the full aperture standard (.945 x .709 inches for the camera, and .906 x .679 inches for the projector). Sound equipment, at least up to around 1951, used the reduced aperture standard (.858 x .631 inches for the camera, .825 x .600 inches for the projector). Not only is the picture frame on sound film reduced, it is somewhat differently positioned on the film strip. Presumably the right sort of equipment could adjust for the differences, but what usually happens when a modern print or master is made on modern machinery from an old silent print is that the original picture is seriously cropped. Usually the top and the left side of the projected frame are most severely cut, which often weakens the symmetrical composition of Keaton's images. Even worse, when a 35-mm. print is run through a modern projector, with a framing aperture fixed at a wide-screen ratio, everyone on the screen is likely to be decapitated, depeditated, or both. Because of this, a 16-mm. showing, which is what most people outside large cities are restricted to anyway, is apt to be preferable to an ineptly or inadequately managed 35-mm. presentation. The 16-mm. prints are also produced on reduced aperture rather than full aperture equipment and are therefore also trimmed on the top and side, but at least they preserve the original silent-screen ratio of length to height, even if something in sweep and detail and probably tonal range is lost in the smaller format. A perfectly managed 35-mm. presentation with an expert live musical accompaniment is, of course, ideal, though like most ideals, it is almost impossible to realize.

Fourth, there is the question of how complete the prints of the features now available are, how closely they correspond to what was first released. Though my interest here is large, my knowledge is small, much more impressionistic than factual, but a few notes can be offered.

In a 35-mm. print of *Sherlock Junior* released by Raymond Rohauer during the summer of 1975, some editing had been done. I assume also that the editing was relatively recent, since the 16-mm. prints distributed by Audio-Brandon, which I have seen in the past, differ. The changes were minor, evidently carried out in an effort to modernize the film, to give it a slicker surface and a more uninterrupted visual flow. My impression as I watched was that up to five titles may have been removed (all those that were not absolutely necessary to an understanding of what is happening), and also that the rather primitive original editing of the film, with its casual jump cuts and raggedly joined pieces of action, had been touched up. The one point where memory and notes are detailed enough to allow me to speak with certainty is near the end of the final chase.

The criminals having been disposed of with a grenade, Sherlock Junior and the girl continue to race along in their car. Then she says, in a title, "Oh, we forgot Gillette. Shouldn't we go back for him?" In the Audio-Brandon print, there follows some awkwardly edited action. In the shot immediately after the title, Sherlock continues to drive. There is then a cut to a new shot as he approaches a curve and slams on his brakes. The awkwardness is caused by a visual ambiguity in the action, an uncertainty whether his slamming on the brakes is a response to the girl's question and signals an intention to turn around, or whether he has ignored her and is simply responding to the curve. Since the car chassis detaches and flies over the curve and into the water, the uncertainty is quickly obliterated in laughter. In the 35-mm. print, however, it is removed altogether. The title is gone and also perhaps a few frames of action, so that now Sherlock drives uninterruptedly from the moment of the grenade throwing to the moment of slamming on the brakes. After the car is in the water, one further title is also removed, Sherlock's assurance to the girl, "Don't be afraid. I'm an experienced sailor." With this additional title deletion, the entire conclusion of the dream chase, from the moment when Sherlock enters the villains' cabin to its waking end, now proceeds without titles, a pure flowing action sequence.

My opinion about such editing as this is mixed. Since it may have been recently done, after Keaton's death, it could be considered a violation of the integrity of his work. But then, it also seems reasonable. The cuts were minimal, discreet, and sensibly managed; the awkward action described might have resulted from damage to whatever surviving print lies behind present ones rather than from original intention; and with the titles removed, the film does have a more modern and therefore more accessible look to it, even a more Keatonesque look (critics, including this one, have perhaps too often applauded Keaton's ability to construct long action sequences that need and use no titles). The editing could also be compared to the handling of an early book in which dated spelling and punctuation (and also occasional misprints) are apt to be silently changed by modern editors to conform to present usage. And if such changes help preserve the film as a viable one, one that is more likely to be accepted, watched, and enjoyed by present-day audiences, they are to be encouraged. But then again, part of the charm of *Sherlock Junior,* it seems to me, is its deliberately casual, deliberately primitive look. To re-edit out all the rough spots is to destroy this level of the film's effectiveness. There is also the fact that the missing titles contain a pleasant laugh, so that to remove them is to make the film less funny than it once was.

The General is another film in which I have noticed differences among available prints, enough differences, I suspect, to make a collation of the prints a highly desirable project. In particular, my impression is that the Blackhawk Films print, which is probably the most widely purchased, is edited a little more tightly than most others and is perhaps as much as a few minutes shorter. Again to limit comments to places where my memory is certain, I can point out two deletions in the Blackhawk version.

First, there is the joke of Johnnie's handcart travels. In the Blackhawk print, he starts his forward roll, there is then a shot of the Union train passing the Kingston station, and in the next shot Johnnie and his handcart reach the missing section of rail and go off the track. In some other prints, there is an additional shot: Johnnie starts his forward roll, Johnnie is shown from a side view moving down the track, and only then is there the shot of the Union train passing the Kingston station.

Second, when Johnnie escapes from northern headquarters, in the Blackhawk print he is shown crawling toward the outside door with a small log in his hand, obviously aiming to attack the sentry there. There is then a cut to Annabelle in her bedroom, and this is followed by a shot of a second sentry by a window, who is approached and knocked out by Johnnie, now dressed in the first sentry's uniform. In other prints, there is also a shot of Johnnie reaching through the door and clubbing the first sentry.

In both these instances, though I wish I knew who made the deletions and when, the Blackhawk print seems to me better than the longer versions. The handcart gag is made more emphatic. There is no unnecessary filler movement between the start and the almost instantaneous end of Johnnie's handcart journey. Similarly, the implied rather than shown clubbing of the first sentry seems to me to improve the escape episode. It increases the comic surprise with which Johnnie appears in Union uniform beside the second sentry. Also, the fact that the audience was denied the sight of the first blow, which it had been expecting, makes all the greater its gratification at being allowed to see the second blow, the unexpected and comic swing of Johnnie's shouldered rifle. Although both cuts seem to me good ones, if they were not approved by Keaton (as I assume they were not), I would prefer that they had not been made.

There is, finally, evidence of another deletion, one present in all prints of *The General*. The music cue sheet originally released with the film contains one action cue to a shot not now there. Cue 19, "JOHNNIE SNEAKS INTO HOUSE," refers to his entry into northern headquarters; cue 21, a title cue, "IT WAS SO BRAVE OF YOU," is spoken by Annabelle after she and Johnnie have escaped into the woods. In between, however, there is action cue 20, "OFFICERS LEAVE TRAIN," and this shot is missing in all currently available prints. Since it is an interruptive and unnecessary one, it might have been removed long ago, perhaps even as a result of some last-minute editing at the time of the film's original release.

My real complaint, I suppose, in this minute brooding over the possible completeness and authenticity of currently available prints, is that films cannot be preserved and studied as easily as books, that all editions from the first to the most recent are not available to the different audiences who might be interested in them. Also, I worry that no record of any sort may even be kept, that eventually, with a film like *Sherlock Junior,* only re-edited prints may survive.

As a last note on the state of present-day prints, it should be added that since *The General* is a film available in many 16-mm. prints from a wide variety of sources, one of them, in order to gain a competitive advantage, has prepared a tinted print (or rather, a bad technicolor imitation). Black and white is absolutely essential to Keaton's films, a simplifying abstraction that reinforces the other simplifications, the stylized shapes and movements of things, in them. They do not work in color, and the "tinted" print should be avoided.

Finally, there is the matter of the actual present and probable future availability of the films for viewing, for rental or purchase. A discussion of this has to begin with copyrights.

In the United States at the time of this writing, a film can be copyrighted for a period of twenty-eight years, and during the last year of this original period, but only in this last year, the copyright can be renewed for twenty-eight years more. Since 1962, however, there has been a moratorium on copyright expirations, in anticipation of a new copyright law. This law, if it conforms to the bills now being considered (H. R. 2223, S. 22), will allow films to be copyrighted for a single period of seventy-five years. Further, films copyrighted under the old law and still in copyright at the time the new law is passed will have their present maximum fifty-six-year copyright period extended by nineteen years to meet the new seventy-five-year standard.

Of Keaton's twelve silent features, from *The Three Ages* through *Spite Marriage,* eight will therefore have their present copyrights extended to about the end of the century. Four, however, will not. There is that nasty catch to the old law, the need to renew the original copyright in the last or twenty-eighth year. It is a catch that caught even that astute businessman Charlie Chaplin, who neglected to renew the copyright on *The Gold Rush* when it expired in 1953. (I assume that his failure to do so is explained by the intolerable harassment he was receiving from the United States government, which not only drove him out of the country and denied him re-entry in 1952, but thus also deprived him of the rights to his greatest work.) It is a catch which has similarly affected *The Three Ages, The General, College,* and *Steamboat Bill Jr.* For whatever reason, their original copyrights were not renewed, and they are now in the public domain.

Public domain is somewhat uncertain territory. To the best of my knowledge, expiration of copyright has not allowed anyone so far to buy or sell 35-mm. prints of the films or to show them in commercial theaters to paying audiences, though it is possible that the hindrances have been financial rather than legal. Anyone attempting these things would almost certainly lose money. On the other hand, their public domain status has permitted the development of a 16-mm. market for three of these features, *The General, College,* and *Steamboat Bill Jr.* In prints of widely varying quality and completeness, these are now available for purchase, at least for noncommercial purposes, by individuals and organizations wishing to build a Keaton film library. Though in the public domain, *The Three Ages* cannot be bought, probably because the only surviving print of it belonged to Keaton and nobody but he could make copies. An apparent and unfortunate side effect of its being in the public domain, however, has been also to make the film generally unavailable for rental in this country. To distribute it widely would be an open invitation to film pirates to make and sell prints, and therefore it has only rarely been shown. Imagination conjures up an armed guard in the projection booth on such occasions, keeping an eye on things and ensuring that the film goes directly from projector to take-up reel rather than into some modern miniaturized copying machine smuggled in by the projectionist.

In relation to film rental, except for the unfortunate impact on *The Three Ages,* public domain status has had so far less effect. *The General* is available from many 16-mm. suppliers, but *College* and *Steamboat Bill Jr.* are available only from Audio-Brandon, now Macmillan-Audio-Brandon, which is the authorized 16-mm. supplier for the nine features discussed in this book and for seventeen of the nineteen Keaton shorts. (With the exception of the chapter on *The General,* which is based on a Blackhawk Films print I own and have memorized, my descriptions of the Keaton features have all been based on close viewings of Audio-Brandon prints.) The two shorts not on the rental list, *Hard Luck* and *The Love Nest,* were long considered lost and are often both still so described. The second, however, has recently turned up, at least in private collections, though so far it has not been made available for public viewing in the United States. The last two Keaton silent features, *The Cameraman* and *Spite Marriage,* can be rented in 16-mm. from Films Incorporated, the distributor for films owned by Metro-Goldwyn-Mayer.

Commercial and theatrical rights in 35-mm. to most of Keaton's silent work, including the nine features studied here, are controlled by Raymond Rohauer on behalf of the Keaton estate. Rohauer worked with Keaton in the nineteen-fifties and early sixties on the restoration of his films and in the recovery of the rights to them. It is a labor for which he deserves and here receives much thanks. We all know now that Keaton's films are classics; at a time when Keaton needed support, when several of his films were in danger of being lost, only Raymond Rohauer cared enough to help him save them.

Index

333